INTELLECTUAL CAPITAL

There is arguably no award more recognized in the academic and professional worlds than the Nobel Prize. The public pays attention to the prizes in the fields of science, literature, peace, and economics because their recipients are identified with particular ideas, concepts, or actions that often inspire or sometimes surprise a global audience. The Nobel Prize in Economic Science established by the Bank of Sweden in 1969 has been granted to sixty-four individuals.

Thomas Karier explores the core ideas of the economic theorists whose work led to their being awarded the Nobel Prize in its first forty years. He also discusses the assumptions and values that underlie their economic theories, revealing different and controversial features of the content and methods of the discipline. The Nobelists include Keynesians, monetarists, financial economists, behaviorists, historians, statisticians, mathematicians, game theorists, and other innovators. Rich in biographical details, illuminating the modern history of the discipline as a whole, *Intellectual Capital* allows an audience of lay and professional readers to readily understand the notions that define modern economic science and practice. It pointedly asks, and answers, whether the prizes have been awarded to those economists "who have during the previous year rendered the greatest service to mankind."

Thomas Karier is a professor of economics and a former associate dean at Eastern Washington University, Cheney, Washington, where he began teaching in 1981. He is also a research associate of the Jerome Levy Economics Institute at Bard College, New York. Professor Karier is the author of numerous scholarly and professional publications and two books: *Beyond Competition* (1993) and *Great Experiments in American Economic Policy* (1997). The topics of his research have ranged from wage policies, international competition, research and development expenditures, and welfare reform to the economic contributions of John Kenneth Galbraith. Professor Karier has conducted policy analysis for the Economic Policy Institute in Washington, D.C., and the Washington State Institute for Public Policy in Olympia, Washington.

Thomas Karier was appointed by the past two governors of Washington to represent the state on the Northwest Power and Conservation Council, which coordinates electric power planning and fish and wildlife recovery in the northwestern United States. He has written on energy and natural resource economics for the leading Washington state newspapers and commented on these subjects in the national media. Professor Karier received his Ph.D. from the University of California, Berkeley, in 1985.

Intellectual Capital

Forty Years of the Nobel Prize in Economics

THOMAS KARIER

CAMBRIDGE UNIVERSITY PRESS

CAMBRIDGE UNIVERSITY PRESS

Cambridge, New York, Melbourne, Madrid, Cape Town, Singapore,
São Paulo, Delhi, Dubai, Tokyo, Mexico City

Cambridge University Press
32 Avenue of the Americas, New York, NY 10013-2473, USA

www.cambridge.org
Information on this title: www.cambridge.org/9780521763264

First published 2010

Printed in the United States of America

A catalog record for this publication is available from the British Library.

Library of Congress Cataloging in Publication data
Karier, Thomas Mark.
Intellectual capital : forty years of the Nobel Prize in economics / Thomas Karier.
p.   cm.
Includes index.
ISBN 978-0-521-76326-4 (hardback)
1. Intellectual capital.   2. Economics.   I. Title.
HD53.K37 2010
330–dc22   2010023541

ISBN 978-0-521-76326-4 Hardback

To Kristin, Isabella, and Hailey

Contents

Preface

There were probably no more than twenty Nobel Prize winners in economics when I first started thinking about this book. Trying to find my way around the catacombs of the University of Illinois library stacks, I came across speeches of the first Nobel Prize winners in economics. Here was a fascinating attempt by the laureates themselves to explain their own contributions to a more general, highly educated audience without the aid of mathematics. While not all the laureates fully succeeded in conveying the significance of their accomplishments, they often revealed much about the state of economics as well as their own character and motivation. I started a file about Nobel Prize winners that accumulated over the next twenty years. A lot has changed over this time, including the fact that source documents, once only available in a restricted area of a university library, became widely available on the Internet.

The concept for the book finally took shape after I read something totally unrelated to economics, *A Brief History of Time* by Stephen Hawking. This extraordinary book explained scientific theories without mathematics and included lucid explanations of the achievements of Nobel Prize winners in physics. If it was possible to explain the great ideas of physics, the general theory of relativity, and quantum mechanics, then surely it was possible to explain the great ideas of economics. The period of accumulating documents came to a close and I started writing about the contributions of all sixty-two Nobel winners in economics for the first forty years of the prize, which was first awarded in 1969. Astute readers will note that the winners in the forty-first year are also included, since they were announced while the book was still in production.

Any project that spans such a long period of time incurs many debts and this one is no exception. I especially appreciate the intrepid readers of the first drafts who helped me fine-tune the focus and tone. Paul DePalma and

Doug Hammond read early drafts and are responsible for more changes in the book than they will probably ever appreciate. The Honorable Lisa Brown provided invaluable suggestions for both content and presentation, including the unusual suggestion that I consider the achievements of Nobel Peace Prize winner and economist Mohammed Yunus, who is now a major part of the final chapter. Other readers were helpful in reviewing selected chapters and I appreciate the time they dedicated to the effort, including Doug Orr, William Milberg, Clair Brown, George Akerlof, Zohreh Emami, John Davis, and Teresa Ghilarducci. All of their comments were appreciated and if the book falls short in any respect, it is only because of my failure to adhere more rigorously to their advice. The team at Cambridge University Press was a pleasure to work with and I have to thank both Scott Parris and Adam Levine for making this publication process so effortless. The fine artwork on the cover was donated by Karier Design and my creative sister Nancy.

My deepest appreciation, however, is reserved for my family, who tolerated and encouraged my immersion in this marathon project. Victor, Mirna, Jose, Marco, and my wife Maria Ester never seemed to mind when I was lost to the world, sorting out the great Nobel ideas, and for this they have my love and gratitude.

Economic Nobel Laureates

Year	Nobel Laureate	Country	Chapter
1969	Frisch, Ragnar A.	Norway	13
	Tinbergen, Jan	The Netherlands	13
1970	Samuelson, Paul A.	United States	7
1971	Kuznets, Simon S.	United States	9
1972	Arrow, Kenneth J.	United States	11
	Hicks, John R.	Great Britain	5
1973	Leontief, Wassily W.	United States	9
1974	Hayek, Friedrich A.	Great Britain	2
	Myrdal, K. Gunnar	Sweden	7
1975	Kantorovich, Leonid V.	Soviet Union	9
	Koopmans, Tjalling C.	United States	9
1976	Friedman, Milton	United States	2
1977	Meade, James E.	Great Britain	12
	Ohlin, Bertil G.	Sweden	12
1978	Simon, Herbert A.	United States	6
1979	Lewis, Sir W. Arthur	British West Indies	12
	Schultz, Theodore W.	United States	3
1980	Klein, Lawrence R.	United States	7
1981	Tobin, James	United States	7
1982	Stigler, George J.	United States	3
1983	Debreu, Gerard	United States	11
1984	Stone, Sir J. Richard N.	Great Britain	9
1985	Modigliani, Franco	United States	7
1986	Buchanan, James M. Jr.	United States	2

(continued)

Year	Nobel Laureate	Country	Chapter
1987	Solow, Robert M.	United States	7
1988	Allais, Maurice F.	France	11
1989	Haavelmo, Trygve M.	Norway	13
1990	Markowitz, Harry M.	United States	4
	Miller, Merton H.	United States	4
	Sharpe, William F.	United States	4
1991	Coase, Ronald H.	United States	3
1992	Becker, Gary S.	United States	3
1993	Fogel, Robert W.	United States	14
	North, Douglass C.	United States	14
1994	Harsanyi, John C.	United States	10
	Nash, John F.	United States	10
	Selten, Reinhard	Germany	10
1995	Lucas, Robert E.	United States	8
1996	Mirrlees, Sir James A.	United States	5
	Vickrey, William S.	United States	5
1997	Merton, Robert C.	United States	4
	Scholes, Myron S.	United States	4
1998	Sen, Amartya K.	United States	12
1999	Mundell, Robert A.	United States	12
2000	Heckman, James J.	United States	13
	McFadden, Daniel L.	United States	13
2001	Akerlof, George A.	United States	6
	Spence, A. Michael	United States	6
	Stiglitz, Joseph E.	United States	6
2002	Kahneman, Daniel	United States/Israel	6
	Smith, Vernon L.	United States	5
2003	Engle, Robert F.	United States	13
	Granger, Sir Clive W. J.	United States	13
2004	Kydland, Finn E.	United States	8
	Prescott, Edward C.	United States	8
2005	Aumann, Robert J.	Israel	10
	Schelling, Thomas C.	United States	10
2006	Phelps, Edmund S.	United States	8
2007	Hurwicz, Leonid	United States	10

Year	Nobel Laureate	Country	Chapter
	Maskin, Eric S.	United States	10
	Myerson, Roger B.	United States	10
2008	Krugman, Paul R.	United States	12
2009	Williamson, Oliver E.	United States	14
	Ostrom, Elinor	United States	14

ONE

An Economic Prize

Alfred Nobel was probably the richest man in Europe when he died in 1896. A serious scientist and inventor, he had taken great personal risks in his early experiments with the unstable explosive nitroglycerine. In fact, during a low point in his career, he lost his younger brother in a laboratory explosion and came close to losing his own life. But because of a stubborn dedication to his work and a confidence in his own ability, he persevered, overcoming technical difficulties and ultimately succeeding in creating a more stable and more practical explosive, dynamite. Equally powerful as nitroglycerin but many times more useful, dynamite would revolutionize mining and construction of canals, roads, and railroads. It was one of the great discoveries of the nineteenth century and would open the door to the industrial revolution and the modernization of industry and transportation.

The potential uses for dynamite were almost immediately apparent, creating a huge demand and opening up a great business opportunity. Unlike many inventors, Alfred Nobel easily made the transition to business and found that he was just as good at manufacturing and marketing as he was in the laboratory. He built factories to produce dynamite, fought to protect his patents from rivals, and developed a sales program to sell dynamite across the globe. Like his father, he also dabbled in the development of military explosives, but it was dynamite that made him rich.

As Alfred Nobel neared the end of his life in the late nineteenth century, he recognized that he had accumulated one of the greatest fortunes in the world but had no heirs. He had never married or had any children, so he decided to give his fortune away. His will of 1895 provided the largest philanthropic gift ever made to that point in history, when he established a series of five Nobel Prizes, the first three of which – physics, chemistry, and physiology or medicine – reflected his own professional passion as a scientist and inventor. But Nobel had more interests than just work; he had been

1

a prolific reader and writer in his entire life and left behind an immense and eclectic personal library. He wanted to honor great writers who had inspired him during his lifetime, and therefore he created a prize for literature. His final prize became known simply as the Nobel Peace Prize. You might wonder why the inventor of dynamite and other explosives created a "peace prize." Was it penance for the military weapons he had invented or was it a concession to his close friend, Bertha von Suttner, a prominent pacifist writer? Historians have speculated about both possibilities without any clear resolution. These five were the only prizes requested by Alfred Nobel. The first prizes were awarded in 1901 and were accompanied by a significant financial award equal to the sum of the interest on his gift.

This constituted the entire list of Nobel categories, at least until 1968 when the Bank of Sweden (Sveriges Riksbank) persuaded the Nobel Foundation that they needed one more award; they needed a Nobel Prize in economics. More importantly, the Bank offered to come up with the money every year to match the financial award of a Nobel Prize (valued at $73,000 in 1969 and growing to $1.4 million in 2008). It was an offer too good to refuse. Beginning in 1969, economics became the sixth prize granted by the Nobel Foundation to be awarded to those economists "who have during the previous year rendered the greatest service to mankind."

And what was their service to mankind? How is the world a better place because of the contributions of these scholars? What are the mysteries that these Nobel laureates have solved for the human race? The explanations in the media and editorials are seldom enlightening. The typical Nobel laureate in economics is acclaimed for "inspiring an outpouring of future research" and sometimes for creating a new field of study within economics. We are told that the work is seminal or path breaking, as when the media reported that laureate James Buchanan "had a great seminal influence,"[1] or that laureate Joseph Stiglitz "shared the prize for seminal work,"[2] or that laureates Robert Engle and Sir Clive Granger did "their seminal work in the 1970s and 80s,"[3] or that laureate Ronald Coase wrote a "seminal book."[4] But none of this tells us what they discovered. It only begs the question, what did they actually do? What did they discover that benefited mankind? This book is about those discoveries, the Nobel Prize–winning ideas in economics and the economists who won the awards.

Economists may not be universally held in such high esteem, but every October with the announcement of a new Nobel Prize winner the profession gains a little respect as yet another economist, or two, or three, join the exalted ranks of the Nobel laureates. Albert Einstein and Marie Curie were Nobel Prize winners, as was Enrico Fermi, who probed the mysteries of nuclear fission, and Albert Michelson, who measured the speed of light. Writers Ernest Hemmingway, Toni Morrison, and John Steinbeck were also winners. Winston Churchill, Theodore Roosevelt, and Barack Obama won as well. With the creation of the economic Nobel Prize, economists were invited to join the small but elite party of some of the greatest scientists, authors, and peace advocates in modern history.

How did professional economists respond to this invitation? It wasn't long before they started to bet on the winners. People organize pools and bet on the National Collegiate Athletic Association (NCAA) basketball tournament, the Super Bowl, and the Kentucky Derby; economists enjoy betting on themselves, and the Nobel Prize offered the perfect opportunity. Every year, students and professors at top U.S. economics departments enter a pool and bet on who will win the prize.

All of the first sixty-two winners of the Nobel Prize in economics during its first forty years, which is the time period covered in this book, were men. The streak was finally broken in its forty-first year, when Elinor Ostrom from Indiana University won the 2009 Nobel Prize in economics for the study of voluntary cooperative organizations. Why so few women? The record isn't much better among the other five Nobel categories, in which women have won only 4.4 percent of all Nobel Prizes. Most of these have been in the categories of peace (twelve women), literature (ten), and physiology and medicine (eight). Physics has had only two female winners and chemistry three.

There were earlier opportunities to honor great women economists. Cambridge Professor Joan Robinson was a giant in the economics profession and could have won the award for several different achievements including contributions to monopoly theory, Keynesian economics, and the theory of economic growth. Her own path-breaking work in monopoly theory has been included in almost every economics principles textbook since she and Harvard economist Edward Chamberlin separately discovered it in the 1930s. She was also a colleague of John Maynard Keynes and provided the sounding board he needed to refine his revolutionary theories. But apparently that was not enough for the small group of Swedish economists that constituted the Nobel Prize committee. Professor Robinson's work made her eligible for the Nobel Prize for fourteen years until 1983, the year she died. Posthumous awards are not permitted under Nobel rules.

There was some speculation that Joan Robinson was rejected because she was too political or because the committee was afraid that she might reject the prize. Assar Lindbeck, a chair of the selection committee, confessed that Robinson was excluded because he "feared that she would either refuse it, or worse, use the Nobel limelight to attack mainstream economics."[5] Neither reason had anything to do with her contribution to economic sciences, nor was this standard applied to other winners. Fear of rejection didn't stop the Nobel committee from awarding the Prize in Literature to Jean Paul Sartre, who actually did reject it. For whatever reason, one of the top economists of the twentieth century did not win the Nobel Prize, and she also happened to be a woman.

The list of Nobel Prize winners in economics is not by any means a complete list of the most important economists of modern times. The Nobel committee has its biases, which caused it to pass over another one of the most famous and admired economists of the twentieth century. Harvard economist, advisor to President Kennedy, and past chair of the American Economics Association, John Kenneth Galbraith stands out as one of the greatest economists of the twentieth century whose work addressed the big issues facing society, including poverty, income distribution, and unemployment. His academic work on financial bubbles, countervailing power, and the internal operations of the modern corporation was supplemented by his many popular books. His fame as a leading economist and writer earned him access to the highest levels of national politics and society, making him something of a national celebrity.

One of Galbraith's important books was *The Great Crash* about the stock market collapse of 1929. Some fifty years after it was first published, *The Great Crash* remains one of the most important historical and economic accounts of the catastrophic event that ushered in the decade of the Great Depression. His unique literary style allowed him to write about sophisticated economic topics while still attracting a large popular audience. Galbraith also brought economic issues into the mainstream through his memorable debates with Nobel laureate Milton Friedman. But his popularity may have actually worked against him when it came to the Nobel Prize. More conservative economists were known to grumble about his popularity and to suggest that this popularity was evidence that his work was not sufficiently "rigorous." Perhaps he was also too liberal or not mathematical enough for the Nobel committee. Whatever the reason, his name is another conspicuous omission in the roll call of laureates. His death in 2006 brought an end to speculation that the Nobel committee would remedy this omission.

In 1968, when the Nobel Foundation accepted the Bank of Sweden's offer to fund an award and medallion for economics, it decided to model it after the original five prizes contained in Alfred Nobel's will. Like the other prizes, the winner of the economics prize is formally notified by the Nobel committee in October, followed by an announcement and press release. The winner receives the same amount of money in Swedish kronor as the winners of the original five categories and a gold medallion presented by the King of Sweden in the same formal ceremonies held in December. Just like the other categories, the winner in economics is given an opportunity to present a lecture and is identified as a Nobel laureate on the official Nobel website. With all these similarities how could there be any doubt that the economics prize enjoys equal standing with the other prizes? Not everything, however, is exactly equal.

A closer look reveals some differences. The Foundation couldn't quite see its way to giving the economics winner the same medallion as the original science and literature categories. This isn't such a big deal since the Nobel Peace Prize medallion is also unique. The more significant difference, however, is that the formal name of the economics prize is unlike any other: "The Sveriges Riksbank Prize in Economic Sciences in Memory of Alfred Nobel." So is it a Nobel Prize or is it a Bank of Sweden Prize? Even more striking is that the Nobel Foundation seldom, if ever, uses the term "Nobel Prize" in reference to the economics award, nor is the term uttered by members of its official committees. The official Nobel website lists the "Nobel Prize in Physics," the "Nobel Prize in Chemistry," and so on, but when it gets to the last category, it is the "Prize in Economics." All of the other laureates give "Nobel Lectures"; but it is only called the "Prize Lecture" when it comes to economics.[6]

In contrast, the press accounts have ignored this nuance and routinely refer to the award as the Nobel Prize in Economics. From their perspective, it is a prize issued by the Nobel organization in Sweden, so that makes it a Nobel Prize in Economics. No one has succeeded in correcting them; even the Nobel Foundation doesn't seem to mind. The term "Nobel prize" is used in this book, but in recognition of the fact that it is not the official title of the economics award, the "p" is not capitalized. It is not, apparently, the formal title of the award. The formal title is the Sveriges Riksbank Prize, which does have a capital "P."

Economics: A Science?

Is economics a science? Does it deserve the same scientific award for its contribution to society as Alfred Nobel envisioned for physics, chemistry, medicine, and physiology? The other Nobel sciences are dedicated to uncovering the hidden nature of matter, energy, and the human body. No one doubts that this nature exists, more or less independent of time and place, and that this nature is amenable to discovery. The relentless application of the scientific method slowly unravels these mysteries until basic truths emerge. In this process, theories are either confirmed or on occasion refuted, creating opportunities for new hypotheses.

So how does economics stack up against the sciences? Can economists simply follow the scientific method and create a science? Economics is a field of ideas about how people organize themselves through institutions and rules to meet their various wants and desires. People organize themselves in businesses, markets, and governments to produce goods and services, and to distribute the outputs among themselves. If there are basic laws in economics, as in the sciences, then these laws must be derived from human behavior because people are the essential building blocks of all businesses, markets, and governments. But human behavior is notoriously fickle and difficult to summarize with a few fundamental equations. This is one of the most difficult challenges facing economics and also what distinguishes it from the sciences.

The Bank of Sweden and the economists who awarded the Nobel Prize were not interested in differences; they were interested in similarities. Toward that end, they ensured that the award was granted for "economic sciences" and not just "economics." They also wanted the winners to "appear" like scientists, and that meant that there was an immediate preference for academics whose work emphasized mathematics and statistics. They hoped economics would join the ranks of physics, chemistry, and medicine, even if it is somewhat compromised by the caprice of human behavior.

Mathematics

Almost all of the Nobel winners in economics had strong mathematical backgrounds, and most of their theories were originally presented as formulas that emulated those in physics and other sciences. As you will see, a surprising number of the winners of this prize began their training as majors in physics, engineering, mathematics, or related sciences. Economics was already moving toward a greater mathematical rigor, but this emphasis in the Nobel Prize has no doubt reinforced the trend. In fact, some laureates like John Nash, featured in *A Beautiful Mind*, and Robert Aumann had doctorates in mathematics and almost no formal education in economics.

The economic ideas in this book are described in words, not formulas. Where prize winners simply took an idea and translated it into mathematics, it is relatively easy to explain the original concept. It may seem odd that translating ideas into mathematics can qualify for a Nobel Prize, but that is, in a sense, a large part of modern economic theory. Economists find a high degree of satisfaction from converting familiar ideas into mathematics and an even greater sense of accomplishment from proving mathematically what anyone else might recognize as common sense.

Mathematics has the advantage of requiring precise definitions and providing a common language for a diverse and multinational profession. While there is no doubt that mathematical representations appear more scientific and are favored by the Swedish Nobel committee, they do have their limitations. For example, formulas, with their underlying assumptions, tend to overstate the degree of precision that can realistically be expected from an economic theory. And the introduction of advanced mathematics, like topology, has completely transformed some fields in economics. It is safe to say that this development has placed full comprehension of many of these theories beyond the grasp of a large number of professional economists.

As a result of these developments, many economic theories tend to be less about any actual economy and more about an entirely imaginary world. And herein lies the danger that economic models may become little more than castles in the sky – elaborate constructions with limited real-world application. This book, however, is about economic ideas, not mathematics, so all the theories and insights are described in the English language.

Another danger in the mathematical approach to economics is the fact that it can create a false impression of objectivity and truth. When an economic theory is cast in a mathematical formula, the presumption exists that it is unbiased. This is not necessarily so. On the one hand, economists who favor free markets are more likely to make assumptions that present markets in the best possible light. For example, they would be more likely to assume that people are completely rational and behave with complete information and objectivity so that markets work efficiently. Perfect outcomes are more likely under perfect conditions.

On the other hand, skeptics of free markets are more likely to assume less than perfect behavior and conditions, and are less likely, as a consequence, to find perfection in free markets. Both kinds of economists have been awarded Nobel Prizes over the past forty years, and while both groups start with similar equations, they can modify them and steer their models in different directions. For this reason, it is possible for two economists to achieve mathematically correct conclusions that are, nonetheless, entirely contradictory. You would expect to see few contradictory theories among the winners of the Nobel science awards, but such conflicts are common among economics laureates. The most notable was the 1974 prize that was shared by Friedrich A. von Hayek, an outspoken antisocialist, and Gunnar Myrdal, a socialist. Neither winner that year had anything good to say about their co-winner.

Origins

A surprising number of Nobel Prize winners in economics can trace their work back to one of two giants in the profession, Adam Smith and John Maynard Keynes. Smith, of course, presented a remarkably compelling argument in favor of free markets in his classic volume *Wealth of Nations* published in 1776. By means of simplifying assumptions, he described the operation of a stylized market driven by the forces of supply and demand. Prices played a central role in his eighteenth-century model economy as they signaled either scarcity or surpluses and provided desirable market outcomes. Smith's primary theme was that free markets effortlessly and efficiently regulated production and distribution in an economy, as if guided by an invisible hand. The villain in Smith's narrative was generally played by government, which interfered with price signals and tended to disrupt the otherwise ideal outcomes generated by free markets.

Many Nobel economists owe an intellectual debt to Adam Smith because they share his belief in the superiority of free and unregulated markets. Several of these free-market economists, featured in Chapter 2, fought a high-profile campaign against government and in defense of private markets. These economists, including Milton Friedman who was a leader of the Chicago School of Economics, invoked abstract models of perfect competition to defend their vision of a market economy.

Adam Smith's influence is even greater because of his effect on the development of *neoclassical economics*. Smith's depiction of a market economy provided the inspiration for a more mathematical representation of markets in the late nineteenth century. Neoclassical economists simply assumed rational behavior that was consistent, predictable, infallible, and deeply rooted in self-interest. The assumption that human beings acted in this way was so prevalent in economic models that it was represented by the term *homo economicus*, a mythical creature combining all of these characteristics.

These ideas followed one evolutionary path toward English economist Alfred Marshall, who consolidated the theories of nineteenth-century economists into what eventually became known as *microeconomics*. He introduced new ideas related to supply and demand, and showed how they could be applied to taxes, trade, and other economic policies. Following in this tradition, many Nobel Prize winners in economics were micro-economists who developed new concepts or simply applied the concepts to completely new areas. Chapter 3 describes the application of microeconomics by Chicago School economists to a broad range of topics including the family, crime, education, pollution, and the public airwaves. Other Nobel laureates who focused exclusively on applying microeconomics to financial markets are presented in Chapter 4. Their work, once lauded for expanding markets for stocks, mutual funds, and derivatives, have recently been questioned because of the instability of these same markets. There were still other "micro" laureates, described in Chapter 5, who continued to refine formulas or to apply the theory to determine optimum taxes or understand auctions.

Not all economists were entirely convinced that perfect rationality was the best model of human behavior. Several Nobel winners, called behaviorists, challenged some of these microeconomic assumptions; their work is described in Chapter 6. These economists were interested in the effects on markets when people act like people, imperfect and sometimes lacking complete information and perfect foresight.

Not all economic theory can be traced back to Adam Smith. An entirely different type of economics was pioneered by Cambridge economist John Maynard Keynes, a student of Alfred Marshall. The starting point for Keynes was not the hypothetical operation of perfect markets; it was the reality of failed markets that struck the industrialized world in the 1930s. In the end, Keynes produced a very different theory that was not limited by homo economicus or any of the other assumptions of neoclassical economics.

Keynes' approach appealed to a new generation of academics, and his ideas spread from Cambridge to economics departments across America. In a familiar pattern, one of the first actions taken by the new Keynesians was to translate the theory into mathematical formulas and geometric figures. This allowed for more precise definitions and further refinement. It also created opportunities for Nobel awards for some economists featured in Chapter 7 who defended and expanded Keynesian economics. Like many revolutionary ideas, it inspired a reaction from free-market economists, who objected to both the theory and the policy implications. In its place they attempted to revive classical economic ideas in the 1970s, as described in Chapter 8.

A special group of Nobel laureates invented tools that were uniquely suited to analyzing economic problems. Although influenced by Smith, Keynes, and other economists, they relied on their own detailed observations of the real economy to produce their own original insights. These economists, described in Chapter 9, invented national income accounts, input-output analysis, and linear programming – tools used by many economists to probe contemporary economic problems.

One particular field of economics was highly influenced by the concept of rational behavior but proceeded to develop its own original approach. Game theory was essentially the mathematical depiction of simple games as pioneered by John von Neumann, who wasn't an economist at all. He was a brilliant Princeton mathematician who would have been a contender for a Nobel Prize except that he died in 1957, eleven years before the prize was created. Chapter 10 describes the contribution of the Nobel laureates who followed in his very large footsteps.

While one road led from Smith to Alfred Marshall, the other headed toward French economist Leon Walras, who in 1874 successfully translated Adam Smith's depiction of market behavior into mathematical formulas. Where Smith's book was a great, rambling text that described all sorts of human behavior and motivations, Walras' book was a dry compendium of mathematical formulas and proofs. With enough supply-and-demand equations, Walras was able to represent the entire economy, giving birth to the concept of a *general equilibrium*. Where Walras saw an opportunity to translate Smith's market models into equations, later generations of mathematicians saw an opportunity to translate Walras' equations into even more advanced mathematics. The result has been an ever-increasing level of mathematical abstraction and more than a couple of Nobel Prizes, as described in Chapter 11.

Most economic theory is expected to apply to any market economy, but the world of international trade and development presents a unique set of problems. Economists have been interested in these issues since Adam Smith, and a number of such economists described in Chapter 12 have won Nobels. Also, practicing economists rely on statistical analysis as well as theory to gain insights into real-world activity. Some of the Nobel awards documented in Chapter 13 recognized innovations in statistical techniques.

Throughout its history, the Nobel Prize in economics has been surrounded by unsettled debates and competing theories. The primary debate has always revolved around the appropriate role for government. How much reliance should we place on free markets versus government to repair market failures or fix inequitable outcomes? Many of the economists who have won the Nobel Prize have had a strong belief in how to answer this question, with some of them strongly favoring markets and others favoring government intervention. For several years, the Nobel committee tried to strike a balance by honoring leaders of both competing camps. This may have seemed like the fair thing to do, but it didn't do much for the reputation of economics as a science because both theories could not be right simultaneously. There are several other issues of contention, and those are also illustrated in this book. Even the two economic historians presented in Chapter 14 could not agree on the fundamental importance of the railroads in the nineteenth century. This same chapter documents the contribution of the two 2009 laureates, who asked interesting questions about the governance of firms and cooperative organizations.

The final chapter summarizes the performance of the Nobel Prize in economics and assesses how well it has identified those who have rendered the greatest service to humankind. While some great work has been recognized, there is room for improvement.

Relevance

Few of the Nobel laureates mentioned in this book were ever particularly famous, except for those who wrote for general audiences such as Milton Friedman, Paul Krugman, and Paul Samuelson. For many winners, the most fame they ever achieved was the day they won the Nobel Prize. The majority of Nobel laureates in economics were academics whose lives revolved around universities run by provosts, deans, and department chairs. They were accustomed to presenting their ideas in conferences, academic journals, graduate seminars, and scholarly texts, where brevity and clarity were less valued than mathematical rigor and abstract generality. Few were prepared to explain their work to the entire world in the early morning hours in October when their prize was announced. When the national press descended on their living rooms or college offices and asked them why they won the Nobel Prize, few economists were prepared with an answer. Their responses were often disappointing, usually too vague or too obscure to pass for an acceptable sound bite. It soon became apparent to the news media that they hadn't discovered anything tangible, such as dynamite.

In 1991 the newly announced Nobel Prize winner James Tobin was quoted in a radio interview saying something to the effect, "I guess I proved that you shouldn't put all your eggs in one basket." That was the same year that the medicine/physiology Nobel winners had identified the different functions of the left and right sides of the brain; the winners in physics had studied the property of electrons blasted from atoms by lasers; and the peace prize went to the United Nations High Commissioner for Refugees for its work with millions of displaced refugees wandering the planet. And the economics Nobel laureate proved you shouldn't put all your eggs in one basket! The author Miguel de Cervantes had a similar idea when he wrote, "It is the part of a wise man to keep himself today for tomorrow and not to venture all his eggs in one basket." Cervantes has prior claim on the idea since he wrote this around 1600.

What Tobin accomplished was, of course, far more significant than this, but the comment illustrates how economic achievements can come across as ridiculously trite just as easily as they can be frustratingly incomprehensible. The reality is that Nobel economists have ideas that can change the way we think, and they can influence government policies in very significant ways. These Nobel laureates' ideas have contributed to the intellectual capital from which we draw to inform our political and social policies. Without economic ideas we are assured of falling victim to our own ignorance. We may unwittingly expose ourselves to hyperinflation, stock market crashes, financial crises, or even great depressions. Today there is general agreement that the Federal Reserve should have reacted faster after the stock market crash of 1929 in order to avoid what became known as the Great Depression, but at the time the Reserve lacked a clear theory of what it was supposed to do. That came later. Only by considering economic ideas, right or wrong, can we forge strategies and policies necessary to create a more prosperous society.

When a national government or a national bank embraces a certain economic theory, it can have broad impacts on individuals, entire nations, or even the entire world. A farmer in India may find that his access to credit is determined by World Bank policies that are informed by an obscure Nobel Prize–winning theory. Or when you use a cell phone you are using radio spectra that were auctioned using principles of game theory. Nobel Prize–winning theories even have been used to design auctions on eBay and to inform proposals to trade CO_2 emissions credits. Some Nobel economists helped to fashion Cold War strategies in the standoff with the Soviet Union. It would be a mistake to underestimate the influence that these seemingly obscure economic theories can have on the well-being of millions of individuals across the planet.

The fact that some Nobel ideas are important does not necessarily mean that they are *all* important or even original. There are some examples in the cases that follow where the ideas had a limited influence on the economics profession itself, much less the outside world. In those cases, the ideas faded quickly into history, along with the Nobel Prize winners themselves. Their primary legacy is a gold medallion with their name on it and a brief entry in this book. There are also cases where an important idea was recognized by the Nobel committee, although the laureate was not the first to describe it. In some of these cases this fact is obvious, and in other cases it was pointed out by the Nobel committee. For some of these awards it is not always easy to state definitively which part is original and which part is not. As you can see from the quote above from Cervantes, Tobin may have "proved" the concept about the wisdom of not putting all your eggs in one basket, but he clearly didn't discover it. That discovery predates Tobin and even Cervantes for that matter.

Finally, the fact that economic ideas can be important and have far-reaching repercussions is not the same as saying that they are always correct. Just because economic theories are presented in complex mathematical formulas or win a Nobel Prize does not guarantee that they will always work in the real world. In fact some of them have not fared particularly well. Although economists expend considerable effort "proving" concepts in the abstract, the ultimate test of an economic idea is its value in the real world. What better place to review these ideas than from the insights, large and small, of Nobel Prize winners in economics.

TWO

Free-Market Economics

Friedrich A. von Hayek (1974)

Milton Friedman (1976)

James M. Buchanan Jr. (1986)

In 1947, Friedrich A. von Hayek convened a meeting of fellow economists and academics in Montreux, Switzerland to discuss what they feared most in postwar Europe and America. It was not hunger, or unemployment, or even communism. It was government. They all took great pride in their individual points of view but they collectively agreed that the increasing role of government posed the greatest threat and that "The central values of civilization are in danger."[1] They complained that "Over large stretches of the earth's surface the essential conditions of human dignity and freedom have already disappeared...."[2] The reason for their pessimism was "a decline of belief in private property and the competitive market; for without the diffused power and initiative associated with these institutions it is difficult to imagine a society in which freedom may be effectively preserved."[3]

With these words, the Mont Pelerin Society was born and promptly elected its first president, Hayek. The society insisted on personal liberty and saw "danger in the expansion of government, not least in state welfare, in the power of trade unions and business monopoly, and in the continuing threat and reality of inflation." The philosophy that united Pelerinists was classical liberalism (almost the opposite of modern liberalism), a philosophy more commonly referred to today as libertarianism. Named after the mountain near its first meeting, the society continues to meet in various locations around the world to share stories and research about individual freedom. In total, eight Nobel winners in economics have been presidents or members of the Mont Pelerin Society, which never counted more than 500 members worldwide.[4] Hayek was its first president, Milton Friedman was the seventh, and James M. Buchanan Jr. was the fourteenth, all Nobel Prize winners in economics.

The defining feature of libertarians is their willingness to resolve complex political and economic issues based on the answer to a single defining question: Does the policy encroach on any individual's freedom of choice? If it does, then they will, in all likelihood, oppose it. Using this litmus test, libertarians can arrive at policy positions that range from ultraconservative on economic issues to extremely liberal on social issues.[5] For example, it would be considered unusual for a person to oppose the military draft and favor legalization of marijuana on the one hand and oppose the minimum wage and public education on the other, but not if the person was a libertarian. These were all positions endorsed by Milton Friedman at some time during his career. The common denominator in these positions is that they are all consistent with the theme of removing the influence of government from individual choice. According to libertarians, whether one fights in a war, smokes marijuana, or pays low wages, should be the choice of an individual, not the government. Libertarians start with a principle that places individual freedom above all else. Positions are not determined by popularity, compassion, the greater good, altruism, equal opportunity, or even strategic advantage. They are all decided by a single factor: individual liberty.

In reality, many individual freedoms can cut both ways; for example, the freedom to smoke cigarettes for one person will violate the freedom to breathe smoke-free air for another. But these are generally not the issues that preoccupy libertarians. They are usually more interested in eliminating public education, low-income housing, food stamps, and public health care, even for low-income children. They reject the concept of providing services for some at the expense of others no matter how great the need. Their quest to preserve individual freedom places them in a holy war against almost all public programs.

Friedrich A. von Hayek (1974 Prize Winner)

Officially, Friedrich A. von Hayek won the 1974 Nobel Prize for his work dating back to the 1920s and 1930s on money, prices, and the causes of the business cycle. In all honesty, however, any insights he may have had on these particular topics some forty years earlier were probably a distant memory by 1974. His Austrian theory of trade cycles and arguments for fixed exchange rates were not on very many reading lists by the 1970s.

Instead Hayek was remembered for his criticism of Keynesian theory in the 1930s and 1940s, a role that earned him a small but deeply devoted following. He was even better known as the author of *The Road to Serfdom*, published in 1944. The book was an impassioned warning to the Western world that their experiments with democratic socialism in Europe and the New Deal in America were heading down the road to totalitarianism. It was, according to Hayek, only a short step from Social Security and nationalized medicine to the ruthless dictatorship of Soviet Communism or German Fascism. He urged the Western world to reject government programs and embrace free markets and individual liberty as the only means of avoiding the slippery slope that led to the abyss of totalitarianism. In a purely ironic gesture, Hayek dedicated his book to European and American socialists. The road to serfdom or totalitarianism, as Hayek claimed, was paved by the good intentions of unwitting socialists.

Fortunately, Hayek's dire warning has not come to pass. Denmark, for example, continues to enjoy a successful democratic political system even with taxes in excess of 50 percent and a full menu of government programs. But in 1944, with World War II still raging and fear of Nazis and Communists still extremely high, this thesis attracted a sizeable and sympathetic audience in Europe, England, and the United States.

Hayek was born into a middle-class family in Vienna in 1899. His father, Dr. August Hayek, was a doctor and professor at the University of Vienna, the same institution where Friedrich received his doctorate in jurisprudence and, early in 1923, another doctorate in political science. Hayek found a job in 1921 in the Office of Accounts as a legal consultant, where he engaged in the task of clearing debts that had been blocked during World War I. Getting the job was tough but it helped that he knew several languages – French, Italian, and later English – and that he received a recommendation from Ludwig von Mises, a prominent Austrian economist. Von Mises had a strong influence on Hayek through his books on monetary theory and socialism.

In 1923, Hayek traveled to New York City and, like a true scholar, spent most of his time in the public library. He was impressed by the American newspaper accounts of World War I which he found far superior to what he had seen in Austria during the war. He was dismayed that the Austrian people should be denied this important information and blamed the shortcoming on the Austrian government. This was just one of many failures that Hayek would attribute to government. While in New York, Hayek registered for the doctoral program in economics at New York University with an expectation of writing a thesis but nothing ever came of it. He attended a lecture by Thorstein Veblen, the great American economist and sociologist, and several lectures by Wesley Clair Mitchell at Columbia. By that time, Mitchell was already in full swing at the National Bureau of Economic Research, mining data to track business cycles.

Returning to Austria in 1924, Hayek resumed his government job. As an aside, it is interesting to note that Hayek did not look favorably on government employment. In fact he later claimed, "I've a theory that all economists who serve in government are corrupted as a result of serving in government."[6] Evidently his assignment in Austria was either too short or too insignificant to incur any permanent damage. The same was not true for his friend, Lionel Robbins. Government service, Hayek contended, had contributed to the corruption of Robbins who worked with Keynes during the war and signed on with the Keynesians. Equally corrupting according to Hayek was the "popular lecturing and writing," which, coincidentally, he also tried in the 1940s when he wrote and lectured on *The Road to Serfdom* and ultimately rejected for more academic pursuits.[7] There is probably no better way to fully appreciate the corrupting influence of something than actually to experience it.

On his return to Europe, Hayek had the opportunity to follow up on what he had seen in New York. With the help of von Mises, he established his own institute to study business cycles, which consisted primarily of Hayek authoring papers. His work caught the attention of Lionel Robbins at the London School of Economics who invited Hayek to give a series of lectures. The lectures led to a job offer, which Hayek accepted and held from 1931 to 1950. He characterized the early 1930s as "the most exciting period in the development of economic theory...." It may have been exciting but not necessarily productive, as he also concluded that this period marked an end to "a high point" in economic theory before it was overrun by what he considered to be inferior Keynesian ideas.

From his position in London in the 1930s, Hayek had a ringside seat to watch the unfolding of Keynesian theory at Cambridge. He met Keynes in 1928 at a meeting on business cycles and continued to encounter him at King's College and even claimed to be a "great friend" of Keynes and his wife, Lydia Lopokova. The two economists were in closer proximity in 1939 when the London School of Economics temporarily moved its campus to Cambridge in anticipation of the war. Keynes' critics and detractors may have vehemently disagreed with his theory and reasoning, but they seldom criticized the quality of his scholarship. Hayek was different. Of his "friend," Hayek simply said that "I liked Keynes and in many ways admired him, but do not think he was a good economist." Hayek also criticized Keynes for having little familiarity with economic history, including most English economists other than Marshall.[8] Hayek's low opinion of Keynes was apparently reciprocated. Harold Laski, a colleague at the London School, told Hayek on one occasion that Keynes had called Hayek "the most distinguished muddle-head in Europe."[9] Hayek didn't believe this, calling Laski a "pathological liar."[10] In fact, many of Hayek's disparaging comments were leveled at his colleagues at the London School, including Laski and the School's director, Lord William Beveridge. Hayek claimed that Beveridge "... was completely ignorant of any economics what[so]ever."[11]

Hayek's attempts to refute Keynes' ideas failed to garner much attention and certainly failed to prevent the landslide of Keynesian theory as it took hold in Cambridge and rapidly spread to the United States and much of the world. Hayek had written a critique of Keynes' earlier work, *The Treatise on Money*, but that attracted little attention at the time or subsequently. One of Hayek's serious regrets, he would later say, was that he hadn't done a better job criticizing Keynes' theories. The problem was that Hayek did not offer a very convincing alternative. Another Nobel Prize winner, Paul Samuelson, claimed that Hayek's solution to the Depression amounted to simply sweating it out.[12]

During one of his lecture tours in the United States, Hayek befriended Henry Simons who helped land him a job at the University of Chicago. Hayek arrived in April 1950 but not as a professor of economics. The faculty of the economics department considered themselves to be respectable, scientific scholars and were concerned that Hayek was a little too political and perhaps even a little too popular since the publication of *The Road to Serfdom*. While the economists welcomed Hayek to the University of Chicago, they did not necessarily want him in their department. Instead, Hayek was a professor of social and moral science, which was more closely related to philosophy and psychology than economics.

Hayek did not hold the Chicago economics department in such high esteem either. Although Hayek and Friedman shared many similar views, Hayek rejected Friedman's two major contributions to economic theory, positivism and monetary theory. He dismissed this work as simply another failed attempt to explain all economic phenomena from over-simplified cause and effect. While complimenting Friedman on his expository writing (probably a backhanded compliment), Hayek regretted not writing a formal critique of Friedman's *Essays in Positive Economics*, which he considered to be "quite as dangerous a book," as Keynes' *Treatise*.[13] The member of the Chicago School that Hayek respected most was Gary Becker, another Chicago Nobel Prize winner, whom he considered to be "... a more sophisticated thinker" than Friedman or George Stigler.[14]

There was a brief revival of interest in Hayek's ideas after the fall of Communism in Russian in 1991 and in Eastern Europe shortly thereafter. In November of 1991, President George Bush recognized Hayek with the highest civilian award given in the United States, the Medal of Freedom. The White House spokesman simply claimed that "More than almost anyone else in the twentieth century, this guy was vindicated by the events in Eastern Europe."[15]

By the time of his Nobel award in 1974, Hayek had long abandoned hope that anything useful could be found from the quantitative analysis of business cycles, and he devoted most of his Nobel lecture to this point. In particular, Hayek believed that mathematical economics was an unsuccessful attempt to emulate physics and the other physical sciences. While he did not object to using mathematics to demonstrate the "general character of a pattern," it was the failure to appreciate its limits that concerned him.[16] Game theory, he thought, had crossed that limit. Commenting on *Theory of Games and Economic Behavior* by John von Neumann and Oscar Morgenstern, Hayek wrote, "while I think his book is a great mathematical achievement, the first chapter which deals with economics is just wrong. I don't think that game theory has really made an important contribution to economics, but it's a very interesting mathematical discipline."[17]

Convinced that it was impossible to predict market outcomes or prove market superiority, Hayek also did not believe it was necessary. Only markets, he argued, could convey information from thousands of business and millions of consumers, information about what consumers wanted and what businesses were willing to produce. It was, in his view, enough to simply appreciate the superiority of free markets. It was neither necessary nor possible to prove it.

Hayek elaborated on this idea with a sports analogy. It is possible to collect a great number of statistics about two teams in a sporting contest and use that information to predict the winner. Hayek called such an exercise *pattern prediction* but claimed that it was not scientific. What actually determines the outcome of a game are an infinite number of factors including the physiology of the players and many arbitrary human choices. The billions of details that actually determine the outcome of a game can simply not be modeled "scientifically." It just isn't possible. And markets, involving even more people and even more decisions, are similarly beyond the scope of science, at least according to Hayek.

Described as infinitely urbane, Hayek was imbued with an air of elitism that was reinforced by his classical education. Although neither of his degrees was in economics, he was clearly well read in nineteenth-century economic theory. He judged other economists by whether they agreed with his own ideas, as well as the depth of their classical training. He expressed shock after using a Latin phrase from Cicero that none of his colleagues at the London School of Economics understood.

Many years after retiring to Freiburg, Germany, in the 1960s, Hayek died in 1992 at the age of 92. Throughout his life, Hayek fought an uphill battle against the Soviet industrial machine, the popularity of Keynesian economics, the spread of government programs, and the growth of mathematical economics. His own voice was generally lost in the roar of these dominant trends. But his legacy persists as an early and important patriarch of a conservative, libertarian tradition in economics. His unyielding opposition to most public services and the taxes that paid for them provided an inspiration for the Chicago School economists who continued the campaign.

Milton Friedman (1976 Prize Winner)

Perhaps the most famous and probably the most controversial economist to win the Nobel Prize in economics was Milton Friedman, the sole recipient of the award in 1976. It would not be an exaggeration to claim that Friedman was one of the few economists who inspired a major shift in economic theory, as well as a shift in national economic policy. He became a modern version of Adam Smith, spreading the message that markets can be powerful tools for generating economic efficiency and prosperity. Friedman's uncompromising campaign for free markets and his relentless attacks on government may remain his most enduring legacies, but he also made important and wide-ranging contributions to macroeconomic theory. While history has not validated the details of many of these theories, his innovative arguments almost always provoked useful and spirited debates. As well, because of his disciplined and aggressive approach, Friedman forced even his academic adversaries to become better economists.

Government intervention is not the solution to all economic problems and Friedman certainly forced policy makers and economists to face up to this fact. The best example may be his work on monetary policy. Today, it is generally understood that there are limits to how much the government can increase the money supply without creating economic turmoil, but this was less clear in 1963 when Friedman published a massive study with Anna Schwartz. *A Monetary History of the United States 1867–1960* proved an invaluable resource to understanding the nature of money over almost an entire century. Friedman's warnings about the dangers of unlimited currency expansion were supported by actual historical examples. No one doubts today that an uncontrolled expansion of the money supply can have devastating economic consequences.

The same historical accounts also fueled Friedman's skepticism about a stable relationship between inflation and unemployment as represented by the Phillips Curve. We are now aware that the Phillips Curve is not stable and Friedman deserves credit for making this point before historical events convincingly demonstrated it. Friedman also anticipated the difficulties of maintaining an international system of fixed exchange rates. The Bretton Woods system, which established fixed rates of exchange between national currencies, was established after World War II with support from Keynes. But after several decades, this system started to fail and eventually collapsed in the early 1970s. It was replaced with a system of floating exchange rates, which Friedman strongly supported. Once again, Friedman successfully identified a problem and anticipated the solution.

The Nobel Prize highlighted these contributions and – because Friedman enjoyed a long and productive career – many others by Friedman as well. If Friedman had been content to settle for these broad macroeconomic contributions he might have achieved universal recognition as one of the great economists of the twentieth century. But in all of his work, Friedman was inclined to carry his theories and policy recommendations to extremes. It wasn't enough to warn about the dangers of excessive monetary expansion, he had to claim that *all* efforts by the government to manage the money supply were counterproductive. This turned an otherwise plausible economic concept into a hotly debated topic. Friedman created a similar controversy over floating exchange rates. While many economists also supported floating exchange rates, Friedman distinguished himself by condemning *any* government effort to avoid naturally occurring currency crises. It was his inclination to take extreme positions that rallied his supporters and enraged his critics.

Because of this, even Friedman's errors were newsworthy. Leonard Silk, writing in the *New York Times* in 1976, noted that "in the summer of 1974, Friedman predicted that the international oil cartel would soon break up and prices would fall close to where they were before the Yom Kippur War. Two years later, it still had not happened."[18] Certainly OPEC has had its ups and downs over the years but it still exists as I write today, some thirty-five years later. This was no small mistake. Friedman and his free-market Chicago colleagues had convinced themselves that cartels in any form could be safely ignored because they were theoretically unsustainable. Any cartel will ultimately collapse, they argued, because the individual members will ultimately act in their own self-interest. This was another case of taking a reasonable theory and pushing it to an extreme. Cartels may have an internal conflict but real-life circumstances do not always destroy them, with OPEC being a good example. If theories are to be evaluated based on their predictive accuracy, then this one failed the test.

Others of Friedman's theories didn't fare much better when tested in real-life experiments. According to his Nobel Prize–winning theory called *monetarism*, the money supply had to increase at a steady rate – approximately 2 to 5 percent a year – to avoid the risk of high inflation or recession. When Paul Volcker took charge of the Federal Reserve in 1979, he began by testing this policy prescription, only to abandon it in 1982 after pushing unemployment to record levels. The ever-vigilant Friedman observed Volcker's large increases in the money supply after 1982 and warned that this would cause inflation, if not in 1983, at least by 1984. Friedman's warning became increasingly vociferous as the Federal Reserve continued a rapid run up in the money supply well into 1983.

As economic recovery appeared to be taking hold, the Federal Reserve abruptly changed course again, rapidly slowing the growth of the money supply. This, according to Friedman's monetarist model, was even worse. The inconsistency in federal policy was going to cause unemployment as well as inflation. The myopic policies of the Federal Reserve, according to Friedman, were "bound to be renewed stagflation – recession accompanied by rising inflation and high interest rates."[19] He wrote several articles in *Newsweek* during this time reiterating his prediction, which was counter to all other forecasts, and he even berated the Federal Reserve for ignoring him. What was inevitable in the monetarist model, however, failed to make even the slightest appearance in the real world. Contrary to Friedman's prediction, unemployment rates continued to fall, economic growth was robust, and inflation remained low and steady in 1983, and 1984, and beyond. The model that had earned Friedman the Nobel Prize had let him down. The lesson was not lost on the Federal Reserve, which has continued over the past few decades to use monetary policy to counterbalance tendencies toward recession or inflation.

Part of the opus by Friedman and Schwartz, *A Monetary History of the United States*, provided an important historical account of some of the major innovations in money and currency. Another part of the book was more provocative, blaming the Federal Reserve for the Great Depression. The authors argued that the Federal Reserve should have seen the Depression coming and should have immediately taken steps to prevent the decline in the money supply. The failure to do so, they argued, converted a "garden-variety recession" into a "major catastrophe." Milton Friedman could not accept the possibility that the Great Depression had resulted from free markets, so he found fault in government – in this case, the Federal Reserve.

Trying to identify the primary cause of the Great Depression is difficult if not impossible. It is well-known, however, that the money supply was falling in the early 1930s because banks were failing and bank accounts were disappearing. Eventually the government did act and in 1934 offered deposit insurance to shore up the banks and help restore confidence. Although it was too late to prevent the bank panic in the early 1930s, this action did prevent a reoccurrence in the future.

But none of this was sufficient for Friedman. On the one hand he objected to the government not doing enough to rescue private banks, and when the government did do something – provide deposit insurance – he objected to that, too. He did not believe the government should interfere in the operations of private banks. In hindsight, the Federal Reserve probably should have acted more quickly to rescue the banking system but why did the banking system need to be rescued in the first place? Friedman ignored this problem because it would have forced him to acknowledge an important market failure.

In his prime, Friedman showed great inventiveness by explaining rather simple economic behavior with elaborate stories. Two of these theories were cited by the Nobel committee. For example, it was well-known that poor families saved very little, being more likely to live hand-to-mouth, compared to rich families who typically had significant savings. Setting aside the obvious reason for this, Friedman invented an explanation that became known as the *permanent income hypothesis*. He theorized that poor families may have been wealthier at one point and accustomed to receiving a higher *permanent income*. Even though their new, *transitory income* was lower than before, they continued to spend like the old days, leaving nothing for savings. Friedman thought that was the reason poor families had such low savings. Perhaps – or perhaps they just had little left after buying necessities.

Friedman offered another story to explain the short-run *Philips Curve*, the tendency for unemployment to fall when inflation rises and vice versa.[20] In order to account for this phenomenon, Friedman claimed that businesses were temporarily fooled by higher prices into hiring more workers during inflation. This meant that unemployment would fall (at least temporarily) with inflation. It was an unusual story, especially for Friedman, because it required businesses to make systematic mistakes.

While most of Friedman's theories were intensely debated within the economics profession, it was his affiliation with a military dictatorship that sparked his greatest public controversy. In an unusual event, several Nobel Prize winners in science protested Friedman's Nobel award in letters published in the *New York Times*. George Wald, winner of the Nobel Prize in Medicine in 1967 and Linus Pauling, winner of two Nobel Prizes, Chemistry in 1954 and Peace in 1963, wrote a letter objecting to Friedman's award because of his prominent relationship with the military junta in Chile during the early 1970s. Likewise, Nobel Prize winners David Baltimore (Medicine 1975) and S. E. Luria (Medicine 1969) added their objections to Friedman's award. They, too, focused on Friedman's association with the Chilean junta and its sad record of human rights violations. They characterized Friedman "as a supporter of the enemies of democracy" and claimed that giving the prize to Friedman was "an insult to the people of Chile ... especially to those Chileans who are in jail or in exile as a result of the policies of the military government."[21]

In another rare protest of a Nobel Prize, thousands of demonstrators marched in Sweden in opposition to Friedman's award because of his association with the military in Chile. The 300 policeman called out to maintain control were not entirely successful. One motivated protester slipped through the lines incognito, sporting the white tie and tails required for the exclusive party. The protestor was whisked away only after shouting out at the end of the ceremony, "Friedman go home" and "Long live the Chilean people."[22] Friedman denied serving as an advisor to Chile, but he didn't help his case by adding that he "had no further contact" after spending six days in Chile in 1975.[23]

In fact, Friedman was doing more than enjoying a Latin American vacation during his trip to Chile. He held a whirlwind series of seminars and meetings with government officials during the early days of General Augusto Pinochet's military coup d'état. Friedman was accompanied by his friend Arnold Harberger who was the link between the University of Chicago and the Pinochet government.[24] Harberger had secured financing for University of Chicago faculty through the U.S. Agency for International Development under an agreement with the Catholic University of Chile.[25] Some of the meetings were with government officials and members of the military junta, culminating in a private meeting with General Pinochet to discuss economic conditions in Chile.

While the substance of the policies recommended by Friedman were typical of his economic philosophy, the magnitude and swiftness with which they were implemented in Chile were unprecedented and controversial. The tough medicine recommended by Friedman was characterized as "shock treatment" in order to end inflation in a few months. He advocated an across-the-board reduction in government spending by 25 percent in six months, limits on the money supply, and continuation of what was essentially a free-floating currency. A democratically elected government would have run into trouble implementing such harsh measures, but Pinochet's totalitarian government found the recommendations appealing and had no trouble implementing them. The actions were supported by a coterie of native economists, called the *Chicago Boys* because many were graduates of the University of Chicago. Friedman may have denied advising the junta, but someone forgot to explain this to the General. Pinochet wrote to Friedman, expressing "gratitude for your personal contribution to an analysis of the economic situation of my country, I am also taking this occasion to express my highest and most respectful regard for you."[26]

So how did these policies work? Apparently the Chilean "economic miracle" was underperforming by 1982. Writing in *Newsweek*, Friedman conceded that "Chile is currently having serious difficulties – along with much of the rest of the world.... This temporary setback will likely be surmounted."[27] But in other respects, Friedman was delighted to see his favored policies being implemented, such as school vouchers and an opt-out provision for Chile's social security system. Assessing this political program, Friedman called it an "amazing political miracle," a generous compliment to a military dictatorship with a long record of human rights violations.

While Friedman was reticent on commenting on human rights in Chile, he had plenty to say about the protests in Stockholm. He was outraged by the demonstrators at his award ceremony. They were, according to Friedman, "hoodlums" that reminded him of Nazi Germany.[28] He was quoted as saying, "There is a stench of Nazism in the air. Our nostrils are full of it. Freedom of speech must be accompanied by freedom to listen. Freedom of speech does not mean freedom to use force or coercion to prevent people from speaking."[29]

As this example illustrates, Friedman moved effortlessly from his economic theories to political advocacy. He ventured into high-stakes politics in 1964 when he signed on as an advisor to Senator Goldwater's failed presidential campaign and again with the more successful Nixon campaign in 1968. His resume also included serving as an economic advisor to the South-African government at a time when it was internationally condemned for its apartheid policies. In 1966, he began writing a regular column for *Newsweek*, which gave him a forum for his controversial opinions that included opposition to Social Security, the minimum wage, unions, and public education. But true to his libertarian philosophy, he also opposed politically motivated tax deductions, oil company subsidies, and the military draft. Friedman seemed to stir up controversy with everything he did.

It was easy for Hayek and Friedman to merge a libertarian philosophy with a passion for free markets, because they both required less government. It was more difficult, however, to combine a libertarian philosophy with the principle of scientific objectivity. What do you do, for example, when your economic research conflicts with your libertarian values? How do you choose between scientific objectivity and libertarian principles? Hayek and Friedman had different answers to this fundamental question. Hayek, who was probably the better philosopher, resolved the dilemma by claiming that attempts to maintain scientific objectivity in economics were a waste of time. He was comfortable with his philosophical preference for unregulated markets and discouraged others from believing that it required scientific justification. He also doubted that economists could find truth embedded in economic data – an interesting perspective for a Nobel Prize winner in economics.

Milton Friedman, however, did not surrender his scientific aspirations so easily. Friedman made a name for himself through the promotion of *positive economics*, the idea that economics can be objective and scientific, uncontaminated by politics or personal bias. He insisted that he could separate his scientific work from his political and philosophical positions. When he wore his science "hat," he was capable of developing theories and objectively testing them with data. He called this positivism. When he wore his policy hat, he was free to express his political opinions even if they weren't necessarily scientific. He called this *normative*. It didn't matter if there were inconsistencies between Friedman the scientist and Friedman the policy advocate, because the former was science and the latter was opinion. Therefore, he claimed there was no contradiction between being an objective scientist and a libertarian, as long as he had two hats in his closet.

There is a certain irony about Friedman – one of the most politically motivated economists – winning professional acclaim for writing a book on the virtues of politically neutral economics. There were other economists in addition to Hayek who could not accept this. Friedman's teacher at Chicago, Henry Simons, was equally skeptical. He was convinced that economic discourse was, by its very nature, based on "prejudices and preconceptions."[30] Simons complained about economists who thought they could be scientifically objective, writing "The emptiness of this pretense among economists is notorious."[31]

Even Friedman seemed to have second thoughts. Writing his memoirs in 1998, Friedman noted that his wife and co-author, Rose, didn't believe that economics was objective.[32] Over the years he had gradually moved toward Rose's position and in a rare moment of candidness, Milton confessed that "I am much less confident now that I am right and she wrong than I was more than four decades ago when I wrote the methodology article...."[33] Friedman might not have entirely abandoned this concept, but he seemed to lack confidence in it. Nevertheless, positive economics was cited by the Nobel Prize committee as one of his major contributions to economics.

There was another aspect of positive economics that disturbed critics. Friedman proclaimed that it didn't matter how unrealistic assumptions are in economic models as long as the predictions are useful. While this appears to be an obvious lapse in common sense, it is worth noting that all economic models generalize in some way about human behavior and generalizations can't always be perfect. However, most economists would like to believe that their assumptions are reasonably accurate. But Friedman wasn't going to waste his time defending his assumptions, no matter how unrealistic they might appear. It was almost as if Friedman, according to Leonard Silk, was trying to make a "virtue out of 'unrealistic' assumptions."[34]

Friedman's parents were both immigrants from Carpatho-Ruthenia which at various times was part of Hungary, Czechoslovakia, the Soviet Union, and after that collapsed, the Ukraine. Milton Friedman was born in 1912 in Brooklyn, New York where his mother ran a small dry goods store and his father commuted to Manhattan as a day laborer. Bills were sometimes difficult to pay but the store provided a modest income with little room for luxuries except the music lessons for Milton and his three older sisters. Milton's violin lessons revealed little musical ability and equally little music appreciation. During his early school years he converted from something of a religious fanatic to an agnostic with antireligious tendencies.[35]

With the help of a New Jersey state tuition scholarship, he attended Rutgers University where he studied both mathematics and economics. He supplemented his scholarship with income by working as a waiter, selling socks, used books, and fireworks, and tutoring high school students in Rahway.[36] But what began as a prospective career as an actuary took an abrupt detour a couple of years later after he failed some qualifying exams.[37] Although his math skills were a little low for an actuary, they were more than adequate for an economist. After graduating from Rutgers in 1932, Friedman accepted a scholarship to attend the University of Chicago in the fall where he was exposed to some of the leading economists of the day. Friedman quickly attached himself to the free-market clique led by Frank Knight and Jacob Viner and took enough courses in mathematics, according to his estimate, to have earned the equivalent of a master's degree. He also had the good fortune to sit next to a young Ukrainian immigrant in his first theory class, Rose Director, who became his wife and partner on some significant projects.

During graduate school, Friedman had the opportunity to work with some prominent economists including Wesley Clair Mitchell at Columbia, Simon Kuznets at the National Bureau of Economic Research, and George Stigler, a fellow graduate student at Chicago. After a few government and university jobs, Friedman accepted a more permanent position in the economics department at the University of Chicago in 1946. Over the years, Friedman helped to populate the department with like-minded economists, creating what became known as the Chicago School of Economics.

Friedman was hardly the first economist to promote free, unregulated markets but it could be said that he was one of the most effective. Both his academic work and his popular writing and speaking were all directed toward this goal – which was more of a political campaign than a scientific program. He ignored examples of market failures and insisted that free markets were better than government. This "extreme" approach did not go unnoticed. On the occasion of Friedman's Nobel award, the *New York Times* editorial questioned "whether an exaggerated version of the efficacy of the market may not serve the public badly – by leading to the neglect of social actions needed to protect the public health and welfare in a highly industrialized and mass-organizational world."[38] It was an obvious and poignant question.

When Friedman was informed of his selection for the Nobel Prize he was surprisingly aloof. "It is not the pinnacle of my career," he announced. Nor did he accept "the particular seven people who make the awards as the jury to which I would want to submit my scientific work."[39] He seemed to appreciate the prize more after a little reflection and after they wrote him a check for $160,000. In 1977, Friedman retired from the University of Chicago but continued his association with the Hoover Institution at Stanford University. Milton Friedman died in 2006 at the age of 94.

James M. Buchanan Jr. (1986 Prize Winner)

Although he had a grandfather who was governor of Tennessee in the 1890s, James M. Buchanan Jr. was still a poor Southern farm boy who earned spending money by milking cows. He later enrolled in a relatively obscure college, Middle Tennessee State. After graduating in 1940, he earned a master's degree from the University of Tennessee in 1941 and spent five years in the Navy, including a stint serving on the staff of Admiral Chester Nimitz during World War II in the Pacific operations. Education opened up new opportunities for Buchanan, and after the war he received his doctorate from the University of Chicago in 1948.

When it was announced he had been awarded the Nobel Prize, including the entire $294,000 allocated for that year, Buchanan was a professor at George Mason University in Fairfax, Virginia. He was in fact the first and only economic Nobel Prize winner from George Mason, which was primarily an undergraduate teaching university as opposed to a top-ranked research school. He was, at the time, also the General Director of the Center for Study of Public Choice, an institute and discipline of his own creation.

Buchanan had worked hard for what he achieved and was inclined to resent those who had not. Associates of Buchanan commonly referred to him as having an austere, even intimidating personality. One economist who knew Buchanan as a fellow officer of the Southern Economics Association described him as "one of the coldest people I ever met...."[40] Making personal connections was not one of his strengths. Invited to participate in a panel to honor the contribution of economist Armen Alchian on his 80th birthday, Buchanan gave short shrift to personal anecdotes and instead launched into pointed questions for Alchian and challenged some ideas only remotely related to his work – not exactly a birthday celebration.

James Buchanan was truly a product of the University of Chicago's economics department. He eagerly absorbed microeconomic theories, embraced libertarian beliefs, and adopted Friedman's positivist philosophy. Like Friedman, Buchanan insisted that his work represented objective science, all the time reaching conclusions consistent with his own devotion to free markets and his disdain for government. The same formula that had worked so well for Friedman – claims of scientific objectivity combined with libertarian values – worked equally well for Buchanan.

The primary challenge for new doctoral students who became disciples of the basic market model was to seek out new applications. Their goal was not to revise the model but to apply it to new areas and hopefully discover new insights. Some chose to focus on the macroeconomy while others applied the ideas to social institutions. Buchanan's choice was to apply microeconomic principles to the behavior of individuals in government service. What happens, for instance, when all government agents – elected officials and bureaucrats – act in their own self-interest? Here was a simple application of the basic economic model to government agents and it was one of the primary reasons cited by the Nobel committee for Buchanan's award.

What insights came from the assumption that public servants are motivated by self-interest? The primary discovery seems to be basically the assumption itself, that is, public servants have their own self-interest. Although *public choice* advocates seemed genuinely surprised to discover that it was possible for public servants to act in their own self-interest and ignore the will of the people when setting public policy or spending public money, it is safe to say that this possibility was not entirely unknown prior to the development of the theory.

The Nobel committee was impressed that public choice theorists generalized this observation to all organizations, concluding that the self-interest of leaders in any organization may conflict with the interest of the membership. The Nobel committee considered this discovery to be an "important scientific achievement," but stopped short of claiming that Buchanan discovered this more or less obvious fact.[41] What he and his public choice advocates did, according to the Nobel committee, was to build on this relatively simple concept and construct a comprehensive theory of politics and economics.

These ideas were used to oppose government actions, even those intended to correct clear market failures. According to Buchanan, it may be better to live with a flawed market than to expect government, with its self-interested bureaucrats, to solve the problem. It's not enough, he argued, to have a legitimate role for government; there also has to be a mechanism to compel the government to serve the public interest.

There is in Buchanan's work and in public choice theory in general a curious preference for consensus in public decision making. Consensus was also championed by Buchanan's hero, early twentieth-century philosopher and economist Knut Wicksell.[42] While support for consensus may sound virtuous, it is in truth just another strategy to limit the role of government. The practical effect of consensus is that it grants veto power to each individual, ensuring a minor if any role for the state. Such a voting standard would limit most government activities, even those with great public benefits.

Buchanan backed consensus requirements but not for all decisions, only for what he called constitutional issues. One way to explain this concept is with the example of a basketball game. When observers recommend strategies about how to win a game – zone or man-to-man defense – they are merely offering opinions about strategies. However, when observers recommend changes in the rules – the three-point circle, twenty-four-second shot clock – they are raising constitutional issues. Because the rules of an economy are constitutional issues, Buchanan argued, they should be subject to a consensus requirement.

Buchanan was particularly fond of balanced budget rules because they eliminated the potential for the government to run deficits. He complained that current voters support budget deficits because they reap the benefits while the costs are left for future generations that do not yet vote. The nation had apparently lost its fiscal discipline, according to Buchanan, and the economist who "must bear substantial responsibility is Lord Keynes himself."[43] By making deficits politically acceptable, Buchanan believed that Keynes had committed an "intellectual error of monumental proportion(s)...."[44]

Buchanan's animosity for Keynes was as much personal as it was about economics. He concluded in one essay that "Keynes was not a democrat, but, rather, looked upon himself as a potential member of an enlightened ruling elite."[45] This illustrates another dimension of James M. Buchanan's character, a strong dislike for intellectuals from elite universities. As a graduate of a small Southern college, he felt discriminated against by Harvard and Yale graduates. He blamed elitism for the reason that he was passed over for cadet officer in midshipman school and why he was not treated fairly even at the University of Chicago.[46]

If the Great Depression hadn't devastated his family's financial circumstances, Buchanan might have attended Vanderbilt University and become part of the academic elite himself. Instead, he was forced to attend the more affordable Middle Tennessee State and milk cows morning and night for four years to pay for his books and fees.[47] He described himself as a "member of the great unwashed" and continued to rail against the Eastern academic elite.

Buchanan complained in 1986 that his libertarian ideas placed him outside the mainstream of economics. His position at George Mason University also denied him the kind of respect that came from a Harvard, Chicago, or Berkeley professorship. As a consequence, his students from Virginia, Virginia Tech, and George Mason faced difficulty securing academic appointments. According to one of his students, Paul Craig Roberts, "We were all heretics who were excluded from academic life by the pure thinkers. That's why so many of Jim Buchanan's students turned up in the Reagan administration."[48] In fact, up to the time of the Nobel award, many economists considered Buchanan to be something of an eccentric gadfly.

It might seem odd that Buchanan's public choice theory did not receive a more favorable response from the vast majority of economists who favor conservative, antigovernment theories. Two years before the Nobel award Buchanan gave a speech expressing hopelessness for ever achieving the recognition he thought he deserved. Other economists were critical of his work, in part because it relied on philosophical arguments that looked more like editorial writing than mathematics. But he held firm and criticized conventional economists who seemed to get "their kicks from the discovery of proofs of propositions relevant only for their own fantasy lands."[49] He criticized other economists for being a "stubborn lot," and even worse, "ideological eunuchs."[50]

Friends claimed that Buchanan never really stopped trying to prove that he deserved a place among the "front ranks of academe."[51] His frustrated ambition, however, motivated him to work even harder. He became a prolific writer, producing twenty-three books including his major work, *The Calculus of Consent*, with co-author and frequent collaborator Gordon Tullock. Buchanan also produced hundreds of written and edited papers and groomed a cadre of students through his Center for Public Choice.[52]

What Buchanan characterized as a lonely and frustrating thirty-year struggle to gain recognition ended in 1986 with the announcement of the Nobel Prize. The initial announcement created a stir among reporters who knew little about George Mason University. The university had only started three decades earlier, but it had already earned a reputation as a school that was willing to pay generously for its conservative stars. In 1986, Buchanan earned $114,130 a year, making him one of the highest paid professors anywhere in the United States, with one-third of his salary paid by donations from private foundations.[53] The Nobel Prize rescued Buchanan from the professional fringe and put him right in the middle of consideration by mainstream economics.

Buchanan's supporters insisted on characterizing his message as important even if they conceded that it was sometimes self-evident. His work neatly reinforced the basic market model and the antigovernment theme so popular among the Reagan administration, libertarians, and the University of Chicago. Balanced budget amendments, spending caps, and tax cuts were the vehicles for carrying out this goal, and all of these gained political momentum in the 1980s. There was no real effort to distinguish between useful functions of government – such as funding Middle Tennessee State College – and less useful functions, such as providing subsidies and tax breaks to otherwise successful corporations. Instead, the message was a broad condemnation of all government functions, a message that resonated with wealthy libertarian benefactors.

Historical events have a way of turning the tables on economic theories. Buchanan had originally blamed Keynesians for budget deficits and the mounting national debt. But in the 1980s, Buchanan's allies in the Reagan administration, some of whom were his own students, engineered some of the largest budget deficits in American history. The deficits were so large that they persisted through four years of the ensuing Bush administration and eight years of the Clinton administration before they were finally eliminated. In 2003, the second Bush president took his turn, cutting taxes for the wealthy, launching a prolonged war in Iraq, and sending deficits to new highs. During these years, Republican administrations were responsible for creating much larger deficits than the Democrats.

The announcement of a Nobel Prize for the founder of public choice was not greeted with universal acclaim. Michael Kinsley, writing in the *Wall Street Journal*, decided to lampoon the entire business. From what he could gather from the press accounts, the Nobel committee decided to honor an eccentric academic who discovered that he could explain all political behavior as motivated by self-interest. Kinsley concluded that perhaps it was not so difficult to win a Nobel Prize and chastised himself for not having thought of this theory first. Just to make sure it didn't happen again, Kinsley proposed several of his own theories, positing that self-interest also motivated the Nobel committee that selected Buchanan, the universities that hired him and paid his extraordinary salary, and even the editorial committees that praised him.[54]

A good parody will often hit a soft spot and Kinsley hit the bull's eye, eliciting a barrage of indignant letters to the editor including one from Milton Friedman. Rallying around the University of Chicago alumnus, Friedman condemned Kinsley's column as cute, malicious, and ignorant.[55] Puerile scribbling was the characterization offered by David Shapiro from San Francisco State, and gratuitous snide remarks was the analysis from Thomas DiLorenzo of Washington University.[56] If any evidence was needed to confirm that public choice theory deserved respect, the only proof needed was the fact that it was represented in "all the top academic journals in both economic and political science," according to DiLorenzo.[57] This has always been an important litmus test for Nobel Prizes, notwithstanding what economist Armen Alchian once said, "95 percent of the material in economics journals was wrong or irrelevant."[58]

Robert Lekachman, writing in *The New York Times*, concluded that if the Nobel Prize was actually awarded for economic ingenuity, "it would cease to be embarrassingly easy to ridicule."[59] In his view, it was painfully clear from Buchanan's work that economics is permeated by political values, no more a science than history or political science. He particularly mentioned the Nobel committee's infatuation with the basic competitive model, essentially giving awards to theorists who merely rediscover Adam Smith every few years.

THREE

Micro: The Chicago School

Gary S. Becker (1992)

George J. Stigler (1982)

Theodore W. Schultz (1979)

Ronald H. Coase (1991)

Most of what conventional economists know about markets can be found in the field of microeconomics. Adam Smith launched it in the eighteenth century with his description of market behavior, and Alfred Marshall made it popular in the early twentieth century with a more modern representation of supply and demand. Microeconomics has continued to thrive in universities, and the Nobel Prize has been awarded to one group of economists who translated the basic concepts into higher levels of mathematical abstraction, and to a second group who applied the concepts to problems unrelated to formal markets. This chapter is about the latter, those economists who have won Nobel Prizes by discovering new applications for microeconomics.

Supply and demand, a simple notion, informs many economic models. It easily explains all kinds of basic economic behaviors in all kinds of situations. But microeconomics, especially the perfect competition version, went far beyond that, providing a mathematically precise description of idealized market behavior. Perfect competition relied on simple, but highly abstract, assumptions, namely, a very large number of firms and consumers who act rationally with perfect information. Even firms entering new markets are assumed to know exactly what to do. Under these ideal conditions, it was possible to derive mathematical conclusions about the economy. But what did they actually mean? If the models weren't based on reality, what insights could they provide about the real world?

The four Nobel Prize–winning economists presented in this chapter, Gary S. Becker, George J. Stigler, Theodore W. Schultz, and Ronald H. Coase were all from the University of Chicago. This was no coincidence. Under the command of its most famous member, Milton Friedman, the economics department at Chicago for many years hired and retained only those economists who shared his strict adherence to the model of perfect competition and a political preference for free markets. These four economists were some of the giants of the Chicago School, and they all had a mind for micro.

Gary S. Becker (1992 Prize Winner)

While teaching at Columbia University, Gary S. Becker found himself looking for a parking spot in New York City one day and accidentally stumbled onto a topic that would lead to his Nobel Prize. Because Columbia did not provide parking for faculty, he had to find his own space on this trip into the city for a student's Ph.D. oral examination. As he approached the campus he faced a choice, not unlike those facing commuters every day – park legally in a lot or take a chance and park illegally to get a little closer and hopefully save a little money. The decision, he reasoned, rested largely on the probability of getting a ticket and the size of the ticket. The problem seemed good enough to ask the Ph.D. candidate, which Becker did. Not entirely satisfied with the answer, he puzzled over the problem for the next few years, resulting in a number of path-breaking publications on the economics of crime.

Becker's understanding of criminal activity began with a classic microeconomic assumption, perfect rationality and perfect information. He presumed that criminals objectively calculate the probability of getting caught and of serving a prison term before deciding to commit a crime. Initially, this theory struck many people, including many economists, as ludicrous. In fact, there was initially some question as to whether Becker was serious. It turned out that he was serious enough, even if he seemed to enjoy his role as an academic provocateur. His effort to extend Chicago School's economics into the realm of topics traditionally reserved for sociology earned him a place in history and the entire 1992 Nobel Prize worth $1.2 million.

Becker's parents may have only had eighth grade educations but their son Gary showed a talent for school, especially for mathematics. Becker's father was a businessman who kept track of the financial news even after he lost most of his eyesight. To keep informed, he relied on Gary to read the financial papers to him, and although the young man found it a little boring, he was exposed to economics through these business and financial reports.

Becker majored in economics at Princeton as an undergraduate and managed to graduate in only three years while taking additional mathematics courses beyond the core requirements. He was accepted by the University of Chicago for graduate studies in economics, even though he conceded that his interest in the subject had started to wane during his final year at Princeton. His enthusiasm was restored in 1951 when he took his first class by Milton Friedman. Becker acknowledged the "profound effect" that Friedman had on him, and underwent a complete transformation into a Chicago School economist. Friedman in turn praised his prized student, calling him "far and away the most creative economist of his generation." When Becker's Nobel was announced, Friedman confessed that he had "been recommending him for the prize for years."[1]

Like Friedman, Becker served as president of the Mont Pelerin Society and opposed most government activities, preferring instead the operation of private markets. He also opposed Social Security and the minimum wage while supporting school vouchers, individual retirement accounts, and the economic policies of Chilean dictator General Pinochet. He even endorsed Friedman's more controversial positions like legalizing marijuana.[2]

While a student at the University of Chicago, Becker took classes by Theodore Schultz who taught him the concept that education is an investment in *human capital*. After only three years of graduate study Becker accepted a position at Chicago as an assistant professor. What was shaping up as a fast track to academic success took an odd turn when Becker did something that would surely have violated his own economic models: He left a higher paying job at the University of Chicago to take a lower paying job at Columbia. The reason, he explained later, was to leave the nest and prove that he could make it on his own.

Becker's long string of controversies began with the publication of his first book, *The Economics of Discrimination*, in 1957. His ideas about discrimination were developed for his doctoral dissertation at Chicago. He started with the notion that discrimination was caused by individuals having a preference for their own race. People with this preference were willing to accept an economic loss simply to avoid contact with individuals of other races. Becker's theory of discrimination assumes that workers turn down higher paying jobs to avoid working with other racial and ethnic groups, and businesses reject some productive workers because of their race and accept a lower profit rate.

This may have been a curiously narrow view of discrimination but by itself it wasn't particularly controversial. The next part of the theory, however, is what set off Becker's critics. According to his definition, discrimination only took place when the discriminator suffered an economic loss. Everything else was just good business! If for example, a business hires only white applicants and does not suffer an economic loss then there is no discrimination according to Becker. Or if a landlord always chooses white renters who always pay their rent and maintain the property, then that would not qualify as discrimination. In Becker's theory, the business or landlord would need to make a decision that harmed them economically before it would qualify as discrimination.

Becker proceeded to combine his definition of discrimination with the theory of perfect competition. His conclusion offered a remarkably simple solution to discrimination. According to Becker, any business that discriminates will earn lower profits than its competitors, which will eventually force it out of business. Therefore, one needn't worry about businesses discriminating because they will suffer lower profits, and if they persist in discriminating, they will soon find themselves out of business because of competition in perfect markets. In this case, there is no need for affirmative action, an Equal Employment Opportunity Commission, or government enforcement of antidiscrimination laws because a competitive market will regulate itself.

A narrow definition of discrimination in the workplace combined with an unrealistic economic model may not sound like a useful theory, yet it was cited by the Nobel committee as a major achievement. At first, Becker's book was ignored and, as he noted, "for several years it had no visible impact on anything."[3] But as it became better known, the response was generally hostile, except of course from Friedman and others at the University of Chicago. As Becker explained, "Support by people I respected so highly was crucial to my willingness to persevere in the face of much hostility."[4] The real problem was that the theory explained why discrimination could not exist in competitive free markets, when, in fact, discrimination was a fact of life. One might think it would have been difficult to defend a new theory when counter examples were ubiquitous.

While teaching at Columbia University, Becker also accepted an appointment with the National Bureau of Economic Research in Manhattan where he pursued Theodore Schultz's ideas about human capital. This work became the basis of his second book, *Human Capital*. Working collaboratively with faculty at Columbia, Becker not only continued to promote the Chicago School philosophy, he also recreated the Chicago School's method of instruction, the graduate workshop where students presented and discussed their work.

Becker's approach involved the construction of mathematical formulas weighing the costs and rewards of undertaking a specific act, including crime, education, and even suicide. Let us look at his examination of crime in more detail in order to understand the simplicity of the approach. Most of the conclusions drawn from this exercise "made sense" to many people,

and this combined with the simplicity of the approach made Becker's theories easy to teach. For example, the poor are more likely to commit serious
crimes because they are often less educated and have fewer alternatives with
less to lose. And teenagers are more likely to commit crimes because they
seem to have so little concern about future consequences.[5] Similarly, drug
users commit more crimes because they also live in the here-and-now and
care little about what happens next.[6]

Becker's approach to crime depends entirely on the assumption that
criminals are rational. Criminals may be strategic, they may be crafty, and
they may even be smart, but are they really rational? Of all occupations,
criminals may well be the most predisposed to irrational behavior. In
fact some criminals – serial murderers, for example – are almost by
definition irrational. For some smaller fraction of the criminal population generally involved in less serious crime, like university professors
contemplating parking violations, rational behavior may be a perfectly
valid assumption. In such cases, the probability of getting caught and
the level of punishment may be decisive. But are these the crimes that
matter to society? How many communities live in fear of serial parking
violators?

Becker even used criminals' high recidivism rates as confirmation that
criminals are rationally assessing costs and benefits because they keep coming to the same conclusion – crime pays. An equally plausible explanation is
that criminals are irrational, making the same mistake over and over again.[7]
Wouldn't a scientist consider both possibilities?

Whether a person is predisposed toward crime largely depends, according to Becker, on how much they value the future. Individuals who place
little value on the future are more likely to smoke, take drugs, and commit crimes because they are prone to ignore future consequences such as
cancer, death, and prison. In economic terms, they have a high *discount
rate*. Becker claimed this as the reason why so many drug addicts are also
criminals. Because we cannot directly observe discount rates, economists
can attribute a high discount rate as the cause for almost anything. Thus,
criminal behavior must mean high discount rates. This economic theory
of crime overlooks the fact that drug addicts also have a strong need for
money to support their habits and few rational inhibitions about how to get
it. The theory also ignores the role of dysfunctional families, domestic violence, child abuse and neglect, drug and alcohol abuse, and gang activity, all
of which may be connected with criminal activity. I also suspect that there
may be some people with high discount rates who manage to live perfectly
happy, crime-free lives.

Having cultivated a reputation as a crime expert, Becker offered his opinion on a wide range of policy issues. He was skeptical of the three-strike laws that require a stiff penalty for anyone committing a third felony. The law, he explained, should focus on serious, violent crimes, not just any felony. Becker would also grant police more freedom to conduct searches for concealed weapons based on only "reasonable suspicion." On the other hand, he made it very clear that he supported the right to own and carry weapons that were not concealed. And consistent with his libertarian principles, Becker confessed that he was "not an enthusiast about giving people long prison sentences for drug activity."[8]

Families

When he was still teaching at Columbia, Becker married and had two daughters. Years later, after his first wife died, Becker married Guity Nashat, a Middle East historian, and became father to two stepsons. All this gave Becker some first-hand knowledge about families that would become the subject of his next major work.

By the late 1960s, Becker grew increasingly dissatisfied with Columbia University. He didn't like his commute from the suburbs or the way the university handled the student antiwar demonstrators in 1968. He thought the administration made a mistake by not taking a "firm hand" against the demonstrations, which he characterized as riots. He criticized the faculty for behaving "no better than the students" and the administration for failing to control the situation and being "incompetent."[9] In 1970 he returned to a position at the University of Chicago and refocused his attention on the family, exploring the motivation behind marriage, divorce, altruism, and investments in child quality. This research culminated in the publication of *A Treatise on the Family* in 1981.

In order to develop a unique theory of the family, Becker borrowed concepts from microeconomics typically used to describe factory production in a competitive market. Karl-Görän Mäler, a member of the Swedish Economics Nobel committee said, "Becker broke down the traditional concepts of what a family actually does. A family produces what it needs, and one should look at a family as a kind of factory."[10] A similar description was offered by Assar Lindbeck of the Royal Swedish Academy of Sciences when citing the highlights of Becker's academic work. He made a special point to recognize Becker's discovery that every household is essentially "a small factory."[11]

Why do couples get married instead of remaining single? Setting aside the ostensible reasons for marriage – love, infatuation, procreation, wealth, and companionship – Becker focused on economic criteria. Being married allows more specialization and improved efficiencies in the family's use of time to raise its standard of living. One partner can specialize in paid work and the other in unpaid work at home, and collectively their use of time and money can create their highest standard of living. The office worker can work longer hours knowing that domestic chores will be done by the house worker.

This sort of analysis leads to some interesting "scientific" conclusions. Becker presumed that beauty and intelligence were responsible for higher productivity at both work and home, and for that reason smart and beautiful people make desirable marriage partners. According to Becker, "Presumably this helps explain why, for example, less attractive or less intelligent persons are less likely to marry than are more attractive or more intelligent persons." A footnote concedes that this conclusion about attractiveness is "not based on any statistical evidence."[12]

The theory explains why beautiful people get married but can it explain polygamy? If gains from marriage apply to two individuals, then why not to three, four, or more individuals? This was an obvious question that Becker felt compelled to answer. The problem, he argued, with a marriage containing multiple husbands is that it "makes it difficult to identify the father of a child." And having multiple wives would result in diminishing returns – again assumed and not shown with data – and therefore one man and one woman were "the most efficient marital form." This may constitute the first "scientific" defense of monogamy.

Crazy and Controversial

In his personal statement for the Nobel committee Becker confessed, "For a long time my type of work was either ignored or strongly disliked by most of the leading economists."[13] Popularity, however, was never his goal. As he explained in an article in *Business Week*, "I get a little bit uncomfortable when identified with the conventional wisdom," and added, "I enjoyed being unpopular." In the same article, it was noted that "Early in Becker's career, most economists viewed him as brilliant, but wacky." He declared, "I had fun going against the Establishment." Audiences would laugh when he explained "that parents would have fewer children as the cost of raising them increased."[14] Economist Sherwin Rosen said, "People thought he was nuts to treat children as durable goods."[15]

In an interview with the Federal Reserve Bank of Minneapolis in 2002, Becker expressed enough doubts to make you wonder how much of this he actually believed. "How many people," he questioned, "sit down before they marry and say, oh these are the reasons I should marry this woman, these are the reasons why I should not marry her, then weigh these and see if the pluses exceed the minuses? Very few people do that."[16] In fact, Becker acknowledged how offensive even conducting this process would be to a prospective spouse. The real question, Becker acknowledged, is quite simply "Are they in love?"[17] But that question doesn't make a very interesting economic theory, does it?

Becker's work on the family also led him to consider questions involving children: How many children should a family have and how much should they invest in their development? In answer to these questions his models churned out few real insights. Most of his highly quoted statements were simple observations of prevailing trends in developed countries. For instance, as families achieved higher levels of education and as children became more expensive to raise, families were choosing to have fewer of them. Replacing quantity with quality, many families chose to invest more in their children, including everything from athletic programs and music lessons to higher education.

Becker also followed the lead of Theodore W. Schultz at Chicago in studying the returns to education called human capital. Taking the same approach as he did in his other work, Becker disregarded many of the other reasons for attending college and focused on one motivation, albeit an important one – financial returns. Becker joined a number of economists who attempted to measure the specific return to education, which is not as easy as it may sound. While it was possible to compare the lifetime income of college graduates to high school graduates, it is a mistake to attribute the entire difference to education. The reason is because those who attend college may be different from those who don't. They may be more ambitious, harder working, or even more talented on average than the cohort that opts for only a high school degree. A proper measure of the return to education has to compare exactly identical individuals – identical in ambition, work ethic, and talent – with the sole difference being that one went to college. The statistical method to do this calculation is still not perfected as of today and was even less reliable when Becker did his work in the 1960s.[18]

In 1992, the Nobel committee announced that Gary S. Becker was the sole recipient of the Nobel Prize in Economic Sciences. In announcing the award, Assar Lindbeck cited Becker's success at extending the "economic approach" to broader social issues. Becker expressed surprise, not at receiving the prize, but at receiving it that particular year. It was the third year in a row that the prize had gone to free-market theorists associated with the University of Chicago. Becker had thought that the Academy would try to avoid the symbolism of repeatedly honoring the same department, explaining, "I didn't think they would give it to us three years in a row."[19]

A standard question for Nobel recipients – and lottery winners, for that matter – is how they plan to spend their prize winnings. Hope springs eternal that economic laureates will say something interesting to add to a potentially bland, academic story. Becker, however, gave reporters little to work with: no interesting charitable contributions, no philanthropic donations to the university. Instead Becker patiently explained to the press that he would have no trouble spending the money because his wants, like those of other consumers in rich countries, were nowhere near being "satiated."[20] This large sum, $1.2 million, was diminished by what he described as the "very large bite" that Uncle Sam was going to take in taxes.[21]

Becker insisted that his work was objective and scientific, and he criticized those Nobel laureates who exploited their award to promote political points of view. He humbly stated that "I hope my Nobel prize doesn't delude me into thinking I have all the answers...."[22] And yet, Becker could not resist offering a few opinions. In his *Business Week* column he recommended that colleges pay athletes, argued for a volunteer army, advocated for competition in schools through the use of vouchers, and compared affirmative action to crop subsidies.[23] He endorsed the "Chicago Boys'" work with the Pinochet dictatorship in Chile, supported privatization of Social Security, argued for the legalization of some drugs, and criticized the New York Federal Reserve for bailing out Long-Term Capital Management and his fellow Nobel laureates, Robert Merton and Myron Scholes.[24] Finally, he opposed no-fault divorce laws because he expected them to "worsen the plight of divorced women with children."[25] This is the same Gary S. Becker who embraced the Nobel award as "an occasion to avoid political propaganda and to convey to the public some flavor of the scientific quality of economics."[26]

Becker was never reluctant to share his opinions before, but once he was a Nobel Prize winner they somehow seemed newsworthy. He expressed frustration with the inept economic reasoning of his fellow Nobel laureates who were not economists. Becker complained, "I have dealt a lot with Nobel laureates in physics, chemistry and other fields who have very strong opinions on economic issues and usually they are terrible."[27] Intellectuals and even fellow economists were not exempt from Becker's criticisms. He did not like the fact that "Many intellectuals, many economists, use obscure language when they write. Sometimes it is a way of disguising that they are not saying a heck of a lot."[28] Becker even criticized the study of law and economics, pioneered by his Chicago colleagues, because it had grown stale. He claimed that it had entered "a more static, more sterile period" and needed to take a fresh look at real issues.[29]

Asked to comment on Becker's Nobel Prize, the chief economist of First National Bank of Chicago, James Annabale, referenced a quote from a more famous Nobel Prize winner, Albert Einstein. Annabale said, "Einstein once said that genius is when you ask questions that a child would ask. In the nicest sense, that's what Becker was able to do. He asked very important questions and came up with very interesting answers. They weren't always right, but they were always stimulating."[30]

George J. Stigler (1982 Prize Winner)

For his Nobel lecture in 1982, Chicago School economist George J. Stigler decided to do something a little different; he decided to define science. He might have underwhelmed his audience when he opened with "A science is an integrated body of knowledge, and it is pursued and developed by a group of interacting practitioners called scientists."[31] Because this was the same body that awarded Nobel Prizes to Albert Einstein and Marie Curie, it is probably safe to assume that they already knew what a scientist was. Stigler may have caused many in the audience to wonder what he meant when he claimed that scientists were, of course, pursuing "whatever personal goals such as prestige, reputation, and income the scientists seek." Income? Some were no doubt wondering who let economists into the Nobel club.

Throughout his career, Stigler thought it was important to explain how economics, at least the way he practiced it, could be an objective science. In his book *The Economist as Preacher*, he celebrated "the relative precision and objectivity of economic analysis."[32] But Stigler's economics had little to do with the day-to-day world. He suggested as much in his Nobel lecture when he claimed that "The scholars who create economic theory do not read the newspapers regularly or carefully during working hours." And why don't they? Because, he explained, "A viable and healthy science requires both the persistent and almost timeless theories that naturally ignore the changing conditions of their society...."[33] Is it really desirable for economists to ignore society and its changing conditions?

George Stigler's father was a brewer from Bavaria, but after Prohibition ended his career in the United States, he tried his hand at many jobs, settling on housing renovation. Stigler described his childhood as comfortable but nomadic because his family moved on average every year for the first sixteen years of his life. His father would buy a house and fix it up, only to sell it and move on.[34]

After attending public schools in Seattle, Stigler earned a degree from the University of Washington and an M.B.A. from Northwestern University in 1932. He was hooked on economics and accepted a scholarship from the University of Chicago. Here he came under the spell of the first generation of Chicago luminaries including his dissertation advisor, Frank Knight. Milton Friedman pointed out that only about three or four students successfully completed a dissertation under Knight's demanding supervision during his twenty-eight years at Chicago, and Stigler was one of them.[35] Stigler hints at his own travails when he acknowledged Knight's many talents but explained that intellectual history was not one of them. Stigler's dissertation topic, production and distribution theories from 1870 to 1915, unfortunately fell into that category.[36]

Stigler became fast friends with fellow students W. Allen Wallis and Milton Friedman when their graduate studies in the University of Chicago Ph.D. program coincided in 1934–5. Wallis went on to become dean of the business school at Chicago and president of the University of Rochester, while the friendship between Stigler and Friedman continued as their careers intersected over the decades. In his eulogy for Stigler, Friedman referred to him as "my closest friend or one of my closest friends" for sixty years.[37]

After the war, Stigler was almost hired by the University of Chicago but was rejected at the last minute when the university president, Ernest Colwell, concluded that Stigler was too empirical. The job went to the next in line who happened to be Milton Friedman. In jest, Stigler cites this story as evidence of how he helped launched the Chicago School.[38] About twelve years later, he formally joined the University of Chicago when he accepted an offer by the dean of the business school, his old friend Allen Wallis.

The economics department welcomed the return of Stigler as a pivotal member and made him the editor of their primary publication, *The Journal of Political Economy* (*JPE*), a position he held for nineteen years. Publication in the *JPE* became a standard that was used to hire, promote, and tenure economists at many universities and Stigler was the gatekeeper. It was also a useful vehicle for Stigler's own publications, which he took advantage of twenty-two times during his career, averaging more than one article per year.[39]

Stigler received many honors including the National Medal of Sciences awarded by President Ronald Regan (1987) and was elected president of the Mont Pelerin Society from 1976 to 1978. But his most significant award was the Nobel Prize in Economic Science issued in 1982. Lars Werin of the Royal Academy of Sciences listed Stigler's two major accomplishments under the headings information and regulation. As Werin noted, Stigler's ideas consistently fall squarely within the tradition of "the basic theory of markets and price formation which originated over 200 years ago with Adam Smith...."[40]

In fact, it was neither information nor regulation that launched Stigler's reputation; it was calories. In 1939 Stigler calculated the cheapest possible diet that still met the minimum caloric and nutritional requirements recommended by the federal government. The calculation was developed as an option to feed army troops and produced an adequate but boring daily menu that cost only ten cents a day in 1939. The minimum-cost diet was also an important number because it was used to calculate the poverty threshold for government statistics and programs. According to Milton Friedman, Stigler demonstrated that previous, more costly government diets were inflated to improve taste and variety, but did not represent a "scientific" minimum.[41] Apparently the poor could manage their budgets more efficiently if they would eat the same cheap meal every day.[42]

In 1939, Stigler did not have the right mathematical tool to solve this problem precisely. George Danzig later invented the simplex method and one of its first applications was by Jack Laderman of the National Bureau of Standards who solved Stigler's minimum-cost diet problem in 1947.[43] In the absence of computers, the calculation was time consuming, requiring 120 man-days using desk calculators. The result was a diet that cost $39.69 per year, only 24 cents higher than Stigler's original estimate. These low-cost diets have been criticized by nutritionists for containing unhealthy ingredients such as lard.[44] Apparently, economists do a better job telling us how to live cheaply rather than healthily.

Information and Regulation

Stigler dedicated his career to attempting to reconcile inconsistencies between the real world and the basic competitive model in microeconomics. For example, it is obvious in the real world that prices are not always the same for the same product. Firms often allocate scarce goods by forcing customers to wait rather than by increasing prices, and firms do not reduce wages and thus maintain queues of prospective employees, all of which are inconsistent with the basic competitive model. In theory, these problems would not occur if everyone had complete or perfect information and responded only to prices. No one would buy a higher-priced television if they knew a less-expensive version of the same model was readily available. Is this evidence of market failure or – worse – irrational behavior? Stigler was a staunch defender of the competitive model and promoted an alternative explanation: All of this could be explained by the cost of acquiring information.

Information is not perfect, nor should it be, said Stigler. It is like any other commodity, he argued, purchased only if the benefits of using it are greater than the cost of acquiring it. With this simple insight, Stigler attempted to resolve a troublesome inconsistency between the real world and the basic competitive model. He also launched a new field: the economics of information. Conventional economists jumped at the opportunity to apply their mathematical tools to developing search models that would determine the ideal level of information. People would want to avoid not only having too little information but also too much. Either mistake could be costly. This idea was the primary reason for his Nobel Prize, and Stigler himself thought it was his most important contribution.[45]

There was little controversy over Stigler's observation that information often comes at a cost and will, therefore, be limited. This much is obvious. But do people acquire information optimally, that is, up to the point where the value of additional information exactly equals the cost of acquiring it? How do you know, for example, that one more call to a local retail outlet won't turn up a lower price for a flat screen television? Well, in fact, you don't know. You have to guess. In fact, the market for information is no more optimal than the market for televisions or anything else. Stigler's fix for the competitive model required a new and equally challenging assumption, perfect information about information. Absent this condition, markets continue to fall short of perfection.

Not all economists accepted the idea that information costs could explain all price differences. Joseph Stiglitz, another Nobel Prize winner, claimed that this was not an adequate explanation for the wide variations in wages. We know that wages and salaries are different for the same jobs in different businesses, and sometimes even in different departments of the same business. Is this really because of lack of information? Stiglitz didn't think so. He explained that if economists can find out that wages are higher in some enterprises, then employees can find this out, too. If this is true, then Stigler's model was not the right explanation for the wide range of wages paid for comparable work.

The second reason for Stigler's Nobel Prize was his work on government regulation. This work consisted mostly of an attack on all forms of government regulation, whether it was intended to limit monopoly activity or protect consumer safety. He suggested a new idea – that regulation actually benefited the companies under government control. Stigler wrote that "as a rule, regulation is acquired by the industry and is designed and operated primarily for its benefit."[46] One might think that such a sweeping statement would be based on a comprehensive review of government regulation, but that was not the case. It seemed to originate as a theoretical concept unrelated to actual observations.

In reality, government regulation did protect some industries such as airlines, telecommunications, and trucking from competition. Deregulation in these industries ushered in a new era of innovation and competition. But in other cases, government regulation was probably no better than the integrity of the regulators, and holding them accountable is why we have elections and laws about ethics and public disclosure. But Stigler was not interested in improving government; he was interested in minimizing it.

Why can't voters in a democracy hold elected officials accountable to serve the public interest? On this topic, Stigler quoted his mentor Frank Knight who said that voters were "ignorant, emotional, and usually irrational."[47] According to Knight, the incompetence of the voters generally allowed "public servants to pursue chiefly their own interests."[48] Stigler seemed to endorse this point of view. But voters are the same people that also make economic decisions. Why are people so ignorant and irrational when making political choices, but so astute and rational when making economic decisions?

The Nobel Committee also credited Stigler with a surprising discovery, proving that there were no benefits from large-scale production, in other words, economies of scale. Stigler attempted to demonstrate that whether a firm succeeds or not has little to do with its size. Again, according to Werin from the Nobel committee, "Stigler found that …[the] ability to exploit conventional economies of scale in production is rather unimportant. Thereby he toppled what was an established doctrine in unsophisticated textbooks…."[49] Yet sixteen years later, in 2008, the committee seemed to reverse itself when the Nobel Prize went to Paul Krugman for applying the concept of economies of scale to international trade.

Some have called Stigler's microeconomics the counterpart to Milton Friedman's macroeconomics. Both mechanically applied the competitive model to important economic issues, and, like Friedman, Stigler collected data and conducted statistical analysis in what he claimed was objective science. And in both cases, these economists were key participants in the Chicago School of economics, devotees of Adam Smith, and committed members of the Mount Perelin Society dedicated to free markets. They sincerely discussed the meaning of objective science, but not once, beginning with their graduate school days at Chicago in the 1930s, did their science deviate from their personal commitment to individual liberty and free markets.

In his book *The Economist as Preacher*, Stigler complained about the lack of objectivity of intellectuals. He said, "In short, the intellectuals are the beneficiaries of the expansion of the economic role of government. Their support is, on this reading, available to the highest bidder, just as other resources in our society are allocated. Have not the intellectuals always been respectful of their patrons?" Stigler was obviously directing this critique at *other* intellectuals. He was all but certain that his own rewards – a tenured position at a major university, the editorship of a prestigious journal, and the Nobel Prize in economics – were based on merit.

People who knew Stigler often commented on his acerbic wit. He claimed that he was an intellectual because he owned more books than golf clubs.[50] More common were his comments ridiculing his academic colleagues or adversaries. He once made the comment that if *Hamlet* were showing on one television channel and a comedian on the other, he wished he "could be confident that less than half the professors were laughing."[51] Another time he offended his conservative friends in the Reagan administration when he characterized supply-side economics as a "gimmick."[52] Even his best friend, Milton Friedman, acknowledged that "Many who knew him only casually, especially in his younger years, were offended by his wit, which could be biting...."[53] More direct was Paul Samuelson who said, "His wit has a point, and it's drawn blood."[54]

Over his lifetime Stigler supervised many dissertations and taught and inspired a generation of conservative thinkers, including economist and columnist Thomas Sowell. "Stigler really taught ... intellectual integrity, analytical rigor, and respect for evidence," explained Sowell.[55] Beginning in 1971, Stigler joined his colleague Milton Friedman as a fellow at the Hoover Institution at Stanford, where he spent part of most years until his death in 1991.[56] On the event of his passing, columnist George Will praised Stigler for his "intellectual defense of markets."[57]

Theodore W. Schultz (1979 Prize Winner)

As a teenager during World War I, Theodore W. Schultz was faced with a choice of attending high school or staying home to work on his family farm in South Dakota. There was a labor shortage everywhere including in the Dakota farm country, so he chose to work on the farm and never attended high school. Despite this choice, Schultz eventually went on to attend college, received a Ph.D. and won a Nobel Prize in economics.[58] As luck would have it, those extra years on the farm were not wasted; his major field was agricultural economics.

It's not generally easy for an agricultural economist to win recognition from the wider economics profession, much less a Nobel Prize. Agricultural economics is typically considered too practical and too concerned with corn and hog prices to earn much respect from traditional economists. Schultz managed to overcome that hurdle, as well as another: He wasn't particularly mathematical. Unlike many of his contemporaries who either studied a lot of mathematics or wished they had, Schultz wished he had studied more history.[59] Despite these differences, Schultz's research caught the attention of the Nobel committee. He did this by applying the perfectly competitive model in microeconomics to new areas, a familiar theme of Chicago School economists.

Schultz's first appointment was at Iowa State College in 1930 where he rose to department chair and set out to build a strong academic department. At one point he tried to recruit a young agricultural economist named John Kenneth Galbraith but lost him to Harvard. Schultz's career at Iowa State came to an abrupt end in 1943 during a fierce debate over butter and margarine. A colleague had written about the benefits of margarine as an alternative to butter, which seemed perfectly reasonable considering all commodities were in short supply during World War II. But this was Iowa State College. The Iowa dairy industry would have none of this and they pressured the college to suppress the report. The department fought back in the name of academic freedom with Schultz leading the campaign.[60] Margarine and academic freedom won the day but only after Schultz and several colleagues resigned as a show of protest. Schultz immediately accepted a more coveted position with the department of economics at the University of Chicago.[61]

At Chicago, Schultz again rose quickly to become department chairman and was soon credited with calming down a fractious, bickering faculty.[62] Despite his administrative responsibilities, he continued his own research and advised many students working on their Ph.Ds.[63] While Schultz never did much with mathematics himself, he attracted talented graduate students who did. One of those was Gary Becker, who provided some quantitative estimates for Schultz's idea of treating education like an investment in capital. This turned out to be one of Schultz's most important ideas.

In the 1950s, economists like Nobel laureate Robert Solow were using their newly invented equations to track economic growth throughout the world. Inputs like labor and capital were measured and plugged into formulas to determine economic output such as gross national product.

In these so-called growth models, more labor and more capital produced more output, but there was a discrepancy: Economic growth far outpaced the growth of the inputs for most countries, especially Japan and Germany.[64] The world economies were growing faster than could be accounted for by simple quantitative increases in workers, equipment, factories, and resources. This led to the observation that something called "technological change" must be taking place to increase the productivity of labor and capital.

Schultz offered the simple observation that the inputs were not always the same but were generally getting better. Capital was always improving because of technology, as economists noted, but so was labor. Schultz argued that as people improved their health and expanded their knowledge, they became more productive inputs. The idea that education can enhance production was certainly not new. Three decades earlier, Alfred Marshall had observed, "Knowledge is the most powerful engine of production; it enables us to subdue Nature and satisfy our wants."[65] What Schultz suggested was that education was like any other investment and people were like machinery. His first article on the subject was published in 1958 under the title "The Emerging Economic Scene and Its Relation to High School Education."[66] With this inauspicious beginning, Schultz launched the theory of human capital, although he didn't initially call it that.[67] He simply applied a theory, which was developed by economists such as Irving Fisher to describe how businesses make investment decisions for factories, to describe how people make investment decisions for education. There are obvious parallels. For example, human capital can also depreciate as anyone who has forgotten some of the things learned in college knows. The invention of this new concept helped to solve Solow's statistical discrepancy: Economies grew primarily because of more productive people, not just because of more inputs and better technology.

Setting aside all its other benefits, it should seem obvious that education makes people more productive and allows them to qualify for higher paying jobs. Schultz and his human capital colleagues focused on this single aspect of education. They measured the higher earnings of college graduates and distilled it into a single indicator – a rate of return. In this form, a return on human investment could be compared to investments in anything else: the stock market, real estate, or pork bellies. Was your college education a smart investment, or would you have been better off using your tuition to buy stocks or commercial real estate? These are the types of questions they could answer. The return on education, incidentally, was often found to exceed returns for most other kinds of investment.

There were, of course, some problems with human capital theory. Some academics questioned the wisdom of ignoring all the other benefits of education and health care, while others objected to the assumptions of perfect competition in the theory. For example, if college graduates earned 50 percent more than high school graduates, then human capital theorists would conclude that college graduates were also 50 percent more productive. Wages must be proportional to productivity under perfect competition, but such an exact relationship may not exist in reality. For Schultz and Becker, who assumed that competition was always perfect, it wasn't even an issue.

Developing Countries

In 1979 Schultz was awarded the Nobel Prize along with Arthur Lewis. Both were intellectually interested in poor, underdeveloped countries but they advocated very different remedies. Schultz was imbued with the free-market approach of the Chicago School while Lewis was more inclined to encourage the opposite, enlightened government intervention.

The continued poverty of many nations and the chronic stagnation of their agricultural sectors were well known but received relatively little attention from economists. Microeconomists like Schultz were inclined to believe that economic growth failed to take hold in these countries because their governments were insufficiently committed to free enterprise, again echoing the doctrine of Adam Smith. The arguments were familiar: Governments were excessively taxing or regulating businesses according to Schultz, misguidedly trying to promote some businesses over others, or worse, trying to reallocate incomes for humanitarian purposes.

Schultz used his Nobel lecture to complain about governments in poor countries that were trying to hold down agricultural prices, usually with the effect of favoring the urban population at the expense of the poorer, less politically powerful, rural population. He claimed, "The effect of these government induced distortions is to reduce the economic contributions that agriculture is capable of making."[68] Furthermore, he criticized economists and "donor agencies" that continued to support such regulations.[69] One of those other economists could have been his co-winner in the shared prize, Arthur Lewis.

Combining his interest in human capital and agricultural development, Schultz was a strong advocate for education, especially for rural populations. He explained that "The decisive factors of production in improving the welfare of poor people are not space, energy and cropland: the decisive factor is the improvement in population quality."[70] He also chided those who failed to count spending on education as an investment. This champion of free markets from Chicago who opposed government in general seemed to support government spending if it were for education. As he said, "It is misleading to treat public expenditures on schooling as 'welfare' expenditures, and as a use of resources that has the effect of reducing 'savings.'"[71]

Efforts to improve health and increase longevity help stimulate other worthwhile investments. Better health insurance and more frequent health care tend to increase life expectancy and, in response, Schultz expected that people would make even more investments in their own education because they would have more years to reap the rewards.[72] The problem has always been how to secure better health care if the market isn't providing it, a topic that Schultz did not address.

When it came to having children, Schultz perceived that there was a growing interest in quality over quantity. He expected people to spend more on their children for health and education and have fewer of them. To put it bluntly, he observed that people wanted better, not more children. In the language of microeconomics, "quality and quantity are substitutes and the reduction in demand for quantity favors having and rearing fewer children."[73]

At his memorial service in 1998, Schultz was remembered for his leadership at the University of Chicago, for his research, and for his teaching. He helped to promote microeconomic theory by applying it to education, health care, and developing countries.

Ronald H. Coase (1991 Prize Winner)

Ever since its inception in 1968, the Nobel committee on economics struggled to emerge from the shadows of the hard sciences: physics, chemistry, biology, and medicine. The ideas behind the economic prizes were often difficult to explain and seldom inspired the same respect as their counterparts. What the rewards lacked in substance, the committee often tried to compensate with rhetoric. Few depictions were as grandiloquent as those reserved for Ronald H. Coase. The Nobel committee claimed that "... Coase may be said to have identified a new set of 'elementary particles' in the economic system."[74]

The Nobel committee cited two particular ideas associated with Coase, which corresponded to two different articles, one written in 1937 and the other in 1960. The first was an answer to the fundamental question: Why do firms exist? More precisely, why are some firms so large and do so much work that could be contracted out? Coase's not-so-surprising answer was that the firm does whatever is cheaper. For some businesses, it may be cheaper to create a large company like Microsoft, General Motors, or Union Carbide. For others, it may be cheaper to rely on subcontractors, as is the practice of many real estate developers. While everyone understood the obvious costs of hiring, training, and supervising employees to do the work in-house, Coase thought that the cost of negotiating and enforcing contracts was underappreciated. He called these marketing costs, but later they became known as *transaction costs*. According to Coase, large firms exist when transaction costs are high. It was a simple answer that just seemed right, even if it was difficult to prove or disprove.

Coase's second idea proposed a unique solution to problems such as pollution. In order to illustrate this idea, consider a steam locomotive that spews sparks along its path, threatening to start fires on adjacent farms. This is a classic example of an *externality*, where one party creates a cost that is born by another party. If this becomes a big enough problem, the government could regulate the railroad company and prohibit sparks. English economist Arthur Pigou suggested another solution: The government could tax any locomotive that spewed sparks. The tax would discourage the behavior and, if desired, provide revenue to compensate the farmers that were affected.

Coase had yet another idea. The government could issue the railroad the right to emit sparks and if the farmers wanted the sparks to stop, they could buy the rights from the railroad. This was a little unusual, but Coase argued that it could efficiently solve the problem. Or, he argued, the government could give farmers the right to be spark free and let the railroad buy the rights from the farmers if they wanted to continue emitting sparks. In theory, either approach could solve the problem. The important thing was that the government had to issue a property right to one of the parties, either the farmers or the railroad. Once that was done, the government could step aside and let the market work. This was, of course, a popular idea among free-market economists.

In order for Coase's solution to work, farmers and the railroad had to negotiate honestly and openly and arrive at a solution. In practice, it's difficult to imagine the farmers agreeing among themselves much less striking a deal with the railroad. A sarcastic reviewer wrote that he was sure it would work, and "pigs could fly, if only they had wings."[75] In order for the theory to work in practice, the parties had to have perfect information and zero transaction costs. These conditions are unlikely to be met, especially because both parties might want to withhold information from the other. In a perfect world, property rights could efficiently solve this externality problem; in the real world, perhaps not. Coase seemed to understand this limitation when he explained that government action, including regulation, taxation, subsidies, and even outright ownership, may lead to a better result than "relying on negotiations between individuals in the market."[76] But the members of the Chicago School were less willing to accept the limitations to what George Stigler christened the *Coase Theorem*. In Coase's words this theorem states that "in a regime of zero transaction costs, an assumption of standard economic theory, negotiations between the parties would lead to those arrangements being made which would maximize wealth and this irrespective of the initial assignment of rights."[77]

All of this put Coase in a rather awkward position. His first idea cited by the Nobel Committee claimed that transaction costs exist and are important in determining the existence of firms. But his second idea, as interpreted and embraced by the Chicago School as the Coase Theorem, only works when there are no transaction costs. When there are transaction costs, which there may be always, the Coase Theorem doesn't really apply.

Many free-market advocates ignored the limitations on Coase's idea and embraced it as a solution to many real-world problems. They also emphasized Coase's point that either party could be given the property right to achieve economic efficiency. As one observer noted, this means that "a nearby homeowner's ownership rights over the air are no greater than those of the factory."[78] The decision of who got the property right was considered a question of fairness, a topic more appropriate for philosophers than economists. The rush to create property rights and get them into private hands has proceeded quickly.

One of the best examples of Coase's ideas can be seen in the *cap and trade system* developed in the 1990s to regulate the emissions of sulfur from the nation's coal burning power plants. The government created permits to emit a ton of sulfur, which were considered property rights, and then gave most of them to the industry for free. Remember that according to Coase's theorem, it doesn't matter who holds the right. The permits could be bought and sold relatively freely, but by the end of the year each polluter had to have a permit for each ton of sulfur emitted. The actual amount of sulfur emitted decreased as the number of permits issued decreased but also because power plants came under increasingly strict regulations. A similar system is being used to regulate carbon dioxide (CO_2) emissions in Europe and is proposed for regulating CO_2 in the United States. Coase's proposal provides a philosophical justification for all of these systems.

Despite the grounding of Coase's ideas in microeconomics, his ideas were not immediately popular with conservative economists. In fact he struggled in relative obscurity for the first thirty years of his career. Born in 1910 in the London suburb of Willesden, there was very little in his childhood that would have suggested that he was a future Nobel Prize winner. Neither of his parents continued in school past the age of twelve, and his father worked for the post office as had his mother before she was married. While his parents enjoyed playing sports, like tennis, Ronald's interests were more solitary and academic. Even when he learned to play chess, he was more likely to play against himself than a real partner. By his own account, he attended a "school for physical defectives," because of a weakness in his legs. He was forced to wear leg irons like the character in the movie *Forrest Gump*.

After ruling out a number of majors because of his lack of interest in Latin and mathematics, Coase decided in 1929 to study the competitive economic system and Adam Smith's "invisible hand" at the London School of Economics. He claimed these subjects changed his life and made him a believer in competitive markets. In 1931 Coase was awarded a "traveling scholarship," which he used to tour the United States for a year, visiting large corporations and determining why they existed. His answer was the article "The Nature of the Firm," published in 1937 in which he first described the concept of transaction costs.

Between academic assignments in England and the United States, Coase did statistical work for government agencies during World War II, a curious assignment given his lack of interest in mathematics. A future colleague at the University of Chicago, Richard Epstein, apparently unaware of Coase's earlier occupation as a statistician, claimed that "he never looked at a number in his life."[79]

The Dinner Party

After World War II, Coase returned to academics and took up the subject of public utilities, writing a book about British broadcasting and an article in 1959 on the Federal Communications Commission. As a rule, in the competitive model of Adam Smith, productive resources should always go to the highest bidder. Because Coase considered the radio spectrum a productive resource, he figured it too should be sold in a competitive auction. This was a significant departure from the way the Federal Communications Commission then allocated licenses, which required the holder to meet public standards and provide public benefits.

Not everyone immediately accepted this idea. Coase submitted his paper to the *Journal of Law and Economics* at the University of Chicago, which published it but the editor of the *Journal*, Aaron Director, still had questions. He invited Coase to his house for a dinner party along with a few of his friends, including George Stigler, Milton Friedman, and other economics

faculty from Chicago. What a party! It quickly turned into a debate between
Coase and more than twenty members of the Chicago School. When all was
said and done, the consensus was that Coase was right. According to George
Stigler, "Milton Friedman opened fire and the bullets hit everyone but
Coase."[80] He had convinced the entire party of skeptics including the most
aggressive questioner, Milton Friedman. The concept of converting public
resources into private property rights and auctioning them off to the highest
bidder became part of the Chicago School canon literally overnight. It was
a celebrated moment of intellectual history, at least for the Chicago economists, inspiring two members of the dinner party to write up the whole event
for a special issue of the *Journal of Law and Economics* in 1983.

The original resistance to Coase's ideas from the Chicago School reflected
more a lack of familiarity than a philosophical difference. With his newly
won respect, Coase was offered a position at the University of Chicago in
1964 – this offer came not from the economics department, but from the
law school. Coase accepted the position and immediately became the editor
of the *Journal of Law and Economics*, a position he held until 1982.

Did Chicago simply make a better offer or did a plot drive Coase out
of the University of Virginia? Paul Craig Roberts, an economist partial to
supply-side economics and conspiracy theories, promoted the idea that
Coase was targeted by a socialist cabal. In an article in *Business Week*,
Roberts claimed that Coase was the victim of "a secret plot hatched by the
university administration to purge the 'right-wing' economics department
of its leadership...."[81] According to Roberts, the University of Virginia drove
Coase out in 1964 and James Buchanan in 1968 because the head of the Ford
Foundation complained about them and the department for "expressing
hostility to socialism...."[82] Perhaps predisposed toward hyperbole, Roberts
once blamed the 1981–2 recession on fellow Reagan Republican, David
Stockman.[83]

In some respects, Coase was not a typical Nobel winner. Like Hayek, he
did not use statistics or mathematics to make his economic arguments. In
his Nobel speech he insisted that he was not opposed to the use of mathematics by economists. In fact, he suggested that a time would come when
mathematics would be necessary in economics, implying that perhaps that
time had not yet come.[84] He once recalled, "In my youth it was said that
what was too silly to be said may be sung. In modern economics it may be
put into mathematics."[85] David Warsh, a former writer for the *Boston Globe*,
speculated that Coase would have won the Nobel Prize earlier if his work
had been more mathematical. As it was, he was eighty years old when he
won the prize.

Coase's writing often included hypothetical examples such as the railroad and the farmers rather than real life cases. While he encouraged other economists to look more closely at the actual economy, he did relatively little of that kind of work himself, with the exception of his visits to large corporations from 1931 to 1932. His writing was also distinctive because it was comprehensible. A colleague from the University of Chicago, Richard Epstein, commented, "Anybody can understand it with a tenth-grade education."[86] In academic circles, that is not always a complement.

The Nobel Committee had some difficulty locating the eighty-year-old economist on that particular day in October of 1991 when his award was announced. He and his wife had chosen that day to leave their vacation home in France to tour the ancient city of Carthage in Tunisia.

Coase was not a particularly prolific writer during his long career. He wrote the two articles cited by the Nobel committee and relatively few other works of distinction. His saving grace was that one of the two articles, *The Problem of Social Costs*, is often described as one of the most cited articles in economics. This fact prompted Robert Cooter, an economist at Boalt Law School at Berkeley, to comment, "Most economists maximize the amount they write. Coase maximized the amount others wrote about him."[87]

Coase provided a theory for those who wished to privatize "something" where markets had historically failed. His modest proposal of creating property rights and auctioning them off to the highest bidder has led to the privatization of the airwaves, pollution rights, natural monopolies, and more. Even the right to name public places or public events is fast becoming the right of the largest donor. There are many more areas where property rights are nonexistent, vague, or restricted from sale that may someday be up for auction. Water rights, rights to human organs, and adoption rights have been exempt from free markets, but all that may change some day. And if that happens, someone will cite Ronald Coase as the genius who saw no limits in what could be auctioned to the highest bidder.

In addition to his vacation home in France, Ronald Coase maintained a position of Senior Research Fellow at the Hoover Institution like his former colleague, Milton Friedman. Coase himself said, "People have not thought (my work) was wrong, but they had not seen its importance."[88] The Nobel Prize certainly helped to win Coase more attention and accelerated the infusion of his ideas into mainstream economics.

FOUR

Stock Market Casino

Merton H. Miller (1990)

Harry M. Markowitz (1990)

William F. Sharpe (1990)

Myron S. Scholes (1997)

Robert K. Merton (1997)

On October 14, 1997, the Swedish Academy of Sciences announced the winners of the Nobel Prize in economics, Myron S. Scholes and Robert K. Merton. They were honored for developing ingenious formulas for calculating the value of financial instruments, including options, a simple but difficult contract to value.

Less than one year later, however, there was a sudden turn of events. The Federal Reserve Bank of New York quietly convened high-level negotiations to avoid one of the largest bankruptcies to ever threaten Wall Street involving the same two Nobel Prize winners. The company causing the trouble was Long-Term Capital Management (LTCM), which not only applied the theories of laureates Scholes and Merton, but also counted them among the company's principals. In less than a year, they became famous for winning the Nobel Prize and then infamous for one of the most spectacular business failures in history. The Nobel laureates at LTCM looked like geniuses until the market destroyed them financially. Why did Merton and Scholes receive a Nobel Prize? And why did their ideas fail so miserably in the real world?

The stock market has always attracted the attention of economists as both an essential economic institution and as a testing ground for new ideas. Although you might think that familiarity with the great theories of economics would be an advantage in the market, the actual track record of economists has been mixed. At one extreme, John Maynard Keynes established himself as a shrewd and successful investor in the stock market as well as the more challenging market for international currencies. He would, according to legend, make his investment decisions and call them in every morning before rising from bed. Keynes sometimes lost money, especially during the stock market crash, but he was always able to recover and greatly improve his position.

Keynes did not diversify his portfolio, as many advisors recommend today, but instead concentrated his investments in a few select companies that he believed had potential for growth and a solid balance sheet. It was a strategy that worked so well that King's College in Cambridge asked Keynes to invest its endowment. Over a period of twenty-two years that included the Great Depression, Keynes managed to average a 12 percent annual return for the college's funds. This was a remarkable accomplishment given that the overall British stock market fell by 15 percent during the same time. Keynes' investing strategy was emulated by other investors, including the legendary American investor Warren Buffett.

At the other extreme was the unfortunate Irving Fisher, a prominent mathematical economist from Yale University. Professor Fisher was heavily invested in the stock market in 1929 and tried heroically to reassure investors that the stock market was not overvalued and that it could continue on its remarkable trajectory. His status as a Yale economist and his impeccable academic qualifications were not enough to prevent the stampede of investors to dump stocks, and the market collapsed in October of 1929. Valuable life savings were lost by many, including Professor Fisher. Like Fisher, Myron S. Scholes and Robert K. Merton also believed that they had a special gift for understanding the operations of financial markets, and they believed that it could make them rich.

Previous Nobel laureates in financial economics helped to pave the way for Merton and Scholes. In 1990 the Nobel Prize went to three pioneers in mathematical finance: Merton H. Miller, Harry M. Markowitz, and William F. Sharpe. These three economists in particular launched the effort to apply microeconomics to the stock market and other investments. The theories attributed to these Nobel laureates attempted to uncover valuable secrets and, in the process, contributed to what became an immense financial industry.

Merton H. Miller (1990 Prize Winner)

Merton Miller attended Harvard University, graduating magna cum laude with a degree in economics in 1944.[1] At Harvard he took an introductory economics class with a fellow student and another future Nobel laureate, Robert Solow. The class might have seemed a little tough to the other students with two future Nobel Prize winners setting the curve.

Miller took a position at the Carnegie Institute of Technology (now Carnegie Mellon University) where he crossed paths with future Nobel laureate, Franco Modigliani. His association with Modigliani was particularly fruitful because of their overlapping interests in corporate finance. After publishing their first article together in 1952, the two continued to collaborate during the 1950s and 1960s. When Modigliani received a Nobel Prize in 1985 for some of their shared work, Miller figured that he had missed his chance, "I thought that was it for me."[2] But in 1990, Miller had a second chance when the Swedish Academy honored the leading pioneers in finance and included him.

Miller's work with Modigliani is largely credited with establishing several basic principles about corporate finance. Most importantly, they proved that in a microeconomic world, the only thing that determines stock value is profitability. Whether a firm finances its expansion with debt or equity, or whether it pays dividends is irrelevant.[3] Many economists thought it was interesting that these results could be derived from microeconomics regardless of whether they had any relevance in the real world.

In 1961, Miller took a position at the Graduate School of Business at the University of Chicago where he embraced the Chicago School philosophy as "an activist supporter of free-market solutions to economic problems." To this end, he wrote about the problems of government regulation and offered his support for shielding trading institutions from regulatory oversight. He had a direct interest in these issues as a public director of the Chicago Board of Trade and later as a public director on the Chicago Mercantile Exchange.

Harry M. Markowitz (1990 Prize Winner)

Miller and Modigliani weren't the only economists thinking about how to apply microeconomics to corporate finance in the 1950s. Microeconomics provided economists with a powerful tool, but it required some creative thinking about how to apply it. Harry M. Markowitz was one of those creative thinkers, and he focused on questions involving *risk* and *diversified portfolios*. Risk wasn't a new concept, but Markowitz gave it specific meaning when he used a familiar statistical value, variance, to measure it. Wall Street was impressed and quickly adopted it as a standard measure of risk.

Harry Markowitz grew up in Chicago during the Depression. His parents owned a small grocery store that provided sufficient income for him to have his own bedroom in the family apartment but few real luxuries.[4] Like other Chicago kids, Harry played baseball and football in the local park, but unlike other kids he enjoyed reading science and philosophy. Charles Darwin's *Origin of the Species* and the works of philosopher David Hume were among his favorites.

After two years at the University of Chicago, Markowitz discovered economics. He was drawn to the theories of mathematician John von Neumann and was inspired by Milton Friedman and other future Nobel economists teaching at Chicago. Markowitz became a student member of the famous Cowles Commission for Research in Economics. Despite being a relatively small group, the Cowles Commission produced many Nobel laureates who specialized in mathematical economics and econometrics.

For his dissertation, Markowitz decided to apply mathematical methods to the stock market. This led him to develop a portfolio model where a bundle of investments are characterized by two numbers, average return and risk. Markowitz believed that earlier investment models had overemphasized the importance of returns without sufficient concern for risk. His model, he argued, was more consistent with what investors seemed to do in the real world; they diversified their portfolios in order to reduce risk. Markowitz was able to show that by adding or subtracting stocks from a portfolio, investors could obtain different combinations of expected returns and risk.

William F. Sharpe (1990 Prize Winner)

A key consideration when buying a stock is to understand how it will add to the risk of a portfolio. Obviously a risky stock may make the portfolio riskier as well. There is a subtle, but more important characteristic, and that is how much the price of the stock tends to move with the other stocks. The price of a stock may be volatile, but if it tends to move counter to other stocks in a portfolio, then it can actually reduce overall volatility. This insight, included in the now well-known Capital Asset Pricing Model, earned William F. Sharpe his Nobel Prize in 1990.[5]

The cornerstone of Sharpe's analysis was the *beta factor*, which is now widely used by Wall Street investors, novices and wonks alike. The idea behind the beta factor is fairly simple. The return on any portfolio of stocks, like the Dow Jones Average, will trace out a historical pattern with some degree of volatility. Some individual stocks in that portfolio will contribute significantly to that volatility but others will not if they are more independent. The beta factor measures this degree of independence. When properly measured, the beta factor is a useful indicator of how the addition of a stock may alter the risk of a larger portfolio. When betas are estimated relative to the Standard and Poor's 500, they essentially measure the degree to which the stock tracks the overall market.[6]

The development of the beta coefficient is widely credited with stimulating and redirecting investments. According to Noble laureate Kenneth Arrow, "Sharpe's work provided a very practical guide to portfolio diversification for the modern investor."[7] According to James Risen, writing in the *Los Angeles Times* in 1990, the work of Sharpe and Markowitz contributed to the "success and popularity of mutual funds," although mutual funds didn't really take off until several decades after their work was first published.

When Sharpe enrolled in the University of California at Berkeley in 1951, he intended to major in science and pursue a medical degree. Instead, he transferred to University of California at Los Angeles where he received a bachelor's degree in economics in 1955 and a master's degree in 1956 before serving in the army.

Like a number of other Nobel laureates, Sharpe joined the Rand Corporation, which in the postwar years offered the opportunity to pursue academic problems in computer science, game theory, linear programming, and economics. While at Rand, Sharpe learned computer programming, an exotic skill at the time. His job at Rand also allowed him sufficient flexibility to pursue a doctorate in economics, which he received from UCLA in 1961. After a false start on a dissertation topic, Sharpe consulted with Markowitz, who was also working at Rand. Acting on Markowitz's recommendation, Sharpe used microeconomics to calculate the value of capital, an exercise that served as the basis for his Capital Asset Pricing Model.

The brain trust at LTCM also relied on the Capital Asset Pricing Model, which claimed that more volatile stocks should also have higher average returns. Volatility became synonymous with risk, and it soon became just as important to measure stock volatility as it was to measure rates of returns. Even if you didn't believe the math, there was a good reason to believe that risky stocks needed a higher rate of return. Why, for example, would anyone buy a more volatile stock if it did not also have a higher rate of return?

The central idea of this theory was that the difference in returns between two assets is determined by the difference in risk. When the gap in the returns widened or narrowed between two different bonds, for instance, the statistical wizards at LTCM saw a profit opportunity. They could make money, lots of money, if they could count on relative earnings to return to historical values. It was the failure of this concept, in combination with some of the other principles of financial economics that led to the crisis at LTCM.

Myron S. Scholes (1997 Prize Winner)

This brings us to Myron Scholes, a Canadian and one of the later generation of finance economists. Scholes inherited his mother's enthusiasm for business as he watched her operate a chain of small department stores with her uncle.[8] He loved anything associated with business, including trading, investing, and even gambling. While he was still in high school, his parents set up a stock market account for him so he could pursue this passion. He traded stocks through high school and college, and eventually made it his profession as a finance economist and consultant.

Scholes attended McMaster University where he studied liberal arts and majored in economics. Inspired by the work of Milton Friedman and his colleagues, Scholes signed up for the graduate program in economics at the University of Chicago. After the first year, he was hooked; he had considered returning to Canada to work for his uncle but instead took a position as a computer programmer. This made him invaluable to the Chicago faculty in the early 1960s, including Merton Miller. It was Miller who encouraged him to pursue a doctorate at the University of Chicago. Scholes received his degree in 1968 and took a position at the Massachusetts Institute of Technology (MIT) as an assistant professor. There he met Robert Merton and Fisher Black, the other half of the Black–Scholes theorem.

Options

The name Scholes had considerable cachet in the business world even before his Nobel Prize because of the famous Black–Scholes pricing model for financial options developed in the 1970s. The formula claims to provide an objective value for an option, the right to buy a stock at a particular time at a particular price. The formula was proposed shortly after the creation of the Chicago Board Options Exchange in April of 1973 and is largely credited with the explosive growth of this market from virtually zero in 1973 to $15 trillion in trades by 2006. There may be some truth to this story because the Black–Scholes formula became ubiquitous on Wall Street when Texas Instruments programmed it into its early business calculators.

Options were central to Scholes and Merton's Nobel Prizes, as well as their business escapades. While options are relatively simple financial instruments, placing a precise value on them is difficult. An option is simply the right to buy or sell something in the future at a given price that may be exercised or not. They can be traced back as far as ancient Greece when they were used to capture the potential returns from trading vessels as they set sail. In the modern world, option trading represents a multibillion dollar enterprise with the center of the universe being the Chicago Board Options Exchange. Options trading simply gives investors more choices by allowing them to bet on the increase or decrease in an asset at a particular point in time. While a futures contract may obligate an investor to buy an asset (or stock) sometime in the future, an option only involves a purchase if the investor chooses, hence the name option. It is one type of investments known more generally as derivatives.

There are two kinds of options, the option to buy (a call option) and the option to sell (a put option). A call option is purchased if the asset is expected to go up in the future. For example, you might pay $1 for an option to be able to buy a stock for $5 three months from now. If the stock actually sells for $8 three months from now, you make a profit by exercising the option. You have made $3, less the $1 you paid for the option, for a $2 profit. If the stock price doesn't rise, you don't exercise your option and you are out the $1 paid for it. This is simply another way to speculate in the stock market with just a little more complexity.

In 1973, Black and Scholes wrote an article in the *Journal of Political Economy* that included a formula for the value of an option. Although this appeared to be a rather difficult problem to solve, it turns out that it is equivalent to a problem in physics related to the transfer of heat, which does have a solution. Fischer Black, with a background in physics, deserves some credit for recognizing the similarities and providing the answer. Laureate William Sharpe helped to simplify the mathematics sufficiently to make it more useful for investors.

The University of Chicago, MIT, and Stanford University were the centers for the development of the new finance economics, and Scholes moved easily among them. In 1973, he returned to the University of Chicago as a visiting professor and then took a job at Stanford in 1981. By the 1990s, Scholes' academic work and business ventures started to blend together. While continuing to study derivatives at Stanford, he also consulted for Salomon Brothers and eventually took on a managing director position. All this was good preparation for becoming a founding partner in LTCM in 1994 and the opportunity to turn his Nobel Prize–winning ideas into gold, or so he hoped.

Robert K. Merton (1997 Prize Winner)

Scholes' partner at LTCM was an equally motivated and mathematically inclined finance professor, Robert K. Merton. When he was still a student, Merton was interested in engineering and applied mathematics, which he pursued at Columbia College and California Institute of Technology, one of the top engineering schools in the country.[9] He had always been attracted to numbers and math, whether he was memorizing batting averages and pitching records or car engine specifications. He also had a penchant for banking and the stock market. At the age of nine, Merton was balancing his mother's check book and inventing fictitious banks. Ironically the IRS accused his company, LTCM, of a similar practice to avoid taxes many years later.[10] At the age of eleven years, Merton bought his first stock and by nineteen he had implemented his first "risk arbitrage."

Merton was accepted by MIT for graduate studies in economics primarily on the strength of his recommendations from mathematicians at California Institute of Technology. He was advised to take an economics class taught by Nobel laureate Paul Samuelson who immediately recognized his talents and recruited him as his research assistant. Samuelson and Merton shared a mutual interest in esoteric stock market instruments and were soon collaborating on research. Merton was only a second-year graduate student but he was so good that Samuelson allowed him to present their joint paper to several Nobel Prize winners at the inaugural session of the MIT–Harvard Mathematical Economics seminar.

Although Merton had no formal training in finance, MIT's Sloan School of Management hired him to teach finance because mathematical proficiency was the critical requirement. When he commenced full-time teaching in the fall of 1970, Merton spent much of his time learning the material to present to the students in his graduate classes. At MIT, Merton was surrounded by talented finance analysts including Myron Scholes, Franco Modigliani, and Fischer Black.

Long-Term Capital Management
Investors are always looking for some advantage over their competition, and sometimes they seek that advantage in academic venues. Tapping into the skills of reputable scholars to make money is not a new strategy, but it was applied with gusto in the 1980s and 1990s by John Meriwether, an investor from Salomon Brothers. Meriwether was a gambler from the start and an early disciple of using mathematical modeling to guide his investments.

When Meriwether later built his own investment firm, he followed the same strategies that he found so successful at Salomon: hedging, leverage, and risk. He also continued the strategy of recruiting the finest minds in finance theory by courting Merton from Harvard and Scholes from Stanford. As Merton put it, Meriwether and LTCM "attempted to marry the best of the finance theory with the best of finance practice."[11] Of the experience, Merton gushed, "It was deliciously intense and exciting to have been a part of creating LTCM."[12] Meriwether added to the brain power of his new enterprise with other high-powered academics from MIT and Harvard Business School. The all-star cast was recognized by *Institutional Investor* as "The best finance faculty in the world."

Meriwether cashed in on his stable of top academics in two ways. First, he had the fire power for high-level calculations and modeling, but more importantly, the prestigious professors contributed to the company's reputation of having an advantage over the average investment house. This was essential for recruiting investors and their money. The razzle dazzle of intellectual talent worked on Wall Street and successfully carried LTCM to the top even before it made its first investments in 1994. Without a proven track record, LTCM was still able to create a one billion dollar investment fund and to win concessions from banks and others on the fees normally charged for this kind of business.

Among the principles that LTCM tried to exploit was hedging, the simple art of offsetting one investment with another to reduce overall risk. It often involves selling short, which means borrowing a stock to sell it immediately. You buy a stock if you think it will go up, but you sell it short if you think it will go down. In 1949, Alfred Winslow earned recognition as the father of hedge funds when he offset his investment in stocks by selling other stocks short. With four friends and $100,000 he created what may have been the first hedge fund.

Hedge funds are typically less volatile than other investment strategies and as a consequence, they also don't do as well on the upswing or as badly on the downswing.

The only way to make a lot of money quickly on most hedge funds is through leverage, borrowing money to make an investment. Leverage is a simple but important concept in finance. One dollar earned on a $100 investment doesn't add up to much – only about 1 percent. But if you personally only invest one dollar and borrow the other $99, then the return is extraordinary. In the case where you invest one dollar and earn an additional dollar, the return on your investment would be about 100 percent![13] The financial geniuses at LTCM combined their understanding of earnings, risk, hedge funds, and leverage with the goal of beating the market and their competitors. It was a clever strategy and worked well for a while. In the first few years, LTCM earned impressive returns in double digits.

But none of this helped when LTCM failed to anticipate or respond to an increasingly dysfunctional market related to a default on Russian bonds. No formulas, no computer model, and no high-level mathematics could

change the fact that the market was at times unpredictable, even irrational. There is no rule that markets will respond in a rational way, especially
in times of crisis. And even if the market does eventually regain a rational
footing where prices make sense, there is no way to know how long irrational prices will last. Keynes described this problem many years earlier when
he said, "markets can remain irrational far longer than you or I can remain
solvent."

Throughout the summer of 1998, LTCM hemorrhaged more and more
capital while its positions continued to lose value. As the company's crisis
grew, it became clear to the outside world that LTCM was leveraged to the
extreme, and that the debt it owed was held by some of the nation's largest banks. Even those banks, Salomon, Merrill Lynch, Goldman Sachs, and
Morgan Stanley, were in no position to write-off loans of this magnitude.
Having leveraged its original investment by twenty-eight to one (borrowing
$28 for every dollar put up by investors), the company's crisis became a
national crisis almost overnight.

Most companies in a similar position would have been forced to liquidate
their assets in order to pay off their lenders; if they were unable to raise
sufficient funds, they would have landed in bankruptcy court. The court
would then allocate whatever funds were available to all appropriate parties, effectively assigning losses. But LTCM was too big, it owed too much
money, and it had to liquidate too many positions to begin paying off investors. With $100 billion of debt, they were large enough to wreak havoc in
world financial markets. Insiders complained of a lack of liquidity because
there simply weren't enough investors to buy LTCM's assets at prevailing
prices. The mere act of selling these immense positions threatened to start a
downward spiral in prices that could have easily gotten out of control.

At least this was the assessment made by the New York Federal Reserve
Bank when it called together the big lenders and negotiated a slower and
more systematic strategy for liquidating positions and dismantling LTCM.
Warren Buffett even entered the picture with a last minute offer to take over
the company. Meriwether rejected the offer out of hand because it offered
nothing to him and the other principals. That killed Buffett's offer and the
bankers got down to business and provided a voluntary, private bailout of
LTCM with encouragement from the New York Federal Reserve but no
public money. Over the course of one year, LTCM lost $7.5 billion of its
$8 billion in capital.

There was still one unresolved issue that took many years to straighten
out – taxes. Although LTCM failed in 1998, the Internal Revenue Service
(IRS) was still trying in 2002 to recover $70 million in taxes that it believed

had been improperly handled. Roger Lowenstein, in his fascinating book about LTCM, claimed that Nobel Prize winner Scholes "regarded taxes as a vast intellectual game" and apparently said, "No one actually *pays* taxes."[14] David Wessel, in the *Wall Street Journal*, called the IRS investigation a "glimpse into the way big guys get out of paying taxes."[15]

The transaction described by Wessel is as complex as it is fascinating. To start with, General Electric and First American National Bank leased computers, presumably entitling them to deductions for rent and depreciation. From this simple operation, a San Francisco investment bank, Babcock and Brown, created something called "lease stripping" that moved taxable income overseas, out of reach of the IRS but which retained deductions for U.S. companies exposed to profit taxes. The vehicle for this was a London-based corporation, Onslow Trading & Commercial LLC, consisting of a post office box, tax lawyers, bankers, accountants, and not much else.

Long-Term Capital Management got involved when Onslow, the London-based corporation, swapped their preferred stock for a stake in LTCM. When LTCM sold the preferred stock at a great loss in 1997, they reduced their tax liabilities. The IRS disagreed and successfully challenged this scheme in court in 2003.[16] David Wessel covered this story for the *Wall Street Journal* and concluded that "… paying taxes ought not to be a vast intellectual game in which millions are spent to create complex 'sham transactions' that the creators know will take the government years to untangle."[17]

After LTCM, Nobel Prize winners Merton and Scholes went back to their universities and resumed providing expert advice on investment opportunities. For a fee, Scholes would advise clients on their portfolio strategies and explain how to legally reduce their tax exposure.

Doubts

Each of these Nobel laureate economists from the University of Chicago, Stanford, MIT, and Harvard contributed in some way to the development of finance economics, and to some degree or another, they were associated with the booming markets for mutual funds, derivatives, and stock options. What they did was to apply microeconomics and advanced techniques from calculus to financial markets. In the process they convinced many investors that they had discovered objective formulas to value stocks, options, risk, capital, and other securities.

Commenting on the role of the new finance economists, Robert Brusca, chief economist at Nikko Securities International in New York, said "their contributions have helped make everybody's life a lot better."[18] There is no question that the market for mutual funds and option trading is much larger than it once was, and it is also quite likely that the development of these financial models probably encouraged that growth. The market for derivatives, for example, is estimated to be approximately $70 trillion a year, nearly ten times the U.S. gross domestic product.[19]

But is all this good? Remember that finance formulas are only as good as their assumptions. The derivation of the Black–Scholes formula, for example, is so abstract and complex that it is quite possible that the average investor fails to understand that it is not always true. The actual assumptions behind the formula are probably no more transparent than the Ito calculus used to prove it. Is it possible that Nobel laureates have systematically understated risk by using overly optimistic assumptions, thus luring investors into taking excessively risky positions. Isn't this much like what went wrong with LTCM? Is all this risk taking adding to the net wealth of the nation and the world, or has it evolved into some sort of monumental gambling operation?

One of the central assumptions in finance economics is the *efficient market hypothesis*, which claimed that the price of a stock is the best measure of its present and future value. Originated by Eugene Fama from the University of Chicago, this theory assumes that the stock market rationally processes all available information and always produces the "right" price. But this assumption requires a lot of faith. In order for the stock market to be perfectly rational, it cannot be influenced by exuberance, fear, euphoria, superstition, panic, second guessing, or many other human emotions.

There were reasons to be skeptical about the reliability of the efficient market hypothesis, but these problems were generally ignored by the new finance economists because without the assumption of efficient markets, many of the principles, proofs, and formulas, including the Black–Scholes formula, would have been impossible. With no obvious alternatives, economists continued to construct an elaborate mathematical theory that rested precariously on the assumption that financial markets were essentially perfect. At stake were more than a few academic reputations and many billions of dollars in options trading.

According to the efficient market hypothesis, only new information can change stock prices; however, prices can sometimes bounce around almost randomly without any clear linkage to significant new information. This discrepancy between theory and reality becomes most pronounced during stock market crashes.

On October 19, 1987, the Dow Jones Industrials fell 508 points for a record 23 percent decline in a single day, yet there was no new information that anyone could identify as its cause. The collapse seemed to come out of the blue. One of the interesting findings from the ensuing investigation was the role of computer trading in the downturn. The computers, programmed with financial models, were authorized to buy and sell orders automatically. When they registered the market decline they immediately authorized more sales that caused further price decreases. This created a downward spiral in the market that stopped only after the exchanges curtailed trading.[20] Ironically, one of the culprits in this crisis was a computer program that featured the Black–Scholes formula.

According to David Dreman, writing in *Forbes* magazine, these models interacted with each other to create havoc in a market that should have been stable. Furthermore, the collapse created a challenge for advocates of the efficient market hypothesis. How can a market be worth 2,500 points one day and 1,800 a few days later when nothing else really changed? For the Nobel Prize winners in finance economics, the crash of 1987 was a dramatic, conspicuous, and bewildering counter-example to their life's work. Nobel laureate Sharpe is quoted as saying, "We're all totally perplexed."[21] He weakly suggested that there might be some new information behind this collapse, as the theory requires. "It's conceivable that a change in the well-informed forecast of future economic events moved the market as it did: you can't prove it one way or the other. On the other hand, it's pretty weird," conceded Sharpe.[22]

Professor Fischer Black responded to the 1987 crash by suggesting that increasing volatility leading up to the October crash created a need for lower stock prices.[23] But that begs the question of why volatility increased in the first place. Another explanation would be that markets are sometimes irrational and unpredictable, making them susceptible to occasional crises. But this explanation would violate the efficient market hypothesis.

Keith Devlin reported Scholes' explanation for the stock market crash in 1987.[24] Scholes said it wasn't so much the formula that was to blame, but rather that market traders had not grown sufficiently sophisticated in how to use it. But what sophistication was lacking? Is the market perfect in every other respect except when it comes to how to use a formula? Certainly it wasn't the actual calculation, because all that required was the purchase of a Texas Instrument calculator.

In the aftermath of the crash, another, more subtle development occurred that continued to cast doubts on the validity of the efficient market hypothesis and the finance models; the current value of stocks were diverging from their indexed future contracts. At this time, the discrepancy was running between 10 and 20 percent. According to Professor Black, "That shouldn't have happened."[25] This fact was reinforced by Harvard economist Lawrence

Summers, who claimed that it was "... a clear gap in the theory," and that for years "every finance professor in America has taught that can't happen."[26]

Lawrence Summers and other critics challenged the basic premise of the efficient market hypothesis. They claimed that there are basic human behaviors such as fear, panic, or exuberance that can drive markets and that are quite capable of overriding the perfect rationality of the mathematicians. Yale University professor Robert Shiller claimed that "The efficient market hypothesis is the most remarkable error in the history of economic theory. This is just another nail in the coffin." The importance of this event was also emphasized by Summers who concluded, "If anyone did believe that price movements are determined by changes in information about economic fundamentals, they've got to be disabused of that notion by Monday's 500 point movement."[27] Keynes was not under any delusions that the stock market was rational, which he described using terms such as "animal spirits." At one point he warned, "When the capital development of a country becomes a by-product of the activities of a casino, the job is likely to be ill-done."

How did Nobel economists get into this trouble? The whole endeavor started out innocently enough when mathematically oriented academics started to apply principles of microeconomics to financial markets. There should be no doubt that this exercise can lead to interesting ideas and insights. But an astute investor would understand the limitations of these theories and not make the mistake of blindly accepting them as absolute truth.

The theories of financial economics, or any economics for that matter, are no better than their assumptions. To their credit, most economists are scrupulously careful to document their assumptions in academic papers. But who actually reads this fine print or even understands it? Certainly not the general public or even investors, unless of course they are proficient in Ito calculus. Instead, investors have relied on academic reputations, mathematical prowess, and of course, Nobel Prizes as indicators of quality.

Fully understanding the limits of modern economics may be just as important as understanding its insights. Where were the critics of the efficient market hypothesis before the 1987 crash? They certainly weren't published in major economic journals. David Dreman claimed that the academic system is, in effect, rigged to limit criticism. He wrote, "The academic journals have become a tight elite that allow only the approved academic theorists of the day or other believers to publish. They don't burn the work of dissenters. They don't have to. They just don't publish it."[28]

Scientists appreciate thoughtful criticism and see it as an opportunity to strengthen their theory or develop new ones. Economics seems to be different. For lack of any better standard of quality, the value of an economic idea is often determined by the opinions of colleagues. While criticism and dissent may be a hallmark of modern science, it is seldom encouraged by economists or the Nobel committee.

The new finance model did not do a very good job of protecting LTCM in 1998, or explaining the stock market crash in 1987. However gloomy the prospects looked for this theory after 1987, it did not stop the Nobel committee from honoring yet again two more of its proponents in 1997. The Nobel committee appeared to be too easily seduced by mathematical rigor at the cost of ignoring real-world economics. Economic theories should do more than solve mathematical puzzles; they really should explain actual economic events.

One of those actual economic events is the great stock market collapse of 2008. When faced with such a dramatic crisis, it is natural for the press, politicians, and businesses to turn to Nobel Prize–winning economists to explain what went wrong and how to make it right. But those Nobel laureates who were honored for the new finance economics would have a hard time explaining an event that, in their theory, just wasn't supposed to happen. In this case, the Nobel Prize fell short of providing the greatest service to mankind.

FIVE

More Micro

Sir John R. Hicks (1972)

William S. Vickrey (1996)

Sir James A. Mirrlees (1996)

Vernon L. Smith (2002)

Not all Nobel Prize–winning microeconomists were part of the Chicago School of Economics or were focused on the stock market. Some, like Sir John R. Hicks, simply applied the microeconomics that they learned in doctoral programs to interesting problems. Microeconomics is a standard part of all advanced studies in economics, and like mathematics or physics, it has a certain appeal because of its well-defined problems and solutions. Hicks was initially attracted to this work and made significant contributions to some of the subfield's basic concepts. While he was never a great mathematician, he had a talent for translating his ideas into simple equations and graphs, providing important tools for other economists. His contributions were not limited to this one field, however, and he was properly recognized by the Nobel Prize committee for equally important contributions to Keynesian economics and general equilibrium.

Another example of a Nobel economist with strong microeconomic skills was William S. Vickrey who used these tools to explore the nature of auctions. He made the surprising discovery that very different auctions will, on average, result in the same revenue. This is a very interesting result and would also be very useful if it were true, but unfortunately the idealized world assumed in microeconomics does not always apply perfectly to the real world. Vickrey also believed that microeconomic analysis could identify the optimum tax, the one that would benefit the most people and do the least damage to the economy. While Vickrey was able to formulate the problem, it took the finer mathematical skills of Sir James A. Mirrlees ultimately to solve it.

The final laureate in this chapter, Vernon L. Smith, attempted to demonstrate the relevance of microeconomics and game theory by simulating markets and games with real participants. The approach was innovative because it allowed Smith to test certain simple economic behaviors in an experimental context. Does economics have a future as an experimental science? Smith's work gave us a glimpse of that potential. His experiments became particularly interesting when they produced some unexpected results that seemed to conflict with Smith's own strong preference for free markets.

Sir John R. Hicks (1972 Prize Winner)

There was something unique about Sir John R. Hicks that earned him great respect from almost all economists. He was knighted in 1964 and won the Nobel Prize in economics in 1972, but more importantly, he was one of the last Renaissance economists equally proficient in history, mathematics, and philosophy. He was also one of the few economists respected by neoclassical and Keynesian economists for his work in both areas. In neoclassical economics, he resurrected interest in general equilibrium theory and uncovered fundamental microeconomic concepts. In Keynesian analysis he invented concepts and diagrams that helped to explain and expand upon Keynes' original theory.

In microeconomics, prices are the essential mechanism for sending signals to consumers and businesses and thus guiding their behaviors. Economists have given considerable thought to the role of prices in organized markets, especially in allocating resources and balancing supply and demand. All of this scrutiny has produced some curious insights. For example, an increase in gasoline prices can be thought of as having two separate effects. The first effect, called the *substitution effect*, is rather obvious. Higher prices cause people to look for substitutes, like ethanol or mass transit. The second effect, called the *income effect*, is more subtle.[1] With higher gas prices, families generally spend more of their income on gas and have less income to spend on everything else. It was considered a major breakthrough in microeconomics when Hicks and his colleague, R. D. G. Allen, were able mathematically to separate responses to price changes into substitution and income effects.[2]

One application of the income effect is in the area of *welfare economics*. When economists use this term, they are not referring to government programs that provide aid to the poor and indigent, but instead are referring to attempts to measure changes in the general welfare of society. For example, how much do people value a 20 percent reduction in food prices? In the 1920s, Alfred Marshall invented a practical way to measure this, which he called *consumer surplus*.[3] Hicks provided two related measures to value the same price change based on his income effect.[4] It was a little disconcerting for economists to have multiple values for the same thing, but Hicks' explanation made it clear that this outcome was unavoidable.

A concept related to Hicks' income effect is used to value certain types of government actions. For example, it is sometimes useful to know how strongly people would object to the construction of an airport in their neighborhood. One way to estimate that is to ask people how much money they would require to offset the inconvenience of living next to an airport. Because the amount of compensation should leave people as content as they would have been before the airport was built, it is in a sense another cost of the airport. For many decades economists have used surveys like this to value these impacts. However, this approach may not be very reliable, according to Nobel laureate Daniel Kahneman, who suggested several reasons why it is difficult to get honest answers from these surveys.

Hicks and R. D. G. Allen thought they had discovered the mathematics of the substitution and income effects in the 1930s, but they found out later that they weren't the first. Eugene Slutsky, a Russian statistician, had worked out the basic results quite a bit earlier and published them in 1915. Probably because the article was published in an obscure Italian journal, it remained outside the economic mainstream until Allen, Paul Samuelson, and others came across it in the 1930s.

General Equilibrium

Economists had already invented equations to represent supply and demand, and in the 1930s, Hicks added more equations to represent the production of goods and services and the utility, or satisfaction, gained from consuming them.[5] These equations were important for microeconomics but they also helped to complete the general equilibrium model Leon Walras had constructed in the 1800s to represent the entire economy. Hicks provided an important bridge between Walras' work in the 1870s and the sophisticated mathematical proofs of Nobel laureates Kenneth Arrow and Gerard Debreu in the 1950s. The Swedish committee cited this work as one of the reasons for Hicks' Nobel award.

All of this early work in microeconomics and general equilibrium theory was rooted in the assumption of perfect competition, a concept for which Hicks had little regard later in his career. Perfect competition was an essential part of his first book, *Theory of Wages* (1932), which Hicks described in 1986 as "a perfect competition book, running that particular assumption, a very convenient assumption, to the death."[6] Even though this assumption was essential to this book and many of his Nobel

Prize-winning ideas, Hicks candidly admitted, "I don't believe in it." He went on to describe this book as one that "even to this day people continue to use. I now think it is a piece of rubbish."[7] His other acclaimed book, *Value and Capital* (1939), was also, in retrospect, too neoclassical for Hicks. He insisted that "My own thinking had been proceeding on rather different lines."[8]

Hicks was drawn toward a competing paradigm when *The General Theory* was published in 1936 – Keynesian economics. The *Economic Journal* invited Hicks to write one of the earliest reviews of the book, an invitation that he later described as "one of the greatest honors I have received."[9] Hicks' comments were supportive and provided additional explanations of some concepts and simple, geometric representations of others. One of those representations – now called the *IS-LM model* for investment, savings, liquidity, and money – illustrated Keynes' central idea that the economy could end up in equilibrium despite persistent unemployment. The model was independently created by Alvin Hansen at Harvard whose name for the model is the one that stuck. Hicks also provided a more detailed description of the *liquidity trap*, a desperate case suggested by Keynes when unemployment is high but the national bank is incapable of pushing interest rates any lower.[10]

Even Hicks' venerable IS/LM model was not exempted from the author's second thoughts. In an interview, Hicks explained the mistake that he had made. "Those two curves do not belong together. One is a flow equilibrium, the other a stock. They have no business being on the same diagram."[11] But second thoughts or not, the two curves continue to be reproduced in many modern intermediate macroeconomic textbooks almost seventy years later.

Second thoughts were part of Hicks' assessment of his own legacy, as described in his acceptance speech for his Nobel Prize. He briefly explained his discoveries, followed by another brief explanation of why he no longer found them useful. In particular, he no longer thought it made sense to talk about capital as a single number, which is essential in neoclassical economics. He claimed that he could no longer justify the practice of adding up all factories, equipment, machines, and vehicles into a single variable called capital, and concluded, "Capital, thus arbitrarily valued, carries no conviction; there is no reason why it should exist."[12] This argument originated with Joan Robinson, and to the extent that it was true, it made much of neoclassical economics meaningless. Consequently, Hicks dedicated the balance of his Nobel lecture to topics that were not recognized by the Nobel committee but that he felt were "more promising."[13]

During an interview in 1986, Hicks suggested that he would have preferred the Nobel committee to honor him for his later work, specifically mentioning his book, *Theory of Economic History*.[14] It wasn't one of Hicks' more popular books, nor would it have been considered very "scientific" by the Nobel committee. Instead of equations, Hicks analyzed actual economic behavior. For example, Hicks observed that despite the power and authority of kings, they were often in dire financial conditions.[15] How do you explain that? He attributed some part of the problem to the difficulty of collecting taxes when economic activity was widely dispersed around the countryside and record keeping was poor or nonexistent. The growth of trade helped to alleviate this problem because it concentrated economic activity in a few geographic locations. The development of joint stock companies also made it easier to collect taxes because of the careful bookkeeping required for stockholders, although it was unintentional. Finally, Hicks noted that kings often found it difficult to borrow money. This made sense to him because it would be difficult to enforce a contract with a sovereign. A contract is generally enforced by appealing to a higher authority, but when the contract is with a king, there is no higher authority. As a result, lending to a king was ironically perceived as a high risk. As these examples illustrate, Hicks observed real economic patterns and then tried to explain them. The Nobel committee was not impressed and did not mention this work, much to Hicks' disappointment.

Born in 1904 in Warwick, England, John R. Hicks was the son of a journalist. His original studies in mathematics at Clifton College and Balliol College, Oxford, proved to be both expensive and uninspiring. He solved the first problem with a scholarship and tried to solve the second by switching fields in 1923 to a new major at Oxford – philosophy, politics and economics. He hoped the new major would satisfy his broader interests in literature and history, but for Hicks, the move was "not a success."[16] The resulting education left him with a second-class degree and, in his own judgment, ill-prepared in any of the subjects.

Fortunately for Hicks, economists were in short supply in the late 1920s and he was able to secure a position as a temporary lecturer at the London School of Economics. He taught labor economics and industrial relations and initiated research projects but soon realized that his mathematics training was inadequate. Hicks claimed that he abandoned the formal study of mathematics at about the age of nineteen, and was forced to learn more on his own. The mathematical appendix in the *Theory of Wages* was one of his earlier works and was something he was "rather ashamed of." Although his skills improved over time, he had respect for economists like Samuelson whom he described as "a much better mathematician than I am."[17]

The 1930s was a good time to be at the London School. It was evolving into a formidable center of economic theory with the presence of Nobel laureate Friedrich A. von Hayek and others. Ursula Webb also taught there, and she and Hicks were married in 1935, the same year that Hicks was offered a position at Cambridge University. Cambridge, however, did not appeal to him. He found it a "horrible place to live" because of both the physical and intellectual environments. The faculty had withdrawn into two warring camps, and they weren't talking very much to each other. Hicks left Cambridge in 1938 for the University of Manchester and then for Oxford in 1946.

There was a particularly long interval between the time when Hicks published his Nobel ideas and when he actually won the award. Most of his acclaimed work in microeconomics, general equilibrium, and Keynesian economics was completed in the 1930s, nearly forty years before his work was recognized with a Nobel Prize in 1972. The Nobel Prize in economics was still relatively new and was still catching up with the backlog of past achievements.

While a prolific contributor to economic theory, Hicks was not the type of economist to venture an opinion about real-world economic policy. He was confident of his understanding of theory and economic principles, but "reluctant to pronounce on larger issues of practical economics."[18] He was a rare example of an economist who believed his deep understanding of economic theory did not automatically qualify him to offer opinions on current events, even those related to economics.

William S. Vickrey (1996 Prize Winner)

The Nobel Prize in economics is announced every year early in October and formally awarded by the King of Sweden at a lavish ceremony in December. One of the two 1996 winners didn't make it to the formal award. William S. Vickrey died on October 11th, three days after the announcement.

The Nobel committee's citation of Vickery's award noted two distinct accomplishments, the development of optimal auctions and framing the problem for the optimal tax rate, later solved by his co-winner, Sir James A. Mirrlees. In economics, auctions are broadly defined as everything from competitive bids on defense contracts to silent auctions at church fundraisers. Auctions have become more common and more important since Vickrey first put them under the economics microscope. His major article, "Counterspeculation, Auctions, and Competitive Sealed Tenders," was published in 1961, long before the government auctioned off the radio spectrum and off-shore oil leases, or before eBay created the famous online auction.

There are many different ways to hold an auction but what is the best way? Is it best to generate the most revenue or to ensure that the "right" bidder wins, the one that stands to profit the most? Will the best auction minimize the incentive to collude or reduce the occurrence of second guessing? In 1961, Vickrey evaluated several types of auctions with these questions in mind. A little later he earned the distinction of having one named after him, the *Vickrey auction*.

Traditional microeconomists before Vickrey had relatively little interest in the nuts and bolts of how prices were actually set. Like Adam Smith, they were inclined to believe that markets determine an efficient price through trial and error and through the active participation of many buyers and sellers. But the reality is that many products do not lend themselves to this simple scenario. Take the radio spectrum for example. Only a handful of companies exist with enough capital and knowledge to bid on this esoteric resource. The supply is also limited because we can't create more frequencies no matter how popular it is. Under these conditions, there is no guarantee that markets will operate smoothly or efficiently.

Auctions provide one way to determine a market price, and Vickrey identified three primary auctions and proposed a fourth. The *English auction* is the one we are most familiar with – a continuous stream of bids, one just higher than the next until the highest bid is reached. The *Dutch auction* runs in reverse with an auctioneer announcing prices that steadily decline until the first and final bid is made by the winner. Finally, there are the *sealed-bid auctions*, which are won by whoever submits the highest bid. A further distinction is the first-price and second-price sealed-bid auction. In the former case the winner pays the price they bid, and in the latter case, the winner with the highest bid only pays the price of the second highest bid.

In the English system, so popular on eBay, bids are taken in ascending order until no more bids are offered or until time runs out. If a pair of Elvis Presley's sunglasses is worth $1,000 to you, then you should stay in the bidding until you win or the price reaches $1,000, at which point you would drop out. If you win this auction, however, you will only have to pay one dollar more than the second highest bid. For example, if the next highest bid is only $499 you can win it for $500. Vickrey wondered if there wasn't an analogous sealed-bid approach that would produce the same result as the

English auction. He proposed the second-price sealed-bid auction in which the winner pays one dollar over the second highest bid. This variation of a sealed-bid process should produce the same outcome as an English auction and is sometimes called the Vickrey auction.

There is one particularly desirable feature of the English auction and the Vickrey auction: In neither case do you need to guess the strategies of your competitors. In fact, it doesn't even help to know their strategies. In the English auction, you simply bid until you win or you reach your maximum price. You should follow the same course of action whether you know your opponent's strategy or not. The same is true in the Vickrey auction, because your bid only determines whether you win; someone else's bid determines what you pay. The Vickrey auction, like the English auction is, in theory, a good way to ensure simple, honest bids.

The Dutch auction and the first-price sealed-bid auction are different. In these auctions, naïve participants might bid their top value but more than likely they will bid less than that based on a guess of what the next lowest bid might be. In effect, they don't want to pay $1,000 dollars for Elvis' sunglasses if they suspect they can get them for $500. But how much lower will they bid? If they actually knew the second highest bid, then the decision would be easy. But what if they only knew the probability distribution of all bids? Vickrey was able to demonstrate that under this assumption, the price will on average tend to equal the second highest bid. In this case, the expected price from all four types of auctions would be identical, which is the origin of his *revenue-equivalence theorem* and a major reason for his Nobel Prize.[19] While the price would not necessarily equal the $500 bids for the sunglasses in the Dutch auction and first-price sealed-bid auction, it would, in theory, equal $500 on average. The practical value of this surprising result is severely limited because, in reality, the distribution of other bids is generally impossible to know. In fact, economists have run experiments and found that the results of actual auctions generally violate Vickery's equivalence rule.[20] The problem seems to be that the theory doesn't capture real-world behavior as people start creating their own strategies based on rather poor expectations of other bids.

It would be easy to presume that Vickrey invented the Vickrey auction but in fact he did not. The Vickrey auction, or second-price auction, had been around for many decades before Vickrey wrote about it in his 1961 article. A more appropriate name would probably be a stamp auction, because the practice was originally developed to sell postage stamps bought by collectors. Astute research by David Lucking-Riley identified the use of the Vickrey auction as early as 1893, long before Vickrey was born.[21]

While Vickrey did not invent this particular auction, he was one of the first to seriously analyze it. Was he familiar with the stamp auctions or did he invent the concept without knowing that it already existed? Either scenario is possible. Outside of the stamp auctions the Vickrey auctions were never very common so it would have been easy to overlook.

Although used for stamps, the Vickrey auction was never particularly popular for other purposes. Lucking-Riley suggested that such auctions may not live up to their potential if bidders don't trust the auctioneers. After all, it is in the interest of auction operators to fabricate a high second bid when their income is based on a percentage of the bid. If auction operators lie and claim that the second highest bid for Elvis' glasses is $900, they make more money. Lucking-Riley actually found a stamp auction operator who ran Vickrey auctions and confessed to cheating in just this manner.[22]

Introducing a Vickrey auction on eBay would make some sense. In theory it should provide the same essential result without all the time required to monitor the bids down to the wire. And in fact eBay introduced something called proxy bidding that simulates a Vickrey auction. Of course, even eBay had to assure parties that it was honest and above board, and did that by publishing a list of all losing bidders and bids so they could be verified.[23] While the Vickrey auction requires less time than a traditional eBay auction, it also takes some of the drama and luck out of last-second bidding. Some people may miss that.

Vickrey's youth could be characterized as one of privilege, culminating in his graduation from Phillips Andover Academy in 1931. Andover is, to this day, one of the most prestigious boarding schools in the United States and it is the oldest, dating to 1778. Vickrey attended Yale University as an undergraduate, received a bachelor's degree in mathematics in 1935 and a master's in economics in 1937.

At Yale, Vickrey came under the influence of the prominent economist Irving Fisher, who may be best known for his failed attempt to reassure investors just prior to the stock market crash of 1929.[24] Fisher is credited with inspiring Vickrey in his quest for the optimum tax, defined as the tax that creates the least distortion in the economy.[25] This achievement, cited by the Nobel committee, was the topic of Vickrey's doctoral dissertation "Agenda for Progressive Taxation." Although largely ignored by policy makers, this work became a minor classic among those economists who still believed that the rich should pay higher taxes.[26]

Because Vickrey died only three days after the announcement of his Nobel Prize, a fellow economist was invited to give the prize lecture, which included auctions and some of his other interests. Vickrey was especially passionate about his proposal to use prices to reduce traffic congestion in crowded cities and to improve New York subways. Later in life, he seemed to lose interest in microeconomics altogether, including a concept he helped to develop, *asymmetric information*, which simply means that some people have more information than others. He apparently dismissed this idea for having little relevance, although it later became an important economic concept and was cited as a reason for his Nobel Prize.[27]

In some respects Vickrey was a crusader. He was a Quaker and a conscientious objector during World War II, and was willing to criticize some of his fellow economists, even his fellow Nobel laureates. He condemned economists who showed a "callous tolerance of unemployment ... most of whom would not share in the sacrifices they recommend for others."[28] Unlike other economists who would be satisfied with unemployment rates in the 3 or 4 percent range, Vickrey didn't think we should give up until the rate was down to 1.5 percent. He did not live long enough as a Nobel laureate to make his case for this ambitious goal.

Sir James A. Mirrlees (1996 Prize Winner)

Is there such a thing as the perfect income tax? If there is such a thing, should the tax rates be higher for those with high incomes or with low incomes? Is there a tax that would increase the overall well-being of society or at least minimize losses to society? These questions have been explored in great detail by microeconomists, including Sir James A. Mirrlees who won the Nobel Prize in 1996.

The basic objection to high *marginal tax rates* has been around for a long time. Marginal tax rates are defined as the amount paid by individuals on the last dollar of income earned. Taxing income might possibly discourage high-wage earners from working as hard or as long as they would otherwise, or discourage investors from making investments or taking risks that promise high returns. If high taxes cause workers to cut back their efforts and investors to cut their investments or risk, then the results may be undesirable: less private sector output and less revenue for the government. Not surprisingly, high-income earners tend to be the strongest advocates of this concept. On the other side of this argument was John Kenneth Galbraith who noted that very high marginal tax rates existed in the United States in the 1950s and 1960s without any observable shortage of talented business executives, entrepreneurs, inventors, or movie stars.

The ideal tax is fairly simple if everyone earns about the same income before taxes. Imagine a case where the government needs approximately one thousand dollars from each person to pay for its expenditures. The government can simply levy what is called a *lump sum tax* of one thousand dollars on each individual and there is no adverse incentive because the marginal tax is zero. In other words, if an individual decides to work a little harder or longer they don't pay any more in taxes, just the thousand dollars. In theory, a lump sum tax can raise revenue without discouraging work, which makes it an efficient tax.

In the real world, people earn a wide range of incomes before taxes so a lump sum tax doesn't see very fair. Consider another example: Suppose you knew that the highest income earner is expected to earn exactly five billion dollars next year. It would make some sense to set the marginal tax rate for that individual to zero but only for income over five billion dollars. That creates an incentive for that individual to work harder or longer and to generate more output for the economy, a net benefit for society. Government revenue from that individual wouldn't go up, of course, but it wouldn't go down either.[29] This policy is efficient but also not particularly realistic because tax collectors don't know exactly what incomes will be in the future. Both these examples illustrate how microeconomists think about the effect of taxes on incentives.

Does this mean that the optimal tax should have lower marginal rates for high-income earners, the opposite of the U.S. federal income tax? Not necessarily. It may make sense to take relatively more money from high-income earners if you believe they will miss it less. You would expect one thousand dollars to mean more to a poor family than to a billionaire and economic theory suggests that may be true. Increasing amounts of anything, including income, are likely to result in diminishing increments of satisfaction. We might assume that one thousand dollars means less to Bill Gates than it does to a family living in public housing on the south side of Chicago. This concept is used to defend our progressive income tax that has higher rates for those with high incomes.

The optimum tax schedule has to take all this into account: the potential disincentives to work and invest (efficiency) and the relative satisfaction gained from a more equal distribution of income (equity). There are other factors to consider, however, with efficiency and equity two of the most important. William S. Vickrey was one of the first economists to formulate this mathematical problem, but it was Sir James A. Mirrlees who had the mathematical talent to solve it. So what is the optimum tax rate? It actually depends on the relative importance of these two factors, efficiency and equity. Depending on their relative strength, the ideal tax could be *progressive*, higher rates for high income, or the opposite, *regressive*. Because the ability to measure these two factors accurately is extremely difficult, if not impossible, the ideal income tax remains hard to pin down.

At the age of fourteen, Mirrlees claimed to have "acquired a strange enthusiasm for mathematics," and aspired to be a professor of mathematics.[30] He was of Scottish origin and attended the University of Edinburgh and then Cambridge University in the 1950s to study mathematics and later economics. Cambridge had gained a reputation for macroeconomics because it was the birthplace of Keynesian economics, but Mirrlees was not impressed. When his first teacher at Cambridge advised him to read Keynes' *General Theory*, he claimed, "That may not have been the best advice, but it did no great harm and one day I hope to finish it."[31] Instead, Mirrlees gravitated toward microeconomics where he found problems to solve.

Economist Hal Varian has suggested a reason why economists may tend to understate the merits of a progressive income tax.[32] In the real world, incomes are determined by more than an individual's productivity and their tax rates. For example, there is also luck. The fact that some people are in the right place at the right time may explain as much about their economic success as their productivity. Luck might also explain the variation in individual income over time and the widely different incomes for brothers, even though they may share similar talents and work ethics. This issue is important because if high incomes are explained by luck, there is less of an efficiency loss from a progressive income tax. There may even be some justification for taxing such windfalls. Varian's point was that conventional microeconomics is likely to miscalculate optimum tax rates when it overlooks important factors like luck.[33]

Determining the importance of efficiency is difficult enough but at least in theory it should be observable. You need to measure how much people work under different tax rates. Attempting to place a value on equity is far more challenging because it is neither observable nor measurable. How can you mathematically compare Bill Gates' decrease in happiness from having $1,000 less to an increase in the happiness of a poor child having $1,000 more? Such a comparison may be essential in a qualitative sense when debating the merits of a progressive income tax, but is it reasonable to presume it has a precise mathematical value?

In much of his later work, Mirrlees extended his analysis of taxes and incentives to take into account market imperfections related to uncertainty.[34] In this respect, he had something in common with the Nobel laureates described as behaviorists. As he introduced different forms of uncertainty into the basic model, the results changed, reminding us once again to pay less attention to the results and more attention to what we might learn along the way. Results in any model may change or even reverse with the modification of a single assumption.

As an expert in tax rates and a Nobel Prize–winning economist, Mirrlees' opinions about taxes became newsworthy. At a seminar in Hong Kong, Mirrlees reportedly suggested that the country could stand to raise its income tax rate. At 15 percent he believed it was relatively low by international standards and could be raised as high as 20 percent, the rate in Singapore, but probably not as high as the 40-percent rate in Britain.[35] He had a similar recommendation for China. He did not consider the then-current taxes of 25 percent of gross domestic product to be particularly high, and recommended that China raise the personal income tax to pay for education, health care, and cash subsidies for the poor.[36]

Microeconomists are trained to think objectively about incentives and certainly the Nobel Prize itself creates something of an incentive. Because a Nobel Prize includes a large sum of money and great prestige, it should stimulate additional effort. But what happens after you win a Nobel Prize? Does the motivation for hard work dissipate? As Mirrlees explained, "according to economic theory, a prize once awarded should actually induce a recipient to work less hard and is therefore supposed to be not entirely good."[37] But then he quoted a colleague to the effect that "I am of the opinion that … it is not entirely bad, either."[38]

Vernon L. Smith (2002 Prize Winner)

Vernon L. Smith could remember exactly when he got the idea that would lead to his 2002 Nobel Prize in economics. The light bulb came on while he was in graduate school at Harvard University in 1952. He was taking a class from Edward Chamberlin who was already famous for inventing the monopoly model in parallel with Joan Robinson of Cambridge. As an introduction to imperfect markets, Chamberlin ran a little demonstration with his students to simulate a simple Adam Smith–kind of market. Half the students were designated as buyers, assigned a secret maximum price, and half were sellers, assigned a secret minimum price. Chamberlin instructed the students to mill about the room and negotiate in pairs as if they were horse trading. If they didn't strike a deal, they moved on; if they did reach a deal, then the sale was posted for the rest of the class. On paper there was a supply and demand curve that should have produced a neat equilibrium in price and quantity. In practice, the prices were all over the map and did not usually converge in a predictable or efficient manner.

By demonstrating that free markets don't always work, this exercise provided Chamberlin a segue into his own theories. But Vernon Smith didn't like the message. How could the free markets of Adam Smith and his own idol, Austrian philosopher Hayek, be dismissed with one contrary example? He resolved to design a different exercise to give markets a better opportunity to prove themselves. Four years later, in 1956, Vernon Smith conducted his own classroom exercise with twenty-two buyers and sellers. This time, though, they followed the rules commonly used in more formal stock exchanges, known as a double auction. Buyers post their prices (*bids*) and sellers post theirs (*asks*); with only a few iterations, the market would converge to the *competitive equilibrium* price. As Smith said, "Thus did I seem to have stumbled upon an engine for testing ideas inside and outside traditional economic theory."[39]

Gradually, this simple class exercise evolved into more sophisticated experiments with subjects using computers and receiving actual cash rewards to simulate markets. The Noble prize committee commented that "Economics used to be regarded as a non-experimental science," but this is no longer the case because of the work of Vernon L. Smith.[40] His exercises offered a vehicle for testing human behavior under the rules and incentives suggested by microeconomics and game theory.

Smith was a big fan of game theorists and enjoyed testing their ideas in his laboratory. There was a problem, however, because most of what game theorists did was too abstract for a laboratory. When they did propose a real game, it was generally very simple because anything more complicated often couldn't be solved mathematically. While these simple games could be tested, they also had relatively little economic relevance. Smith conceded that sometimes game theorists built "castles in the sky" and then started to believe in them.[41] While their ideas were not always validated in the laboratory, game theory played a big part in Smith's experimental economics.

Boom and Bust

As he had done in his first experiment, Smith was most interested in using his laboratory to demonstrate that markets work. In particular, he set out to show that even without all the conditions necessary for perfect competition, a properly organized market could still be efficient. With this mission, it was particularly surprising when Smith's own experiments reproduced the irrational boom-and-bust cycles evident in many financial and real estate markets. In one experiment Smith allowed his test subjects to trade a simple financial instrument. Traders bid the price up higher and higher until buyers eventually got cold feet and the market crashed. In an effort to make the market more stable, Smith told his subjects exactly what the security they were trading was worth. But even this addition did not put an end to speculation. At first, Smith used graduate students as the test group; then he thought it would be interesting to bring in finance professionals. The result, however, was worse, with the professionals creating even bigger price swings. As Smith concluded, "It is pretty easy to get bubbles and crashes."[42]

Multiple iterations of the same experiment showed that people eventually wise up, and the bubbles get smaller and eventually disappear. But still, Smith observed that "people are myopic," and "if the price is going up, they think it will keep going up."[43] None of this was very helpful for free-market advocates. Speculative bubbles and crashes are quite the opposite of the efficient market hypothesis and microeconomics. According to the efficient market theory, the stock market absorbs all the information from participants and accurately reflects the "true" value of stocks at any moment in time. But if markets are driven by myopic, irrational exuberance as revealed by Smith's experiments, then they fall short of that ideal.

Smith was reluctant to concede this market failure although it was demonstrated by his own experiments. Instead, he looked for a positive outcome from a boom-and-bust cycle. He concluded that the busts were useful because they cleared out the dead wood. "The excesses of high tech's early days," he reasoned, "have been thankfully driven out, leaving the strong."[44] But this is what a well-functioning competitive market is supposed to do without an erratic boom-and-bust cycle. It's not easy to put a positive spin on speculative bubbles and financial crashes that produce obvious economic waste and inefficiency.

Too Much Cooperation

Rational behavior is the essential starting point for most microeconomics and game theory, but it didn't fare very well in Smith's experiments. This result could not have been any clearer than in the so-called ultimatum game. In this game, a player is given $100 and must decide to keep some fraction of it and offer the rest to the second player. The second player can only decide to accept or reject the offer; if rejected, neither player gets anything. The game is played once.

How would a rational person play this game? The first player would assume that the other player is also rational and will accept any amount of money rather than nothing. So the first player should offer the minimum amount possible, say $1. Being rational, the second player should accept the dollar and the first player makes $99. Really? Smith found that the second player would react negatively to such inequity and often reject such an offer even if it meant a loss to them. The first players generally understood this better than the economists and would consequently offer significantly more than the minimum but not always enough to avoid rejection. In one experiment reported by Smith, the average offer was $44 and even that was not always accepted.[45]

Smith and his colleagues ran many variations of this game. They changed the amount of money, changed the wording of the instructions, introduced anonymity, and even eliminated the single decision of the second player, which changed the ultimatum game into the so-called dictator game. They also tried limiting the allocation choices for the first and second players, creating what they called the trust game. Despite all this effort, it was impossible to avoid the obvious conclusion: People do not act rationally in these laboratory experiments. "We find that people are more trusting and achieve more cooperative outcomes more often than game theory predicts," said Smith.[46] People seemed to trust each other and cooperate with each other even when the other person was anonymous, and they acted out of a sense of fairness, sometimes to their own detriment.

In his Nobel Prize acceptance speech, Smith asked the question, why so much cooperation?[47] He suggested that much of it was based on a sense of reciprocity. According to reciprocity, individuals make sacrifices for others only if there is an opportunity for others to pay them back at least as much or more than they sacrificed. While some of the experiments cited by Smith supported this explanation, they didn't seem to be enough. Is it possible that people simply find satisfaction in helping others and treating them fairly? People leave tips in restaurants every day, even when they have absolutely no expectation of returning. Increasingly complex variations in the games have yet to fully explain this behavior. But whatever the reason, human behavior is clearly not consistently rational in the conventional economic sense of the word. In addition, Smith cited research that showed that monkeys also seem to be motivated by fairness and inclined toward cooperation.[48]

There were some exceptions to this behavior, however. For instance, research showed that individuals with antisocial personality disorder or sociopaths demonstrate little evidence of cooperative behavior. Joseph Stiglitz, the 2001 Nobel Prize winner, suggested that economists could add themselves to this list of exceptions. According to Stiglitz, "Among the more amusing results that have come out of experimental economics are those concerning altruism and selfishness. It appears (at least in the experimental situations) that experimental subjects are not as selfish as economists have hypothesized, except for one group – the economists themselves."[49] In his Nobel speech, Smith reported that faculty with a knowledge of game theory cooperated less and, as a result, made less money in these games when compared to undergraduate students. Curiously, they also required more time to make a decision.[50]

Auctions

One of the more practical applications of experimental economics has been to provide trial runs for auctions, which can have many complex rules. These tests may not predict how auctions will work in reality, but they may identify potential flaws, much the same way as a wind tunnel is used to test airplane designs.[51] One example is a combinatorial auction, like the one used to sell the wireless spectrum for cell phones and other gadgets. Combinatorial auctions, in fact, have been used by many entities including Sears when they contracted out shipping jobs and NASA when they auctioned off payload space on the Casini mission to Saturn.[52]

Not all examples have been entirely successful. One author speculated that the wireless auction might have worked too well, causing excessively high bids that contributed to the widespread bankruptcy of telecom companies.[53] Another example was the deregulation of the electric power industry, which included complex auctions to promote more competitive markets. The actual auctions in California worked fine for a brief time with relatively low and stable prices. But when a heat wave in California coincided with a drought in the Northwest hydropower system, the market experienced soaring prices, rolling blackouts, and massive fraud by unscrupulous energy traders like Enron. The resulting energy crisis created billions of dollars of losses for utilities that may take years to pay off. Economists tested some of these auctions implemented by the state of California. While many of the flaws in the new markets were identified in hindsight, they unfortunately weren't predicted in advance.

Smith was not impressed by the psychologists and behavioral economists who challenged the model of rational behavior, including Daniel Kahneman who shared the Nobel Prize with Smith in 2002. Smith was concerned that behavioral economists were spending too much time highlighting the limitations of markets by documenting human errors. As he said, "Research strategies that focus on the study of errors, however, can distort professional beliefs, to say nothing of popular representation...."[54] In his Nobel speech he summed up the difference between psychologists and conventional economists as follows: "Many psychologists appear to find irrationality everywhere, and many economists appear to see the findings as everywhere irrelevant."[55]

Furthermore, Smith was not persuaded by the survey method often used by behavioral economists and psychologists. In his view, "Sometimes what people actually do completely contradicts what they say, and sometimes you cannot find [that] out by asking because the agents themselves do not know what they will do or are doing."[56] At another time Smith directly accused Kahneman and his collaborator, Amos Tversky, of "ignoring contrary interpretations and evidence over extended periods of time."[57] Despite all of these harsh criticisms, Smith graciously toasted Kahneman at the Nobel banquet for his ingenuity and understanding.[58]

Smith closed his lengthy, fifty-two-page Nobel Prize lecture with a few comments on what he considered the next frontier in economics, neuro-economics. Economists and psychologists have teamed up to test which parts of the brain are activated when people make economic decisions. For example, one study seemed to find that the right hemisphere was lit up by economic gains while losses lit up the left side. This tracking has been made possible by adding functional magnetic imaging to the toolkits of curious experimental economists.[59]

During his career, Smith might have been less successful if he hadn't been willing to break the rules and follow his own course. He eschewed more conventional approaches to economics in favor of experimental economics at a time when it was not very well accepted. But Smith's maverick behavior went even further. His long hair, usually tied in a pony tail, and his silver inlaid Hopi Indian jewelry made him look different than most economists. But it was the cowboy boots that most worried the Nobel committee. According to Smith, "They were scared to death that I was going to wear my cowboy boots.... I couldn't believe it. Who cares?"[60] Smith wasn't worried about what to wear to the prize ceremony but he was concerned about the tax on his prize money. "Right away, you hit the alternative minimum tax," he complained.[61]

There are, of course, some rules of behavior that should be followed. The University of Arizona, where Smith was employed for twenty-six years, had a rule common to most public universities: prohibiting employees from financially benefiting from the use of university facilities and other resources. While Smith and three of his colleagues were employed by the university, they were also involved in a for-profit company called Cybernomics that developed computer software for economic and market analysis.[62] A concern raised by a suspicious faculty member sparked a university audit to investigate whether the four professors had violated the rule. Three years after leaving the University of Arizona and two years after winning the Nobel Prize, Smith and the other faculty paid $75,000 in a mediated settlement to reimburse the university for part of their salary but did not admit any wrongdoing. The audit placed part of the blame on the College of Management because it "did not monitor for compliance or provide adequate guidelines to employees regarding outside consulting."[63]

For Vernon Smith, life started with few advantages. As he stated in his autobiography for the Nobel committee, "Like many of my generation I am a product of the strange circumstances of survival, and of success built on tragedy." Smith's mother became a widow at age twenty-two with two daughters when her first husband, a fireman on the Santa Fe railroad, died in a train wreck in 1918. Later, she met and married Smith's father, a machinist, and when he was laid off in 1932, they moved to a farm outside Wichita.

Fortunately Smith was a standout student in his classic one-room schoolhouse and again as an undergraduate at Caltech and later Harvard University. Starting out as a physics major, he switched to electrical engineering and received his baccalaureate degree in 1949. He also started out with his mother's politics, casting his first vote for Socialist Norman Thomas.[64] But Smith became intrigued by economics and converted to a more pro-market, libertarian philosophy when he discovered Paul Samuelson's *Foundations* and Ludwig von Mises' *Human Action* in the Caltech library. In order to learn more economics he attended the University of Kansas and earned a master's degree. From there he enrolled in the Harvard doctoral program where he studied under Alvin Hansen, the leading American Keynesian and took classes from Nobel Prize winner Wassily Leontief. But it was in Chamberlin's class that he saw his future: using students to test market outcomes.

Smith spent an important year at Stanford where he became aware of economic experiments being conducted by game theorist and future Nobel laureate Reinhhard Selten. Although experimental economics appeared to be a very small field, at least it was a field. The experience convinced Smith that experimental economics could be more than a hobby.[65] The laboratory was an ideal setting for Smith to pursue his free-market convictions. Even when markets burst from speculative bubbles or participants chose cooperation over competition, Smith never lost his enthusiasm for free markets. Where Adam Smith saw an invisible hand, Vernon Smith saw a "kind of magic."[66]

There have been some interesting spin-offs from Smith's work in experimental economics. If markets truly channel large amounts of information, then perhaps they can be used to make predictions. Some economists have invented markets to do just that. The basic idea draws upon Hayek's optimistic view of markets as a vehicle for aggregating information. One example is the Iowa Electronic Market (IEM), a venture by some faculty of the business school at the University of Iowa to create a futures market for predictions. The IEM has been used since 1988 to predict a variety of events, including the popular vote for presidential elections. The market allows investors to buy and sell shares on the internet that are associated with each of the candidates in a particular election. The payout per share is designed to be proportional to each candidate's share of the popular election. Therefore, money is made whenever the purchase price of a share is proportionately less than the candidate polls in the final election. In an efficient market, the price per share should be a good predictor of the outcome of the election. The Iowa faculty claim that this is, in fact, the case and that their electronic market does a better job of predicting elections than exit polls conducted during an election.[67]

Inspired by this new forecasting tool, the U.S. Department of Defense seriously considered creating an artificial market to predict where a terrorist might strike. The plan was dropped after a group of U.S. senators found the concept "immoral," but it would have raised some interesting questions.[68] Would investors need to see a terrorist strike to reap their profits? Could Osama bin Laden and his business associates buy shares to throw the United States off track? And would the Pentagon's use of this method unintentionally send a signal to terrorists that they lacked confidence in their own conventional intelligence gathering tools?

SIX

Behaviorists

Herbert A. Simon (1978)

Daniel Kahneman (2002)

George A. Akerlof (2001)

Joseph E. Stiglitz (2001)

A. Michael Spence (2001)

Does anyone doubt that people can make irrational choices based on bad information? And yet, for more than 100 years, free-market advocates were content to assume that people made perfectly rational decisions based on perfect information. The human beings that populated these microeconomic models were immune to jealousy, spite, procrastination, whims, regret, caprice, ignorance, and even errors. In other words, they were not really human at all. They were more like machines, programmed to always make the best choices in their own self-interest.

Not all economists were equally persuaded by this vision. Karl Marx in the mid-nineteenth century certainly harbored no illusions about capitalists making perfect decisions, but then again, he had no effect on mainstream economics. In the early twentieth century, Thorstein Veblen found a popular audience for a theory based on the idea that workers were motivated by a sense of workmanship. He also thought that consumers derived as much satisfaction from impressing others with their purchases as they did from the purchases themselves. This concept, which he called *conspicuous consumption*, seemed to explain some real but distinctly irrational behavior. He also left no lasting mark on conventional economics.

The economist who achieved the most success in changing this academic view of human nature was John Maynard Keynes. In his theory, Keynes saw animal spirits driving the stock market and faulty human judgments driving savings and investment decisions. According to Keynes, businesses and consumers might have expectations about what the future could hold, but those expectations were not always fulfilled. In other words, people could make mistakes. With a few simple, practical assumptions like these, Keynes was able to turn much of conventional economics on its head.

Neoclassical economists, including free-market economists, members of the Chicago School, and microeconomists generally, resisted this new theory and clung to their belief that competitive markets were always superior to government intervention. While free-market advocates effectively lost the field of macroeconomics to the Keynesians, they fought to defend microeconomics from the corrupting influence of more plausible assumptions. In this mission they were more successful. For many years they stifled most challenges to microeconomics with the exception of a few talented individuals who managed to publish their work in respected economic journals, and some of them even received Nobel Prizes.

One of the intellectual leaders of this group of challengers was a prominent economist from Stanford University, Kenneth Arrow. In 1963, Arrow published a ground-breaking article about the problem of uncertainty in medical insurance and brought the concept of moral hazard into mainstream economics. Moral hazard is an old term dating back to the 1600s that described people with insurance who took more risks and on average experienced more losses. If you ever heard people say, "don't worry about it, it's insured," then you have witnessed moral hazard. In other research, Arrow probed the way that people made decisions with imperfect information and incorporated the concept into a theory of statistical discrimination. He also considered how individuals who know something signal to those who don't. These signals are only useful when information is unevenly distributed, or as economists describe it, *asymmetric*. Arrow received a Nobel price in 1972 for these contributions and many others, which are more fully described in the chapter about general equilibrium.

Other Nobel Prize winners, Daniel Kahneman, George A. Akerlof, Joseph E. Stiglitz, and A. Michael Spence followed Arrow's lead and considered a broad spectrum of plausible human behavior in their economic theories. Another leading contributor to this effort was Herbert A. Simon, a brilliant thinker who made significant contributions to both economics and computer science.

Herbert A. Simon (1978 Prize Winner)

How do people really make decisions? Consider a catcher in baseball. Not only does he wear a lot of unwieldy armor and squat in an uncomfortable position in front of a screaming pitch next to a swinging bat, but he also has to think. Taking into account the abilities of the pitcher and batter – right-handed or left-handed, runners on base, number of outs, and the current count of strikes and balls – he has to provide a signal for every pitch. How does he decide in a split second whether to call for a fast ball inside, a curve ball high and outside, or an inside slider? Does he make this decision like a perfect calculator, as presumed in classical microeconomics, or does he make the decision using more practical "rules of thumb," as suggested by Herbert Simon?[1]

In the world of classical economics, the catcher would select the optimum pitch for the situation, analyzing all existing information including statistics on all meetings between this pitcher and this batter. This is obviously unrealistic for a catcher who needs to make each decision quickly, but it is equally unrealistic, according to Simon, to expect every individual consumer and firm to make every decision in the same manner. And yet that is precisely what thousands of microeconomic students are taught every day in the nation's universities. Economic decisions, they are told, are based on perfect information, made by rational individuals who optimize their utility or profits.

Microeconomics had been criticized previously because actual decision making clearly falls short of this ideal. The best defense of this practice was offered by Milton Friedman in his theory of positive economics. Friedman claimed that unrealistic assumptions can be safely ignored as long as they generate accurate predictions and useful explanations. Simon didn't buy this, and he used his Nobel Prize lecture to explain why.

Beginning his Nobel lecture, Simon pointed out the obvious; it was possible to observe how people actually make decisions and it wasn't the way Friedman thought they were made. There is too much uncertainty in the real world and even if all the information was available (which it's not), it would be too costly to obtain and process. While perfect information and perfect rationality may thrive in the minds of economic theorists, they are relatively scarce in the real world. His final point was that there is no conclusive evidence that perfect rationality is necessary or even useful in predicting actual economic outcomes. In summary, Simon concluded that perfect behavior didn't really exist, it wasn't necessary for making predictions, and it wasn't very useful for explaining actual decisions.

Simon believed that it was human nature to make decisions that are good enough, not necessarily perfect. This rule, Simon argued, applies to all human beings, even economic theorists, like Milton Friedman. Simon cleverly noted that even Friedman defended his theory, not because it was perfect, but because it yielded predictions that were "good enough" or at least "better" than alternative theories.[2]

Simon may have rejected perfect rationality but he certainly didn't believe that all decision making was completely irrational either. He coined the phrase *bounded rationality* to characterize the actual decision-making process. People are neither perfectly correct nor perfectly arbitrary; instead they are reasonably efficient. They rely on short-cuts or "rules of thumb" to make many decisions or even rely on "habit" where the problems seem to be fairly routine. Simon described this as *satisficing behavior* in contrast to maximizing behavior in traditional economics.

When looking at the behaviors of Grand Masters in chess, Simon was struck by how quickly they could decide their next move, often in a matter of seconds. The same speed was evident whether the masters were playing a single game or many games simultaneously. When asked how they make their decisions, the players would more than likely attribute it to "intuition" or "professional judgment."[3] Simon didn't stop here but continued to probe what individuals meant by intuition. What is the human mind doing when it surveys information, like a chess board, and comes to a snap decision without consciously thinking through every analytical step? The answer, he concluded, was subconscious pattern recognition, a specific form of human thinking.

Simon had an ulterior motive for trying to distill the process of decision making into its fundamental elements; he wanted to program computers to "think." He identified three basic elements of thinking: scanning data and looking for patterns, storing the patterns into memory and then applying the patterns to make inferences or extrapolations. In the case of intuition, these steps are conducted essentially subconsciously and rapidly. Intuition arises from experience, for example, when a chess player recognizes a familiar pattern on the board and recalls the appropriate response. There is a second kind of thinking that relies more on systematic "analysis," utilizing more formal calculations. Most decision making, according to Simon, involves a combination of both types of thinking: intuition and analysis.[4]

It is not uncommon for chess masters to decide the next move in a matter of seconds, but then take a longer time to evaluate their "educated hunch" against all possible responses. Only then do they conclude that their hunch was in fact correct.[5] The same general combination of intuition and analysis is used to solve problems in many different fields including physics. While studying problem solving in physics, Simon compared the performance of a novice to that of an expert. The expert relied on intuition, which draws more rapidly on memory and stored patterns, thus producing short-cuts and faster solutions. The novice had to resort more often to tedious analysis and calculation.[6]

In 1933, during the depths of the Great Depression, Simon finished high school and headed to the University of Chicago with a mission: to raise the mathematical standards in the social sciences.[7] His plan was to learn economics, political science, mathematics, and symbolic logic, as well as graduate-level physics to sharpen his mathematical skills and familiarize himself with the characteristics of a "hard science." After receiving his doctorate degree in political science in 1943 from the University of Chicago, he took a position at the Carnegie Institute of Technology (later named Carnegie Mellon University) where he combined his new ideas about business management with emerging computer technologies.[8] Although he started his career doing conventional economics, he gradually drifted in the direction of decision-making theory, encompassing psychological concepts and *artificial intelligence*.

Beginning in the 1950s, Simon dedicated much of his time to designing computer programs that could "think." He was interested in computers that could do more than simply calculate; he wanted them to prove theorems and discover principles. He believed it was possible to take the "mystery" out of thinking and simply reproduce the same steps that humans follow. One of his first efforts in this regard was his work with Allen Newell and programmer J. C. Shaw in 1956 to develop a program to "prove" the mathematical theorems of Bertrand Russell. The program, *Logic Theorist*, was doing some fairly sophisticated "thinking" even on a fairly unsophisticated computer by today's standards. Another program, the *General Problem Solver*, tried to solve mathematical problems by working in reverse. It essentially started with the answer and then worked backward to the original problem. Other programs focused on pattern recognition, analogous to chess players. These were followed by more sophisticated programs that attempted to "rediscover" fundamental laws of physics from Galileo, Keppler, Boyle, and Ohm. All of these required rules of thumb or *heuristics* to increase the efficiency of an otherwise cumbersome process of trial and error. If, for example, a program found that two different theories could account for the same result, a rule of thumb might be to choose the simplest theory, a principle known as Occam's razor.[9]

Swept up in the excitement of his work, Simon made a prediction in 1957 that within ten years, a computer would be able to beat the best chess player in the world. At the time it was a startling idea given the state of computers and the intellectual demands associated with chess. Although wrong about the date, Simon's prediction eventually came to pass. A computer, IBM's Deep Blue, did in fact defeat the human champion, Garry Kasparov, but not until 1997.[10] By that time, computer power and sophistication had improved so dramatically that few people were probably surprised that such a feat was possible.

Can computers actually *think*? Are they potentially smarter than humans? While some people may claim these questions are still open to debate, Simon had little doubt. In 2000 he was asked when he thought a computer would make a Nobel-worthy discovery. His answer was that he needed a minute to think about whether that had already happened. When asked whether a computer would someday deserve a Nobel Prize he responded that he saw no reason why not.[11] To the extent that computers achieve these goals, Simon will deserve some of the credit as one of the widely recognized founders of the field of artificial intelligence.

Simon was honored to receive the Nobel Prize in 1978, but he was not the type of person to take it or himself too seriously. The morning his prize was announced, the usual paparazzi of television and newspaper reporters converged on his office. In the midst of answering a few questions, Simon suddenly looked at his watch and excused himself to go teach a class, "After all that's what they pay me for."[12] The reporters protested and were astonished when he actually left. He would later say to an interviewer, "Forget about Nobel Prizes; they aren't really very important."[13]

When he received the prize, there were some who questioned whether Simon was really an economist. Although he received his doctorate in political science, Simon began his career doing fairly traditional mathematical economics in the 1940s and 1950s.[14] He conducted a wide range of research during those days, including the proof of the Hawkins-Simon theorem used to determine the existence of a solution to Leontief's input-output model. The theorem stated that as long as industries didn't use less of any input as they expand, the model had a mathematical solution. Simon gradually came to the conclusion that economics did not need more mathematics; rather, it seemed to have enough. According to Simon, "The flowering of mathematical economics and econometrics has provided two generations of economic theorists with a vast garden of formal and technical problems that have absorbed their energies and postponed encounters with the inelegancies of the real world."[15] Simon claimed that it was as if economists were studying a falling body in molasses. They were dutifully applying Newton's laws for falling bodies without taking the molasses into account.[16]

Simon expressed frustration with conventional economists when they failed to entertain more realistic models of human behavior and when they tried to emulate the hard sciences. "The social sciences have been accustomed to look for models in the most spectacular successes of the natural sciences," Simon observed. He went on to caution his fellow economists, "There is no harm in that, provided that it is not done in a spirit of slavish imitation."[17] Newtonian physics, Simon claimed, "is not the only model for a science, and it seems, indeed, not to be the right one for our purposes."[18] Simon's dissenting view on this key issue caused a columnist for the *New York Times* to characterize him as a heretic.[19] Modern economists would probably agree and they would further describe Simon as a behaviorist because of his interest in a broad range of human behaviors.

Many of Simon's ideas have been preserved and expanded through the Summer Institute on Bounded Rationality in Psychology and Economics at the Max Planck Institute in Germany. The Institute encourages creative exploration of all kinds of decision making and is not limited to the practice by humans. Honeybees, for example, make an important collective decision about where to move the hive. After sending out several hundred scouts to assess prospective sites, there is a group dance that determines the outcome. It seems that the most-inspired scouts from the best sites dance longer and with more frenzy, ultimately recruiting the less-inspired scouts to join them. While it may sound a little like a political convention, the bees actually use this process to decide where to move the hive, not necessarily to the optimum site, but to one that is certainly good enough.[20] Apparently, bounded rationality applies to bees as well as humans.

Simon spent fifty-two productive years at Carnegie Mellon University, teaching, establishing and chairing the computer science department, working with interdisciplinary groups, and writing and publishing nearly 1,000 articles![21] Because of his eclectic interests he frequently visited other departments including social and decision sciences, philosophy, statistics, and physics. As a specialist in decision making, Simon noted that one of his best decisions was to persuade Dorothea Pye to marry him, which she did on Christmas day in 1937. They had three children who managed to live "interesting and challenging" lives outside of academia.

While Simon's resume reflects his broad diversity of interests, he claimed that each topic really addressed the same question: How do people make decisions or solve problems? Even though he retained this overriding theme, it is nonetheless remarkable that he achieved acclaim in many different disciplines. He not only won the Nobel Prize in economics in 1978, he was also awarded the American Psychological Association's award for outstanding lifetime contributions to psychology in 1993, the A. M. Turing Award for work in computer science in 1975, and many other significant honors.

Simon died in 2001 at the age of 84 while still pursing his passion for research and writing at Carnegie Mellon. He also inspired many students and colleagues during his lifetime who spoke highly of his influence. Two of his students who later became psychology professors at Carnegie Mellon described him as "the consummate intellectual and academic."[22] He was both a skilled technician and a broad-thinking visionary. In his speech at the Nobel Prize awards, he called on his fellow economists to "broaden and deepen our knowledge of Nature's laws, and we must broaden and deepen our understanding of the laws of human behavior."

During his career, Simon's concept of bounded rationality was given professional respect but was embraced by relatively few economists. It did not change the basic core of microeconomics. What Simon did manage to do, however, was to break the lock on rationality and open the door for future challenges like the one from Daniel Kahneman, the 2002 Nobel Prize winner.

Daniel Kahneman (2002 Prize Winner)

Few Nobel Prize winners in economics have captured the imagination of the popular media as has Daniel Kahneman. Writers from the *Wall Street Journal* to the *Tulsa World* and every publication in between took advantage of Kahneman's examples of odd and quirky human behavior to embellish their stories about the Nobel Prize in economics that year. Kahneman became a popular reference point for any idea that involved people acting less than rational.

The enthusiastic reception for Kahneman's ideas by the popular press was not shared by a significant part of the economics profession. One problem was that he was a Princeton psychologist, not an economist. The other problem was that the odd and quirky behavior that he documented was inconsistent with what most economists believed to be human nature. Kahneman's real human subjects did not come close to living up to the expectations of homo economicus, the cold, calculating agent in microeconomic models.

Kahneman was careful not to overstate the significance of his work. He simply provided a dazzling number of examples of plausible human behavior that were not rational by economic standards. With simple surveys and controlled laboratory experiments, he demonstrated that people are neither infallible nor free of bias. As unremarkable as these ideas may sound, they helped spawn an entirely new field called behavioral economics, which was based on the way people were actually observed behaving rather than how economists thought they should.

Intuition and Framing

A starting point for Kahneman's theory was the distinction between quick responses based on intuition (System 1) and the more systematic deliberative reasoning (System 2). The psychology of quick responses is by now fairly well known, developed by Herbert A. Simon and popularized by Malcolm Gladwell in his best selling book *Blink: The Power of Thinking Without Thinking*.[23] People make all sorts of choices throughout their day, mostly minor, characterized by a rapid assessment of a situation followed by an immediate decision. This behavior probably had important evolutionary value and continues to be used for many human decisions. But as useful as it is, reflex responses are not always correct or free of systematic bias. Consider a quick answer to the following question: "A bat and a ball cost $1.10 in total. The bat costs $1 more than the ball. How much does the ball cost?"[24] If you said 10 cents then you are like most people, using a reflex response that gets you close but not quite right. You need to kick the problem over to your System 2 process, check the answer, find the mistake, and fix it. The correct answer is 5 cents. The point is that human reasoning, especially System 1, is prone to such errors, which may be, as in this case, predictable.

Like Herbert Simon, Kahneman assumed that people rely on rules of thumb, or heuristics, to arrive at speedy decisions. One of those rules he called the *law of small numbers*, in which people are quick to base decisions on a single personal experience rather than a larger sample of information. An investor may be convinced that her broker is a genius because last year's return exceeded the market index. But in fact that sample is too small – one observation – to reach a valid conclusion. People seem to disregard the fact that a single observation is generally not significant whether it is based on personal observation or not.

To make matters worse, it is not clear that people understand that larger samples provide more meaningful information. For example, the percentage of male babies born in a large urban hospital is much more likely to come close to the national average than in a small rural clinic simply because of the larger number of births. But most people when surveyed did not recognize that fact.[25] There is a principle in statistics called the *law of large numbers* that can demonstrate that this is, in fact, true. But in the practice of making real decisions, people are quick to generalize from personal experience and ridiculously small samples even while overlooking evidence from larger, more meaningful ones.

Many of the errors that Kahneman identified fall into a category he called *framing*. When we are fooled by an optical illusion it is generally because of the context or the framing of the objects that we are looking at. Two squares of equal darkness will look different depending on the shade of the background. Just as visual perception can be intentionally distorted by context, so can cognitive perception. Consider the following: In an experimental survey, students were asked, "How happy are you with your life in general?" and "How many dates did you have last month?"[26] When asked in this order there is virtually no correlation between the two answers, but if you reverse the order of the questions the correlation suddenly jumps. Whatever you ask first – dating activity or anything really – can easily affect the perception of well-being. Framing, or context, is important.

In some settings, framing can be a problem. Should a doctor tell you that you have a 90 percent chance of surviving your surgery or a 10 percent chance of dying? Both are accurate but a study cited by Kahneman showed that patients were more likely to choose surgery when presented with the survival rate than the mortality rate.[27] If framing can influence life and death decisions, why can't it influence mundane economic choices? We know, for example, that advertising has turned framing into a fine and lucrative art, and yet it is largely ignored by economists.

Loss Aversion
In microeconomics, an individual's level of well-being should be objectively determined by their accumulated goods and wealth, not by the order that they accumulated them. Consider another Kahneman example. Two people receive a report from their broker: One has $3 million and the other has $1.1 million but the first one just lost $1 million and the second just earned $100,000. Which one should have the higher level of satisfaction, the one with the most money? Probably not. Context is again important because we know people are happier when they make money and quite unhappy when they lose it. Ironically, even though the first person is much wealthier, we expect the second one to be happier. Kahneman pointed out that this reasoning challenges the fundamental premise of expected utility theory, which has changed little since it was first formulated by Daniel Bernoulli in the eighteenth century.[28]

Underlying this example is a particular attitude that Kahneman believed is universal, *loss aversion*. Where economists embrace the concept of risk aversion – in other words, the reluctance to take risky chances – Kahneman refocused attention on the strong reaction that people have toward loss, financial or otherwise. He illustrated this with a very simple exercise. A sample of students were split into two groups; one group was given a decorated mug and was asked what minimum price would they accept to part with the mug and the other group was asked how much money they would accept instead of the mug. The only difference between the two groups was possession. And because people have a hard time parting with things – loss aversion – the first group required $7.00 to part with their mug while the other group was willing to accept $3.50 instead of the mug. This specific application of loss aversion became known as the *endowment effect*.

Home owners, in particular, are averse to losing money on their houses. One study showed that home owners came up with different selling prices depending on how much they had paid for their houses. In this case, comparable houses were priced higher if the owner had paid more for the house. The higher listing price typically resulted in a longer time to sell the house, but in the end, if it did sell, it would in fact receive a higher price.[29] In microeconomics, rational homeowners are not supposed to care what they paid for their house, which is a *sunk cost*, something they can do nothing about. According to microeconomics, they should only care about what they think they can get for their house.

Related to loss aversion is the finding that people don't assign the same weight to the importance of opportunity costs as to actual out-of-pocket costs. For most people, counting something as a loss that you never really had is a questionable practice. Economists may be among the only people on earth that consider an opportunity cost equivalent to all other costs. For example, a power utility can help migrating salmon by either spilling water over a dam or by paying for habitat restoration. The cost of the first action can be calculated as the value of the electricity that is not produced when water is diverted over the spillway and the cost of the second action is a financial payment. The issue of whether the opportunity cost of spilling water is sufficiently real to be compared to the cost of habitat improvement remains a highly contested issue in the Northwest. In other words, people question whether the loss of something counts as a cost if you never really possess it. Kahneman described these phenomena as the "economically irrational distinction that people draw between opportunity costs and real losses."[30]

Have you ever wondered whether those extended warranties offered for new appliances or computers are good deals? On average they are not actuarially fair and although sometimes they may payoff you are quite likely to be better off during your lifetime if you don't buy any of them. And yet people buy them. Why? Behavioral economists have suggested that the answer is loss aversion. Because consumers hate the idea of losing the value of a purchase, they are willing to pay an unrealistically high price to insure it. Not surprisingly, businesses are more than happy to accept the money.[31]

Anchoring

An important form of framing with implications for the business world is called *anchoring*. This is the tendency for people to start with a particular number in mind and only slowly move off that number. This makes the starting point of an estimate, target, or negotiation a very important number, even if it has little or no basis in fact. In one experiment, psychologists showed that they could influence a subject's estimate of the number of physicians in Manhattan by first asking them questions about their social security number. Remarkably, the two numbers were correlated just because the Social Security number was planted in the subject's mind before questioning them about the number of physicians.[32]

Kahneman suggested that anchoring is prevalent in big executive decisions like acquiring other firms, entering a new market, or making a major new investment. These business initiatives have caught the attention of economists because they seem to fail more frequently than they should.[33] In an article for *Harvard Business Review*, Kahneman cited a major new computer system for Oxford Health Plans that failed and sent the company's stock into a tailspin, eliminating $3 billion of equity in a single day.[34] There is also the fact that 70 percent of new manufacturing plants in North America don't make it through the first decade and 75 percent of mergers and acquisitions don't pay off. One problem, Kahneman suggested, was that executives are often anchored on the first cost estimate they see and are reluctant to move off of it when considering real-life contingencies and risks. Being anchored in a particular number can also create problems for naïve investors. They become fixated on the price that they paid for a stock, making them reluctant to sell losers before they sink lower. Just as often, naïve investors may be too quick to sell winners once they exceed the purchase price. Of course, knowing which stocks are going to be winners and losers is no easy trick either.

Contingent Valuation

A small but rewarding industry for economists has been assessing nonmarket values for public policy or for legal settlements involving pollution or endangered species. We know that people value clear skies, clean water, and species survival, but there are no market mechanisms to indicate just how valuable these are to society. Economists commonly estimate these values by simply asking people, a method called *contingent valuation*. This usually involves simple survey questions such as "How much would you be willing to pay to have a clear blue sky instead of a dark, polluted one?" Pictures usually help.

Because of his expertise in using surveys to measure attitudes and biases, Kahneman was critical of this method. For starters, people consistently exaggerate the importance of things that are called to their attention. When asked how they would feel if one candidate or another were to win an election, people typically respond that the outcome will make them considerably happier or considerably unhappier than they are then. But follow-up surveys after elections show little real change.[35] Kahneman concluded that "Nothing in life is as important as you think it is when you're thinking about it."[36] And when you are asked a question by a surveyor, you are forced to think about it.

Compounding this error is the fact that people are generally not very good about anticipating how they will adjust to changes, referred to as *adaptation*. Whatever makes you happy or sad at the moment may have no bearing next year, next month, or even next week. In other words, people adapt to change.[37] Finally, there is the problem that providing a range of numbers creates an anchor and steers responses toward a particular answer.[38] Even worse may be not providing a number at all, in which case the response may be completely arbitrary. People will simply choose some arbitrarily high number if the issue is important to them.[39]

When all of these biases and problems are considered, the results of contingent valuation surveys may provide little meaningful information to guide court decisions or public policy. Economist Matthew Rabin concluded that "It is now widely accepted that the methods of 'contingent valuation' used by courts and government agencies to elicit such preferences are flawed."[40] Despite these problems, contingent valuation continues to be used in a wide range of cost-benefit studies, not because it is accurate, but because there are few alternatives.

Happiness

A belief that underlies conventional economics is that people are motivated to work and invest because the money they earn will make them happier. Kahneman decided to test even this seemingly obvious principle. Psychologists have been evaluating what makes people happy for many years and have raised as many questions as they answer. Why, for example, is Minnesota one of the happiest states? Or why does happiness decline until age 45 and then start to rise again?[41] But more importantly, why doesn't income seem to be a significant determinant of happiness? Admittedly, very low-income individuals, those making $12,000 or less, are not very happy. But outside of that range there is not a significant correlation between income and happiness within countries or even among countries.[42] Why is that?

Kahneman suggested that the explanation has something to do with adaptation. Once someone becomes accustomed to a new income level, they revert to a level of happiness that is more closely related to their natural disposition or their original circumstances. As evidence of this, one study showed that lottery winners, after the initial euphoria had time to wear off, were not much happier than a control group.[43] For that matter, paraplegics were not much more unhappy than anyone else. With the exception of poverty or painful health problems, it seems that people are fairly resilient and eventually adapt to their circumstances. As a result, people are more likely to report that they are happy if they slept well last night than if they are millionaires.[44]

Adaptation may have been a new concept for economists but not for psychologists. Kahneman described the exercise of putting one hand in a bucket of hot water and the other in a bucket of cold water. When both hands are then put into a single bucket both hands feel distinctly different temperatures that are correlated with the previous buckets. The body clearly adapts to outside stimuli much as the mind adapts to its current situation, which includes having a lot or little money.[45]

If money isn't the primary source of happiness, then what is? In a carefully conducted study of 909 working women in Texas, Kahneman believed he found an answer. He speculated that only by asking people how happy they are throughout their day do you get an accurate record of their happiness. His results were also derived from surveys about how people recalled feeling during the prior day's activities or what Kahneman called the "day reconstruction method." He found, of course, that people are generally happier in certain activities. At the top of the list were intimate relations, socializing, eating, relaxing and exercising and at the bottom of the list were work and commuting. The same women were quite happy interacting with other people but not indiscriminately. Some groups were more enjoyable than others. In order of preference were friends, relatives, partners, children, clients/customers, and finally coworkers.[46] It might seem surprising that children fell fairly low on the list but this result was consistent with the relatively low ranking of childcare on the happiness scale, which fell slightly below housework.[47]

All this knowledge about how people recall levels of satisfaction has put Kahneman on a new quest: to develop a national well-being account as an alternative to the familiar national income accounts. The basis for this account will emphasize how people allocate their time between enjoyable and less-enjoyable activities.[48] Wealthy individuals, for example, may end up in more stressful and conflict-ridden situations as compared to blissfully happy underachievers.

The flip side of happiness is pain, and Kahneman applied his survey expertise to this emotion as well. Perhaps his most unusual test was the experiment to see what made a patient recall a medical procedure – in this case a colonoscopy – as particularly painful. What he found from this study was that duration of the procedure made little difference to the overall assessment of the experience. What did matter was the peak level of pain and the pain at the conclusion of the procedure. He called this the Peak and End Rule. In what has to be counted as one of the more extraordinary experiments in psychology, he was able to convince a sample of doctors to leave the colonoscopy probe in place for an additional minute at the conclusion of the procedure for some patients. His surveys confirmed that these patients had a better overall recollection of the experience because it ended on a better note, discomfort rather than pain.[49]

Fairness

Fairness has not traditionally been part of microeconomics but maybe it should be. In the exercise called the "ultimatum game" individuals often sacrifice their own gains in order to either punish or reward others. In particular, people did not like being treated unfairly and were willing to forego money to even the score.[50] A related problem for business is the perception that price increases caused by higher costs are fair, but price increases caused by higher demand or shortages are unfair.[51] Additional surveys showed that people thought cutting wages for current employees was unfair but lowering the wage for a new position was understandable. Employees strongly object to wage cuts when they are expected to work as hard as they did before. The fear of a hostile reaction from employees may explain why companies often avoid wage cuts even during recessions, a phenomenon Keynes and his cohorts referred to as *sticky wages*. While some companies obviously do cut wages as we have seen in the 2009 recession, the practice seems to be tempered by a concern about employee reaction.

Finally, Kahneman challenged the idea in conventional economics that business leaders are exceptional and deserving of their high salaries. Economists typically assume that CEOs are competent and efficient or else they would not make it to the top. Kahneman was not so sure. First, most people have an unrealistically high appraisal of their own abilities. A survey of one million students in the 1970s conducted by the College Board found that 70 percent thought their leadership skills exceeded the average. Only 2 percent thought they were below average.[52] Why, Kahneman wondered, should CEOs have any less hubris? There is a possibility that many successful CEOs have benefited from good luck during their climb to the top.

In fact, studies cited by Kahneman showed that executives often took full credit for successes but blamed failures on bad luck. This exaggerated sense of one's own ability can lead CEOs to make grand mistakes, the kind that end in bankruptcy or government bailouts.

Kahneman would have been born in Paris in 1934 if his mother hadn't been on an extended trip to Tel Aviv. Instead he was born in what later became Israel and spent most of his early years in Paris where his father was in charge of research at a chemical factory. Being Jewish, Kahneman's family was in jeopardy when the Germans rolled through France in 1940 and occupied it. The eight-year-old Kahneman experienced a tense moment one evening after curfew. A German soldier waved him over, which terrified him until he realized the soldier simply missed his own son who was about the same age. Fortunately Kahneman had taken the precaution of turning his sweater inside out, thus hiding his Star of David identifying his Jewish heritage.[53]

Although Kahneman's father was picked up along with other Jews and for all intents and purposes appeared to be headed to the concentration camps, he was released through some complicated intrigue.[54] The family fled to Vichy France on the Riviera and later to central France before his father died from diabetes, less than two months before D-Day.[55]

The family moved to Palestine where Kahneman eventually attended Hebrew University and in two years received his first degree in psychology and mathematics. The following year he was drafted into the Israeli defense forces and assigned to their psychological branch where he was given an assignment of selecting candidates for officer training school. They did this by assigning candidates to groups and giving them challenging assignments, like moving a telephone pole through an obstacle course. Any participant that demonstrated natural leadership skills was recommended for the training program. It was a lesson in humility that the training school found virtually no value in these carefully constructed recommendations from the psychologists. Kahneman called it "the illusion of validity." But the army assignment allowed him to develop psychological survey instruments, a skill that proved invaluable in his future academic work.[56]

Leaving the army in 1956, Kahneman headed to Berkeley for graduate school with his wife, Irah. After intense years of courses and reading, Kahneman claimed to have written his doctoral dissertation in eight days by typing it directly onto ditto paper. This was not great literature and even his teacher said reading it was like "wading through wet mush."[57] In 1961, after receiving his degree, Kahneman returned to take a teaching position in the psychology department at Hebrew University. Here he developed many of the ideas and techniques that fueled his research for the next forty years. Building on his earlier work, he refined a research approach that he called the "psychology of single questions." The simplicity of this approach made his results self-explanatory and more convincing.

In 1968, Kahneman began an important collaboration with friend and fellow psychologist from Hebrew University, Amos Tversky. Kahneman worked with many individuals and almost all of his major works were coauthored, but his collaboration with Tversky was, in his view, his most important and most successful collaboration. Virtually all of the work that was cited by the Nobel committee for Kahneman's prize in 2002 was coauthored with Tversky, who, unfortunately did not share in the award because of his untimely death in 1996.

On his way to a tenured position at Princeton University, Kahneman began collaborating with economist Richard Thaler, and together they invented much of behavioral economics by studying actual human behavior and applying it to economic theory.[58] Although Kahneman was careful not to overstate the significance of this work as a challenge to microeconomics, others made the case for him. This made him a target for conventional economists who accused him of creating "artificial puzzles designed to fool undergraduates," and he was snubbed by one critic who was "not really interested in the psychology of stupidity."[59] After initially engaging his critics, Kahneman came to the conclusion that traditional debate in academic journals was usually a waste of time. It almost never settled an issue, and so he left much of the criticism unanswered as he moved on to other projects. He did, however, explore something he called "adversarial collaboration" in which he would invite a critic to join him in conducting an experiment specifically designed to resolve an issue. Kahneman offered to work with his critic to design an experiment, conduct it, and then jointly author an article reporting the results. He found this approach more interesting and productive than the traditional academic debate.

The general public was not as difficult to convince as economists. Concepts like loss aversion, anchoring, and framing all seemed to resonate with the way most people understand human nature. Kahneman's theories have been widely cited in the media on topics ranging from the best way to deter crime, to strategies for successful investing. The Nobel Prize helped immensely to raise the visibility of his work. As the Nobel committee concluded, "With increasing confidence, researchers in psychological economics have been able to demonstrate that in some situations individuals do not behave like homo economicus."[60] Some of the shortcomings of conventional economics could be avoided, as Kahneman demonstrated, by simply paying more attention to actual human behavior.

Despite significant resistance, Kahneman was successful in penetrating the protective shield around microeconomics. He was able to publish his ideas in some of the leading economic journals and to force debate within the profession about how people actually behave. How did he do it? Kahneman certainly had a lot of talent and a strong reputation in psychology, but that wasn't necessarily enough. He was well aware of what he called the tribal nature of the social sciences that normally kept psychology and economics effectively isolated from each other. He described the "ritual rule of competence" practiced by each of the social sciences that provided a "screening function" having "little or nothing to do with substance."[61] He claimed that "It is a strange and rather arbitrary process that selects some pieces of scientific writing for relatively enduring fame while committing most of what is published to almost immediate oblivion."[62] Perhaps like some of the CEOs that he studied, Kahneman may have enjoyed a little luck as well.

Kahneman and Tversky's first break in economics was the publication of an article in *Econometrica* in 1979.[63] But a major breakthrough for them was the publication of another article on fairness in the top economic journal, the *American Economic Review*, in 1986. Kahneman was surprised that both of the reviewers of this article recommended immediate acceptance. He later learned the names of the reviewers and realized how fortunate he was to have a sympathetic reader like future Nobel Prize winner George A. Akerlof, who was no stranger to challenging conventional wisdom.[64] The article may not have faired so well if the reviewers had been from the University of Chicago. Looking back on his good luck, Kahneman graciously acknowledged that "The church of economics has admitted and even rewarded some scholars who would have been considered heretics in earlier periods."[65]

George A. Akerlof (2001 Prize Winner)

If we all had perfect information, we would never pay more for something than we should. This was an important assumption in microeconomics, but it was more self-serving than accurate. It allowed economists to prove that free markets were theoretically efficient and better than any other system. Unfortunately information is no more perfect than people.

One of the first economists to confront this problem seriously was Nobel laureate George Stigler from Chicago. He suggested that information is like everything else, a scarce resource that will be acquired strategically by weighing its benefits and costs. Stigler thought that this solved the problem but it didn't really. How much information is enough? To answer this question requires even more information. Stigler's attempt to rescue microeconomics from this conundrum did not get very far. He could not avoid the fact that markets will be inefficient as long as information is limited, including information about information.

In the 1960s, a young economist from Berkeley started thinking seriously about information, or more accurately, the lack of it. George A. Akerlof was close enough to mainstream economics to ponder such questions but not so close that he believed in the perfection of free markets. He wanted to know what happened to markets when information was not perfect, or more specifically, when one party had more information than another. Because of the imbalance, he referred to it as *asymmetric information*. He found that markets characterized by asymmetric information were no longer ideal. As anyone might have guessed, imperfect information leads to imperfect markets.

Akerlof came from a family of scientists and was probably expected to follow in that tradition. His father and uncle were chemists, his brother a physicist, his great-grandfather a doctor and medical professor, his grandfather a professor of pharmacology, and his mother a chemistry graduate student at Yale until she met his father. Bucking family tradition, George Akerlof became an economist.

A self-described nerd, Akerlof excelled in school and avoided the physical training program. He followed his brother to Yale where he developed an interest in economics that he described as "more closely linked to substantial policy issues and less tied to the official (competitive general equilibrium) model and its assumptions."[66] Because of his firm grasp of economics and math, Akerlof had no problem getting into the doctoral program at Massachusetts Institute of Technology (MIT) in the fall of 1962. He spent a lot of time during his first year mastering algebraic topology with the belief that this would give him a better understanding of the economy. MIT was also a good fit for Akerlof personally as he made friends with a number of the graduate students including Joseph E. Stiglitz who would later share the Nobel Prize with him in 2001.

The Market for Lemons

Soon after graduating from MIT in 1966, Akerlof received an appointment at the University of California at Berkeley where he wrote "The Market for Lemons" during his first year. This single article was the primary reason for his Nobel Prize. As Akerlof later explained, he was originally thinking about how car sales were related to the business cycle. He figured that new car sales were influenced by consumers weighing the options of leasing a new car or buying a used car. But the market for used cars was impaired because sellers have such an information advantage over buyers. This meant that buyers might make mistakes or sometimes simply shun the used car market altogether. He thought this was an interesting idea and sat down and proved it mathematically. While the proof focused on used cars, the conclusion suggested that similar problems could occur for people borrowing money or buying insurance. The first version of the draft utilized the abstract mathematics of topology, but after a colleague prevailed upon him to simplify it, he rewrote it using conventional supply and demand curves so that more economists might understand it.

This paper was not an immediate success, and it was rejected by three journals. The leading journal in the field, the *American Economic Review*, rejected the paper citing the triviality of the topic. The *Review of Economic Studies* also rejected it as being trivial, and The *Journal of Political Economy* rejected it after two reviewers simply concluded that the argument was incorrect. They pointed out that eggs have different qualities and yet they are sorted and sold so why not used cars. They focused on the extreme case in the paper where the market for used cars simply disappeared, which clearly hadn't happened. Finally the paper was published by the *Quarterly Journal of Economics*. Despite the slow start, the sudden popularity of the published article suggested that the time to challenge the assumptions of microeconomics was overdue.

It would be a mistake to presume that Akerlof discovered something unknown in the market for used cars. Common sense could tell you that sellers of used cars know more about the quality of their cars than buyers, and that one of the consequences is that buyers usually pay too much for lemons and too little for real gems. In fact, horse traders for hundreds of years have probably faced and understood the same risks, so none of this was particularly new. What made Akerlof's article important was that he challenged microeconomics in a mainstream economic journal. It was now a legitimate academic topic to consider the effect of limited information. Future Nobel winners A. Michael Spence and Joseph E. Stiglitz benefited from this opportunity and walked through the door that Akerlof opened.

In the real world, the used car market doesn't disappear simply because information is limited. Some dealers that sell quality used cars may offer a warranty because they have confidence in their product while other dealers don't. In my own case, I have bought used cars but not before taking them to professional mechanics for a once over. It has always provided particularly useful information. The point is that in the real world there are usually practical ways to address asymmetric information by either sellers or buyers. But this debate was really more about economic theory than the used car market. Akerlof wanted to convince microeconomists that asymmetric information existed, and in this respect, he was successful.

A year after arriving at Berkeley, Akerlof spent a year in New Delhi searching for the causes of India's poverty. This started him thinking about unemployment and led to his second major contribution to economics. The origin of this idea started with the microeconomic idea that unemployment is essentially voluntary, something anyone with first-hand experience knows is patently false. Equally troublesome was the policy that microeconomists recommended to increase employment: cut wages. This policy was decisively repudiated during the Great Depression when cutting wages did not stop unemployment from rising.

Akerlof was one of the economists who wondered why microeconomics was wrong. Why don't employers simply lower wages when there is a pool of workers who want a job? His answer to that question started with the idea that people are more productive when they are paid more; they are more loyal, they work harder, and they are less likely to quit. All this makes them more valuable. Higher wages can also attract a larger pool of applicants and increase the chance of finding high quality employees. The last thing employers want to do is cut wages and lose all of these benefits. This became known as the *efficiency wage theory* and although it may sound perfectly reasonable, or even obvious, it again stirred up quite a debate.

After he returned to Berkeley in 1968, Akerlof was granted tenure but was rejected for full professor because of insufficient publications. In response, Akerlof redoubled his efforts, creating what he described as a "monomaniacal focus" and got his promotion. In 1978 he married another prominent economist, Janet Yellen, who has the distinction of having held three prominent economic policy jobs: She was a member of the Board of Governors for the Federal Reserve Bank, Chair of the Council of Economic Advisors, and is currently President of the San Francisco Federal Reserve Bank. Their son Robby earned his doctorate from Harvard and is at MIT. Family dinners represented a high-level meeting of economic theory and policy.

Behavioral Economics

Akerlof, along with Herbert Simon, launched the first serious challenges to the basic competitive model since Keynes in the 1930s. The idea of using more realistic assumptions about human behavior is now known as behavioral economics and Akerlof was one of its pioneers. As Akerlof noted, behavioral economics has "been gradually evolving an economics that relies more on careful empirical observation and less on questionable assumption[s] regarding how rational people must behave."[67]

This fact was not overlooked by the advocates of the basic competitive model. Gary Becker, one of the Nobel laureates from Chicago, conceded that "markets are sometimes inefficient," but professed that contrary to the new Nobel laureates, Akerlof and Stiglitz, "I believe the government generally makes things worse."

Behavioral economics was also a threat to the New Classical economists who were trying to resurrect free-market macroeconomics as it had existed before Keynes. Akerlof took advantage of his prize lecture to criticize the advocates of this approach, which included Nobel Prize winners Milton Friedman and Robert Lucas. Their theories, he argued, were only valid under conditions of perfect information and perfect rationality, the same conditions that the behavioral economists were demonstrating were invalid. Akerlof thought the advocates of the New Classical theory had a "common perceptual error: overconfidence." Quoting Oliver Cromwell, he appealed to them to "think it possible you may be mistaken."[68] While the new classical economists and the behavioral economists couldn't both be right, members of both camps won Nobel Prizes in economics.

Akerlof also used his prize lecture to call attention to what he called "the most enduring macroeconomic problem facing the United States," the disparity between the economic condition of white and black populations.[69] Whether measured in terms of income, unemployment, crime rate, incarceration, drug and alcohol addiction, out-of-wedlock births, or virtually any measure of well-being, blacks fell far behind whites. Akerlof concluded that microeconomics was "incapable" of explaining the "self-destructive behavior" at the root of this disparity.[70]

The 2001 Nobel Prizes were celebrated by Nobel laureate Paul Krugman who confessed that he usually felt compelled to lambaste Nobel theories, but not in this case. He claimed that the ideas of Akerlof, Spence, and Stiglitz were the reason that he became an economist. Their theories provided plausible explanations for important issues including insider trading and prescription drug coverage. They successfully identified situations where markets fail, or in Krugman's words, where "the invisible hand drops the ball."[71]

Joseph E. Stiglitz (2001 Prize Winner)

Of the three Nobel Prize winners in 2001, Joseph Stiglitz stands out as one of the more prolific writers, even though none of them could be described as slackers. Stiglitz wrote twenty-four pages for his Nobel autobiography, a record among economic winners. For comparison, James Buchanan only wrote about a page and it was really just a curriculum vitae. Even longer was Stiglitz's prize lecture, which went on some sixty-eight pages, including fifteen pages of endnotes, five of which listed his own publications. Unlike Akerlof, there was no single article that earned Stiglitz the prize. Instead, he wrote scores of academic articles, each one making an incremental contribution, but taken together they constituted a strong argument for government intervention to fix markets that fail because of information problems.

Stiglitz identified a few examples where market information was inadequate, including a concept called *adverse selection*. A common example of adverse selection can be found in the credit industry. Banks and mortgage companies are in the business of lending money, and they like to have some assurance that they will be paid back. Checking credit history is a good start, but it will never guarantee repayment. Knowing that some loans won't be paid back, lenders have to raise interest rates for everyone to cover these losses. The losers in all this are the reliable borrowers who pay higher rates to cover the potential default of others. Adverse selection occurs if the low-risk borrowers simply drop out of the market and leave a pool of only high-risk individuals. In this case, the market doesn't work very well because credit worthiness is basically unknown.

In the real world, banks address this problem by requiring the borrower to put some of their own money on the line in the form of a minimum down payment. This improves the likelihood that the borrower will make a good-faith effort to repay the loans, but it doesn't completely eliminate the risk of default or the potential for adverse selection.

A similar story can be told for insurance; insurers charge premiums that have to cover both high-risk and low-risk individuals. While insurers try to distinguish between the two as best they can by looking at personal characteristics – smokers, young drivers, and males – they can never be exactly sure about individual risk. On average, low-risk individuals are likely to pay insurance premiums that are too high only because they can't prove that they are low risk. As a consequence, a normal insurance market with limited information may drive away low-risk individuals, again resulting in adverse selection.

Insurance markets have developed a method that can reduce this problem – deductibles. Young, healthy individuals may be willing to buy health insurance with a large deductible because they figure that they may never have to pay it. In exchange, the insurer can lower the premiums for those policies. Thus, in theory, insurers can retain low-risk customers by offering policy options with relatively high deductibles and low premiums. High-risk individuals, in theory, would choose a lower deductible because they expect to have to pay it more often, even though the policy comes with higher premiums. Presumably customers would select their insurance plan based on how much risk they think they face.

Stiglitz also studied another market failure, *moral hazard*, which applies to most forms of insurance. When people have theft insurance on their cars they might be a little less concerned about leaving it unlocked or out on the street overnight. Fire insurance may make it less likely that the owner of a wood stove cleans his stove pipe every year. When the International Monetary Fund provides insurance against a currency crisis, they may unintentionally reduce the incentive of a national government to maintain a stable currency. While insurers hope their clients avoid risky behaviors, they are often helpless to prevent them.

The recent bailout of Wall Street banks raised new concerns about moral hazard. If banks expect to be bailed out every time they go bankrupt, then they have little incentive to worry about bankruptcy. Moral hazard weakens their resolve to police their own investments and limit the amount of risk.

This same concept has been applied to almost every form of compensation. A salesman on a fixed salary may have little incentive to make a sale, another form of moral hazard. Some have criticized social programs that provide support for the unemployed or poor, unwed mothers based on moral hazard. They claim that these programs weaken an individual's incentive to avoid such unfortunate situations.

Moral hazard may impair many markets to some degree or another, but it can also be reduced by innovative pricing or pay programs. It makes sense to offer commissions to a sales force or profit shares to managers to boost their motivation. These incentives may weaken or even eliminate moral hazard and preserve a well-functioning market.

In addition to adverse selection and moral hazard, Stiglitz promoted another important new concept, *signaling*. In a world with limited information, it is not only important to have accurate information but also to be able to convince others of its veracity. You send a signal when you take an action that conveys information in a compelling manner.

One of the most creative descriptions of signaling was offered by Paul Krugman in a classic essay about the similarity between a peacock's tail and a college degree.[72] Both, he noted, are ornaments that signal a certain characteristic of the holder. In the first case, a male peacock's elegant tail feathers send a signal to potential partners that the male is a fit and desirable mate. Signaling is one of the few functions that biologists can imagine for the ornate peacock tail feathers. In fact, these elaborate feathers are a nuisance and a handicap in virtually every instance except for one – finding a mate. Likewise, the argument goes, a college education may provide some meaningful skills, but more importantly it signals something to would-be employers or graduate schools. A college degree signals a certain degree of talent and ambition. In a parody of this concept, Krugman cited a line from *Liar's Poker* that claimed that investment bankers studied economics in order to demonstrate their willingness to engage in boring and humiliating activities. No one seriously suggests that a college degree is as superfluous as a peacock's tail, but a diploma probably does signal more than academic acumen.

Signaling can also occur when a firm tries to poach an employee from a competitor. The competitor can try to retain the employee by raising his or her salary, perhaps matching the original offer. If the competitor takes such an action, it signals the poacher that it was probably right in thinking that the employee was valuable. But if there is no attempt to match the offer, the original firm may get the employee but also wonder if the employee is really worth it. This example, referred to as the *winner's curse*, illustrates how actions send signals and convey information. This is a far cry from the world of conventional microeconomics where every firm is presumed to know precisely the productivity of every potential employee.

In the business world, almost any action can send a signal, sometimes inadvertently. CEOs especially don't want to send negative signals about their company. Consider the case of CEOs who have accumulated a lot of company stock through incentive pay and stock options. If they ever try to sell the stock to diversify their portfolios, they might send the wrong message to other investors. Because stock sales by CEOs are publicly reported, other investors are likely to suspect that the stock is overpriced, causing them to sell. As a consequence, executives may be stuck with more company stock than they probably want and that may cause them to favor strategies that produce immediate gains as opposed to long-term growth. Signaling is central to stories like this that try to explain why

CEOs voluntarily hold on to so much company stock and how that may change their behavior.

Paul Samuleson once praised Joseph Stiglitz as the best economist from Gary, Indiana, a witty compliment since Paul Samuelson was himself a Nobel Prize–winning economist from Gary, Indiana. Stiglitz's father was an independent insurance agent and it may not have been a coincidence that insurance played a role in some of Stiglitz's prize-winning ideas.

After attending public schools in Gary, Stiglitz attended Amherst College, an all-male liberal arts college with only 1,000 students. Like other prize winners in economics, Stiglitz was attracted to mathematics and science and started as a physics major. He switched majors late in his third year to economics when he saw the opportunity to combine his talents in mathematics with his interest in social issues.

While at Amherst, Stiglitz demonstrated a willingness to take strong positions and fight for them in the face of great opposition. He was elected to the student council in both his freshman and sophomore years and became president of the council his junior year. He opposed segregation and joined the march on Washington where he heard Martin Luther King, Jr. give his famous "I have a dream" speech. Inspired by these events, he organized an exchange program for Amherst, not with a foreign college but with a "small, African-American" school in the South. In another campaign, Stiglitz attempted to abolish fraternities on the principle that they were "socially divisive" and conflicted with the "spirit of a liberal arts school." He embarked on this effort despite the fact that 90 percent of the Amherst student body at the time lived in fraternities! While his campaign failed, Stigiltz expressed his satisfaction years later when fraternities were ultimately banned from Amherst.[73] Stiglitz's liberal initiatives inspired an organized opposition that attempted to remove him from office through a recall election. Stiglitz survived the challenge and established himself as a fighter that stood for principle, even in the face of what appeared to be overwhelming odds.

After three years, Stiglitz decided to leave Amherst for MIT even though he had not finished his degree, because he was in a hurry to begin his graduate studies. He thrived in the intellectual environment at MIT and took classes from some of the top economists in the country.[74] His first academic presentation was with fellow student and his cowinner for the Nobel Prize, George A. Akerlof. It was an inspiring time for Stiglitz, who believed that the great problems of economic growth – unemployment, inflation, and poverty – could be resolved by mathematical models.

After his second year at MIT, Stiglitz received a Fulbright fellowship to attend Cambridge during the 1965–6 school year. While there, Stiglitz was assigned to work under the supervision of the legendary Joan Robinson, one of the original members of Keynes' inner circle. Unfortunately Robinson considered Stiglitz's MIT education more of a liability than an asset and suggested that he might be better off to just start over. Instead, Stiglitz found himself a different tutor.

After a successful academic career at Princeton, Stiglitz was appointed to the Council of Economic Advisors in 1993 and became its chairman in 1995. He characterized his recommendations as the "third way" because they were neither antigovernment nor always progovernment. Instead, he claimed to support a role for government when it was the only option to solve economic problems. After Clinton's re-election in 1996, Stiglitz was asked to continue on as chairman of the Council, a distinct honor for any economist, but he turned it down in favor of another, more enticing offer, senior vice-president for development policy at the World Bank.[75] As the chief economist for the World Bank, Stiglitz hoped to promote enlightened policies that would encourage economic growth in the underdeveloped world.

World Bank

It didn't take long for Stiglitz to conclude that one of the impediments to economic growth was coming from the World Bank's sister agency, the International Monetary Fund (IMF). He considered the Fund's heavy-handed methods to be outdated and counterproductive. They had adopted what was called the *Washington Consensus* that called for austerity measures like balanced budgets, reductions in government subsidies, and less regulation of capital markets in order to encourage more foreign investment. Stiglitz thought that the indiscriminate application of these policies often made economic conditions worse.

In 2001, Stiglitz wrote an article in the *Atlantic Monthly* taking the IMF to task for trying to impose the Washington Consensus on Ethiopia. According to Stiglitz, the IMF took a relatively well-performing country and tried to force it to change.[76] When Ethiopia refused to yield, the IMF suspended its lending program in 1997. Only after strong pressure from Stiglitz did the IMF abandon this strategy and restore the lending program.

The conflict between the IMF and Stiglitz continued during the East Asia crisis. In response to the crisis, the IMF demanded the usual austerity measures: higher interest rates and less government spending. The result was painful as unemployment more than tripled in Korea and Thailand

and food riots broke out in Indonesia in response to cuts in government subsidies.[77] Once again, Stiglitz objected to the IMF using its economic leverage to impose policies that he was convinced were counterproductive. He pointed out that those countries that rejected the IMF remedies, like Malaysia, recovered noticeably quicker.

Stiglitz advocated for an alternative approach more consistent with the theories of John Maynard Keynes. Ironically, it was Keynes who supported the original idea in the 1940s of an IMF to stabilize international finance and a World Bank to facilitate economic development. By the late 1990s, the IMF had turned full circle and was using its financial power to promote anti-Keynesian policies.[78]

Stiglitz was also a strong critic of the IMF strategy to transform the Soviet economy into market capitalism, the so-called "shock" treatment. Without taking the time to develop functioning markets and honest government oversight, the IMF advocated wholesale privatization of the Soviet economy. Even the IMF would have difficulty denying the complete and utter failure of this strategy. There are probably few times in history when an economy collapsed so rapidly and poverty climbed so high that life expectancy actually fell. Once again, Stiglitz lambasted the "cookie-cutter" economics of the IMF that tended to ignore history, social conditions, institutional factors, and what he called information asymmetries.

The IMF did not take all this lying down. Kenneth Rogoff, the head of research at the IMF, counterpunched. Rogoff defended the IMF's general policy of budget cuts and high interest rates for countries undergoing economic crisis and asked, "Do you ever think that just maybe Joe Stiglitz might have screwed up?"[79] Rogoff complimented Stiglitz for his academic achievements, calling him a "towering genius," but panned his policy recommendations as "just a bit less impressive." Rogoff scoffed, "The laws of economics may be different in your part of the gamma quadrant," an apparent reference to the mathematics in Stiglitz's academic work.[80]

The IMF was still clearly stinging from Stiglitz's characterization of the staff as "third rate economists from first rate universities."[81] Rogoff defended the IMF staff as "superb professionals" who worked long hours and endured cold weather and disease to do their jobs.[82] Finally, in an open letter to Stiglitz, Rogoff recounted a private conversation when Stiglitz asked a question about the intelligence of former Federal Reserve Chairman, Paul Volcker.[83] Stiglitz responded that he was "dumbfounded" by the personal attack and wondered if the IMF was seriously "willing to engage in a substantive discussion."[84]

Stiglitz's tenure at the World Bank was explosive and short. Although he claimed that the President supported both his policies and the values they were based upon, the same was less true for U.S. Treasury Secretary Lawrence Summers who did not appreciate being dragged into the scuffle. Stiglitz learned later that Summers called his boss at the World Bank, James Wolfenson, to express his displeasure.[85] It was time for Stiglitz to leave the World Bank, which he did in January 2000.

Others have criticized the IMF for many of the same reasons, but no one elicited a response like Stiglitz. It was unprecedented for such direct criticism of the IMF to be launched in such a public arena from such a highly regarded academic. It was equally unprecedented that such criticism would come from a high-ranking official in the IMF's sister agency, the World Bank. Most attempts to question IMF policies have been ignored, or at least they were until Stiglitz started throwing punches.

The controversy did not seem to do any harm to Stiglitz's career. He moved on to Columbia University, and in October 2001, it was announced that he, along with George A. Akerlof and A. Michael Spence, had won the Nobel Prize. The award that year was widely perceived as important recognition for those economists who supported government intervention when markets failed. It also showed that the Nobel committee was willing to recognize Stiglitz's important contributions to economics and was not deterred by his recent imbroglio with the IMF.

Winning the Nobel Prize also did nothing to dampen Stiglitz's willingness to challenge the IMF. He went after them again when they attempted to rein in government deficits in Argentina. Stiglitz argued that the deficit wasn't the problem; it was only 3 percent of GDP while the U.S. deficit had risen as high as 4.9 percent only a decade earlier. At some point, he argued, the IMF had to stop forcing policies on countries in recession that were likely to make matters worse.[86]

Stiglitz continued to argue passionately about many other issues. Since winning the Nobel Prize, he has claimed that the Iraq war constituted a drain on the U.S. economy,[87] argued that Iraqi debt should be forgiven because it was created by dictator Sadam Hussein,[88] condemned the Bush tax cuts for endangering future growth,[89] puzzled over the jobless economic recovery of 2003,[90] and advised Japan to print more money as a solution to their deflationary doldrums.[91]

It is not uncommon for economic Nobel winners to challenge each other in academic journals, but Stiglitz took on a couple of them in court. When the IRS accused the investment company of Nobel Prize winners Myron Scholes and Robert Merton of using an illegal tax shelter, Stiglitz provided the technical arguments for the government's case. Stiglitz parsed through the complicated records and found no economic justification for the operation, concluding that its true purpose was to avoid taxes.[92] His testimony helped the government win its case, pitting Nobel Prize winners against each other. One of the losing strategies for the defense was to complain that Stiglitz's objectivity was compromised by his $1,000 per hour compensation as an expert witness. But the defense should have thought about what kind of *signal* they were sending to the judge. Was it possible that maybe he really was that good?

Like some fellow economists, Stiglitz was well rewarded for his achievements and was cited along with Saul Bellow, Jeffry Sachs, and Cornel West as among the "trophy professors" that are snagged by competing universities with extraordinary salaries. Although his salary wasn't mentioned, Columbia University enticed Stiglitz away from Stanford at about the same time that they lured fellow economist Jeffrey Sachs from Harvard. Columbia in particular appeared to be trying to reassert a prominence it once had in economics. [93]

How new are the concepts of adverse selection, moral hazard, and signaling? Some 230 years ago, Adam Smith wrote that the best borrowers drop out of the market when banks charge higher interest rates.[94] This was almost a perfect description of adverse selection. It also did not take a Nobel Prize winner to discover that car owners with theft insurance might be a little less likely to lock their car doors. Nor was it the first time that someone recognized that a corporate executive can send a negative signal by selling company stock. What Stiglitz and other behaviorists did was to translate these concepts into the mathematical language of microeconomics and to give them a name. In the process of developing these ideas, they also weakened the traditional defense of free markets; they weren't always perfect, even in theory.

The name of one of these concepts resonated with popular culture. At least two music groups named themselves Moral Hazard, one a punk rock band from Canada recording under the Pesticide Records label, and the other a somewhat eccentric a cappella group from Georgetown University Law Center. This is just a small example of how theoretical economics can enrich everyday life.

A. Michael Spence (2001 Prize Winner)

A. Michael Spence recalled his advisor suggesting to him that he read a new article entitled "The Market for Lemons" by George A. Akerlof. He did and it ignited a flood of ideas. At the time, he was trying to understand how employers figure out who is a good worker and who isn't. He thought he could solve this problem by applying game theory to labor market signals. Akerlof's article provided just the framework he needed to develop the concept of signaling.

The basic problem is this: Employers want to hire the most productive workers and are willing to pay a premium to get them, but they don't always know who they are. If employers don't know who the good workers are, they simply offer the same average wage to everyone, thus overpaying bad workers and underpaying good ones. In this case, people are not paid what they are worth and the market fails.

Spence speculated that productive workers don't fare well in this situation, and they will want to signal employers that they are more productive. How do they do this? By going to college and earning a degree. Employers will hire them at the higher wage because their credentials demonstrate that they are, in fact, good workers. This was the essence of the idea that Spence developed for his doctoral thesis and his Nobel Prize.

Spence was once asked by a perplexed journalist if he was awarded the Nobel Prize "for simply noticing that there are markets in which certain participants don't know certain things that others in the market do know."[95] The journalist found this incredible although he didn't get it quite right. That was actually what Akerlof discovered. What Spence discovered was that sometimes people who know things will send signals containing that information to those who don't.

The value of education in improving productivity is one thing; the role of education as a signal is something else. Spence argued that even if education had no effect on productivity, there would still be a possibility that workers would go to college merely to demonstrate their superiority and earn more money.

What does this type of analysis tell us about the real world? For one thing, if this actually occurs it would be inefficient because workers would be wasting their time and money going to college only to demonstrate a superiority that already existed. A second lesson is that these signals won't work if bad workers have equal access to college. If they did, then they would go to college and the college degree would no longer mean anything. In order for signals to work effectively, they must be cheaper or more accessible for more productive workers. It would be a mistake to try to probe this example any deeper with the hopes of finding some new, hidden purpose for education. The point was simply to illustrate that information gaps can make markets inefficient, and they can become even more inefficient if participants are forced to rely on costly signals.

When market signals are inefficient, Spence suggested that a government tax or subsidy could help. But he was careful not to overstate the significance of his research. It is difficult to claim that these highly abstract models apply in any meaningful way to the real world. For his part, Spence was satisfied to conclude that "there exists a tax/subsidy scheme that produces a fully efficient, separating outcome as an equilibrium" and leave it at that.[96]

There were critics of this point of view. Gene Epstein writing for *Barrons* called this a "bit confused" even for a "frail insight."[97] David Henderson, writing in the *Wall Street Journal*, acknowledged that markets can fail due to a lack of information, but he warned against assuming that government can do any better. In his opinion, most government information was "almost useless."[98] Did Henderson really mean *most* government information or was he just being rhetorical? Perhaps he wasn't fully aware of the immense wealth of government information covering economic data, basic research, public health, space flights, weather, and the census, to name a few areas.

Spence attended Princeton University where he majored in philosophy and played hockey for four years, a testament to his Canadian heritage.[99] After graduating, he attended Oxford as a Rhodes Scholar, this time collecting credentials in mathematics. It wasn't until he entered the Ph.D. program at Harvard that Spence finally concentrated on economics as his major. After receiving his doctorate, Spence took his first position as an associate professor at Stanford University and then returned to Harvard as a professor in 1975. Taking his graduate theory course at Harvard were two industrious young undergraduates, Steve Ballmer and Bill Gates. The two succeeded in getting "A"s in the class and later launched a small startup company, Microsoft.

Spence's climb into administration started early. In 1983, at the age of forty he became the chairman of the Economics Department at Harvard and a year later was asked by Derek Bok, the president of Harvard, to serve as Dean of the prestigious faculty of arts and sciences. When asked why Spence was the third economist in a row to hold the position, Bok answered evasively that it was a "statistical aberration."[100] The press saw this appointment as an opportunity to grill the young economist, asking what he planned to do about increasing the number of minority faculty and students. Spence replied, "The honest answer is, I don't know." It was this kind of unassuming honesty that characterized his management style. A colleague at Harvard called him a nice guy who finished first.[101]

SEVEN

Keynesians

Paul A. Samuelson (1970)

Robert M. Solow (1987)

James Tobin (1981)

Franco Modigliani (1985)

Lawrence R. Klein (1980)

K. Gunnar Myrdal (1974)

A number of Nobel economists came of age during the coincidence of two powerful movements: the Keynesian revolution and the quantification of economics. Keynes had rewritten economic theory and challenged the principles of the old guard from Adam Smith to Alfred Marshall. He explained why free markets didn't always work, and, if there were any doubt, the Great Depression proved it. Gunnar Myrdal, a Swedish socialist and Nobel Prize winner, articulated a similar thesis in the 1930s.

Most of the new Keynesians, however, were in graduate school when they first heard the radical ideas coming out of Cambridge University in the 1930s and from Harvard University in the 1940s. Armed with their new theory, young economists like Robert M. Solow, James Tobin, Franco Modigliani, and K. Gunnar Myrdal set out to change the world. They summarized, refined, and extended Keynesian economics while Lawrence R. Klein tried to program it into his big economic models with mountains of data.

The Keynesians were also part of the generation that believed that economics was a lot like physics. They saw little difference between calculating the maximum trajectory of a rocket and the maximum welfare of a nation. Almost immediately they translated Keynesian economics into variables and formulas, but they didn't stop there. Any economic idea that could be represented by an equation was fair game, including business and household behavior, economic growth, and international trade. For the most part, this work did not require original economic ideas, just really good math skills. Like most economists, they were convinced that simply translating economics into the language of physics had value in and of itself. The undisputed leader in both these movements in macroeconomics – spreading Keynesian economics in America and translating economics into math – was Paul A. Samuelson who won the Nobel Prize in its second year.

Paul A. Samuelson (1970 Prize Winner)

At a young age, Samuelson was already carefully observing economies in transition from his home in Gary, Indiana. He remembered "the disappearance of the horse economy, the arrival of indoor plumbing and electric lighting. After that radio waves through the air or TV pictures left one blasé."[1] He also recalled the economic boom in Gary as the U.S. steel mills surged to support production for World War I. When Paul was ten years old, the family lived in Miami Beach, Florida, where he watched a real estate boom provide riches and the ensuing bust take them away. That was a good primer for the hardships that he witnessed as a young college student during the Depression of the 1930s.[2]

Samuelson was also good in school. He reported that "As a precocious youngster I had always been good at logical manipulations and puzzle-solving IQ tests."[3] Backed with a scholarship, Samuelson attended the University of Chicago, graduating in 1935. Two early members of the Chicago School, Frank Knight and Henry Simons, had the first crack at recruiting Samuelson to their version of free-market economics.

The next stop for Samuelson was Harvard University for a doctorate. At Harvard, Samuelson was exposed to very different economics from professors Joseph Schumpeter and Wassily Leontief, and, even more importantly, the leading Keynesian in America Alvin Hansen.[4] Samuelson realized that his classical Chicago training clashed with this new Keynesian approach. As he described it, "I first resisted the Keynesian revolution and was finally won over."[5] This was not an easy conversion, as Samuelson recounted, "My Chicago-trained mind resisted tenaciously the Keynesian revolution; but reason won out over tradition and dogma."[6] Harvard was teeming with young Keynesian graduate students at the time, including future Nobel Prize winners Robert M. Solow and James Tobin. Because of his education at the University of Chicago and Harvard, Samuelson was exposed to economic ideas from the two major competing schools of economics at the time.

While Samuelson reported little about his formal education in mathematics and physics, he did reveal some of that background in his Nobel lecture of 1970. He mentioned that three decades earlier, he had "thumbed through different physics treatises,..." and also learned thermodynamics from the lectures of Edwin Bidwell Wilson at Harvard.[7] He also took part in physics research at a radiation laboratory at the end of World War II where he studied the "deviation of radar rays."[8] But in case there was any doubt about his background, Samuelson felt compelled to explain to his audience in Sweden during his Nobel lecture that "I am not a physicist."[9]

Physics, however, had a lot to do with his address to the Swedish Academy. In his brief lecture he managed to mention many great scientific theories and the scientists who discovered them: Galileo, Newton, Heisenberg, Fermat, Maxwell, and LeChatelier. In a later essay for the Nobel committee, he made sure to add more famous names in science including Planck, Bohr, Schrodinger, de Broglie, Feynman, Fermi, and Crick. He must have been very proud when the *New York Times* in 1970 described him as "the Einstein of economics for developing a unified field theory of economic activity."[10]

Samuelson was hired by the Massachusetts Institute of Technology (MIT) in 1940 where he remained for the rest of his academic career, which was, by any standard, a very successful one. He won the John Bates Clark medal in 1947, served as president of the American Economic Association, published his famous scholarly work *Foundations of Economic Analysis* in 1947, and advised Presidents Kennedy and Johnson on economic matters. His advice to President-elect Kennedy in 1960 was to increase government expenditures to reduce unemployment. Specifically he suggested that the government could spend more on defense, foreign aid, education, urban renewal, health and welfare, public works, and highways while lowering mortgage costs and fixing the balance of payments problem.[11]

During his career, Samuelson was extremely productive, authoring hundreds of articles – more than 300 by the time he won the prize in 1970 – and four books. But there was more to Samuelson than just work. He and his wife, the former Marion Crawford, had six children, including four boys, three of whom were triplets. He estimated that he spent about three Saturdays a year in emergency rooms having the boys stitched up or otherwise evaluated for minor athletic injuries. Despite his many obligations, he took time to read detective novels and play tennis on nearly a daily basis. On the day his Nobel Prize was announced, the press caught him having a toast with his staff at MIT, sipping his favorite drink Hawkers Amontillado sherry.[12]

The Textbook

While Samuelson won a Nobel Prize for his mathematical economics, it was his textbook that made him famous. The book was so ubiquitous on college campuses that it was often referred to simply by his name, for example, "we used *Samuelson* in my college economics class." The actual book, entitled

Economics, An Introductory Analysis, was such a phenomenal success that it changed the textbook industry forever. It sold more than four million copies in forty-one different languages over a period of about fifty years starting in 1948. It was perhaps the first textbook to set these kinds of sales records and publishers learned that there was real money to be made in textbooks. Even before Samuelson's *Economics* reached its final twelfth edition with him as the sole author (William Nordhaus joined him as coauthor for later editions), economics publishers were wondering who would be the next Samuelson.

Modern economic textbooks owe a debt to Samuelson for the format of his book. Neatly divided into microeconomics and macroeconomics, his text covered the basic ideas necessary for an introductory undergraduate course. The macroeconomics section was composed of standard definitions and Keynesian theory, and the microeconomics section would have looked familiar to Alfred Marshall. Samuelson described this as a *neoclassical synthesis* in the sense of a single, unified economic theory. But the synthesis that Samuelson sought was largely elusive because neo-Keynesian economics and microeconomics remained, in important respects, incompatible.

Although *Economics* aspired to be scientifically objective, it couldn't help but reflect some of the values of its author. The textbook included Samuelson's solutions to economic problems. He supported *progressive taxes*, which taxed the rich at a higher percentage, because he believed they might make some people "work harder in order to make their million."[13] He supported Social Security with its pay-as-you go model, pointing out that it could not be undermined by inflation, like other savings systems. Antipoverty programs also met with his tacit approval, claiming that "we insist upon providing certain minimum standards of existence for those who are unable to provide for themselves."[14] These recommendations were presented in the spirit of self-evident truths rather than provable hypotheses.

Conservatives, no doubt exasperated by the book's unprecedented commercial success, bristled at the few liberal positions in Samuelson's *Economics*. Critics at Oklahoma A&M University banned it in the early 1950s, and William Buckley pilloried it in his own book, *God and Man at Yale*.[15] A more contemporary critic, Mark Skousen concluded in 1997 that "its advice has contributed to certain of the economic problems that the United States faces today."[16] Samuelson clearly saw himself at odds with the more conservative, libertarian wing of the economics profession, including Milton Friedman and the Chicago School. At the conclusion of his Nobel lecture, he quoted an obscure economist who said, "There is no reason why theoretical economics should be a monopoly of the reactionaries."[17] Samuelson confessed that "All my life I have tried to take this warning to heart...."[18]

But was his textbook really that liberal? A good part of its hundreds of pages described the traditional theory of perfect competition and market dynamics. Samuelson had very favorable things to say about free trade and unregulated markets while questioning the wisdom of agricultural subsidies. He was certainly no hero of economists from the left who were uncomfortable with his enthusiasm for free markets.

Astute readers have documented changes in Samuelson's thinking on some subjects over the fifty years of his authorship of the book. He came to recognize that stabilization policy, which was once implemented by the federal budget in the 1940s, had been effectively transferred to the Federal Reserve by the 1950s. He also seemed to develop a stronger appreciation for the role of money, and recognized the necessity of savings for economic growth. As his success grew, he generously included more references to opposing views espoused by Irving Fisher, Friedrich A. von Hayek, Ludwig von Mises, and, in the ninth edition, even a favorable mention of the book *Capitalism and Freedom* by Milton Friedman.[19] But the primary purpose of Samuelson's textbook never changed; it provided him with a special podium to communicate his version of Keynesian economics and microeconomics to many generations of college students. In an interview with Sylvia Nasar, he explained, "I don't care who writes a nation's laws – or crafts its advanced treaties – if I can write its economics textbooks."[20]

Assar Lindbeck from the Nobel committee pointed out that Samuelson, unlike other leading economists, did not invent a new field of economics but rather made major contributions to many of them. Whether he solved problems set up by others or set up problems for others to solve, he pushed forward the frontiers of mathematical economics. His contributions were in consumption theory, general equilibrium, capital theory, and economic growth and dynamics. But what does this mean?

Many of Samuelson's contributions were abstract formulas or mathematical proofs, although some were based on relatively straightforward concepts. An example is his theory of *revealed preference*. Suppose you listed all of the items that you purchased yesterday. This particular list, quaintly referred to by economists as a basket of commodities, is preferred over all other combinations of goods that you could have purchased with the same amount of money. How do you know that? Because you didn't choose the other goods. In economic language, you have a revealed preference for what you actually purchased over anything you chose not to purchase. This may not seem like a great discovery, and in fact it seems to be valued more for its mathematical innovation than any real economic insight.[21]

The Nobel committee also recognized Samuelson for his models of economic growth. Two approaches to economic growth were particularly interesting to economists during Samuelson's era: the *golden rule* and the *turnpike theory*. The whole issue started with the question of what savings rate would provide the highest level of prosperity that could be sustained every year into the future. A savings rate of zero was too low because it left nothing to replace worn out capital and equipment, and a savings rate of 100 percent was too high because nothing was left to consume. So the optimum savings rate had to be somewhere in between, but what was it? Economists defined the golden rule savings rate as the one that produced the highest sustainable level of economic prosperity for every future generation. More analysis showed that the golden rule savings rate had to be higher if the population was growing or capital was depreciating, but lower if technology was improving. All this seemed reasonable.

The turnpike theorem introduced another concept. If you wanted to do better than the constant per-capita consumption rate as represented by the golden rule, then current generations had to save more to benefit future generations. Economists asked the question: Which was better, a slightly higher savings rate for a long period of time or a much higher savings rate for a short time? After much analysis economists found it could go either way, but that there were at least some instances when a very high savings rate for a short time was the optimal way to bump the economy up to higher prosperity. This became known as the turnpike theory, because you take the turnpike when you want to move quickly even if the distance traveled is farther.

The consistent theme in all Samuelson's work was to set up physics-like problems and solve them. Even the language of economics started to imitate physics. Where elementary physics covered statics (objects at rest) and dynamics (objects in motion), economics started to distinguish between statics (markets in balance) and dynamics (economic growth). This is what Assar Lindbeck was referring to when he said, "Samuelson's contribution was to some extent an application of an analogy between processes and dynamic systems in classical mechanics."[22] How far could you push this analogy between physics and economics? It certainly gave economics a scientific appearance, but did it reveal important insights about the real world?

Economists are at a disadvantage because they don't have the same laws of nature that physicists have. Instead, they had to invent them. Samuelson, like other economists, simply assumed the formal relationships that allowed them to formulate and solve interesting problems, including the secrets to economic growth. Whether or not the results had any relevance to the real economy was not their concern. Economic theory, they would explain, is supposed to be abstract and it was someone else's job to apply the theories using real data.

While Samuelson received much acclaim for treating economics as a physics problem, he didn't necessarily value this kind of work from others. He once complained, "There is really nothing more pathetic than to have an economist or retired engineer try to force analogies between the concepts of physics and the concepts of economics."[23] You couldn't just translate any economics into a physics problem and solve it, according to Samuelson; you had to understand the difference between a valid analogy and mere whimsy.

In the real world, optimizing economic growth was not so easy. Turnpike strategies may work quite well for some countries such as Japan, but fail miserably for others such as the Soviet Union. Both countries were characterized by high rates of savings and investment, but their performance could not have been more different. Japan thrived while the Soviets floundered. There is obviously more to economic growth than finding the perfect savings rate. How a country invests that savings and organizes its economy also seems to matter.

There is still an unsettled question about the value of economic research that attempts to closely imitate physics. No one questions the value and necessity of advanced mathematical techniques in studying physics, but what does it really tell us about the performance of economic systems? The question occurred to Leonard Silk of the *New York Times*, who queried, "is this really the way people and institutions behave?" Will the same tools used to explore the secrets of thermodynamics and classical mechanics also provide insights that will improve the quality of economic life for mankind? Silk noted that whatever the answer turns out to be, this is "an empirical question which Professor Samuelson has not really explored."[24]

The press frequently sought out Samuelson for a quote or an interview. Among his favorite targets were political leaders who didn't seem to understand even elementary economics. At a press conference following his Nobel award, Samuelson was quoted as wondering "why Mr. Nixon doesn't rejoin the human race and join the campaign to get the economy moving again."[25] He showed no more restraint twenty-three years later when he chastised President Reagan for bamboozling his constituents into believing that tax cuts would increase revenue without creating massive deficits.[26] He explained, "People have the wrong idea that God will forgive Reagan. They say he didn't know what he was doing. It's true he didn't know a lot of what was going on, but he was directly responsible."[27]

Samuelson's witty comments were not reserved only for presidents. In the 1980s and 1990s, supply-side economists popularized the notion that taxes were too high and responsible for our poor economic performance. Samuelson shot back, "America is not remotely near the limits of taxation, and one more pfennig is not going to break the camel's back."[28] The Vietnam War impressed him as a conspicuous waste of money. He complained, "There is so much work to do in this country that the notion that we've got to put something down a rat hole in Vietnam is ridiculous."[29]

No one was surprised when Samuelson won the Nobel Prize in 1970, along with the $78,000 that came with it. He was already famous for his textbook and well-known in the profession for his neo-Keynesian economics. If there was any surprise it was only that he wasn't honored with the very first prize in 1969. In many ways, he was the economists' economist, the model of academic success. His great contribution to economics was rightfully acknowledged following his death at age ninety-four in 2009.

Robert M. Solow (1987 Prize Winner)

Why do some economies grow quickly while others languish? Why do some countries grow rapidly for a while and then slow down? Determining the reasons for growth is at the very foundation of economics and is the same question that preoccupied both Adam Smith and John Maynard Keynes. Smith's efficient markets and Keynes' aggregate demand are both important elements of long-term economic growth, but there must be more to it. What is the secret to growth and national economic wealth? This was the question that confronted "growth theorists" in the 1940s and 1950s when Robert M. Solow was still a young economist at MIT.

One of the first major contributions to this question was made in about 1939 by two economists working separately, Sir Roy F. Harrod and Evsey Domar. The resulting *Harrod-Domar model* was the first of its kind to link mathematically a country's growth rate with two simple measures: its savings rate and the productivity of capital. They proposed to have discovered the secret to economic growth: Save more and invest in more and better capital. This was not a particularly surprising conclusion. Countries that do not save cannot invest in roads, railroads, offices, factories, business computers, or anything else because, by definition, they are consuming everything they produce. The Harrod-Domar model had two things in its favor: It was remarkably simple and it made sense.

That wasn't the end of it. While the basic results were plausible, the mathematical qualities of the growth equation were not. Balanced growth could only occur if the growth rate of the economy just happened to exactly equal the growth rate of the labor force. When the two growth rates (economy and labor force) diverged, the model spun off in the direction of steadily rising unemployment or steadily increasing inflation. That part of the model was implausible.

One of the young economists troubled by this shortcoming was Robert M. Solow. In his prize lecture, he mentioned that this concern was one of the reasons why, in the 1950s, he started "tinkering with the theory of economic growth." The other reason was that he was troubled by the strong relationship between growth and savings implied by Harrod and Domar. Why exactly did the role of savings bother him? Unfortunately, by the time of his Nobel speech he could "no longer remember exactly why" it troubled him, it just did.[30]

Because the Harrod-Domar model started with such simple assumptions, it was easy to modify. Solow made a few different assumptions and derived a very different result. Resorting to microeconomics, Solow assumed that capital and labor were substitutes and that each were paid in proportion to their productivity. In the resulting model, growth no longer depended directly on the savings rate nor the productivity of capital. In fact, neither made any difference anymore. In the new model, economic growth depended on only three variables: the growth in the labor force, the productivity of labor, and technological progress. Solow's model was also stable, tending to regain equilibrium if it was ever bumped off course. The resulting equation, published in a series of articles in 1956 and 1957, became known as the *neoclassical growth model*.

Almost immediately Solow started having regrets about this innovation but it was too late. The neoclassical growth model was immediately popular with microeconomists who were looking for a stable model to replace the Harrod-Domar model. It was stable, in fact, almost too stable. It effectively eliminated the potential for recessions and depressions that had been the hallmark of Keynesian theory. This point was clear to Charles Schultze, a former chairman of President Carter's Council of Economic Advisers. Schultze commented that Solow explained why small declines in investment did not produce recessions, counter to what Keynesian theory might suggest.[31]

Solow, a Keynesian economist, had developed a long-run growth model that ignored – or worse, contradicted – Keynesian theory. Only later did

Solow confess that he should have paid closer attention to Keynesian concepts like effective demand. It was not entirely accidental, however, as he confessed, "I can honestly say that I realized the need at the time."[32] Solow's model was essentially a microeconomic model of the macroeconomy without the messy, real-world problems of unemployment and inflation. In Solow's opinion, the problem of reconciling his long-run model with Keynesian economics "has still not been solved."[33]

Solow's growth model had other curious characteristics. "The moral of Solow's story was that savings wouldn't greatly influence the rate of growth," according to David Warsh, writing for the *Boston Globe*.[34] But is that true? Are national savings really irrelevant when it comes to growth? Solow justified this result by claiming that a higher savings rate could increase the level of economic activity for a short time, but "it will not achieve a permanently higher rate of growth of output."[35] Not only did this contradict the assumptions in the golden rule savings rate and the turnpike theory, it was rather hard to believe. We know that a zero savings rate will guarantee no growth, because everything that is produced is immediately consumed. There must be some savings to generate investments for the future, so growth and savings should be related. At least in this one respect, the Harrod-Domar model seemed more realistic.

A particularly important innovation in Solow's neoclassical growth model was the idea of technological change. Harrod and Domar's model had been so simple that they had related output only to savings and capital productivity, but Solow included technological progress as a source of growth. Later estimates by Solow and others validated this assumption. They found that one-half to three-fourths of U.S. economic growth could be attributed to better technologies. This was higher than most economists expected. Assar Lindbeck, a member of the Nobel committee, claimed that "When these results came out in the '50s, they had a very strong impact on people's thinking because then many governments drew the conclusion that they should push higher education and technological research."[36]

After the announcement of the Nobel Prize, reporters asked Solow to comment on what he had discovered. He explained, "Silicon Valley is an example of the sort of thing I'm talking about."[37] He did not mean to imply that he had any role in discovering Silicon Valley or the computer industry. What he meant was that he prodded economists into appreciating the importance of technology in models of economic growth. The importance of research and development and education was hardly a new idea, but they were surprisingly new to the mathematical growth theorists in the 1950s. Solow's colleague at MIT, Richard Eckaus, admitted that "Everybody knew technology was important, but nobody knew how to bring it into our analysis and how important a factor it was,"[38] "What Bob Solow did was quantify how much the improvement in labor productivity is attributable to capital investment and technological change," according to James Tobin, a Yale University professor and Nobel laureate.[39] The conclusion was that technology was probably really important.

After all of this work, do we now know the secrets to economic growth? Can we prove that growth is caused by technological innovation, education, capital investment, free markets, or high savings, or some combination of these factors? All of these factors seem important – but then they always did. The problem was that none of the models could fully account for what was happening in the real world. As Nobel winner Robert Lucas pointed out, we still don't have a very good explanation of economic growth, especially in the Asian "miracles," countries like Hong Kong, Singapore, Japan, Korea and Taiwan.[40] Why is there growth in these countries and not as much in India?[41] "These economic miracles are still extremely mysterious…. I mean, how did Korea pull it off?" Lucas asked in a lecture given at Cambridge University.[42] After hundreds of articles about Solow's growth models and hundreds more about the meaning of technological change, innovation, invention, and learning-by-doing, can economists say anything with any authority about how to achieve economic growth? Why some countries grow and others don't remains an open question in economics.

Although neither of his parents had attended college Solow performed well in school and by high school had taken an interest in classical literature and ideas in general. His high school literature teacher advised him to consider Harvard University rather than Brooklyn College and he took the advice. With a scholarship to attend Harvard, he enrolled in September 1940 when he was only sixteen.[43] Before finishing college, he joined the army in 1942, serving in Africa, Sicily, and Italy until 1945.

Returning to Harvard at the end of the war Solow still didn't have a major. His wife, who was studying to be an economic historian, suggested that he take an economics class.[44] He did and it changed his life. Solow started his career as a professor at MIT in 1949 and completed his dissertation for Harvard, receiving his doctorate in 1951. At MIT he collaborated and consulted with Paul Samuelson. A university faculty award for Solow noted that "The intellectual partnership of Solow and Samuelson must rank among the most productive of such relationships in the history of economics."[45]

Both Robert Solow and Paul Samuelson were self-described Keynesians, and yet both made major contributions to neoclassical economics as recognized by their Nobel Prizes. They shared a dual allegiance to Keynes and neoclassical economics although, in some ways the, two approaches were incompatible. This contradiction – based in Cambridge, Massachusetts, where MIT is located – came to the attention of the other Cambridge, the Cambridge University in England. Keynes was gone but his colleagues Joan Robinson and Piero Sraffa remained, and they were not in the least impressed with Samuelson and Solow's so-called neoclassical synthesis. While they disagreed on many issues, the most prominent disagreement was an eso-teric debate about how to define capital. The MIT Keynesians relied on an abstraction that allowed them to add up all productive resources such as factories, equipment, office buildings, and computers into a single number called capital (not the dollar value of capital but just capital). The English Keynesians thought that was entirely meaningless.

After many years of bitter debate and increasingly obscure arguments, the so-called "Cambridge Capital Controversy" ended more from sheer exhaus-tion than from a decisive victory. Solow concluded in his Nobel speech that the "whole episode now seems to me to have been a waste of time."[46] It appeared that both sides lost sight of the purpose of models, which was to represent what was happening in the real world. Without this practical compass, the entire debate became painfully academic.

While Solow's Keynesian views were sometimes omitted from his research, they were prominent in his policy recommendations. Starting with a two-year stint at the Council of Economic Advisors, he contributed to a program of tax cuts and spending increases that were designed to boost economic activity. In later years, he adamantly opposed Reaganomics and supply-side economics that called for lower taxes, particularly for cor-porations and high-income individuals. At one point Solow said, "The best thing you can say about Reaganomics is that it probably happened in a fit of inattention." And he warned that because of the large tax cuts and the large federal deficits, "we're going to be a number of years dig-ging ourselves out of a hole that we dug for ourselves over the past six or seven years."[47] His proposed remedy was simply to reverse what the Reagan administration had done. "There has got to be a tax increase," he insisted.[48] In the end he complained, "The most frustrating thing is how difficult it is for academic economic thinking to penetrate the every-day workings of government."[49]

Nearly every article about Solow's Nobel Prize mentioned his good sense of humor and endearing wit. "Those who know him say Mr. Solow is the nicest guy you're ever likely to meet," proclaimed the *New York Times* edi-torial page. Solow enjoyed working with students and continued to teach undergraduate classes long after his status would have exempted him. In his

Nobel lecture, he dryly noted that he had estimated he could have increased his research productivity by 25 percent if he had neglected his students.[50] But that was something he would not do. Outside of his work, he found great pleasure retreating with his wife and three children to their house at Martha's Vineyard to partake in his passion for sailing.[51]

James Tobin (1981 Prize Winner)

The same day that a Nobel Prize in economics is announced in Stockholm, the national media descends on recipients and asks them to explain their work. When this happened to James Tobin from Yale University in 1981, he started to explain his contribution to portfolio theory in the context of general equilibrium, which quickly became incomprehensible to the reporters. After being pressed to explain his theory in every-day language, he might have aimed a bit too low when he said, "You know, don't put your eggs in one basket."[52] I recall hearing a radio report the following day that led with this quote from Tobin and the reporter's comment that, as incredible as it might have seemed, it appeared to be the reason for his Nobel Prize.

Economists seldom talk about putting eggs in different baskets but instead prefer to talk about diversifying a portfolio, which amounts to the same thing. For the record, Tobin wasn't the first to measure the value of a diversified portfolio. That is credited to Harry Markowitz, another Nobel Prize winner. Tobin merely used this idea to solve a puzzle in Keynesian theory and explain why people hold money.

To economists, money generally means a liquid form of payment that you can use at a store, like cash or a check. Cash, as we know, is useful because you can buy things with it. But economists suspected that people were holding on to more money than they needed for this purpose. To economists, this seemed almost irrational because money doesn't typically earn an interest rate or any other return. It would be smarter to hold just as much money as you needed and to invest the rest in a savings account, bonds, or something else. The question was why do people hold more money than they need?

Keynes, like previous economists, understood that there was a demand for money primarily to buy things. He also observed that people held money in case of emergencies and if they feared other assets could soon fall in value. Keynes referred to this as the *speculative or precautionary demand for money*.[53] In particular, Keynes argued, people will hold more money when interest rates are low.[54]

Tobin accepted the idea that the demand for money depended on interest rates, but he thought the reason was simpler.[55] He proposed two additional explanations. First, there is usually a cost of converting money into bonds and back into money again. If the cost of this conversion is high enough, it makes sense to keep more money on hand then trying to extract every penny of interest.

The second explanation treats money like any other asset in a portfolio. Money has a zero rate of return but it also has a low risk. Consequently there is a demand for money as part of a balanced portfolio that includes other assets. When interest rates are low, other assets are less valuable and money becomes relatively more desirable. Here we get the same result as Keynes but with a simpler explanation.[56] Introducing this portfolio concept into Keynesian economics was cited by Assar Lindbeck of the Swedish Academy as one of the primary reasons for Tobin's Nobel Prize.[57]

One of Tobin's other major insights addressed a key business decision. If a business wants to expand, it has at least two options. It can invest in new capacity requiring additional buildings, equipment, and employees, or it can buy existing firms that already have buildings, equipment, and employees. On what basis does a business make this decision? According to Tobin, the choice should depend on the relative cost of the two options.

This is essentially the same decision made by future homeowners. If they can buy a house for $250,000 or build an identical house for $200,000, they should build a house. The comparable cost for buying an existing business is its market value in the stock market, and the cost of starting a new business is its *replacement value*. If the market value is lower, it pays to buy the company; if the replacement value is lower it pays to start a new one. Tobin simplified this comparison by calculating a single value, now known as *Tobin's q*, which is the ratio of the market value to replacement value.

When calculated for a single company, Tobin's q indicates whether it is less expensive to buy a company or build one. When it is calculated for the entire economy, it gives some indication of whether firms, on average, should be buying each other or making new investments.[58] While this may seem a little esoteric, it has important economic consequences. If firms expand by buying each other through mergers, then they are simply transferring ownership, but when they build new factories and buildings, they create new jobs and raise incomes. Tobin's idea was so popular with the economics graduate students at Yale that they started wearing t-shirts with the single letter "q" in his honor.

In reality, there are many reasons why merger activity rises and falls, and Tobin's q counts as only one of them. But it seemed to be a factor in the low investment rates in Sweden during the 1970s, according to Assar Lindbeck. When he announced Tobin's Nobel Prize, Lindbeck complained that low stock market values in Sweden made it less costly for companies to buy stocks than to build new businesses. As a consequence, the country suffered from low investment and low economic growth.[59]

Tobin wasn't just interested in why people want money or how businesses grow. He really wanted to build macroeconomic models to test economic policy. The hope was that by combining these ideas, represented by equations, he could produce more accurate models and provide more useful insights and predictions. For several decades starting in the 1950s, Keynesian economists like Tobin and classical economists like Friedman competed with each other to build the best macroeconomic model. The Keynesian models all "proved" that government actions could improve the economy, and each of the classical models "proved" the opposite. Each iteration of the debate typically produced more complex models but few clear-cut victories. The Nobel committee did not choose sides but simply awarded prizes to both camps.

It is quite possible that two different economic models can reach completely opposite conclusions even when they are produced by Nobel Prize winners. Tobin pointed out that the model he presented in his Nobel speech in 1981, directly contradicted a model developed by Robert Mundell. What made this interesting was that Mundell won the Nobel Prize eighteen years later in 1999 for the very model that Tobin supposedly "disproved."[60] What Tobin really demonstrated is that economists can "prove" almost anything given the right assumptions, making all of this a little suspect. Tobin seemed to sense this in the middle of his Nobel lecture when he observed that "Representation of economics as systems of simultaneous equations always strains credibility."[61]

Tobin's criticism of conservative economic policies started with Friedman and continued through the Reagan administration. He complained that what "Mr. Friedman and his disciples recommend, is likely to damage the economy."[62] He also objected to Reagan's policies that only serve "to redistribute wealth and power to the wealthy and powerful."[63] Tobin was a supporter of the Great Society programs developed during the 1960s, favoring food stamp programs over tax cuts for the wealthy.[64] In 1981, Tobin warned that the effect of Reagan's tax cuts and the Federal Reserve monetary policy "will not bring interest rates down enough to spur economic growth, until the economy suffers a recession."[65] In fact, Tobin was correct; the economy suffered a severe recession in 1981–2 before interest rates came down and restored economic growth.

Tobin had the good fortune to attend a high-powered school in Urbana, Illinois associated with the University's College of Education and largely populated with the children of university faculty. In addition to Tobin, two other Nobel Prize winners, one in physics and one in medicine, also graduated from University High School. This education helped Tobin to qualify for a full scholarship to Harvard at a time when Harvard was trying to diversify the geographic distribution of its student body. In September of 1935, at the age of seventeen, Tobin took the train to Harvard.

Growing up during the 1930s had a profound impact on Tobin. In 1932, during the worst years of the Depression, his mother returned to work directing a family service agency in the twin cities of Champaign-Urbana. Tobin believed that "The miserable failures of capitalist economies in the Great Depression were root causes of worldwide social and political disasters."[66] Economics was attractive to him for its intellectual challenges, but also because he believed "that improved understanding could better the lot of mankind."[67] Growing up with these values, he was easily persuaded by the ideas of Keynes when he first read them as a sophomore at Harvard University. Tobin was also exposed to some of the country's top economists who were at Harvard in the 1930s, including Joseph Schumpeter, Edward Chamberlin, Alvin Hansen, and future Nobel Prize winner Wassily Leontief. There were also up-and-coming faculty and graduate students, including John Kenneth Galbraith and Paul Samuelson.

The economic build-up to World War II created a demand for skilled professionals to coordinate planning and price controls in the federal government. Tobin responded to the call from Washington, D.C., in 1941 to help oversee the conversion of the civilian economy into war production. But his commitment went deeper; he enlisted in the U.S. Naval Reserve. During the war, Tobin rose from a line officer to second in command of the destroyer U.S.S. Kearny, which provided convoy escorts in the Atlantic and Mediterranean, and participated in the invasion of North Africa and Southern France. After the war, he completed his doctorate at Harvard in 1947 and then joined the faculty of Yale University where he spent the remainder of his career.

When asked in 1961 by President John F. Kennedy to serve on his Council of Economic Advisors, Tobin responded with honesty and humility, "I'm afraid you've got the wrong guy, Mr. President, I'm an ivory tower economist." Undeterred, the President responded, "That's the best kind, I'm an ivory tower president."[68] Kennedy's wit carried the day and Tobin climbed down from his ivory tower at Yale to serve on Kennedy's Council. The Council was chaired by Walter Heller and the staff included two future Nobel Prize winners, Kenneth Arrow and Robert Solow. This particular alignment of all-star academics also proved surprisingly effective at getting their ideas heard. They promoted the idea of a tax cut to stimulate the economy, which, by most accounts, seemed to work. Despite this impressive achievement, Tobin didn't stay long. After only one and one-half years, he returned to academics claiming the "fifteen-hour days and seven-day weeks" put a strain on him and his family, which by then included four young children.[69]

The Tobin Tax

In 1972, Tobin floated a proposal that gained surprising popularity but not in the way that he had hoped. Tobin's idea was to limit speculation on international currency markets by placing a small tax on all transactions. These markets are immense, with over one trillion dollars worth of currency changing hands every day, a good part of which is motivated by speculation.[70] Problems occur when rampant speculation creates crises where none actually exist. Tobin's idea was to dampen the animal spirits of international currency traders by taxing transactions.

The so-called *Tobin Tax* was given new life by an anti-free trade group, the Association for the Taxation of Financial Transactions for the Aid of Citizens (ATTAC). The group, located in France and claiming 27,000 members, made the implementation of the Tobin Tax its primary mission. Although the tax was rejected by the French Treasury Minister in 2000, it came within six votes of being adopted by the European Parliament that same year.[71] The proposed tax of 0.25 percent would have raised about $250 billion a year, which ATTAC wanted dedicated to providing international aid.

The tax also had its critics, including the *European Wall Street Journal*, which referred to it as the "vampire that keeps rising from the dead."[72] American economist Rudiger Dornbush of MIT called it "retrograde" and rooted in "reactionary mushy-headed liberalism."[73] Tobin's reaction was to complain that he was not opposed to free trade; all he wanted to do was rein in unproductive currency speculation. He protested, "I have been hijacked. I have nothing in common with this revolution against globalization."[74] In fact, he insisted, "I'm a free trader."[75]

Tobin was awarded the Nobel Prize in 1981.[76] His wife, Elizabeth Fay Ringo, mentioned to the gathering reporters that her husband was accustomed to riding his Sears three-speed bicycle to classes at Yale, but that was interrupted the previous spring when his bike was "taken." Now, she commented, he could afford to buy himself a replacement.[77]

He certainly could afford a replacement and an upgrade if he so desired. Being the sole winner that year, Tobin was entitled to the entire $180,000 prize.

Tobin was a dedicated researcher and an equally committed teacher. Even after formally retiring from Yale in 1988 at the age of seventy, he continued to teach as a professor emeritus.[78] He was lauded by his students and colleagues alike who described him as both brilliant and shy.[79] On March 11, 2002, James Tobin died at the age of 84.[80]

Franco Modigliani (1985 Prize Winner)

It was well-known from early studies of individual family budgets that the rich had the highest savings rate and the poor the lowest. This pattern suggested that rising incomes should cause personal savings rates to increase over time for a country overall. But extensive data collected by Nobel Prize winner Simon Kuznets in the 1940s showed that this was not the case. Despite rising wealth and income levels, the savings rate in the United States had changed little since the 1850s. This was one of those unexpected puzzles that sparked some creative thinking. Milton Friedman offered one theory that contributed to his Nobel Prize, but Italian economist Franco Modigliani offered a simpler, competing explanation that helped earn his Noble prize in 1985.

Working at the University of Illinois in the 1950s with one of his students, Richard Blumberg, Modigliani observed that savings was often determined by a person's age or more precisely, where they were in their life cycle. A young family may borrow money (negative savings) to buy houses, cars, and furniture that they pay off (positive savings) during their lifetime. When they retire, their savings are again negative as they live off their accumulated wealth. Therefore, when a family is most income poor – when they are very young or very old – their savings is negative. At all other times their savings are positive and correlated with their income. Later studies seemed to confirm Modigliani's theory, finding a fairly constant savings rate for the middle-age group and a lower savings rate or even *dissavings* for seniors and the very young.[81] Modigliani's *life-cycle theory* provided a simple explanation for the observed savings pattern.[82]

Modigliani also needed to explain why the national savings rate didn't rise with higher national income. As income goes up for all families, Modigliani observed, their savings goes up but so does their borrowing. The net result had little effect on the national savings rate. This seemed to neatly resolve the puzzle raised by Kuznets.

Because Modigliani's model seemed to be based on reasonable human behavior, it was immediately popular with many economists. Paul Samuelson called it "the best explanation of what has actually been happening in the great swing of American life since the 1950s."[83] Nobel winner James Tobin called it "a good common-sense explanation that said that, unless people are living hand to mouth, they're going to smooth out (their income) so they have something left over when they retire."[84]

Savings was also at the center of an important policy debate over the effect of government retirement programs. In 1985, Assar Lindbeck, the chairman of the Nobel committee, blamed the introduction of a comprehensive pension program in Sweden for the decline in the savings rate from 7 percent in the 1960s to zero. According to Mr. Lindbeck, "When Swedes no longer had to save for their old age, they no longer saved at all."[85] Modigliani, however, was a strong supporter of the U.S. Social Security program because it provided relatively higher benefits to poor people, and he strongly opposed any effort to privatize it.[86] He understood that people might think they had to save less because of Social Security, but he suggested that if it encouraged earlier retirement it might also encourage more savings.

In the 1950s, there was another academic debate about the ideal strategy for funding corporate investment. Businesses can raise money by either selling bonds or issuing stocks. Which one, economists wondered, was the best way to raise money? Modigliani teamed up with Nobel laureate Merton Miller while they were both at Carnegie Mellon University and worked out the answer under perfectly functioning capital markets. The answer was simple: It really doesn't matter whether a company sells bonds or issues stocks. Corporations, they concluded, are valued by their future earnings potential, not by how much or how little debt they have. Moreover, they argued, it is irrelevant whether the company pays a high or low percentage of its profits in dividends. Once again, it is future earnings that are important for determining stock prices, not how generous or stingy a company is about paying dividends.

In retrospect, this answer should have been obvious if you were willing to assume perfect markets, but it still seemed to surprise many economists. By the time that some economists fully absorbed the meaning of this finding, other economists had already modified it. It was clear that Modigliani and Miller's finding only applied to a world without taxes or inflation, and if you took signaling into account, it was even more complicated. But Modigliani and Miller were credited with getting the ball rolling and kicking off modern finance theory by applying conventional microeconomics to financial markets. There was nothing Keynesian about this theory; it was conventional market economics.

When it came to economic policy, Modigliani was clearly a Keynesian and was quick to support government action. But he did not find it necessary to agree with Keynes on every issue. Modigliani noted that "Rather than the Keynesian view that monetary policy doesn't matter, I have always asserted that money meant some[thing] in controlling economic activity and may mean a lot."[87] Historical events have repeatedly confirmed his point of view. But unlike the monetarists, Modigliani didn't believe that the money supply should be locked into a fixed growth rate. As he said, "I don't think we should leave all decisions to a computer programmed by Milton Friedman."[88]

Franco Modigliani was born in Rome, Italy, in 1918 to Enrico and Olga Modigliani during World War I. After struggling for a few years with his studies, he enrolled in the best high school in Rome, Liceo Visconti, and his performance blossomed. The school prepared him for a series of difficult college entrance exams and he was allowed to enroll in the University of Rome at age seventeen, two years earlier than his peers.

When Modigliani was thirteen, his father died and his family pressured Franco to pursue a career in medicine, his father's profession. Shortly after he entered the University of Rome, he realized that he had little tolerance for blood, so he abandoned medicine and obtained a law degree in 1939. Mussolini had been in power for seven years, and Modigliani was Jewish and anti-Fascist. He decided it was a good time to leave Italy, so he and his wife fled for New York in August of 1939. They arrived only days before the outbreak of World War II in Europe.

Having won a prize in Italy for an economic essay, Modigliani decided to pursue a new career in economics. He received a fellowship to attend the New School for Social Research, which was populated with recent European émigrés. There he found great teachers who advised him to study more mathematics although he confessed to initially having "some aversion to it."[89] The advice paid off.

Modigliani's Nobel Prize was the first in economics for an Italian. "In Italy, they just went wild," he said.[90] When asked how he planned to spend his $225,000 he said, "in accordance with my own theories of how people behave – namely distribute it over the rest of my life. I'm not going to go on a binge. I will use it gradually. That's what my theory says people do."[91] He went on to explain, however, that it was his wife who actually managed the family finances. "I give the general ideas, and my wife makes better specific decisions."[92] He was described as a small bouncy man with silver hair in disarray, forgetful and disheveled with a professorial appearance.[93]

Throughout his career Modigliani had a history of acting on principle. During an interview in 1985, he expressed little interest in holding government posts because he had no desire to place limits on his self-expression. Even advisory positions, such as the one he had with the U.S. Treasury, created problems for him. When it was disclosed sometime around 1970 that the United States had invaded Cambodia as part of the war in Vietnam, Modigliani resigned his position. He did not wish to advise a government when he disapproved of its policies.[94]

Modigliani seemed to relish the attention from the press that came with the announcement of his Nobel Prize. With the press in full attendance, he made a point to criticize the economic policies of the Reagan administration. He said, "I think they're making serious mistakes. I think now maybe ... I will speak with a louder voice."[95] He did raise the volume and almost immediately found himself in an acrimonious exchange with Reagan administration spokesman Larry Speakes. Modigliani started off by characterizing the federal deficits as "disastrous"[96] and declared the Reagan deficits "a clear and present danger"[97] before the Joint Economic Committee of Congress in 1985. He suggested the solution was to restore taxes and cut military spending – in other words, to reverse the policies of the Reagan administration. Like Samuelson, Modigliani thought that tax rates were already relatively low in the United States, at least compared to other successful industrialized countries.[98]

A mischievous reporter asked Larry Speakes, President Reagan's spokesman, what he thought of the new Nobel Prize winner's comments. Speakes smugly opined, "Got nothing. I thought he was the fellow that painted the Sistine Chapel."[99] Now it may be impossible to sort out exactly what was going through Larry Speakes' mind but it appeared that he intentionally confused the names of the Nobel Prize winner, Franco Modigliani, with the great Italian painter Amedeo Modigliani as a joke. But at the same time he seemed unintentionally to confuse Amedeo Modigliani with Michelangelo who actually did paint the Sistine Chapel. He seemed to be overwhelmed by too many Italian names that began with the letter "M" and ended with a vowel.

This must have been a slow news day, because the press went back to Modigliani who answered with another volley, "His statement confusing the life cycle hypothesis with alluring nudes in the Sistine Chapel has me seriously worried."[100] And he added, apparently with some prompting by the press, that the joke had "an ethnic connotation," like "an ignorant slur."[101] The media rushed back to Speakes who said he was "offended" that his remark would be interpreted as an ethnic slur and left it up to his deputy to explain that it was nothing more than a joke. Modigliani got the last word with some reference to "abysmal ignorance."

This tussle did not dampen Modigliani's enthusiasm for criticizing the Reagan administration policies, which, he complained, were encouraging people to "enjoy the moment" and show "no compassion for the poor or handicapped, and none for future generations either. People don't make the connection between the deficits and the bad things that are going on – farm failures, the trouble young people have buying houses, loss of jobs."[102]

In his final public campaign in 2003, Modigliani protested the decision by the Anti-Defamation League to award their Distinguished Service Award to Silvio Berlusconi, Prime Minister of Italy. The protest was in the form of a letter to the *New York Times*, cosigned by his colleagues Paul Samuelson and Robert Solow.[103] The three economists wrote that Berlusconi was once quoted as saying that Mussolini did not murder anyone, but rather sent them into long exile.[104] They argued that Berlusconi was wrong to express a view sympathetic to the Italian fascist, and at the very least, it should disqualify him from being honored by the Anti-Defamation League, an organization whose purpose was to protect the Jewish people.

Two days after the letter was published in 2003, Franco Modigliani died at the age of eighty-six.[105]

Lawrence R. Klein (1980 Prize Winner)

Unlike the other Keynesian Nobel Prize winners, Lawrence Klein was not honored for economic theory but for pioneering the art of economic forecasting. Despite the sophisticated statistics, this category of research is called "applied economics" because it uses actual data. Economic forecasting with big models is challenging because of the difficulty of deriving useful and accurate results from hundreds of equations and variables. Like weather forecasts, the predictions tend to be more accurate the closer they are to the present. Near-term economic behavior is apt to be much like the present, so simple extensions into the future are sometimes surprisingly accurate. It is the long-term forecasts that present the biggest challenges. One blessing for long-term forecasters is that no one is likely to remember or care about their predictions for very long.

While a good track record is the goal of all economic forecasters, it doesn't hurt to have a slightly inflated reputation. In 1977, Klein testified at a hearing of the Joint Economic Committee of Congress where he noted that an appreciation of the yen would help the U.S. economy, conceivably by discouraging U.S. imports from Japan. Coincidentally, the yen soared the next day in international currency markets, an event that was light-heartedly referred to as "the Klein shock" by some of his colleagues. Sometime later, a reporter for the *New York Times* took this little anecdote seriously and reported it as evidence of Klein's powerful "international influence" and justification for his Nobel Prize.[106]

Even the most respected forecasting models will occasionally yield totally unrealistic numbers. This is usually an opportunity to make some "adjustment" in order to avoid having to defend some implausible result. The adjustment process relies on professional judgment about what is and what is not reasonable. Most forecasters have to make these kinds of adjustments and the honest ones will describe them to their subscribers. The fact that adjustments need to be made illustrates that forecasting is both a science and an art.[107]

Lawrence R. Klein has been called the "dean of U.S. model-builders," and is responsible for one of the first, major national forecasting models. When he was at the University of Pennsylvania he built the Wharton model, named after the business school, and generated many national forecasts. By 1975, when it was featured in an article in *Fortune* magazine, the Wharton model consisted of 400 equations and some 170 variables.

The complexity of all these equations impressed some businesses that were willing to pay $7,500 a year for access to quarterly forecasts, economic seminars, and data bases. The enterprise was so successful as a nonprofit that it soon spawned copycat for-profit enterprises such as Data Resources Inc. and Chase Econometrics. Michael Evans, who started Chase Econometrics, was a former colleague of Klein's at the Wharton School and admitted that "Klein has a brilliant, well-deserved reputation" but claimed that his mentor and competitor was "a flop as a businessman."[108] Eventually, Klein and the University of Pennsylvania sold the model and Wharton Econometric Forecasting Associates became a for-profit corporation. The revenue from the sale benefited research and instruction at the university.[109]

Assar Lindbeck commented on the "immense amount of very hard, detail work" required to collect all the data for the model and to calibrate it. It involves "extremely complex and tedious material."[110] Despite the scientific and statistical claims of model building, it still relies on many subjective assumptions. Which sectors should be included, at what level of detail, and over what time interval? Some of these assumptions in Klein's models were guided by Keynesian theory but others had to be somewhat arbitrary.

The value of any complex model is ultimately determined by its accuracy. Does the model provide an accurate picture of the future? On this account, econometric models, including Klein's, have had mixed success. In 1980 when Klein won his Nobel, Leonard Silk of the *New York Times* suggested that such models had not lived up to their expectations, creating "a measure of disillusionment among economists, business executives and Government [sic] officials."[111] "The models have sometimes failed to predict major changes in the business cycle and have underestimated rates of inflation," he wrote. "Indeed, the Klein model, with its Keynesian roots and structure, has been relatively weak in dealing with prices...."[112]

A 1975 article about Klein and the Wharton model in *Fortune* asked the question: "But does it really work?" It was common at that time to compare the records of the major forecasters against each other but also to compare them to seat-of-the-pants predictions by "judgmental" forecasters who used no specific model. *Fortune* concluded that "there is no good evidence that they [judgmental forecasters] did worse than the model-builders" for various predictions between 1970 and 1974.[113] The author of the *Fortune* article, Deborah DeWitt Malley, concluded, "And so the failure of the model-builders to demonstrate any special predictive advantages must at least raise a question about their understanding of the economy."[114]

Forecasting models have to assume that human behavior follows fixed patterns. The models are then calibrated using historical data for consumption, savings, and investing. To the extent that people spontaneously change their behavior – buy more appliances, save less income, travel more abroad, invest more in real estate – the models based on the past will not be able to keep up. Models can be very accurate as long as nothing really changes.

A more generous assessment of econometric models is that they provide a useful way to organize a lot of information and force a certain discipline in economic thinking. It is possible to consider such modeling a work-in-progress that will provide more value in the future. Economist R. J. Ball of the London Business School offered a similar opinion by quoting Samuel Johnson who said, "The proper response to a dog dancing on its hind legs was not to observe that he did it badly, but that it was remarkable that he did it at all."[115] Ball also suggested that the journey was more significant than the destination, and that the many specific insights or "spin-offs" provided from this disciplined thinking was more important than the forecasts themselves.[116]

Klein's final project, called LINK, was also his most ambitious: to connect national econometric models from around the world into one gigantic model of the world economy, or at least a large part of it. Models for this immense project represented the developed world, some developing countries, and even socialist countries such as China and the Soviet Union. In total, LINK was an extraordinarily complex model comprised of some 3,000 equations.[117]

Nobel Forecasts

In his Nobel acceptance speech in 1980, Klein took the opportunity to describe his long-term forecasts for the next ten to twenty years based on LINK and the Wharton model. The accuracy of these forecasts illustrates just how difficult it is to predict future economic events.

One problem was that Klein's model assumed "a continuing increase … in the real price of imported oil."[118] His model also expected the federal government to "keep taxes high enough to generate an eventual domestic budget balance."[119] With regard to inflation he foresaw little reduction, expecting it to hit 8 percent by 1985 and 7.6 percent by 1990.[120] There was also no reason in his model that U.S. trade should not remain in balance. As he predicted, "the current account stays close to balance with only slight deterioration…."[121] All of these assumptions and predictions were, at various times during the 1980s and 1990s, completely off the mark. There are distinct turning points in economic performance and 1980 was one of them. When these occur, all bets are off.

An accurate forecast in 1980 of future economic activity would have benefited from anticipating four particularly important events. The first was the dramatic reversal of world oil prices as OPEC's influence began to ebb after six years of record prices. Falling oil prices helped to tame a raging inflation and to stimulate economic activity. The second event was the dramatic run up in interest rates in the early 1980s orchestrated by the Federal Reserve in an effort to choke off inflation. Third, President Reagan with the help of supply-side economists and a willing Congress engineered the largest tax cut in history in 1981 and opened up record budget deficits. Finally, Reagan appointees to the U.S. Treasury embarked on an unprecedented experiment to let the U.S. dollar float freely on world markets.

Together these events brought down energy prices, wiped out inflation, exploded the federal budget deficit and trade deficit, and after a severe recession, put the economy on stable footing for an extended period of growth. Unfortunately, in 1980 Klein did not have a clue that any of these events were just around the corner, but then again, neither did anyone else. Klein's models cranked out predictions based on business as usual, but unfortunately business was anything but usual.

Growing up in Omaha, Nebraska, in the 1930s was a defining experience for Klein who told reporters, "I was a child of the Great Depression."[122] Klein started his undergraduate studies at Los Angeles City College where the quality of his education in economics and mathematics was very good, and then transferred to the University of California at Berkeley where it was even better. After Berkeley, Klein had two lucky breaks. The first was the chance to attend the graduate program at MIT and work with a rising young star on the faculty, Paul Samuelson. Like Samuelson, Klein became a devoted Keynesian and proficient mathematician. The second break came after finishing his doctorate in only two years – a record for MIT. He then joined the econometric team at the Cowles Commission affiliated with the University of Chicago.

While working with the Cowles Commission, Klein developed one of his earliest forecasting models consisting of some twenty equations. On the basis of this model, he forecasted a surge in economic activity after World War II.[123] While others predicted an economic relapse and six million workers unemployed, he anticipated a thriving economy.[124] During his Nobel Prize announcement thirty-four years later, Klein was still proud of this particular forecast.

Klein lived through the anticommunist McCarthy period of the 1950s as a participant rather than an observer. In 1945 while in Chicago working with the Cowles Commission, he was invited to teach a course in Marxian economics to a group in his neighborhood. The class was associated with the Communist party, and they explained to Klein that he needed to be a member to teach. He joined the party and maintained his membership until he left Chicago in 1947.[125] Klein downplayed the membership and insisted that he was "not a politician" but was rather a teacher who eventually "got bored with it" and quit.[126] Because of this two-year membership, Klein was called before the House Committee on Un-American Activities in 1954 where he recounted this story. Unquestionably, Klein had a constitutional right to join a political party, but in the 1950s during the red scare, Klein's membership, even one as temporary and superficial as he described it, had serious consequences. The University of Michigan informed him that because of his testimony they could not promote him when he became eligible for tenure.[127]

Disappointed and disillusioned, Klein left the university and the country. He took a position at Oxford where he studied savings behavior and developed a macroeconomic model of the United Kingdom. He returned to the United States in 1958 and joined the faculty at the University of Pennsylvania where he remained throughout his career.

The Communist party episode surfaced again when Klein was working with the Carter campaign in 1976. Klein was a frequent advisor to President Carter, largely because of Carter's infatuation with numbers and Klein's ability to produce them.[128] When Carter won the election, it was only natural that Klein would be a contender for a presidential appointment. According to a source on Carter's transition team, Klein was considered for an official role in the administration but withdrew his name given the potential for the Communist story to resurface.[129] Klein denied that was the case.

Low-key was the description most often used by his colleagues and even his wife to describe Klein. His wife fully expected that he would do the dishes as usual the day that his Nobel Prize was announced just as he excused himself that day from the press to teach his 1:30 class. While his wife described Klein as slightly stunned that day, his university president claimed that he "knew 10 years ago that they had to give it to him eventually."[130]

K. Gunnar Myrdal (1974 Prize Winner)

The announcement of the Nobel Prize winners in 1974 left a lot of economists scratching their heads. Here were two economists associated with two perfectly contradictory theories, and yet both were honored with Nobel Prizes in the same year. How could both theories benefit mankind if one had to be wrong? As Paul Samuelson observed, "their policy conclusions, if followed literally would be at loggerheads and self-cancelling."[131] One winner, Friedrich A. von Hayek, passionately believed in free markets and equally passionately opposed almost all forms of government intervention. The road to totalitarianism, in his view, was paved by the good intentions of government officials. One of those government officials with good intentions was Hayek's co-winner, K. Gunnar Myrdal from Sweden.

Myrdal was, among other things, a government planner, an elected official, and a high-level executive in the United Nations. His early work on macroeconomics in the 1930s explored the topics of savings and investment to understand better the potential for government action to moderate or reverse economic stagnation. He focused specifically on the benefits of using fiscal policy – government spending or tax cuts – to stimulate economic activity. Like Keynes, Myrdal recognized the "multiplicative" effects of public works expenditures on income and spending as they cycle through a stagnant economy. In 1974, a reviewer noted that Myrdal's book on the topic "contains most of the arguments for expansive fiscal policy that are used today – and that was indeed an achievement 40 years ago."[132]

Myrdal's early Keynesian approach contradicted the pro-market economics of Hayek. While Paul Samuelson welcomed the joint award as a gesture "for tolerance and eclecticism," the two co-winners were less gracious. An editor for the *Wall Street Journal* noted that "Hayek was famously unhappy about sharing his Nobel with Swedish socialist Gunnar Myrdal," and a reporter for the London *Financial Times* stated that "Myrdal wanted the prize abolished because it had been given to such reactionaries as Hayek and Milton Friedman."[133] Both men understood that the joint award undermined their own achievements. How could their ideas be so great if their co-winner contradicted most, if not all, of them? Were they recognized for their scientific discoveries or simply for representing two extremes in an ongoing debate?

Myrdal started out as a macroeconomic theorist in the 1930s and evolved into a self-described economic institutionalist. In fact, as his interests expanded to include history, anthropology, sociology, and politics, he looked back on his early work as "naïve empiricism." He no longer believed that small truths derived from a narrow economic analysis were particularly useful. Instead, his interests turned to big topics including one he referred to as the Negro problem in America. With financial backing from the Carnegie Corporation in 1938, Myrdal began a major study of black Americans after 1870. The results were published in 1944 in *An American Dilemma, The Negro Problem and Modern Democracy.*

In this extensive study, Myrdal analyzed the role that race played in determining income distribution, unemployment, segregation, discrimination, union membership, and education. A good part of the study traced the migration of blacks from the South after World War I and identified some of their economic gains. But while the North had much to offer, it failed to offer economic equality. Myrdal described a vicious circle where discrimination caused economic disadvantages that fed back into poor education and continuing discrimination.[134]

A review of Myrdal's work by Erik Lundberg described one of the difficulties of breaking this cycle. A progressive employer may want to stop discriminating and hire black workers, but being one of the few firms open to blacks, the owner could expect to be inundated with good black applicants. If he continued to not discriminate, he would eventually find that he had an all black-labor force. According to Myrdal this may be more than the employer bargained for, causing him to stop hiring blacks, or worse, not to hire them in the first place.

Myrdal's second major study, supported by the Twentieth Century Fund and undertaken in the late 1950s, investigated poverty and underdevelopment in South Asian countries. This work produced two publications: *Asian Drama, An Inquiry into the Poverty of Nations* and *The Challenge of World Poverty*. It was this work that inspired the topic of his Nobel lecture, "The Equality Issue in World Development." Myrdal argued that poverty in underdeveloped countries was not given sufficient attention by economists. He cited one estimate in 1975 that claimed "as many as 10 million people may starve to death this year, and at least half a billion are hovering on the brink of starvation."[135] Countries south of the Sahara and Bangladesh were particularly vulnerable because of natural catastrophes, war, exploding populations, and the increasing loss of farmland to deserts. The problems were exacerbated in 1975 by high petroleum costs.

Myrdal recommended an increase in the amount of foreign aid, especially from countries like the United States. The existing aid programs in most countries, he suggested, were too small to make a dent in the problem. But he also thought the purpose of foreign aid had to change. Too much foreign aid, he argued, came in the form of military assistance related to the Cold War. Even when the United States did provide useful aid, it was too often directed to the wrong people. Myrdal said, "During the Cold War, particularly the United States' aid and trade became purposely directed upon supporting reactionary regimes."[136] His recommendation to the United States and other countries was to provide aid for humanitarian purposes, not just as a weapon in the Cold War. He was hopeful that the United States could make this change. After all, he argued, Sweden committed a much higher percentage of income to foreign aid. "I cannot believe," he wrote, "that Americans are basically less charitable than Swedes."[137]

In addition to more humanitarian aid, Myrdal recommended other steps, foremost among them being land reform. Breaking up the ownership of large farms and ranches would enhance equality, while better farming practices and more investment in roads, storage, and irrigation would enhance productivity. All of this would be affordable if developed countries were willing to forego some of their massive investments in armaments and, as Myrdal described it, their "lavish food consumption."[138] Not only would a reduction in American consumption of beef, pork, and poultry free up a significant amount of grain for human consumption throughout the world, he said, it would also be good for Americans' health.

Myrdal was clearly frustrated with the lack of interest in solving world hunger. "I am asking myself," he wrote, "what has happened to people's moral valuations." He asked whether the problems with drugs, violence, crime, and war had effectively "blunted our feelings of human compassion and thus made us more prone to opportunistic indifference?"[139] Myrdal described the American war in Southeast Asia as "illegal, immoral, and ruthlessly cruel."[140] All of this contributed to what he admitted was a rather gloomy world view.

When Myrdal's wife Alma won the Nobel Peace Prize in 1982, the Myrdals had the distinction of becoming the third husband and wife team to win Nobel Prizes.[141] Alma was recognized for her efforts to promote nuclear disarmament by the United States and the Soviet Union. The Cold War was in full force in 1982, and the danger of a nuclear war was a serious concern throughout the world. She had the distinction of being the first woman to head a major department in the United Nations, and she used that position to promote the concept of disarmament. This was the culmination of a very successful career that included positions as Swedish ambassador to India, a cabinet member, a member of parliament, and Sweden's representative to the Geneva disarmament conference in 1962.

In Samuelson's essay about Myrdal, he explained that the Swedish academy generally took pains to avoid decisions that "might smack of provincial favoritism."[142] Nevertheless, Myrdal's background and achievements were probably best known in Sweden at that time. During his career he was a professor of political economy at the University of Stockholm, an elected member of the Swedish Senate, Sweden's Minister of Commerce and the Executive Secretary of the United Nations Economic Commission for Europe. He also served as a member of the Board of the Bank of Sweden which created the Nobel Prize in economics and was a member of the Royal Swedish Academy of Sciences, which selects the winners. Myrdal's own reaction to winning the Nobel Prize was mixed. He told one reporter that "the only reason why he accepted the prize was that he was not properly awake on the fateful morning when the Swedish Academy had called him."[143] But another reporter claimed that Myrdal was grateful for the prize because it "rescued him from personal depression."[144]

EIGHT

Classical Revival

Robert E. Lucas (1995)

Edward C. Prescott (2004)

Finn E. Kydland (2004)

Edmund S. Phelps (2006)

In classical economics, unemployment only occurs when wages are held unnaturally high, for example, by a minimum wage or unions. This theory was often a tough sell when applied to the entire U.S. economy, but it was never tougher than during the Great Depression. At the start of the Depression, the minimum wage didn't even exist, unions were hardly significant, and unemployment still soared to 25 percent. Classical economics wasn't just wrong, it was spectacularly wrong, making it easier for Keynesian economics to replace it. Classical economics was dethroned but managed to survive largely intact by retreating to the more limited domain of microeconomics. It was acceptable to use classical theory to explain individual markets but not necessarily the entire economy.

Not all classical economists accepted this demotion willingly. The Chicago School led by Milton Friedman never surrendered although the real economy didn't help their cause. If the minimum wage and unions caused unemployment, then the economy had a strange way of proving it. By the time a minimum wage was passed and union membership began to soar in the 1950s, unemployment fell to historic lows. With so much actual evidence contradicting their theory, it was a tough time to be a classical economist.

The University of Chicago provided a safe haven for classical economists and maintained somewhat of training camp for their assaults on the dominant Keynesian theory. They made relatively little progress until the 1970s when oil price shocks temporarily surprised all economists, including Keynesians. Before a new concept could be developed to explain this development, the Chicago School staged a counter-revolution. In the temporary confusion, they rolled out new versions of classical theories and tried to retake macroeconomics. Their theories, which combined modern mathematics with vintage economics, went by various names including rational expectations, new classical economics, and real business cycles. This effort challenged Keynesian economics and had an impact on policy, especially during the 1970s and 1980s. Eventually many of the proponents, including Robert Lucas, Edward Prescott, Finn Kydland, and Edmund Phelps, won Nobel Prizes in economics.

Robert E. Lucas (1995 Prize Winner)

When Rita and Robert Lucas were filing for their divorce in the late 1980s, Rita insisted on a brief but highly unusual clause in their settlement papers. It simply stated, "Wife shall receive 50 percent of any Nobel Prize...." Whatever Rita might have thought of Robert, she obviously figured that as a conservative economist from the University of Chicago he had a shot at a Nobel Prize. The settlement condition was scheduled to expire on October 31, 1995.

For several years the former Mrs. Lucas must have thought she came close to cashing in when Chicago School economists won the prize in 1990, 1991, 1992, and again in 1993, or she might have thought that her luck had run out when Chicago didn't win in 1994. But pay day came on October 10, 1995, when the Nobel committee announced that Robert Lucas had won the prize only three weeks before the divorce clause was scheduled to expire. It also capped an incredible streak for Chicago in which they won economic Nobel Prizes in five out of six years. Lucas was the sole winner of the million dollar prize in 1995 that he honorably and legally split with his ex-wife. As he explained, "A deal's a deal," and besides, "It's hard to be unpleasant after winning a prize like that."[1]

Not long after Robert Lucas was born in Yakima, Washington, his parents were forced to shut down their family business. The Lucas Ice Creamery could not survive the economic downturn in 1937–8 and the family moved to Seattle. Robert's parents abandoned the Republican principles of their parents and family friends, choosing instead to support Roosevelt's New Deal. As good liberal parents, they encouraged young Robert to think for himself about politics, religion, and even what kind of cigarette to smoke.[2]

Although Lucas voted for John Kennedy in the fall of 1960, he adopted a more conservative outlook after taking a theory course from Milton Friedman at the University of Chicago. He approached Friedman's classes with high expectations, yet he still found them "far more exciting than anything I had imagined."[3]

In 1963, Lucas was offered a faculty position at Carnegie Mellon University where he developed the ideas for his major paper "Expectations and the Neutrality of Money." It was published in 1972 by the *Journal of Economic Theory* and cited as a primary reason for his Nobel Prize twenty-three years later. Lucas' career at the University of Chicago resumed in 1974 when he returned to accept a position as the John Dewey Distinguished Service Professor.

Classical Revival

As Friedman's devoted student, Lucas adopted many of the same beliefs as his mentor. Both started with the classical concept that money was neutral, meaning that increases or decreases could not affect the real level of economic activity measured by production and employment. The idea could be traced at least as far back as philosopher David Hume in the eighteenth century. Hume wrote, "Where coin is in greater plenty, as a greater quantity of it is required to represent the same quantity of goods, it can have no effect, either good or bad...."[4] According to this theory, a doubling of money might double prices, but it was not supposed to boost employment.

This idea is an important element of classical theory called the *quantity theory of money*. Although elegant, it seems for the most part to be wrong. There are just too many counter examples in history when an increase in the money supply resulted in lower interest rates that stimulated economic activity. That didn't stop Robert Lucas; as a new classical economist, he simply believed in the quantity theory of money. He went one step further by assuming that everyone else in the economy believed likewise. He incorporated these ideas in his theory called *rational expectations* to show that whenever the Federal Reserve increased the money supply, everyone in the country knew that inflation would soon follow. While this idea was popular with other classical economists, it missed an important point: The quantity theory of money, on which it was based, did not seem to work in the real world.

My own economics professors at Berkeley in the 1970s were puzzled why anyone would resurrect classical theories that hadn't actually worked. Berkeley professors may have gotten that right, but Chicago got the Nobel Prize. Setting aside the fact that the theory was not necessarily correct, it also appears that Lucas may not have discovered it. Rational expectations was described as early as 1961 by John Muth in an article in *Econometrica*.[5]

One reason rational expectations was popular with Chicago School economists was that it sent a strong antigovernment message. If monetary policy does little more than cause inflation, as rational expectations claimed, then what good was it? Lucas was a free-market economist and cited his theory as a reason why government should refrain from attempting to use monetary policy to stabilize the economy.[6] In fact, it was reported in the *New York Times* that "Mr. Lucas helped lead a shift in the profession away from the government interventionist approach identified with John Maynard Keynes...."[7] While this might have shifted part of the profession in that direction, it had little effect on government policy. By 1995 when Lucas received his prize, the Federal Reserve was routinely adjusting the money supply and interest rates to direct overall economic activity, a practice that continues to this day.

In addition to his classical ideas, Lucas was strongly devoted to using mathematical models to describe economic ideas. Although Lucas borrowed ideas from David Hume, he was not impressed with Hume's expository style. Lucas complained that "this is just too difficult a problem for an economist equipped with only verbal methods, even someone of Hume's remarkable powers."[8] Lucas' original paper on rational expectations was rejected by the major economic journal, *The American Economic Review*, because it was too mathematical. Lucas responded by accusing the editor of a bias for simple articles or, in his words, "of trying to run *Newsweek*."[9] As he explained, "Progress in economic thinking means getting better and better abstract, analogue economic models, not better verbal observations about the world."[10]

Lucas' acclaimed 1972 article is a good example of how difficult it is to apply highly abstract mathematical models to the real economy. He basically constructed equations to represent a population split into two generations, young and old, assigned to two separate islands. In one scenario, no one knows how many young people (workers) there are on each island and they also do not know how much the money supply increased. He assumed that young people will work more if prices rise unless the price rise is caused by more money.[11] Confusion arises when prices rise but people are not sure why. On the basis of this abstract model, Lucas argued that the Federal Reserve should not use monetary policy to rescue a weak economy. It's a little like building castles in the sky and expecting them to play a role in national defense.

The Nobel committee is often guilty of exaggerating the contribution of prize winners, as for example when they claimed that "Robert Lucas is the social scientist who has had the greatest influence on macroeconomic research since 1970." They went on to claim that Lucas' research demonstrated "that employment could definitely not be permanently increased by allowing inflation to rise." In fact Lucas did demonstrate this but only for an imaginary world comprised of two generations living on two islands. Any similarity to the real world would be almost coincidental.

By the time he won the Nobel Prize in 1995, the value of Lucas' contribution might have already reached its high point. He is mostly remembered for his strong conservative opposition to government intervention in the economy and strong professional support for developing new macro models based on microeconomics and mathematics.

Edward C. Prescott (2004 Prize Winner)

Behind most government regulations there is usually a well-intended purpose. Consider the rules about building on flood plains. Despite the obvious risk involved in building houses in potentially dangerous areas, given the opportunity, there will almost always be someone willing to take the risk. And just as predictably, when devastation inevitably comes, you can expect an appeal for government disaster relief. For these reasons, it is usually good public policy to prohibit people from building houses on flood plains in the first place.

Regulations, even this one, are not generally very popular with free-market economists. A free-market approach would allow anyone to build anywhere they choose but make it very clear that the government will not, under any circumstance, bailout victims of inevitable natural disasters. The economists who won the 2004 Nobel Prize endorsed this approach but took it one step further in a paper published in 1977. According to Edward Prescott and Finn Kydland, the government had to do more than state the policy, they actually had to follow it. Otherwise, builders would second guess the government, bet on a bailout, and build in dangerous places.

According to Prescott and Kydland, there is sometimes a good reason why builders second guess the government. In some cases, after the flood has occurred, the best public policy may be to bail out the flood victims. Builders may bet on government being rational after the flood and discount anything said in advance. This makes it particularly difficult for the government to be convincing when it claims to have no intention of bailing out anyone. Prescott and Kydland refer to this dilemma as the *time inconsistency problem*, and the fact that they identified this problem was cited as one of the reasons for their Nobel Prize.

Prescott and Kydland also applied the same concept to fighting inflation. Assuming that the government knows how to control inflation, it will need to convince the public that it is serious about eliminating inflation. Once again the government faces a credibility problem. If government officials are not entirely convincing, they could foster inflationary expectations that actually produce real inflation. The solution, according to Prescott and Kydland, was for the government to adopt a strict rule fixing the rate of increase in the money supply and stick to it at all cost. They thought that this would overcome the credibility problem and successfully contain inflation. According to Prescott, "All that can be hoped for is to follow a good rule, and this requires economic and political institutions that sustain this rule."[12]

This was a clever way to bring classical economics back into economic policy. A fixed rule about the money supply had already been proposed by Milton Friedman and Robert Lucas who derived it from the quantity theory of money. At least this part wasn't new. Kydland and Prescott's contribution was to claim that the only way to convince people that the government would stick to a fixed rule was to, well … stick to the rule. For this, they won Nobel Prizes.

When Milton Friedman won his Nobel Prize in 1976, the Federal Reserve had not yet tested his proposal for a fixed increase in the money supply. At that time, there was still an academic debate over the merits of the theory. But the Federal Reserve actually tested this idea in the early 1980s with dramatic results. The fixed increase in the money supply in 1982 helped usher in the highest unemployment rate since the Great Depression and the economy only began to improve after the fixed rule was abandoned.[13] Was the Nobel committee really unaware that that the fixed rule had failed so decisively with such immense cost to the U.S. economy? They seem to have missed this because they awarded Lucas, Kydland, and Prescott Nobel Prizes for this idea many years after it had failed a real live test.

Whether or not the fixed rule for monetary policy was a good idea, it found considerable support from free-market economists. The idea also found supporters in the U.S. Federal Reserve system, and that support spread to other central banks around the world. There is a certain amount of risk involved in a fixed money policy if it ties the hands of central bankers. When a country is confronted with a deep recession, widespread bankruptcies, an international liquidity crisis, or an exchange rate crisis, should it really wait and see what happens, or should the national bank be allowed to consider the full range of its policy options?

Following fixed rules is not always a bad idea. There are examples where government policies are successful because they are consistent and credible. The best example is patent protection. In order to encourage innovation and invention, the U.S. government allows a patent holder to retain exclusive rights to an invention for seventeen years. But once an invention exists, like a new drug to treat cancer, there is usually a strong interest in seeing more competition to bring prices down. In fact, once the invention exists, a popular social policy may be to violate the patent and allow anyone to produce it. But if that were to happen, investment in future inventions might be stifled. This is another example of the time inconsistency problem. The solution in this case is for the government to stick to its rule, no matter what. As the patent example illustrates, this is neither a new problem nor a new solution. When it comes to patents, that is simply what the government has done for over 200 years.

Rewriting History

Irving Fisher, a Yale economist, was perhaps one of the most visible symbols of the failure of classical economics. Fisher offered the ill-timed observation on October 15, 1929, "I expect to see the stock market a good deal higher than it is today within a few months."[14] With this quote Fisher established himself as a symbol of how far removed economics was from the real world. The stock market crash and the ensuing downward spiral commenced only nine days later. The economist John Kenneth Galbraith commented on this spectacular error in his book, *The Great Crash, 1929*. Galbraith explained that "One problem with being wrong is that it robs the prophet of his audience when he most needs it to explain why."[15]

In 2004, Nobel laureate Prescott wrote an article with Ellen McGrattan that attempted to restore Fisher's reputation. In their article, Prescott and McGrattan applied modern microeconomic analysis to determine whether the market really was overvalued before the 1929 crash. The authors concluded, "with regard to the value of the 1929 stock market, Irving Fisher was right."[16] The conclusion was based on complicated assumptions and calculations that showed U.S. stocks were selling for less than the actual value of corporations in 1929.[17] Theoretically, you could have bought stocks before the crash, sold all the companies' real assets, and made a tidy profit.

If Irving Fisher was right and the market was not overvalued in 1929, then who was wrong? Well, that would have to be the vast majority of investors who proceeded to sell stocks for the next three years. Prescott and McGrattan, like Fisher before them, believed that microeconomics gave them special insight into the true value of the stock market that even the market didn't fully comprehend.

By claiming that the entire market was wrong, Prescott contradicted another theory that was popular with free-market economists – the efficient market hypothesis. According to this hypothesis, the market accurately incorporates all known information and is the best measure of future profitability. But according to Prescott, the market made a spectacular mistake in October 1929. He seems to conclude that free markets didn't work.

One problem with Prescott's analysis was that it ignored the fact that the stock market is supposed to be forward looking, not focused on the past or the present. By this standard it was appropriate for the stock market to crash in 1929 because it properly anticipated a massive fall in corporate profits. The only mistake seems to have been the extraordinary rise in stock prices just preceding the crash.

Prescott and McGrattan probably didn't pick the best model for their analysis. They used microeconomics, based on certainty and rationality, to analyze the stock market that is better characterized by uncertainty and occasional irrationality. Even Prescott realized that his analysis fell short when he conceded, "The excessive volatility of stock prices remains. Indeed our study strengthens this puzzle...."[18] But he wasn't worried about this puzzle because he fully expected "this volatility puzzle will, in the not too distant future, be resolved by some imaginative neoclassical economist."[19]

Real Business Cycles

One of the most conspicuous failures of neoclassical economics has been its inability to account for business cycles. Prescott and Kydland thought they found an answer. They tried to explain most, if not all, business cycles by a random variable that they attributed to changes in productivity. If productivity spontaneously accelerated and then slowed, it could cause the economy to trace out a pattern that looked something like a business cycle. The rest of their model was purely neoclassical, so much so that there was no unemployment in it.[20] A business cycle without unemployment was a very strange innovation but it was the primary reason Prescott and Kydland won Nobel Prizes.

Prescott himself called this approach "a revolution in macroeconomics."[21] As he explained during his Nobel banquet speech, "One of the great joys of research – whether it be in economics, physics, chemistry or any academic discipline – is the act of discovery, those moments when we are surprised by what we have found.... After the initial shock we [Prescott and Kydland] humbly said, 'yes Master,' and we promptly changed our views."[22]

By simply grafting microeconomics onto their *real business cycle theory*, Prescott and Kydland precluded even the possibility of unemployment. This point was clear to Sergio Rebelo, an economist at Northwestern University, who noted that "Most [real] business cycle models adopt a rudimentary description of the labor market. Firms hire workers in competitive spot labor markets and there is no unemployment."[23] Another reviewer noted that the early models, like Prescott and Kydland's, enjoyed limited success because they "had no market imperfections, nor government intervention."[24] Because this model didn't even try to explain real economic conditions, Gregory Mankiw found that "the real business cycle model was not terribly interesting."[25]

According to the real business cycle theory, people don't work less because they are fired or laid off; they work less because wages are too low and leisure looks like a better option. Amazingly, this is the same argument that classical economists tried to make in the 1930s without much success. All this was too much for some economists. Paul Samuelson was quoted as questioning the wisdom of applying this theory to the Great Depression "where at one time in 1929, folks everywhere developed a desire to substitute leisure for good paychecks."[26]

This again looked like a case where the desire to promote free markets was more important than building credible economic models. It was difficult for Prescott to restrain his enthusiasm for free markets. Shortly after receiving his Nobel Prize he announced, "I don't like decentralized market mechanisms, I love them."[27] Could this passion interfere with his unbiased investigation into economic science?

There was something else odd about the real business cycle model; there was no attempt to see how well it explained past events or predicted future ones. Prescott saw no reason to test the model because it was based on neoclassical theory that he believed everyone should simply accept as revealed truth. A frustrated reviewer, James Hartley, asked the obvious question, "if one is not genetically disposed to placing confidence in real business cycle theory, what should convince one of its usefulness?"[28]

In defense of this approach, Prescott explained, "The neoclassical growth model is tested theory" and therefore doesn't require any further testing.[29] Why should he worry about testing an economic theory that he was already certain was correct? As he said in his Nobel lecture, "Macroeconomics has progressed beyond the stage of searching for a theory to the stage of deriving the implications of theory. In this way, macroeconomics has become like the natural sciences."[30]

Not all economists were persuaded by these arguments. Robert Gordon, an economist at Northwestern University, stated that "I am not alone in feeling that the Kydland-Prescott model of business cycles was a significant step backward."[31] Equally unimpressed with this model in particular and macro models in general was British economist Paul Ormerod who claimed, "It's not clear that we understand that much more about macroeconomics than we did 30 years ago."[32] Lawrence Summers, economist and past president of Harvard University, voiced his skepticism: "I, like many others, find their particular theories [about business cycles] implausible."[33] But while Summers didn't believe their theories, he did like their method and thought that Prescott and Kydland richly deserved the prize on that basis alone.[34]

Many advocacy groups appreciate and seek support from Nobel Prize winners, and Prescott lent his name to several conservative causes. He supported private savings accounts as an alternative to Social Security and claimed, "The beauty of individual savings accounts is that each person decides how his money will be invested ... He can then monitor these investments at any time and easily change to react to changing investment news."[35] John Havelock, a columnist in Anchorage, Alaska, responded facetiously, "Sure, like each person was in 1929."[36] Havelock is to be excused if he was unaware that Prescott had already studied the stock market crash in 1929 and proven that it was a mistake.

Endorsements from Nobel Prize winners are especially sought by presidential candidates. Prescott took the high ground when talking to the press after his Nobel award and insisted that an economist should resist political endorsements and stick to policy. But earlier he had signed a letter along with 367 other economists including five other Nobel Prize winners in opposition to Senator John Kerry's economic policies. When asked later to reconcile the two statements he explained that a criticism of one candidate was not necessarily an endorsement of the other.[37]

Edward Prescott attended Swarthmore College where he played on the football team and majored in physics, at least until his senior year when he switched to mathematics because his honors physics program was not theoretical enough for him. He particularly enjoyed microeconomics because it reminded him of conversations with his father about how businesses operated. Swarthmore also cured Prescott of what he called his "socialistic leanings." He found "nearly all" the other students too "idealogical [sic] to carry on an intellectual discussion," and too quick to memorize rather than think.[38] "How anyone could defend the killing of tens of millions by Stalin and Mao," he lamented, "was (and is) beyond me."[39]

Prescott was not trained as an economist. Instead he advanced his statistical and mathematical skills with a master's degree in operations research and a doctorate in a multidisciplinary program at Carnegie Mellon University.[40] Although he did not take many economics courses, he took one in growth theory and another in capital theory from Robert Lucas who became a lifelong friend and collaborator. Prescott was aware that his educational background was primarily in statistics and mathematics, but he claimed that after writing a paper with Robert Lucas in 1969 he became an economist![41]

One of Prescott's first positions was at the University of Pennsylvania where he enjoyed his colleagues but worried that he might not be granted tenure. Rather than wait for a decision, he accepted an offer to return to Carnegie Mellon where he met a graduate student, Finn Kydland, who would be his co-author on the two articles cited by the Nobel committee. This collaboration led Prescott to the insight that "Macro policy is a game, not a control problem as we had thought."[42]

In 1980 Prescott accepted a position at the University of Minnesota and began an association with the Federal Reserve Bank of Minneapolis a year later. The economics department at Minnesota decided to apply the free-market philosophy that they espoused by having no required courses. Students were the customers who should know what they needed to learn, and graduate courses lived or died by their enrollment. This lasted for many years but came to an end when "One group could not attract students."[43] On top of this, the University dramatically reduced the size of the economics department. Prescott looked elsewhere and found a position at the University of Chicago in 1998, which suited him just fine. He had always considered himself to be "more a Chicagoan than a Minnesotan" and observed that "In the single year I was there ... I detected a rise in student morale."[44] He embraced the opportunity to work with Chicago Nobel Prize winners Robert Lucas, Gary Becker, and James Heckman, but inexplicably left Chicago after a year and returned to Minnesota.

In 2003 Prescott took a job at Arizona State University in Tempe while continuing his affiliation with the Minnesota Federal Reserve. One year later he received the Nobel Prize, the first time it was awarded to an economist working for the Federal Reserve or, for that matter, Arizona State.[45] Prescott's Nobel did not come as a great surprise to the profession. By 2004, the market created by economists to predict the future, including Nobel Prizes, was fully operational and he was the clear front runner. Only days before the announcement, Prescott's stock was leading the pack, trading at $63.35. But the market was less successful at identifying the other 2004 winner. Robert Barro was in second place in the market but Finn Kydland ended up as Prescott's co-winner. Markets may be good but they are seldom perfect. Besides, someone suggested, a few mistakes may be useful if it suppresses the gossip about potential insider trading.[46]

Finn E. Kydland (2004 Prize Winner)

What is the purpose of economic model building? Robert Lucas suggested "One of the functions of theoretical economics is to provide fully articulated, artificial economic systems that can serve as laboratories in which policies that would be prohibitively expensive to experiment with in actual economies can be tested at a much lower cost...."[47] One of his students at Carnegie Mellon, Finn Kydland, echoed this sentiment when he described the purpose of his Nobel Prize–winning model building – to create "a framework in which we can evaluate economic policy." Of course such an exercise only works when the model is an accurate representation of the economy.

In addition to his joint work with Prescott that was cited by the Nobel committee, Kydland also studied the performance of the economy of Argentina from 1980 to 2003, and described this work in his Nobel lecture.[48] During the first part of this period, from 1980 until 1990, Argentina suffered such a severe recession that Kydland referred to it as a great depression. This was followed by a dramatic expansion in the 1990s that ended abruptly in another sharp collapse after 1998. All of this represented an interesting period in Argentina's history and suggested some obvious research questions. But Kydland skipped the obvious questions and instead asked why investment wasn't even higher during the brief economic boom since his model "indicated that investment should have been much greater in the 1990s."[49]

The answer, according to Kydland, is "that Argentina still lacked the necessary credibility." Despite all the efforts of former President Carlos Menem, investors simply didn't believe that the threat of defaults and government takeovers had been sufficiently removed to begin investing again in the economy. As Kydland said, "Once credibility has been lost, economists don't know much about how to restore it."[50] Kydland argued that it is not enough to have pro-market policies in place now; you must have had them in place in the past as well. Kydland didn't provide any actual evidence for this idea but suggested that "This conjecture needs to be investigated more rigorously...."[51]

The primary reason for Kydland's Nobel Prize was his collaboration with Edward Prescott in developing the real business cycle model. In order to derive a result that looked like a business cycle, they invented the idea that there were random fluctuations in productivity. When asked to identify specific productivity shocks, Prescott declined, explaining that it was really "the result of the sum of many random causes."[52] One critic thought that this explanation was no better than the one offered by William Stanley Jevons who blamed business cycles on sunspots.[53]

The Nobel Prize in economics has been criticized for honoring theories many years after they were first proposed. In the case of Prescott and Kydland, the honor came twenty-two to twenty-seven years after their most famous articles were written. Why is this so? The conventional answer is that it takes that much time to judge the popularity and influence of the theories. Only if theories inspire new research, create a new field within economics, or influence economic policy are they worthy of a Nobel.

There was nothing in his early background that would have indicated that Finn Kydland was headed for a successful academic career, much less a Nobel Prize. His father avoided taking over the family farm in Norway by buying a truck and hauling agricultural products for local farmers, and his mother worked at home, raising six children. Kydland's rural elementary school combined several grade levels into one class and then only met two or three times a week. None of the students, with the exception of Kydland, went to school beyond the elementary grades. Kydland, however, was a quick study and caught up rapidly in high school and college. In retrospect he thought that a leisurely early education followed by a more intense high school program might actually be an ideal educational strategy.

Although he won the 2004 Nobel Prize in economics, initially Kydland really wasn't that interested in economics. When a professor at the Norwegian School of Economics and Business Administration asked him to become his research assistant, he admitted that "I had not shown any more interest in the economics classes than in business."[54] What really interested him in high school and college were the advanced classes in mathematics and operations research.

After Kydland had completed four years of college, his major professor was hired by Carnegie Mellon University for one year and invited him along. In 1969, Kydland left Norway and enrolled in a doctoral program at Carnegie Mellon where Robert Lucas taught a course in economic fluctuations. Lucas used the class as a venue to develop his Nobel idea about rational expectations, as Kydland gushed, "right there in front of our eyes."[55] But it was his association with a new professor, Edward Prescott, that marked the beginning of a very rewarding collaboration. Together they wrote the two papers about sticking to rules and real business cycles that earned them Nobel Prizes.

In 1973, after four years at Carnegie Mellon, Kydland earned his doctorate degree and took a series of jobs, including work for the Federal Reserve banks in Cleveland and Dallas, before accepting a chair at the University of

California, Santa Barbara. In 2004 he received his Nobel Prize. One of the most enthusiastic endorsements of his Nobel award came from University of Chicago economist, Robert Lucas. "I'm still high. It's a great event," Lucas was quoted as saying in the journal *Science*, "These are great economists."[56]

Edmund S. Phelps (2006 Prize Winner)

The betting pool for economic Nobel Prizes doesn't claim to have a perfect record but top performers in the pool often win eventually. David Romer, an economist at Berkeley and founder of the pool, explained, "Almost everyone who's done extremely well in the pool has gotten the prize."[57] And so it was for Edmund S. Phelps who won in 2006, three years after the pool selected him to win. No one seemed to doubt that Edmund Phelps was a serious contender for the prize. As Robert Solow said, "Ned Phelps was clearly on everybody's short list to win a Nobel."[58]

Phelps was recognized for work that was not necessarily unique or original. He was recognized for "deepening our understanding...." and having "a decisive impact on economic research as well as policy."[59] His macro model strongly resembled one developed by Milton Friedman. They both challenged Keynesian theory by assuming that unemployment was constant over the long run, a rate that became known as the *natural rate of unemployment*. And like Friedman, Phelps devised a model that attributed deviations from the natural rate of unemployment to mistakes made by businesses and workers based on false expectations. In fact it is hard to see that Phelps added much to this theory other than to make it more mathematical and therefore more interesting to microeconomists.[60]

While Phelps' theory was debated in the 1970s, academic interest languished when historical events created problems for his theory. Europe slid into a major slump during the 1980s and no one could identify a false expectation that could have caused it. Alternatively, the United States experienced a major expansion in the 1990s with no apparent role for expectations.[61] If mistaken expectations ever had any real effect they seem to have quickly run their course. According to Robert Solow, "For me there was really only one short period, in the 1970s, when this theory really worked."[62]

There was an important policy implication of this theory, however. If unemployment really is fixed at a natural rate then there is no reason for the government to try to reduce it. As Phelps explained, "The 'natural unemployment rate' leaves people with the idea that there is no hope. It is an act of nature that cannot be repealed by man."[63] The ultimate purpose of devising these models was to discourage government action even when confronted with rising unemployment. For this reason, Jared Bernstein of the Economic Policy Institute concluded that "At this point, the concept does more harm to the country than good."[64]

In the process of studying the operation of a labor market, Phelps described a new idea that would later be called *efficiency wages*. In Phelps' model, firms have options about what wage to offer. They can offer the market wage or, if they want to attract a better workforce that works harder and quits less frequently, they can pay above market wages. When firms pay more than the market rate, they have the additional benefit of being able to hire as many workers as they want.[65]

In announcing the Nobel Prize in 2006, the Swedish committee recognized Phelps for more than just his work on unemployment and inflation. Like many of his generation, Phelps was drawn to the problem of determining the optimum savings rate for a country. The problem was to derive the rate that would maximize consumption per person over time. The proof of this golden rule is relatively simple, so simple that the Royal Academy includes it in a short footnote in the essay describing Phelps' contributions.[66] Unfortunately, neither Phelps nor his other American colleagues were the first to derive this result.[67] Nobel laureate Maurice Allais apparently discovered the golden rule in 1947, well before it was rediscovered by others in the 1960s.[68]

Phelps also took an interest in applying microeconomics to a variety of topics including human capital, discrimination, and monopoly power.[69] For example, he pointed out that increases in economic activity were not only dependent on *increases* in human capital, they were also dependent on the *total stock* of human capital. His point seemed to be an obvious one: An economy with a more skilled and educated workforce can more fully exploit new technological advances.[70]

Phelps was an unusually strong advocate for population growth. According to Phelps, "If I could re-do the history of the world, halving population size each year from the beginning of time on some random basis, I would not do it...."[71] He believed that large populations were necessary to generate the ideas and innovations that have fueled economic growth. Smaller populations risk losing particular individuals who make important discoveries or contributions.[72] "One can only imagine," he wrote, "how poor we would be today were it not for the rapid population growth of the past to which we owe the enormous number of technological advances enjoyed today...."[73]

Phelps also studied discrimination and observed that this can occur when firms apply group averages to individuals. The reason they do this is usually because detailed information about the individual is unavailable. The result is what economists call *statistical discrimination*, developed about the same time by Nobel laureate Kenneth Arrow.[74] Even if applying group averages is unfair to individuals, Phelps proved that it was theoretically efficient for the economy.

Phelps was not impressed by the performance of European economies. The problem, as he saw it, was that Europeans lacked market-oriented values. According to Phelps, "Surveys tell us that fewer French, Italians or Germans than Americans or Britons look for mental challenge, problem-solving, initiative and responsibility in their work.... All these qualities are directly relevant to economic dynamism and innovation...."[75] The result, according to Phelps, is that European economies have relatively high unemployment, low labor force participation rates, and relatively low job satisfaction.[76]

These criticisms resonated with the critics of European economies but sparked a response from some Europeans.[77] Dutch author Donald Kalff thought that the success of the American economy was overrated and mismeasured, and even if partly true, was only a recent phenomenon. He also argued that the large trade surpluses that Europe enjoyed with the United States, even with a strong Euro, contradicted the myth of a vastly superior American economy.[78]

Not all of Phelps' ideas, however, were conservative. In an interview with the *Wall Street Journal* shortly after winning the Nobel Prize, Phelps confessed, "I have the eccentric view that there's too much wealth sloshing around the American economy."[79] The problem is that "This wealth has bad incentive effects on the supply of labor, employee performance and maybe innovation. We have become wealthy thanks in part to unsustainably low tax rates."[80] This rebuke to supply-side economics came as a shock to the *Wall Street Journal*. According to Phelps, some people are becoming so rich that they are losing their incentive to work and innovate. Based on this idea, Phelps supported higher taxes for wealthy individuals. His scheme would raise total taxes on high-income earners.[81] Perhaps in a gesture to appear even-handed, Phelps also said he would raise taxes on lower income individuals. This combination of conservative and liberal policies motivated David Henderson from the Hoover Institute at Stanford to proclaim that "Edmund S. Phelps is difficult to categorize politically."[82]

Besides supporting higher taxes, Phelps committed one more conservative heresy – he supported large subsidies for businesses to hire more workers. In 1997 he wrote a book in which he advocated a "vast subsidy program that would have cost $125 billion in 1997 dollars, a whopping 1.5 percent of that year's GDP."[83] It would work like the Earned Income

Tax Credit (EITC), which augments the earnings of low-income families. Phelps called the EITC "a step in the same direction, but it's aimed toward low-wage parents."[84] Phelps' proposal was broader, open to nonparents, and implemented through businesses. As he explained, "The resulting increase in the demand for those workers would pull up their employment and ultimately give a big boost to their paychecks."[85]

Edmund Phelps' father asked his son for a favor when he was still an undergraduate at Amherst College: Would he please take a class in economics? He did and he loved it; Paul Samuelson became his idol, and economics became his major.[86] From Amherst he continued his studies in the graduate program at Yale University and earned his doctorate in 1959.[87] Phelps took a position at Columbia University in 1971 and was still there in 2006 when he won the Nobel Prize at age 73.[88]

For thirty-two years Phelps and his wife rented an apartment in a New York City overlooking Central Park. As his wife explained, "We never had enough money to buy an apartment as large and as comfortable as the one we live in and the rent for this one is relatively low."[89] The $1.37 million award that accompanied the Nobel Prize that year gave them more options.

NINE

Inventors

Simon S. Kuznets (1971)

Sir J. Richard N. Stone (1984)

Wassily W. Leontief (1973)

Leonid V. Kantorovich (1975)

Tjalling C. Koopmans (1975)

There may have been only three Russian Nobel winners in economics, but their contributions have been substantial on three critical concepts: *gross domestic product, input-output analysis,* and *linear programming.* Two of these important tools were developed in the 1930s by Nobel Prize winners from Harvard University. The first, Simon S. Kuznets, developed the United States' system of national income accounts that included the familiar measure of economic performance, gross domestic product. Without this widely used measure, we would have very little understanding of how well the economy is performing or how fast it is growing. Other economists made contributions to this effort, including the English Nobel laureate Sir Richard Stone, but it was Kuznets who provided the grand design. The second Russian Nobel Prize winner was Wassily W. Leontief who invented one of the premier economic planning tools called input-output analysis. First devised in the 1930s, input-output models continue to be used throughout the world to provide answers to interesting and important economic questions.

These two Nobel economists had something else in common; they were both obsessed by economic data. Kuznets started his investigations by collecting information about economic performance for the U.S. economy in order to track the important but poorly understood business cycles. All of this information had to be collected, categorized, and analyzed. Similarly, Leontief started with the tedious task of collecting information about interindustry sales, that is, the sales of one industry to another, and ultimately to consumers. It was only after collecting data and searching for meaning in the information that they were able to invent something useful.

This approach to economics is surprisingly unique. Adam Smith and John Maynard Keynes certainly observed patterns in the economy and proceeded to develop theories based on those patterns. Their followers and many other Nobel Prize winners presented in this book simply elaborated on those theories, translated them into mathematical formulas, and left it to others to consider how relevant all of this was to the real world. Kuznets and Leontief were different; they started with data.

There was a third, lesser-known Russian Nobel laureate who was also preoccupied with practical questions and data. Faced with the overwhelming task of planning an entire economy, Leonid V. Kantorovich invented an early form of *linear programming* that allowed Russian planners to make sense out of an otherwise bewildering array of information. Linear programming is an analytical method that is indispensable for solving a certain type of problem that shows up frequently in economics, business, and engineering.

The one qualification to this achievement is that Kantorovich's invention, although important in the Soviet Union, had little impact on the rest of the world. Because of the self-imposed isolation of the Soviet Union, his discovery in the 1930s was not initially known to the Western world. Confronted with similar problems, other researchers independently invented linear programming in the United States and improved upon it. Tjalling C. Koopmans, a Nobel laureate honored for promoting the development of linear programming in the United States and Europe, was one of those who rediscovered Kantorovich's prior work.

Simon S. Kuznets (1971 Prize Winner)

One of the most familiar measures in economics is gross domestic product (GDP) or, as its predecessor was known, gross national product (GNP). As any investor knows, announcements about GDP are closely watched on Wall Street and other financial markets. An unexpected change in GDP can move markets around the world by billions of dollars. Since its original development under the direction of Simon Kuznets, it has become one of our most comprehensive and most closely watched measures of economic performance.

Kuznets was a meticulous and prodigious data collector who happened to be in the right place at the right time. He was a graduate student in economics in the 1920s at Columbia University when he met Professor Wesley Clair Mitchell, the director of the National Bureau of Economic Research (NBER). At the time, Mitchell was pursuing his own obsession, tracking business cycles, and he sought out bright young researchers like Kuznets to help him solve this mystery. It didn't take Mitchell long to recognize a talent for data collection, and he invited Kuznets to join his research staff in 1927.

Collecting and tallying detailed economic data from many sources may have been an obscure and routine academic exercise in 1927, but it suddenly rose to a national priority in 1929 as the U.S. economy collapsed into the Great Depression. How could economists begin to understand the crisis, much less determine how to solve it, if they couldn't even measure it?

Senator Robert LaFollette of Wisconsin had an answer. He initiated a resolution in the U.S. Senate in June of 1932 directing "the new Secretary of Commerce to provide national income estimates for 1929, 1930, and 1931," the first three years of the Depression.[1] The Secretary of Commerce, Daniel Roper, recognized that he lacked the necessary expertise in his department and contacted Wesley Mitchell at Columbia for help. Mitchell had one particularly good suggestion; he advised Roper to contact Kuznets who was then teaching economics at the University of Pennsylvania. Kuznets had done some cutting edge work on measuring production and prices for his dissertation at Columbia and was more than willing to advise on the development of a system of national income accounts. He also recommended two of his own students, Robert Nathan and Milton Gilbert, to head up the project.

The resulting national income accounts created by Nathan and Gilbert with Kuznets' guidance were developed in the 1930s and further refined over the next two decades. The basic characteristics of the resulting measures have remained largely unchanged since then, with the exception that GNP (counting production by U.S. companies anywhere) was gradually replaced by GDP (counting production within U.S. borders). Otherwise the approach is basically the same, measuring gross production and assigning it to one of four categories: consumption, investment, government, and net exports.

Collecting all these data for an entire economy is an enormous amount of work, but determining what to count was the challenge facing Kuznets. Suppose for example, an iron company sells $1 million of iron to a steel company that in turn sells $3 million of steel to a car company that then sells $6 million worth of cars to consumers. If you simply add up the value of sales by each company as a measure of gross economic activity ($10 million), you would have an inflated view of the economy. The $3 million of steel sold already includes the $1 million of iron, and so iron is double counted. In fact the proper amount of economic activity in this case is simply the *final* car sales ($6 million). This is the fundamental principle that underlies the national income accounts. In practice the same answer can be found by adding up what economists call the *value added* at every stage of production, which is defined as sales minus material costs.[2]

This is just one example of the painstaking logic and careful thought that was needed to construct a national income account. As well, there were hundreds of other important issues that needed to be resolved. For example, should you count land sales as part of GDP? Should you count sales for both new and existing houses? Should you count inventories or just changes in inventories? All of these issues had to be addressed consistently and logically. Kuznets insisted that there was not necessarily a single "correct" answer to these questions because the answer always depended on one's purpose. The purpose of our national income accounts, largely thanks to Kuznets, is to measure total annual production as represented by final spending on goods and services.

Any measure of economic activity will have its critics. A unique criticism was published in the *Wall Street Journal* in 2001 by economist Mark Skousen.[3] He complained that by eliminating double counting, GDP overemphasized consumption spending and underemphasized business activity. He strongly endorsed adding up all business activity even though it would include a lot of double counting, which in any accounting system is a bad idea. Kuznets would no doubt have been amused by this proposal, as well as the fact that it found its way into the pages of the *Wall Street Journal* almost seventy years after he thought he had settled the issue.

Of course there are deficiencies in our national income statistics, some of which were specifically noted by Kuznets in his Nobel lecture in 1971. In particular, he noted that mass production during the industrial revolution showed up as a huge advance in production, while many of the negative impacts associated with pollution, exhaustion of natural resources, public health problems, and congested urban living were not reflected in these measures. Although economic growth had many positive impacts that were generally accounted for in national income statistics, Kuznets remained concerned about the consistent omission of the negative impacts. For the full picture you need more than GDP.

Since the Commerce Department first started reporting GDP in the 1930s, there have been many proposals to develop a broader measure of economic performance. One example is the "index of sustainable economic welfare" developed by economist Herman Daly and theologian John B. Cobb, Jr. They made a full range of adjustments to GDP by including some valuable nonmarket activity and excluding the production of economic "bads," the opposite of economic "goods." For example, Daly and Cobb included an estimate for the value of unpaid housework but deducted an estimate for environmental damage and natural resource depletion. Where GDP simply includes all government expenditures, they deducted the entire Pentagon budget because, while it may be necessary, it was not necessarily an economic "good." While Kuznets may not have gone as far as Daly and Cobb, he was on record supporting more balance in the national accounts. His influence on the development of the national income accounts was profound but it stopped short of making these types of changes.

In 1999, the Commerce Department celebrated its first century of existence. The Department's most significant accomplishment, according to Secretary William Daley, was the development of the national income accounts and GDP. It was interesting that this accomplishment ranked ahead of all the other important things that the Commerce Department does, such as issue patents, track hurricanes, and conduct national censuses. Without GDP, how would the Federal Reserve Bank know whether to raise or lower interest rates? How would the President and Congress know whether it was time to stimulate or slow down the economy? How would any of us know how well the country was doing economically? During this centennial celebration, Simon Kuznets was duly recognized for his principal contribution.[4]

Because of the importance of this great achievement, it could be possible to overlook Kuznets' many other important contributions to economics. He applied the same meticulous research method to these other projects, an approach that set him apart from other economists. Kuznets was not a typical economic theoretician writing mathematical formulas to represent human behavior, but neither was he a typical empirical economist estimating statistical equations and models. Instead, he was labeled an institutional economist because he was interested in real world economics.

As early as the 1920s, Kuznets collected information about consumption and savings behavior for U.S. households. In the process, he uncovered the fact that the national savings rate was remarkably stable over long periods of time. Despite all the other changes in the economy, the country seemed to save at a fairly constant rate. This was interesting to economists and helped to inform Keynes' ideas, which came some ten years later. Others were a little baffled by the relatively constant savings rate and for good reason. It was well known that rich families save a lot more than poor families, and so economists wondered why the country didn't save more as it became richer. As a testament to his credibility, Kuznets' empirical findings were taken as fact by many economists who set out to reconcile this conflict. Two of them, Franco Modigliani and Milton Friedman, also won Nobel Prizes, in part for their ideas about how to account for the surprisingly stable savings rate.

In his other work, Kuznets focused on the causes and characteristics of modern economic growth. He was among the earliest researchers to conclude, contrary to prevailing belief, that most modern growth was not due to more equipment and larger factories. After carefully considering the data, Kuznets concluded that modern growth far exceeded what could be accounted for by mere increases in the amount of capital or the amount of labor. The key factor was an increase in technology and the ability of an educated labor force to implement it. Kuznets helped the profession to focus on the importance of technology as the primary source of economic growth. This important finding led to yet another question: Since most modern technology, once it is discovered, is available to all countries, why don't all countries enjoy comparable economic growth? According to Kuznets, the missing ingredient was the right alignment of institutions – laws, enforcement, and government – required to exploit the technology successfully. Although these institutions may be critical for economic growth, it is not a topic that economists have traditionally pursued. They typically leave that topic for other social scientists.

Kuznets also studied changes in income distribution over time for a number of different countries. He came up with a simple observation: Income appeared to become increasingly unequal during the initial stages of modern development, but eventually became more equal in later stages of development.[5] According to economists Thomas Piketty and Emmanuel Saez, however, this simple pattern has not held up over time. Instead of more equality in the United States after 1970, they found a significant increase in inequality.[6] Rather than following a fixed pattern, as suggested by Kuznets, income distribution appears to respond to unique historical events. In the case of the United States, the dismantling of progressive taxes and the explosion of corporate salaries after 1970 led to greater inequality. But even in this case, Kuznets asked the right questions and initiated a valuable discussion.

While many economists had great respect for Kuznets and his work, the feeling was not always reciprocated. Bertil Ohlin of the Nobel Prize committee was being diplomatic when he said that Kuznets had "very limited sympathy for abstract and generalizing models." In fact, Kuznets had a strong negative opinion of abstract mathematical models. He had even less tolerance for theories based on concepts that could not even be observed, such as utility.[7]

Born in Russia in 1901, Simon Kuznets lived his youth in a country undergoing a major upheaval. His parents were both Jewish and his father was a skilled furrier.[8] Kuznets studied economics at the University of Kharkov until the Tsarist government collapsed during the October Revolution of 1917 and the university closed. He escaped from Russia in 1922 to join his father and brother in the United States where he finished his undergraduate degree at Columbia University's adult education program.[9] He earned a master's degree at Columbia in 1924 and a doctorate in 1926. After teaching most of his career at Harvard University, he retired in 1971, only three months before he was awarded the Nobel Prize in economics.[10]

Even the Nobel Prize did not make Kuznets the most famous person in his distinguished Cambridge neighborhood. Among his neighbors in the area of Francis Street were famed economist John Kenneth Galbraith, writer Daniel Bell, chef Julia Child, and author Arthur Schlesinger. It was the same neighborhood that once included poet E. E. Cummings and philosopher William James. With Kuznets' award, this neighborhood of celebrities also included a Nobel Prize winner in economics.

Colleagues praised Kuznets for his cultured sophistication and broad academic talents that embraced history, sociology, political theory, and mathematical statistics.[11] He would often inquire about the research of his fellow economists with his trademark question, "Have you found anything you didn't expect?"[12] If they had, then there was something to talk about. An interviewer asked him once why his students weren't more interested in business since it was a more lucrative career than academics. His answer reflected a unique view of human nature, at least for an economist. He said, "The passion for truth dulls acquisitiveness."[13] In 1985, at age eighty-four, Simon Kuznets died in his home in Cambridge.[14]

Sir J. Richard N. Stone (1984 Prize Winner)

Although some referred to Sir Richard Stone as the "father of national income accounting," it is a bit of an overstatement. The tracking of national economic performance has a long history, as Stone described in his Nobel lecture. The real systematic work of defining entries and collecting data for national accounts really got underway in the United States with Simon Kuznets. The first accounts in England were developed by A. L. Bowley and Colin Clark, and were further refined by Stone and James Meade, a 1984 Nobel Prize winner. The information was particularly important to John Maynard Keynes who was trying to track England's war effort from his position at the Treasury. Keynes was fascinated by the flood of important economic data and employed Stone as his assistant to organize the information. At one point Keynes was quoted as saying, "We are in a new era of joy through statistics."[15]

There was still much work to be done to develop a truly modern set of complete national income statistics. Stone's contribution was to help refine definitions, collect data, and devise techniques to estimate missing data. But his most important contribution was to promote the use of double-entry accounting in national systems. Double-entry bookkeeping is a valuable technique in business because it can be used to verify accounts. If one side of the ledger doesn't add up to the other side, then you have made a mistake. Double-entry, or balanced accounts, provide the same benefit for national income accounts. On the most general level, GDP should be equivalent to gross domestic income (GDI). By calculating each one separately, you can check the veracity of the numbers by comparing the totals. The same balance can be part of any national account as long as it is constructed in a particular way. Stone's contribution was to ensure that the systems were all constructed that same way.

The value of this concept can be illustrated with national exports and imports. If all trade balances are properly measured for all countries, then the sum of all balances should be equal to zero because one country's export (positive number) is another country's import (negative number). Adding them all together should equal zero. In practice, they seldom add up to zero, which means there is an error somewhere. The imbalance tells you how large the error is, but you still have to do some investigating to find its source.

Stone introduced a similar bookkeeping model to keep track of national demographic statistics. He used the simple principle that the change in any population statistic starts with an initial value, experiences inflows and outflows, and ends up with a final value. For instance, the initial number of retirees over age 65 in a country plus the inflows (from a birthday, retirement, or immigration) must equal the final number of retirees over 65 plus the outflows (from emigration, returning to work, or death). By constructing an entire demographic picture in these terms, it is possible to double check the numbers by ensuring that they add up. This construction also lends itself to more sophisticated mathematical manipulations that begin to resemble Leontief's input-output tables.

All of this seems fairly simple today. The secretary of the Nobel award committee, Ragnar Bentzel, admitted as much. "The system has become accepted as so self-evident that it is hard to realize that someone had to invent it." Even if Stone wasn't the only one thinking about a balanced national account, he was a strong advocate for its adoption and his version became the standard.

While most Nobel Prize winners in economics are not well known to the wider public, the 1984 winner was probably not well known even to economists, at least outside the field of national income accounts. Because his contribution was primarily applied in Britain and in the United Nations, "American economists expressed mild surprise at Sir Richard's selection."[16] Stone was himself surprised, although he expressed it in a uniquely British vernacular. As he put it, "One is always surprised that things like this happen to oneself."[17]

Although he showed some talent for medicine and the law, which his father encouraged, Stone switched to economics after two years as an undergraduate at Cambridge University. Like many future Keynesians attending school in the 1930s, he was attracted to economics because he believed it held the answers to the Great Depression. He studied under Richard Kahn, a member of Keynes' inner circle, at a time when Keynesian economics was still very much evolving.

Upon graduation in 1935, Stone passed up a research position at Cambridge for fear that he lacked sufficient background. Instead he took a position with Lloyds brokers in London and briefly tried the insurance business, for which he concluded he was not well suited. During that time, he edited a small summary of industry and national statistics for an industry trade publication. This assignment exposed him to economic statistics as they existed then, and also opened doors for him professionally. He was offered a position at the Ministry of Economic Warfare in 1939, which was staffing up in preparation for war. He immediately began to work on national economic statistics with future Nobel laureate James Meade and came under the supervision of Keynes. The United States and Canada had more-developed national accounts than England at the time, and so Stone's assignment was essentially to help Europe catch up.

At the end of the war, a new department was created at Cambridge for Applied Economics and Stone was chosen as the first director. In 1955 Stone gave up the directorship to become a Cambridge professor, working there until his retirement in 1980. His departure did not so much end his work as relocate it to his home, which he much preferred. In fact, he once said that his favorite pastime was "staying at home." When reporters tried to reach him in October of 1984 after the announcement of his Nobel Prize, it was one of those rare moments that he wasn't there.

Wassily W. Leontief (1973 Prize Winner)

Input-output analysis is widely recognized as one of the premier economic planning tools. It has the versatility to address a broad range of economic questions and works equally well for capitalist or socialist economies. The man who invented it, Wassily Leontief, believed that input-output models could contribute to better public policy and dedicated most of his career, including forty-four years at Harvard University, to refining and promoting them.

While Leontief received much recognition during his lifetime, as well as the satisfaction of seeing his model used throughout the world, it was not always easy to sell it to the economics profession. Many economists were inclined to believe that economic planning was a waste of time or perhaps even subversive. The antiplanning sentiment was particularly strong in the United States, one of the least-planned economies in the world. This placed Leontief in an uphill battle for most of his academic life. Input-output analysis was, however, more than a planning tool and had so many useful applications that it eventually prevailed despite its detractors. It continues to be commonly used by economists today to answer practical but difficult questions. Few economists were surprised when Leontief won the Nobel Prize in 1973.

Leontief was born in 1906 in St. Petersburg, renamed Leningrad after the revolution of 1917. Although he was only a child he could recall the mourning over the death of Leo Tolstoy in 1910, bullets whistling overhead during the beginning of the revolution, and Lenin giving a speech from the Winter Palace of the Czar. The son of an economics professor, Leontief showed early signs of brilliance and was permitted to enroll at the age of fifteen in the University of Leningrad in 1921. Although younger than the other students, Leontief was not a typical academic prodigy. He was arrested for posting anti-Communist literature – not on the wall of the university, but of a military barracks. After a few days of solitary confinement he was released but was apparently unrepentant. He persisted in his anti-Communist activities and was arrested several more times.

At a time when many Russians faced the gulag or death for less serious crimes, Leontief was among the fortunate who not only survived but was permitted to emigrate to Germany. He attributed his luck to a tumor on his neck that Russian authorities misdiagnosed as malignant cancer. They were willing to issue him a visa only because they thought he would soon be dead. The tumor turned out to be benign and the contrarian Russian resumed his studies at the University of Berlin in 1925. His parents followed him and he completed his doctorate degree in economics in 1929, the same year as the stock market crash.

In 1931, Leontief moved to the United States and worked briefly at the National Bureau of Economic Research in New York. His analytical skills impressed economists at Harvard University and they hired him. They also gave him an assistant and $2,000 to continue his investigation of production in a modern economy, allowing him to work out the details of what would become input-output analysis.

What Leontief developed was a mathematical description of a production system where some share of output from one industry would be used as input for another. For example, the production of aluminum requires the input of bauxite and electricity, which in turn are the outputs from other industries. Once produced, aluminum becomes an input for the production of aluminum cans, automobiles, electric power lines, and other industries. Leontief thought it was important to track the inputs and outputs from every industry while remembering that the ultimate purpose of this complex flow was to produce goods for *final demand*. Economists consider something part of final demand if it is used by a family for consumption or by a business for investment.

In an input-output model, all of the output of an industry can be accounted for as an input somewhere else in the economy or as a component of final demand. This is the basic idea, although the models can be made larger and more comprehensive by including more detailed industries, multiple regions of the country, and even multiple countries.

While there was an elegant mathematical underpinning to input-output analysis, it depended primarily on large amounts of data that were not readily available. The analysis required a considerable amount of painstaking effort to estimate all interindustry sales. While most academics would consider this work boring, Leontief embraced it and called it a noble effort. In fact, he chastised his academic colleagues for spending too much of their time staring out of office windows in search of great theoretical concepts when they should have been gathering facts about the economy. He knew that he never would have invented input-output analysis if he hadn't been out collecting production data and thinking about what it all meant.

Leontief's invention was truly a unique formulation that viewed the economy as a woven fabric of complex threads connecting industries and geographic regions. What made Leontief's contribution particularly noteworthy was that, unlike many other Nobel ideas, it could not be traced back to ideas from Smith, Keynes, or John von Neumann. Leontief started with an altogether different way of looking at the economy and then devised a mathematical framework to describe it. The result turned out to be surprisingly useful at answering basic and important questions.

Economic historians have noted that input-output resembles the *tableau economique* (economic table) developed by Francois Quesnay in the mid-eighteenth century. Quesnay, a French physician, developed a crude table to reflect the flows between agriculture and manufacturing, as they existed in 1758. But his thinking was flawed by a bias against manufacturing that he thought was incapable of producing anything of value. Manufacturing could rearrange material or fabricate tools, Quesnay argued, but it could not create something from nothing. All value was created, according to Quesnay, from agriculture. This may have been a popular theory among farmers, but it was not very credible to anyone else. It may have been Quesnay's bias against manufacturing that stalled interest in his crude input-output table, but whatever the reason, there was little serious refinement of this concept until Leontief in the 1930s.

Even small input-output tables require a significant amount of information and their analysis requires numerous calculations. Leontief's first project at Harvard was based on only forty-two American industries, but because it included the sales from each industry to all other industries including itself, it could contain as many as 1,764 entries. While many of the interindustry sales are likely to be zero, there are still enough actual entries to require thousands of computations. Although computers make all these calculations effortless today, computers were not available in the 1930s. Leontief relied on state-of-the-art computing machines in 1935, which because they were mechanical and not electronic, still left much work for graduate students.

During World War II, Leontief worked for the Office of Strategic Services where he was able to develop a ninety-two-sector model for the U.S. Department of Labor. The greater number of industries or sectors simply meant that the model contained more detail. For example, a small input-output model might include transportation as a single sector, while a more detailed model would include railroad, air travel, water transportation, and motor freight. In 1943, Leontief gained access to Mark I, the first large-scale electronic computer, which accelerated his calculations.

Almost immediately, analysts found useful problems to study with this new tool. For example, even before the Axis powers surrendered, there was serious concern that a sudden demobilization after World War II would cause a return to the Great Depression. Would the reduction in government demand in the 1940s cycle through the industrial economy and usher in a return to the Depression? Some of these concerns were allayed by a sophisticated analysis using input-output models. In fact, the dire outcomes failed to materialize, as the government replaced some wartime expenditures with Cold War expenditures and the consumer economy surged. Input-output also offered practical insights into understanding the effect of rearmament for the Korean War and other policy questions.

By 1948, Leontief's model-building endeavor was going strong. He established a research project at Harvard with a staff of twenty and more importantly, used another early computer of the IBM punch-card variety. He gained funding from the Ford and Rockefeller Foundations and even the Air Force, until the Eisenhower Administration questioned the need for economic planning and cut the funding.

There was some concern in the early days over the actual purpose of an input-output model. Was it a planning tool that would be more appropriate for communist countries like Russia and China? Was it a tool that could be used to estimate the response of a market economy to changes in public policy? Or was it merely a useful tool for gathering data that could be used to better understand any economy? It was in fact all three. What looked like a socialist planning tool to some looked more like a tool to answer interesting questions about market economies to others. It was in fact the versatility of the tool that made it valuable to countries with very different economic systems.

There were some shortcomings in Leontief's earliest models. They did not generally allow for price changes caused by shifts in supply and demand, nor did they allow for technological change that could increase efficiency. Methods were eventually developed and made available to overcome these limitations, making the models even more complex.

As an undergraduate at the University of Illinois at Champaign-Urbana in the 1970s, I came across a research group using input-output models to analyze different solutions to the energy crisis. One of the more eccentric ideas at the time was a proposal to assemble a large space station comprised of solar cells that would then beam energy via microwaves back to a receptor on Earth. A straightforward application of the input-output model concluded that it took more energy to construct and launch such a collector than it would ever produce. The input-out model was uniquely designed to answer this kind of question.

Input-output analysis would have been useful even if all it did was document interindustry sales but of course it did more than that. Through simple mathematical manipulations it was possible to calculate a new table that showed the total amount of output from one industry required to support an increase in another. For example, input-output analysis might be able to tell you precisely how much steel, glass, paint, labor, and other *direct inputs* would be required to produce one million dollars worth of new office space in New York City. But in order to produce the steel, you needed coal and iron, and input-output analysis could also tell you precisely how many of these *indirect inputs* would also be required.[18] No other economic model was designed to study this particular question.

Another common use of input-output analysis is to estimate the employment effects of changes in the economy. For example, if the Department of Defense closes a military base, this is expected to have some effect on local and regional employment. A military base, like any large operation, requires goods and services as inputs, whether it is food for meals or jet fuel for aircraft. When the military spends money in the local economy, it creates jobs and incomes. Closing the base will eliminate these purchases and the employment associated with them. Input-output analysis is often used to estimate impacts such as these. Of course these models have to be modified to include more local and regional industries, but as Leontief would say, that just means that you need more facts.

When Leontief's Nobel Prize was awarded in 1973, he was just starting to investigate environmental questions. Only six years earlier, the Clean Air Act was passed by Congress and awareness about pollution went from virtually nonexistent in the 1960s to a major issue in the 1970s. This raised a lot of new questions. Which industries produced the most pollution? What would happen to those industries if they were forced to reduce emissions? What would happen to industries that relied on outputs from polluting industries? Leontief also wondered if environmental regulation in developed countries would just shift production and emissions to undeveloped countries. And if it did, how would this affect trade and employment in the world? In order to answer these questions, Leontief built yet another input-output table. This one was even more complex because it was international, accounting for world trade as well as interindustry sales. Leontief took the opportunity to describe the ongoing work in his Nobel Prize lecture in 1973. Here was a compelling and contemporary example of the practical value of input-output analysis.

In 1973, the Nobel committee counted fifty industrialized countries that were using input-output tables for both economic planning and forecasting. China embraced this tool to assist in its economic planning for industrialization in the 1980s, and the United States government maintains one of the most comprehensive and sophisticated input-output models in the world. The 1997 tables, for example, covered 498 distinct industries, including 95 new industries from the previous table in 1992.[19]

Input-output tables are also used to prepare and validate other economic statistics. In particular, the input-output tables prepared by the U.S. Bureau of Economic Analysis provide valuable information for calculating GDP, various price indices, and other components of the national income accounts. The tables have become an indispensable component of the economic statistics necessary to understand and track the performance of the U.S. economy.

In some ways, Leontief was not unlike other Harvard professors. He was a fan of opera and appreciated fine French wines. On weekends he would get away to a summer home with his family in northern Vermont where he pursued another passion, fly fishing for brook trout. In the 1960s, however, he associated less with senior faculty and more with the younger faculty, or the "liberal caucus" as it was called, because he shared their anti-Vietnam War views. He was also highly critical of President Nixon. He told the press, "His short-run program does not run very well and the long-run policy, I am sorry to say, seems to favor people who already have a lot."[20] Leontief encouraged Harvard's economics department to hire more minority faculty and to seek a broader diversity of points of view, even to the point of encouraging them to hire radical economists. He was not impressed with the graduate program where, he contended, teachers didn't teach and researchers didn't do research, at least not the kind he thought was useful. Economists could make themselves more useful, he thought, by getting out of the office and "counting things."[21] He always questioned the value of economic theories that were not based on actual observations.

Many politicians, economists, and economic students, including some of Leontief's own Harvard students, held strong antigovernment opinions along with an equally strong support for free markets. This troubled Leontief. In 1992 he wrote an op-ed article for the *New York Times* lamenting American's loss of confidence in government and indifference about corporate downsizing. He wondered why the government would permit entrepreneurs to profit from the destruction of American jobs.[22]

According to one story, Leontief was in an elevator in New York in 1971 when he heard someone say that the Nobel Prize in economics had been announced and the recipient was a Harvard economist with a Russian name. After quickly buying a newspaper, Leontief realized that it was the other Harvard economist with a Russian name, Simon Kuznets.[23] He had to wait two more years to receive his Nobel and the entire prize money of $121,000.

At the time of his Nobel Prize, the *New York Times* editorialized about Leontief's unconventional approach to economics. Rather than inventing equations based on idealized human behavior, he insisted on a firm grounding in the real economy, one that precisely described what businesses actually do. This information, he claimed was useful and, like the wine at the wedding in Cana, "It cannot be used up ... the same idea can serve many users simultaneously, and as the number of customers increases, no one need be getting less of it because the others are getting more."[24] Leontief died at the age of ninety-three in 1999.

Leonid V. Kantorovich (1975 Prize Winner)

Economists working in the Soviet Union had a far different challenge than those working in the United States or Europe. After the revolution in 1917, the Soviets attempted to develop comprehensive economic plans for the purpose of generating economic growth and prosperity. Given the complexity of the Soviet economy, this was an extraordinary if not impossible task. One of the leaders in this field wasn't really an economist but rather a high-level mathematician. Leonid V. Kantorovich began his career during the Stalin era in 1930 and invented a mathematical technique that would later be called linear programming. While trying to determine the optimum operation of a single factory, he published a general description of the problem and its solution as early as 1939, sooner and in a more advanced form than comparable work in the United States.

What is linear programming? It is a mathematical technique designed to maximize or minimize a variable such as cost or profit under many specific conditions. The name comes from the fact that the conditions are represented by equations that can be graphed as straight lines. In his original study, Kantorovich calculated the optimum assignment of machine tools to maximize the output of a factory, not the stuff of great drama but a very practical problem.[25] Some problems may sound simple but they get increasingly complex as the number of conditions increase. In some cases, a linear programming problem can contain hundreds or thousands of equations. Fortunately, there is a standard method for solving these problems whether there are five equations or five hundred.

Kantorovich's techniques were important for solving micro-level problems for individual factories, but also to solve macro-level problems for entire industries and even the entire economy. For example, the optimum allocation of electrical power to support manufacturing, transportation, and retail sales could be formulated as a linear programming problem.

Because of the isolation of the Soviet Union under Stalin in the 1930s, Kantorovich's discoveries went unknown in the United States where many of the same problems and solutions were also discovered. Only later did Tjallings Koopmans, working in the United States, become aware of Kantorovich's early work and help get it published in English. By then, Americans had independently developed the general linear programming problem, and George Danzig had invented the simplex method, which was widely considered a more elegant solution. Kantorovich's Nobel Prize recognized him as an early pioneer of linear programming.

Mathematical economics became an essential part of Soviet planning but it was also a long way from Karl Marx. Kantorovich was convinced that planners could not possibly include every little detail in their plans and he seemed to favor more decentralized decision making. Such ideas were controversial, even dangerous in the Soviet Union, especially during the Stalin years. Kantorovich also came to realize that certain decisions required prices that did not necessarily exist in a planned economy. For example, Soviet leaders did not look favorably toward rents or interest rates, which were considered to be capitalist tools for exploiting the working class.

This created a dilemma for Kantorovich. In his model building, he recognized that capital had to have some price or else his analysis was meaningless. If capital was free, there would be no limit on the amount desired. Although using an interest rate – even an index – in his models solved the technical problem, it opened him up to criticism from his communist colleagues of drifting too close to "non-Marxist, bourgeois science."[26] To mollify his Soviet critics, Kantorovich would routinely qualify his use of such "bourgeois" concepts by stating, "it was unclear and open to discussion...whether such an index as the interest rate has a right to exist." He even made such a statement in his Nobel lecture in 1975.[27]

Despite the help of mathematical economics and immense linear programming models, the Soviet economy was never very efficient. The Soviets never allowed enough decentralization or use of market forces to handle the complexities of a large modern economy. Many sectors of an economy simply do not lend themselves to centralized planning. Much of the service industry, for example, relies more on personal relationships and cannot be conjured into existence by central planners. The details and dynamics of such sectors were destined to overwhelm even the best planners, and they did. To his credit, Kantorovich recognized these limits and advocated for decentralization but with little success. While he was optimistic that they could do better, he acknowledged that the planning process suffered from "a feeling of dissatisfaction."[28]

Born in St. Petersburg (Leningrad) on January 19, 1912, Kantorovich was five years old when the Russian October Revolution began. For safe-keeping his parents sent him to Byelorussia for a year. At a young age he demonstrated considerable academic talent. He enrolled in the mathematics department at Leningrad University at the age of fourteen and graduated four years later in 1930. In another four years he attained the rank of full professor and a year after that, when academic degrees were officially restored in the Soviet Union, he was given his doctorate.[29]

Kantorovich put his abstract mathematical training to practical use in the 1930s at the Institute of Industrial Construction Engineering and as a consultant for the Laboratory of the Plywood Trust. Despite the pedestrian-sounding nature of these assignments, Kantorovich used the opportunities to pioneer his "method of resolving multipliers," in other words, linear programming. In mathematical jargon "it was a problem of maximizing a linear function on a convex polytope."[30] Also about this time, Kantorovich had contact with some eminent American mathematicians who attended the Moscow Topological Congress in 1935, including A. W. Tucker and John von Neumann. Kantorovich's first major publication on linear programming was a little booklet entitled "The Mathematical Method of Production Planning and Organization," printed by the Leningrad University Press in 1939.

Kantorovich's achievements did not go unrecognized in the Soviet Union. By the time he was awarded the Nobel Prize in 1975 he had already won the Stalin prize in 1949 for mathematics and the Lenin prize in 1965 for great scientific accomplishments. Kantorovich was married to Natalie, a physician, and had two children, both of whom became mathematical economists. He died in 1986 at the age of seventy-five.[31]

Tjalling C. Koopmans (1975 Prize Winner)

The Cowles Commission, which spawned many Nobel Prizes in economics, began with a practical objective. The founder, Alfred Cowles, made his fortune as a Colorado stockbroker but believed that he and his colleagues should have done a better job of anticipating the Great Crash of 1929. Convinced that better forecasting methods would ensure that they would not be caught unprepared again, Cowles established the commission in his name at the University of Chicago.[32] His philanthropy was soon financing the newly formed Econometric Society of Irving Fisher and Ragnar Frisch and the development of increasingly abstract mathematical economics.

Not everyone was convinced by the value of this new approach. Milton Friedman was one of the critics who objected to the Cowles research strategy. His own economic theories were mathematical but they also had a story line that led to specific policy recommendations. On the other hand, the Cowles Commission encouraged more abstract techniques. It was reported that Friedman's relentless opposition was a factor in the decision to move the Cowles Commission (now Cowles Foundation) from the University of Chicago to Yale in 1955.

When the Cowles Commission celebrated its fiftieth anniversary in 1983, it attracted sixty-five alumni including nearly twenty past and future Nobel Prize winners in economics.[33] One of them was Tjalling Koopmans, a Dutch physicist turned economist. Koopmans' first publication was in quantum mechanics and was based on work he conducted with Holland's leading physicist, Hans Kramers. But during graduate school, Koopmans was distracted by the Great Depression, Marxist economic theory, and finally by mathematical economics. Inspired by two other future Nobel laureates, Jan Tinbergen, also a Dutch physicist turned economist, and Ragnar Frisch, Koopmans studied economics and received his doctorate from the University of Leiden in 1936.

Koopmans laid the groundwork for his Nobel Prize while employed by the British Merchant Shipping Mission based in Washington, D.C., during World War II. His assignment involved studying the massive shipping effort underway between the United States and England. Schedules, routes, and cargo were not planned particularly efficiently so Koopmans translated the operations into a series of linear equations and attempted to solve them using numerical methods. Begun in the early 1940s, this was one of the first formulations of what he initially called "activity analysis" but would later name linear programming. He pursued this mathematical approach while at the Cowles Commission during the late 1940s, developing it from a transportation problem into a more general technique. Only later did Koopmans and others become aware that many of these same problems had already been worked out in the 1930s by Russian mathematician Leonid Kantorovich.

Initially there was some question about whether the problems addressed by linear programming should even be considered economics. It was, in a sense, more of an engineering problem for an individual enterprise. Given prices, costs, and production constraints, the technique allowed one to determine the most efficient or profitable operation. In his Nobel speech, Koopmans quoted A. C. Pigou who said, "it is not the business of economists to teach woolen manufacturers how to make and sell wool, or brewers how to make and sell beer...."[34] But these were physicists, mathematicians, and economists who had found an interesting problem and didn't especially care which discipline it fell into. By continuing to apply linear programming to a wide variety of economic problems, Koopmans helped to promote the use of this new tool.

While Koopmans helped to formulate the linear programming problem, it was mathematician George Danzig who invented the simplex method, which later came to be viewed as the best solution. During the late 1940s, while Danzig was developing this solution, he and Koopmans had several opportunities to discuss these problems.[35] Danzig, a statistician with a doctorate from Berkeley, devised his idea while trying to sort out military plans during World War II. He was well prepared to solve this kind of problem, partly because his father, a mathematics professor, gave him thousands of geometry problems during high school, which Danzig believed helped to sharpen his analytical skills.

Danzig is the source of one of the great apocryphal stories in mathematics. While studying statistics with Jerzy Neyman in graduate school at Berkeley, it is said that Danzig came in late one day and just copied the two problems that were on the blackboard. A few days later he apologized to Neyman for taking so long to do the homework but thought they were harder than usual. Several weeks later Neyman came knocking on Danzig's door at 8 A.M. one Sunday morning extremely excited about an idea for a journal article based on Danzig's homework. It seemed that six weeks earlier, when Danzig came in late, Neyman had put two great unsolved problems in statistics on the blackboard. Danzig had solved one of them. Even greater was Danzig's simplex method that solved the linear programming problem in 1947.

One of the first applications of the simplex method was to solve precisely the minimum-cost diet that Nobel laureate George Stigler had first puzzled over in the 1930s. Some of Danzig's colleagues were surprised and even outraged that Kantorovich and Koopman's received Nobel Prizes for linear programming but Danzig did not.[36]

Koopmans, his wife, and six-week-old daughter fled the Netherlands in June of 1940 as World War II was spreading through Western Europe. With the help of a Princeton professor, he was able to secure a position as an analyst with the British Mission in Washington. When that job ended, Jacob Marshak invited Koopmans to join him at the Cowles Commission at the University of Chicago. This was an affiliation that would continue throughout his career. Koopmans succeeded Marshak as director in 1948 and, when the Cowles Commission was renamed and moved to Yale in 1955, Koopmans followed. Tobin became the director at that time, but Koopmans returned as director from 1961 to 1967 and became the first Alfred Cowles Professor of Economics at Yale. Koopmans died in March 1985 at the age of seventy-four.

TEN

Game Geeks

John F. Nash, Jr. (1994)

Reinhard Selten (1994)

John C. Harsanyi (1994)

Robert J. Aumann (2005)

Thomas C. Schelling (2005)

Leonid Hurwicz (2007)

Eric S. Maskin (2007)

Roger B. Myerson (2007)

Eight Nobel Prizes have been awarded for contributions to game theory, although the father of game theory, the brilliant Princeton mathematician John von Neumann, was not among them. He died at the age of fifty-four, twelve years before the first economic prize was awarded. What von Neumann did was to apply the concepts of mathematics with its formal axioms and proofs to the analysis of simple but abstract games. In mathematics, games have a very precise definition. They are presumed to involve players, two or more, and a payoff, gains or losses, with some choice over possible actions. One of von Neumann's first proofs, published in 1928, involved finding a solution to the problem of two players trying to minimize their maximum losses. In this game, players review all of their options with the objective of choosing the strategy that has the smallest possible loss. Von Neumann was able to "prove" mathematically the conditions necessary for a solution to exist, the so-called *minimax theorem*.

From this initial insight, von Neumann explored other variations with more players and less certainty until he had enough different examples to write a book, *The Theory of Games* (1944), co-authored with Princeton economist, Oskar Morgenstern. With that publication, modern game theory was born, setting the stage for other mathematicians to explore variations of these simple games.

If anyone else had invented game theory they would have been celebrated for this single, impressive achievement. But because it was invented by von Neumann, it only registers as one of his many accomplishments and not even his most important. Instead, von Neumann is primarily remembered for his contributions to the invention of the modern computer and the development of the atomic bomb. The fact that he also invented game theory is almost a footnote on his impressive resume of lifetime achievements.

There was little doubt that von Neumann had a talent for mathematics from the start. Legend has it that this precocious Hungarian prodigy could, at the age of six, divide two eight-digit numbers in his head. His teachers were quick to recognize his talent and move him on to more advanced instruction until he received his doctorate in mathematics from the University of Budapest when he was only twenty-three years old. He was hired by Princeton University in 1930 and joined the Institute for Advanced Study in 1933 where his colleagues included Albert Einstein and mathematician Kurt Gödel.

If there is a particular stereotype for mathematical geniuses, von Neumann probably didn't fit it. He liked to drive fast cars although his genius did not extend to his driving skills. He allegedly attributed one of his accidents to a tree unexpectedly stepping in front of him instead of flying by on the side of the road like all the others. He was also known for pithy comments, such as: "There's no sense in being precise when you don't even know what you're talking about."

From the start, game theory had little to do with real economic problems. It attracted the attention of mathematicians, including future Nobel laureates Reinhard Selten, John Harsanyi, Robert J. Aumann, Leonid Hurwicz, Eric Maskin, and Roger Myerson who understood the esoteric proofs and were fascinated by these abstract games. The exception was Nobel laureate Thomas Schelling who skipped the math and simply applied strategic thinking to real-life contests. While game theory fell somewhere between the world of pure mathematics and theoretical economics, it was primarily mathematicians who developed it, starting with John Nash, a troubled Princeton mathematician with a "beautiful mind."

John F. Nash, Jr. (1994 Prize Winner)

Few mathematicians become famous for their economics and even fewer become famous for their life stories. John F. Nash, Jr. became famous for both. Played by Russell Crowe in the 2001 popular movie *Beautiful Mind*, John Nash became widely known as the brilliant mathematical economist who was struck down early in his career by a debilitating disease, paranoid schizophrenia, only to emerge some thirty years later in apparent remission. The movie won four Academy Awards, including best picture. His life had elements of a great story: genius, unlimited potential, a devoted wife, an appointment at Massachusetts Institute of Technology (MIT), work in military intelligence, devastating mental illness, insanity, and redemption. In all likelihood, the story would have gone unnoticed in popular culture except for the outstanding work of the *New York Times* reporter Sylvia Nasar who documented the life of this relatively obscure economist in a widely acclaimed book. What gave this story such a powerful ending was the extraordinary decision in 1994 to award the Nobel Prize to this unusual man.

Nash was an unlikely hero. Largely friendless both before and during the period of his disease, he was known as much for his antisocial behavior as for his mathematics. One can be reasonably certain that Nash could not rely on the strength of his personality to achieve success. Instead, he had to rely on his mathematical abilities, which were, by all accounts, formidable. So what did Nash actually do that qualified him for a Nobel Prize? Answering this question is a challenge because his work is so abstract. Remember it was math that attracted John Nash to game theory, not economics.

In his brief autobiography for the Nobel Foundation, Nash referred to his "beginning as a legally recognized individual," by which he meant his birth.[1] That occurred in 1928 in the comfortable little town of Bluefield, West Virginia. Nash supplemented his public school education in Bluefield by extracurricular reading including *Compton's Pictured Encyclopedia* and a particularly prescient text, *Men of Mathematics*, by E. T. Bell. By the time he was in high school, Nash displayed an exceptional mathematical talent by proving one of Fermat's theorems (not his famous last one). He got a head start on math with a class at Bluefield College before enrolling in Carnegie Tech (now Carnegie Mellon University) in Pittsburgh.[2]

Nash's first major was chemical engineering, but his interest waned during laboratory work and he responded enthusiastically to overtures from the mathematics department. The department appealed to the young Nash by claiming "that it was *not* almost impossible to make a good career in America as a mathematician."[3] Despite the rather lame nature of this overture, he switched majors. Only twenty years old, Nash graduated in 1948 from Carnegie where he received his baccalaureate degree in mathematics and, because of his additional coursework, a master's of science as well.[4] His one course in international economics at Carnegie would constitute the full extent of Nash's formal education in economics.

Mathematicians are expected to be parsimonious with language and R. L. Duffin of Carnegie fulfilled this expectation when he wrote a letter of recommendation for Nash to graduate schools. Duffin's letter consisted of one brief sentence, "This man is a genius."[5] Professor Albert W. Tucker at Princeton found the letter to be eccentric but sufficiently convincing to offer Nash a fellowship, as did Harvard. Nash chose Princeton because of the greater interest expressed by Professor Tucker and Princeton's greater proximity to his hometown of Bluefield.

Princeton was the home of game theory because of von Neumann and his co-author Oscar Morgenstern, but it also housed one of the strongest mathematics departments in the country. Princeton's ability to attract outstanding faculty and graduate students was enhanced by the presence of the Institute for Advanced Study. In 1948 when John Nash stepped onto the campus, the Institute had two legendary figures, John von Neumann and Albert Einstein.

Nash quickly immersed himself in the study of conventional mathematics as well as topics associated with Princeton's two intellectual giants, economic applications of game theory and the physics of quantum mechanics. Lack of background in both economics and physics did not deter the brash young graduate student. Within weeks of being on campus Nash sought and secured a meeting with Einstein with the intention of explaining his idea about the friction that subatomic particles encounter from fluctuating gravitational fields. After devoting a generous amount of his time to the meeting, Einstein offered some advice: "You had better study some more physics, young man."[6] Instead Nash turned to game theory.

Nash selected a dissertation topic in game theory, solved the problem by November of 1949, and submitted it to the Academy of Sciences, all within fourteen months of starting graduate school at Princeton. He was moving fast. The thesis contained his solution to competitive games or what mathematicians refer to as noncooperative games. In a noncooperative game, the players are prohibited from making a binding agreement prior to the game. It was Nash's solution to this problem that was cited by the Nobel committee for his award twenty-five years later. Short theses are the norm in mathematics, and Nash's was only twenty-seven pages. Professor Harold Kuhn joked that the middle fifteen pages was mere "padding," making the remaining twelve pages all that much more important.[7]

Although game theory played a central role in Nash's doctoral thesis and his Nobel award, it was hardly the focus of his academic career. In fact, his celebrated accomplishment in noncooperative games and his article on the bargaining process are his only two substantive publications in game theory, and that work was essentially over by the time he graduated from Princeton.

What had begun as a tumultuous race into the mathematical elite came to a screeching halt near Nash's thirtieth birthday in 1959. His classes, which had never been particularly organized or rewarding for students, became completely chaotic. Upon being offered a prestigious chair at the University of Chicago, Nash politely declined because, as he explained, he had decided to accept a better offer to become Emperor of Antarctica.[8] And with that his tragic slide into mental illness began, ending his career and any hope that his innate brilliance would crack future unsolved problems. His schizophrenia was devastating, causing irrational fears, paranoia, and hallucinations. Long spells of hospitalization and treatment were occasionally interrupted by brief periods of improvement. A good part of his time during the ensuing years was spent roaming the math building at Princeton, earning himself the reputation as the Phantom of Fine Hall.[9]

Nash's Contribution

What was John Nash's discovery and what did it have to do with economics? Game theory was not originally conceived to solve economic problems. It evolved from mathematicians applying the scientific method to human conflicts characterized by simple scenarios or games. Christian Huygens and Gottfield Leibniz, two seventeenth-century mathematicians, were among the first to espouse the benefits of such an approach. A pivotal development in game theory was a theorem proven by Ernst Zermelo in 1912 that finite games such as tic-tac-toe, checkers, and chess have an optimal solution, or strategy. His theorem was not particularly universal because his proof required perfect information about past moves and all possible future moves. Despite this limitation, Zermelo elevated game theory to a higher mathematical level. No longer concerned about merely finding the "optimal" or best strategy for a particular game, he refocused the science of game theory to proving the *existence* of an optimal strategy. Zermelo was solely concerned with whether a winning strategy existed; someone else could take the time to figure out the actual strategy. This led to an even bigger question: If such an optimal strategy existed for all competitive games, why not an optimal strategy for all competitive human interaction?[10]

A second breakthrough came in 1928 when von Neumann published "Zur Theorie der Gessellshaftspiele" (On the Theory of Social Games) in *Mathematische Annalen*. With this publication, von Neumann launched the modern discipline. According to Robert Aumann (quoted by Harold Kuhn), "The period of the late 40s and early 50s was a period of excitement in game theory. The discipline had broken out of its cocoon and was testing its wings. Giants walked the earth."[11] These mathematical giants puzzled over the nature of a two-person game or an *n*-person game, whether the game was a *cooperative game* (involving enforceable contracts) or a noncooperative game, whether there were *pure strategies* or *mixed strategies*, whether outcomes were *symmetric* (equal for each player), whether solutions were *unique*, and if some strategies were *dominant*. They introduced the obscure language of mathematics (topology) to the mundane activity of games and strategies. It was an exciting time for mathematicians and still a rather obtuse exercise to trained economists.

What did Nash add to von Neumann's theories? To begin with, von Neumann found solutions to two-person games in which the outcome was a zero sum, meaning that the competition was over a fixed sum, say \$100. The more one player won, the more the other lost. In some cases, von Neumann analyzed games with more players, called *n*-person games that operated under certain rules. For example, von Neumann analyzed games when there was an opportunity to make deals and to enforce them through contracts. He was particularly interested in mutually beneficial deals that improved conditions for all players. Nash needed to modify these assumptions if he was to say anything new. His particular extension was to assume that enforceable contracts did not exist, which converted von Neumann's potentially cooperative games into noncooperative or competitive games. Add in assumptions of *n* persons and nonzero sums and you have a Nobel Prize in economics.

Game theory might have remained a cloistered mathematical discipline, generating little interest from other academics, if not for a surprisingly modest development: a clever example from a clever mathematician. Albert Tucker was a topologist from Princeton in the spring of 1950 when he was called upon to explain game theory to an audience of psychologists at Stanford University. For his presentation, Tucker invented a very simple game called the *prisoners' dilemma* to illustrate the relevance of game theory.[12] There are many versions of this game but they all make the same point. In general, two partners, both suspects of a crime, are taken prisoners and separated. The rules of the game (an interrogation, really) are laid out in advance. Each prisoner must choose between remaining loyal to his partner, which requires remaining silent, or betraying him. If neither prisoner talks they are both given short sentences; if both betray each other they are given intermediate sentences. However, if one betrays and the other doesn't, the double crosser goes free and the quiet, loyal partner is given a long sentence.

It turns out that whether your partner remains silent or not, your best rational strategy is always betrayal.[13] Taking this one step at a time, if your partner remains silent, you are better off talking and receiving no sentence as opposed to a short sentence. Or alternatively, if your partner betrays you, you are again better off talking and receiving an intermediate sentence as opposed to a long sentence. In either case, it pays to betray.

The advantage of the prisoner's dilemma is that it illustrates some of the concepts of game theory including the abstract concept of a *Nash equilibrium*. The classical prisoner's dilemma is a two-person game because of the two prisoners. It is a noncooperative game because no binding agreements are allowed in advance. It is also a nonzero-sum game because the sum of the punishments for both prisoners is not always the same. And because the strategy of betraying is the best solution to the game for any rational individual, it also qualifies as a Nash equilibrium. A Nash equilibrium occurs when a particular strategy emerges as clearly superior to all others. It was this concept of an equilibrium that constituted Nash's major contribution to game theory. Nash equilibriums were not always this simple; in some games they don't exist and in other games there are many of them. The virtue of the prisoner's dilemma is that this abstract equilibrium concept exists and it offers a single, simple solution: All rational prisoners should betray.

The simple story of the prisoner's dilemma attracted attention from many academics who could understand the basic concept once stripped of the esoteric mathematics. In fact there was an explosion of academic interest in the prisoner's dilemma from a wide variety of disciplines. Thousands of articles have been written about this topic.

Political scientists translated the game into a nuclear weapons context involving two superpowers with two choices, an arms race or a negotiated treaty. No country wants to chose a negotiated treaty if their opponent chooses an arms race. Applying the prisoner's dilemma to such a problem leads to a grim conclusion: An arms race is virtually inevitable.

Academic psychologists took an interest in the prisoner's dilemma but they put their own spin on it. They typically modified the game so that it was not a single episode but rather a series of multiple iterations that substantially changed the nature of the game. Eventually players would tire of being punished for betraying each other. Cooperation, in this version, starts to look like the preferred strategy. Psychologists were interested in how long it would take players to figure this out. They wondered if the best strategy was to be "nice" and "forgive" your opponent, or to employ a "tit-for-tat" strategy by simply following your opponent's previous move.

And what about economists? What did they see of significance in the prisoner's dilemma? Some saw this as a way to understand the market dynamics of a small number of firms. Will these firms compete or cooperate? Take for example two firms in the same market that have a choice of setting a high price or a low price. Without much effort, this situation can be set up to resemble the prisoner's dilemma if you substitute high price for loyalty and low price for betrayal. And, like the prisoner's dilemma, the conclusion is that even two firms, if they act rationally, must compete. This conclusion was welcomed by conventional free-market economists because they liked the idea that firms always compete.

How useful is this in practice? Does the prisoner's dilemma provide an accurate explanation of real-life economic behavior? Do firms always compete through lower prices? Of course not. Sometimes they do and sometimes they don't. Unfortunately, neither game theory nor the parables derived from it, like the prisoners dilemma, are particularly good at predicting actual behavior. The prisoner's dilemma provided a simple metaphor for real life that stimulated some creative thinking, but gave us few tools to predict real economic behavior.

Initially, the United States Air Force and Atomic Energy Commission had great expectations about the value of game theory. They weren't interested in von Neumann's two-person game because they wanted to know how to win at checkers; they wanted to know how the United States could win the Cold War. It gradually became apparent that game theorists envisioned a more modest role for their work. A good example was Nash's seminal article published in the *Annals of Mathematics* in 1951. He applied his proof to the real-world example of a three-man poker game. Nash's poker game had only one card and only two rounds of betting because the analysis of anything more complicated "than the example given here might only be feasible using approximate computational methods."[14]

The most visible benefit from Nash's work was that it launched more work and many more publications by aspiring game theorists. Von Neumann had opened the door for Nash, and Nash in turn opened doors for other game theorists. As fellow mathematician Harold Kuhn explained, "Our ability to ask important game theoretic questions was enhanced by Nash's work."[15] Whether any of this work revolutionized or even changed economics is unclear. Jacob Viner, one of the old-guard economists from the University of Chicago, put it this way, "if game theory couldn't even solve a game like chess, what good was it, since economics was far more complicated than chess?"[16]

To be fair, there have been attempts to apply Nash's equilibrium and von Neumann's principles. Ignacio Palacios-Huerta of Brown University cleverly recognized that the practice of kicking penalty goals in soccer is essentially a very simple game with two basic choices for both the kicker and the goalie. Either player can go right or left. If the ball and the goalie go in opposite directions the chance of scoring is high, but if they go in the same direction the chance is low. Typically, right-footed players tend to kick more frequently to the goalie's right and vice versa, but all players mix it up to keep the goalie guessing. There are two modest predictions from game theory. First, in equilibrium, the chance of scoring should be the same whether the kicker goes left or right. If they weren't the same, then the kicker should be going more often to the better side, eventually evening up the probabilities. And second, the kicker needs to mix it up sufficiently so that there is no pattern from one kick to the next. Palacios-Huerta collected data on 1,417 penalty kicks from 1995 to 2000 in European professional soccer games. He concluded that the predictions appeared to hold up.[17] But as Viner might have said, economics is still far more complicated than penalty kicks.

The Bargaining Problem

Nash's second contribution was to solve a mathematical problem that was supposed to represent negotiations between two parties. To explain this "discovery," consider an example of two parties negotiating an employee's salary. The employee is willing to work for $40,000 per year but hoping to get $50,000. It is just the opposite for the employer who is willing to pay $50,000 but hoping to pay only $40,000. What will the final salary be?

The outcome in this case is mathematically indeterminant because many solutions are possible, not just one. The salary could end up anywhere between $40,000 and $50,000. Although these types of negotiations are ubiquitous in real life, economists tend to steer away from them because the outcomes, at least mathematically, are uncertain.

The fact that two-party negotiations are indeterminant was initially observed by Auguste Cournot in the 1830s.[18] The problem was examined in the 1880s by Francis Edgeworth from Oxford who considered the case of two variables.[19] In our example it would mean that the parties negotiate over salary and benefits. Edgeworth showed that if a solution was optimal, you could not improve upon it within the given budget; that is, you could not shift money between salary and benefits and make both parties happier. This insight was helpful but it did not solve the problem. The absence of a mathematics solution doesn't matter to real-world negotiators who settle issues like this one every day. The outcome depends less on mathematics and more on human factors that encompass the skill and experience of the bargainers.

Always one to seek a challenge, Nash cleverly introduced just enough mathematical conditions to derive a single, unique solution to the bargaining problem. He did this by making assumptions of compactness, convexity, and, most importantly, symmetry.[20] Such simple assumptions are more appropriate in mathematics than as a representation of real-world economics. Why, for example, should the bargaining problem be symmetrical? Why should the final outcome be based on a perfect balance between the two bargainers? Symmetry guarantees a single solution to Nash's bargaining model, but it doesn't really mean much in economics. If there were an economic counterpart to Einstein, he might have advised the young Nash to study more economics. Instead, Nash wrote up his "solution" to the infamous "bargaining problem," published it in an economics journal, and earned accolades from his mathematical colleagues.

Because of mental health problems after 1959, Nash's life spiraled down into an unimaginable nightmare but then two curious events happened. First, Nash began to show signs of remission in the 1980s that became more persistent in the early 1990s. Although rare, remission from paranoid schizophrenia is possible, and Nash was one of the few to enjoy a respite from this tragic disease.[21] The other event was that in 1994, the Swedish Nobel committee compiled a list for Nobel awards in game theory that included John Nash.

Reinhard Selten (1994 Prize Winner)

The sole German to win a Nobel Prize in economics, Reinhard Selten, joined John Nash and John Harsanyi in receiving the 1994 award dedicated to game theory. As a high school student in Melsungen, Selten came across an article in *Fortune* magazine published around 1951 about game theory, which in turn led him to the book by von Neumann and Morgenstern. He was hooked. Most of his academic career was dedicated to working out variations in mathematical games, interspersed with occasional experiments to test the results against actual human behavior.

In the early development of game theory there were many challenges, but one of the most troubling was that there were often multiple solutions to even the simplest game. This was a problem, because all that mathematicians could say in this case was that there were many possible outcomes, all of which are equally possible. Selten's contribution, which earned him Nobel recognition, was to eliminate some of these solutions. The term he used to describe this winnowing process was *subgame perfect*. In more common language, he simply eliminated strategies that were not credible, as, for example, when a competitor might threaten a price war but in fact has no reasonable chance of winning one. Selten's innovation would simply eliminate such strategies, leaving a smaller pool of plausible solutions. As Karl-Göran Mäler of the Nobel committee summarized the contribution, "By excluding such empty threats and promises Selten could make stronger predictions about the outcome...."[22]

The actual significance of such a discovery to human welfare could be considered slight. Even describing this as a discovery may be overly generous since Thomas Schelling of Harvard seemed to have identified the concept earlier but called it "credibility."[23] Certainly other economists, including Schelling, have considered the credibility of threats but none did so with the same mathematical precision as Selten.

Selton was fortunate to have escaped from Germany while the Nazis were in power. During the war, the situation deteriorated for Reinhart when he was banned from his German high school because of his Jewish heritage, but the family managed to flee on the last train out of Breslau. The family survived the war as refugees in Saxonia, Austria, and later Hessia before moving back to Germany. Selten finished high school in Melsungen and college at the University of Frankfurt, obtaining his doctorate there in 1961.

Reinhart Selten was honored with the Nobel Prize in 1994 for "substantially extending the use of non-cooperative game theory." His Nobel lecture provided the opportunity to present yet another innovation. This model introduced the "notion of a delay *supergame* of a bounded multistage game." It was, at the risk of oversimplifying, a game in which a number of decisions have to be made that add up to one supergame. A delay is introduced because although each decision is made at the same time, the outcomes are spread out over time. This is yet another mathematical variation of a game without any obvious application to economics. It is pure mathematics.

The newspaper coverage of the awards in 1994 had a difficult time describing the practical significance of game theory and Selten's discovery. How do you recast *Nash equilibrium* or subgame perfect into something that is comprehensible to the general public? In the absence of clear understanding, reporters tended to exaggerate its importance. After all, it is a Nobel. One publication, *Businessline*, claimed that the effect of Selten's theory was "almost to overwhelm economics."[24] A reporter at the *Economist* proclaimed that game theory "has revolutionized the economics of industrial organization and has influenced many other branches of the subject, notably the theories of monetary policy and international trade."[25] But when it came down to actually describing the theory or its application, examples were scarce. Even the *Economist* concluded, "So far there have been precious few real-life applications. Game theorists have been good at explaining the intricacies underlying strategic interdependence and producing ever more refined concepts of equilibrium, but less adept at giving governments and firms practical advice."[26] Perhaps a more apt assessment was offered by Stefan Szymanski of the London Business School who said that game theory doesn't really solve problems or answer questions, but it is more like "a tool for getting people to think."[27]

John C. Harsanyi (1994 Prize Winner)

When the economics Nobel Committee decided in 1994 to award a prize for game theory, they arbitrarily decided to narrow the field to accomplishments in noncooperative games. This decision may have been intended to benefit John Nash but it also swept in a little-known mathematical economist from the University of California, Berkeley, John C. Harsanyi. Without the name recognition of some other Nobel winners, Harsanyi seemed to be the unintended beneficiary of a decision intended to improve Nash's prospects of winning a Nobel.

What Harsanyi did for game theory was to add a few subtle modifications to Nash's theory. Where Nash constructed games with perfect information, Harsanyi introduced games with incomplete information. More precisely, he assumed that neither player knew what type of opponent he or she confronted. Instead, the type of opponent would be determined by a lottery with known probabilities. For example, if the United States and Russia were negotiating a nuclear weapons accord, neither side would know initially the type of negotiator representing the opponent. Will it be a "hard liner," a "compromiser," a "statesman," or some other type? Not knowing this information can make it more difficult to anticipate an opponent's strategy.

While Harsanyi describes a game in which both sides are uncertain about whom they will deal with, they are certain, however, about the probability that they will face a particular type of negotiator. In other words, the Americans don't know if the Russian is a hard liner but they know that he has, say, a 65 percent chance of being one. Harsanyi was able to demonstrate mathematically that this modest innovation had little effect on the analysis developed by von Neumann and Nash. This outcome was considered a good thing, because it meant that the mathematical analysis did not automatically collapse as soon as a slightly different assumption was made. Harsanyi described his discovery as showing "how to convert a game with incomplete information into one with complete yet imperfect information, so as to make it accessible to game-theoretic analysis."[28] It was a clever solution to an abstract mathematical puzzle. The bigger puzzle remains: What insights does this provide for economics?[29]

More interesting perhaps than what Harsanyi discovered while working at the University of California at Berkeley in the 1960s is how he ended up there. Harsanyi enjoyed a comfortable childhood in Budapest, Hungary, in the 1920s because his parents owned a pharmacy and enjoyed some measure of financial security. He was able to attend the Lutheran Gymnasium in Budapest, which he described as one of the best schools in Hungary. Two earlier graduates from that school also went on to achieve great academic success, mathematician von Neumann and a Nobel Prize–winning physicist. As an early sign of Harsanyi's talents he won a national high school competition in 1937 in mathematics.

Because Harsanyi was Jewish, any comfort that he may have enjoyed during his childhood came to an end with the rise of Hitler in the 1930s. When he enrolled in the University of Budapest in 1937, he would have preferred to major in philosophy and mathematics but instead chose pharmacy because it offered a military deferment. If he had been drafted in 1937, he would not have been permitted to serve in the Hungarian army, but instead, would have been assigned to a forced-labor unit.

Harsanyi's student deferment was good until March of 1944 when the German army occupied Hungary and he was finally assigned to a labor unit. When the unit was reassigned to an Austrian concentration camp, Harsanyi managed a daring escape from a Budapest railway station and, with the help of a Jesuit priest, found refuge in the cellar of a monastery. His good fortune was not shared by others in his work unit, most of whom died in the concentration camp.

After the war, Harsanyi started over in communist Hungary, earned a doctorate in philosophy, and taught at the University Institute of Sociology in Budapest. But he ran into problems because of his anti-Marxist politics. He resigned his position and fled Hungary with his wife in April of 1950. The only route available to them was to cross the border illegally into Austria through marshy terrain guarded by an armed border patrol. Finally free of Nazis and communists, Harsanyi emigrated to Australia where he started over yet again, this time studying economics at the University of Sydney.

Eventually his luck started to turn when he received his master's degree in 1953 and was granted a Rockefeller Fellowship to study economics with Nobel laureate Kenneth Arrow at Stanford University. He was attracted to the "mathematical elegance of economic theory." With Arrow as his dissertation advisor, Harsanyi completed his doctorate in economics and ultimately took a job at the University of California at Berkeley where he remained until he retired in 1990.[30] Four years later, he won a Nobel Prize in economics.

Harsanyi did not often stray from his narrow mathematical work, but he did speculate once that America's great research universities did not have a very bright future. "My feeling is that these institutions won't last very long," he said. "Too many appointments are made on the basis of political criteria – ethnicity, race and gender – rather than proper academic criteria. I don't think this can lead to anything good."[31] John Harsanyi died on August 9, 2000 at the age of eighty.

Robert J. Aumann (2005 Prize Winner)

When the Nobel Prize in economics was announced in 2005, the Nobel committee lauded the application of game theory to the Cold War, but it did not mention its application to the Arab-Israeli conflict. Yet one of the winners that year, Israeli mathematician Robert Aumann, was well known for applying game theory to this conflict. He did not, however, do this in an effort to end the war or to promote peace. Instead, he applied game theory to the Mideast conflict for the purpose of helping Israel win the war. This fact was downplayed by the Nobel committee but it was not overlooked by peace activists in Israel and the rest of the world.

There are militant or "hard-line" organizations on both sides of the Arab-Israeli conflict. "Professors for a Strong Israel" is one of those hard-line organizations because it objects to any concession by Israel, opposes humanitarian aid to the "enemy," and promotes victory through military action. It also counts Robert Aumann among its members. It is clear from Aumann's statements that he believes Israel should be preparing militarily and psychologically for a long and costly war and should resist the temptation to compromise. When asked about the Arab-Israeli war he noted, "It's been going on for at least eighty years and as far as I can see it is going to go on for at least another eighty years. I don't see any end to this one, I'm sorry to say."[32]

Because he did not believe that peace was possible any time soon, Aumann felt obligated to rally his fellow Israelis to prepare for a long war. He was quoted in the *Jerusalem Post* as saying, "We [Israelis] are too sensitive to our losses, and also to the losses of the other side. In the Yom Kippur War, 3,000 soldiers were killed. It sounds terrible, but that's small change."[33] When the

Israeli government under Ariel Sharon decided to relocate Jewish settlers out of the contested Gaza region, Aumann was incensed. He thought this was a sign of weakness rather than a gesture of good will. He opposed the action on political grounds but he claimed that his position was supported by game theory. As he explained, "From a game theory point of view it was a very bad move."[34] He believed that Israelis were making a strategic mistake by not holding their ground and sending a signal that they would never compromise. If Israel demonstrated that it was willing to reverse itself on Jewish settlements in the Gaza region, Aumann feared that it would be interpreted as "saying that everything is reversible. Tel Aviv is also reversible."[35]

How is this position consistent with game theory? Much of the early work in game theory was applied to a single iteration of a game. But what happens if the game is played over and over again? What if decisions have to be made every day, as in war? Do we attack today, tomorrow, or the next day? It was clear to game theorists that rational outcomes change and, in fact, become less predictable with multiple iterations of a game. Strategies under multiple iterations can work like an enforceable contract because now, violators can be punished. A strategy of "tit for tat" can be very attractive in this instance; every time one party attacks, the other retaliates in the next round.

This was essentially Aumann's approach to the Arab-Israeli conflict. As he explained, "To some extent, my political position is informed by my scientific work."[36] The choice between competition and cooperation is like the choice between war and peace. In general, both parties are better off when they both choose peace but it is seldom that easy. Israel adopted a policy of responding to every Arab attack with an attack of its own. The problem was that the Arabs had also adopted the same strategy which guaranteed a prolonged conflict. In order to get out of this destructive cycle, the parties have to pursue an enforceable agreement such as a peace accord, moderate their strategy, or both. Aumann believed that it was not the Israelis' responsibility to change strategies. He strongly defended the state of Israel explaining, "The dreams of thousands of years coming to fruition is something beautiful. That's why I came here. I'm a Zionist. It's very simple."[37]

There is another concept in game theory that Aumann emphasized in his political positions and that is patience. It is possible to show in game theory that a player is more likely to achieve future success if they are willing to hold out for a longer time, a trait you could describe as being patient or stubborn, depending on your point of view. To illustrate this, consider another simple game, the veto game. Play starts when the first player has to allocate $100 between himself and the second player. The second player can only accept the allocation or veto it, in which case both players get nothing.

In a one-episode game, a rational first player will leave as little as possible for the second player, say $1, because he knows that a rational second player should accept it because even $1 is better than nothing.[38]

But in a repeated game both parties start thinking about sending signals and they start thinking about the future. The second player now must consider vetoing any lopsided allocation in order to convince the first player to be more generous in the next round. The second player needs to decide how long to hold out until the first player starts making acceptable offers. It is possible to show in game theory that an impatient player is going to concede sooner and likely earn less money over the entire period. Once again, this has implications for Aumann's position on the Arab-Israeli conflict. He blamed Israel for being "too impatient" in trying to secure a peace agreement too quickly. As he counseled his fellow Israelis, "It's true that people are getting killed ... but I think we still have to say ... peace next year is almost as good as peace this year."[39] His fear was that Israelis were "simply too weary" to continue to fight long enough to defeat the Arabs or win an advantageous settlement.[40] He did not want Israel to blink first.

To some observers this application of game theory sounded more like a war strategy than a peace strategy. Aumann's critics secured nearly one thousand signatures on a petition calling on the Swedish Academy of Sciences to withdraw the prize from Aumann and his co-winner, Thomas Schelling. As the petition read, "Neither of these individuals has contributed anything that improves the human condition; rather, they have contributed to the misery of millions."[41] It also stated "That Aumann uses his analysis to justify the Israeli occupation and the oppression of Palestinians."[42] Many of the signatories were from Israel, but they included individuals from about fifty countries including several Arab states. The press reports described the petitioners as "Israeli peace campaigners, economists, academics, Holocaust survivors and leftwing politicians."[43] Some were members of an organization called Jews Against Zionism.[44]

Aumann refused to "dignify the petition" by commenting on it, and the Nobel Foundation explained that it was impossible to revoke a Nobel Prize. It had simply never been done before.[45] The chair of the Nobel committee, Jorgen Weibull, conceded that he was aware of Aumann's opinions but that it was not the committee's job to evaluate those for political correctness. "Our task," he explained, "is to select the most significant scientific contributions."[46]

Many of the implications of repeated games were known before Aumann started to work on them. The motivation and strategies of each player involved in the games were not hard to figure out. What Aumann did was provide generalized mathematical definitions and proofs demonstrating that cooperation was a possible outcome of these repeated games. Many of these refinements have important mathematical properties without real-world significance. At one point, frustrated at trying to explain his mathematical proofs, Aumann quipped, "If you could say it in a sentence and a half, I wouldn't have gotten the prize."[47] Trust me, he explained, "It's not easy to understand."[48]

The Nobel committee also recognized Aumann's work in studying games with imperfect information. Poker is an example of imperfect information where players know their own hands but not those of the others. In other instances, players have information but would prefer that their opponents not know they have it. When the Allies cracked the German code during World War II, they had very important information but they also had to act strategically not to reveal to the Germans that the code was compromised. Certain actions by the allies would have signaled that the code was broken and prompted the Germans to revise their code. These strategic considerations have always been part of human interactions. What game theorists were able to do was to translate this behavior into mathematics and search for proofs that certain strategies are possible, likely, or inevitable, depending on what assumptions are made about human behavior.

Not all reaction to Aumann's award was critical. There was also considerable pride in Israel that Aumann had won a Nobel Prize. A fellow mathematician, Tamara Lefcourt Ruby, insisted that Aumann's award was an opportunity to raise the standards and relevance of mathematical education in Israel. "We must," she insisted, "seize Aumann's achievement as an opportunity to inspire and educate our children."[49] She suggested that game theory should be taught in the schools and applied to political elections, animal behavior, and ethical conflicts.

Aumann's devotion to Israel was forged from his experience in Nazi Germany. Although his father had fought for Germany during World War I, the family saw the rising Nazi threat and they emigrated to New York in 1938 when Robert was eight. His parents lost everything in their flight from Germany, but they were able to provide their two sons with an excellent education at Jewish parochial schools and later the City College of New York.[50]

There are other Nobel Prize winners in economics whose exposure to economics was fairly minor, but Aumann's background was so minimal it was almost nonexistent. He was so "baffled and bored" by his economics class at City College that he dropped it after a few weeks.[51] Instead he pursued mathematics, eventually earning a doctorate from MIT. He was attracted to the abstract topics of number theory and later knot theory, which was the topic of his dissertation. Knot theory is exactly like it sounds. It entailed very abstract proofs about the property of knots, such as in ropes. He found the work very appealing because it was "both very difficult and deep" and like many topics in higher mathematics, "absolutely useless."[52]

It wasn't until he had his first job after college and was given an applied math problem that he was forced to think about more practical issues. The problem involved a squadron of aircraft attacking a city, only some of which carried nuclear weapons.[53] He was not prepared to analyze this problem but he did recall an analytical method employed by John Nash at MIT called game theory. Aumann studied game theory for this assignment, and it eventually became a lifelong vocation.

Both Robert and his brother Moshe wanted to participate in the Jewish resettlement of Israel after World War II. Moshe was the first in the family to emigrate to Israel in 1950 and Robert soon followed, taking a position at Hebrew University in Jerusalem in 1956. Tragedy struck in 1982 when Aumann's oldest son, Shlomo, died while serving in the Israeli army.[54]

Being an orthodox Jew presented a few challenges for Aumann's participation in the Nobel Prize ceremony. Because Jewish tradition prohibits "sha'atnez," a fabric combination of wool and linen, Aumann had it removed from his customized black Nobel tuxedo coat. And because the ceremony fell on the Jewish Sabbath (Saturday), he was unable to arrive before sundown. Fortunately sundown comes early in Sweden in December so with considerable effort he made it on time. In his banquet speech, Aumann thanked God who is "Monarch of the Universe, who is good and does good," for the return of his people to Jerusalem, and to "the mother of game theory, Oskar Morgenstern."[55]

In game theory there is typically no room for ethical, religious, or compassionate behavior. Players in game theory are not motivated by a higher sense of right or wrong but merely by rational thought. Why then do we see ethical behavior in real life? Aumann explained that some rational behavior may look ethical but in fact be motivated by fear of punishment. He gave an example of this in his Nobel lecture. When stopped by a policeman, a rational person will not offer a bribe, not because he thinks it is wrong, but because he fears that he will be turned in by the policeman. And the policeman in turn would not be likely to accept the bribe, again not because it is wrong, but because he fears being turned in by the driver. So fear and mistrust can lead to what appears to be ethical behavior, even when it isn't. Of course there is also ethical behavior that is not rational, such as self-sacrifice, but that is more difficult to describe mathematically and has not yet been part of game theory.

Given that game theory assumes rational behavior, is it surprising that a game theorist would adhere to religious rules and conventions? Aumann didn't think so. As he explained it, "Game theory says nothing about whether the 'rational' way is morally or ethically right. It just says what rational – self-interested – entities will do."[56] This certainly limits the relevance of game theory if people in fact are concerned about what is morally or ethically right.

Thomas C. Schelling (2005 Prize Winner)

Shortly after World War II, the United States and the Soviet Union began manufacturing nuclear weapons in preparation for a war that could consume and annihilate both countries. Each individual missile could wipe out a major city and the superpowers were stockpiling hundreds of them. The early Cold War was a chilling affair and there were no manuals to explain how to proceed or what to expect. Would the Soviet Union wait to see if the United States attacked first, or would it assume it had a better chance to strike first with a preemptive attack? If the Soviet Union was actually considering a first strike, should the United States consider a preemptive attack to beat them to the punch? These seem like interesting academic questions, but in fact millions of lives in the United States and Soviet Union hung in the balance.

Some careful thinking by a bright young scholar from Harvard University, Thomas Schelling, offered some encouraging, if not slightly obvious, insights. Schelling received his doctorate from Harvard University in 1948 and was looking forward to enjoying his prestigious position as a junior member of the Society of Fellows. But his career path took a detour when he was invited to join U.S. officials implementing the Marshall Plan in war-devastated Europe. Schelling found himself working in Copenhagen under the office of American diplomat Averell Harriman. This exposure to international negotiations fascinated him, and he vowed to pursue this topic when he returned to the United States and took an academic position at Yale University. Armed with first-hand knowledge of negotiating strategies, he proceeded to study the most dangerous international conflict of his day, the Cold War.[57]

The key to understanding the cold war, according to Schelling, was to put yourself in your opponent's shoes.[58] What were the Soviets thinking? What did they want and what did they expect the United States to do? For the most part, Schelling expected that the Soviets were thinking much the same thoughts as Americans. They were, he imagined, rational players in the same high-stakes game. The key, Schelling reasoned, was *deterrence* and that meant that each side needed to be able to retaliate effectively. No rational party would strike first if the opponent was expected to survive and launch an effective counter attack that could obliterate major cities. Second-strike capabilities alone should ensure that neither party would think seriously about a preemptive first strike. And while there was little that either superpower could do to protect its major populations from a first strike, there was a lot they could do to protect their second-strike capability. In order for deterrence to work, the superpowers had to convince their opponents that enough of their nuclear arsenal would survive a first strike to mount a massive retaliation. This, according to Schelling, was the key to peace in the Cold War era.

This and other ideas were lucidly described in Schelling's path-breaking book *The Strategy of Conflict*, published in 1960. Although he did not invent the term, Schelling described the concept of *mutually assured destruction*, or the MAD strategy as it became known. While a MAD strategy decreased the likelihood of a first strike, it had other problems.

"Mistake" may be the wrong word to describe an action that unintentionally causes global obliteration but it was a mistake that worried Cold War strategists. What if one party mistakenly believed that they were under attack and launched their second strike prematurely? The remedy proposed by Schelling was a hot line between the White House and the Kremlin to minimize the chance of such a mishap.[59] No one believed that a hot line would prevent all mistakes but those critical moments before nuclear annihilation is no time to wish for a quicker switchboard. President Kennedy installed the hot line.[60]

It's no coincidence that this sounds like a movie plot. Doomsday scenarios were popular in the 1960s when Schelling wrote a magazine article suggesting several possible scenarios for an accidental nuclear war. Stanley Kubrick read the article and later made the movie *Dr. Strangelove* based on one of those scenarios, which was further dramatized by Peter George in his novel *Red Alert*. In this story the Soviets took deterrence to a new level by inventing a secret device that would destroy the world with nuclear explosions if the Soviets were attacked first. Schelling, who advised on the film, was not entirely happy. "One obvious point in the *Strangelove* movie," he complained, "was that the Soviet doomsday thing is not a deterrent when the other side did not know in advance that it existed."[61] Effective deterrence doesn't necessarily make for effectively dramatic movie scripts.

Avoiding the hostile use of nuclear weapons was described by Schelling in his 2005 Nobel lecture as the "most spectacular event of the past half century ... that did not occur."[62] And why didn't it occur? Certainly deterrence played a part, but Schelling argued that even more important was the emergence of a strong taboo against using nuclear weapons of any kind. Over time, no superpower wanted to break the taboo and risk reaching the place where the use of nuclear weapons would be considered acceptable.

The fact that a taboo against the use of nuclear weapons would evolve was by no means inevitable. In fact, President Eisenhower's Secretary of State, John Foster Dulles, objected to the taboo as an unfortunate constraint on the United States' ability to deploy its nuclear arsenal. If these weapons where held to a higher moral standard than other weapons, then how could American presidents fully exploit their military superiority? In 1953 Dulles argued, "Somehow or other we must manage to remove the taboo from the use of these weapons."[63]

The taboo continued over Dulles' objection and despite an important technical advance. By the 1950s, the military had access to nuclear weapons with explosive power smaller than the largest conventional bomb. The small size eliminated the obvious objection to nuclear weapons and made it possible to use a small, tactical nuclear weapon to protect troops in the field. The use of nuclear weapons was contemplated against mainland China in defense of Quemoy at the time of the Korean War and again to save the French at Dien Bien Phu in Vietnam in 1954. But they were not used, not even a small "nuke." Schelling believed that the American decision to abstain from using nuclear weapons may have influenced the Soviets in Afghanistan in the 1980s and the Israelis in Egypt in 1973 who could have used nuclear weapons but chose not to. By honoring the taboo, the United States and the Soviet Union contributed to an "astonishing sixty years" without a nuclear attack.[64]

How does this strategic thinking apply to the rogue nations of North Korea and Iran or even terrorist organizations like al Queda? For these two countries, Schelling did not expect to see dramatically different behavior. As he explained, "I think if Iran or North Korea gets nuclear weapons they will think of them as deterrent weapons."[65] Schelling believed even these countries would want to avoid obliteration that would surely result from nuclear war. Terrorist organizations, however, without nations or cities to defend, are different. Deterrence doesn't work the same way for a terrorist organization with nothing to lose.

The danger posed by nonnuclear terrorist attacks was not of great concern to Schelling. He pointed out that "with the exception of the Twin

Towers in New York, terrorism is an almost miniscule problem."[66] He cited a study that found more Americans die in their bathtubs than from terrorist attacks.[67] Even nuclear proliferation did not significantly concern him. He suggested that the United States, if it participated in the markets for nuclear weapons components, "would be able to outbid anybody that wanted to buy a nuclear weapon."[68]

The Nobel Committee honored Schelling for applying game-theory concepts to the practical problems of global security and the arms race.[69] But it appeared that game theorists were more beholden to Schelling for his ideas than vice versa. Shelling wrote his first articles about cooperation, conflict, and limited war in the late 1950s, before he was even aware of game theory. He also didn't share a strong interest in the high-level mathematics of traditional game theorists. As Schelling explained to a reporter, "I think math is used too much to show off. It's a lazy way to write an article."[70] His preferred approach was to write clearly and use analogies to establish the wisdom of an argument. This seemed to work, according to Harvard economist Richard Zeckhauser, who described Schelling's games as "richer than most game theory analysis."[71] Similarly, James Tobin claimed that as a result of Schelling's work, "Game theory has never been as much fun or as relevant."[72]

Unencumbered by the constraints of formal mathematical proofs, Schelling was able to consider many more factors in strategic negotiations. He discussed the importance of credibility in negotiations and defined it as the ability to follow through on a threat or a promise. For instance, a military commander might achieve a strategic advantage by convincing his opponent that he will not retreat but how does he do this? One strategy would be for the commander to put himself in a position that makes retreat impossible, such as burning bridges behind his advancing army. The ancient Greek historian Xenophon once described the value of this very strategy.[73] Credibility was also behind the U.S. decision to place seven divisions in Western Europe after World War II, according to Schelling. Was there any better way to convince the Soviets that we were serious when we said that an attack on Western Europe would be considered an attack on the United States?[74]

Trust is an equally important concept in negotiations. How far is a party willing to go in an agreement when success rests entirely on the other party fulfilling its obligations? One way to ensure compliance is to implement an agreement in stages, as the Israelis and Palestinians did in the Oslo accords.[75] By taking small steps both parties could avoid a major embarrassment if one party did not follow through.

How important was all this theorizing? Did it actually prevent a nuclear holocaust? Many of the media reports of the 2005 Nobel awards were extremely generous in crediting game theory and Schelling for "the stunning achievement" of helping to avoid nuclear war for fifty years.[76] One headline from the *Irish Times* proclaimed, "Schelling Helped Stop the Cold War From Turning Very Hot."[77] All this was too much for a pair of Swedish politicians who complained that it was "far-fetched to argue that game theory played any significant role" in actually preventing nuclear war.[78]

In some ways, Schelling's model of the Cold War was not much more complicated than two gunslingers with pistols pointed at each other. Shooting first only makes sense if the other cannot retaliate. In 2006 Schelling explained, "When I used to theorize about a nuclear standoff, I didn't really have to understand what was happening inside the Soviet Union."[79] Of course the Cold War was more complicated than a couple of gunslingers; therefore, some understanding of what was "happening inside the Soviet Union" might be useful.

The arms race was only one of many topics that interested Schelling. In his 1991 presidential address to the American Economic Association, he focused on a topic that he thought required serious attention, global warming. In his assessment, the real brunt of the impact was not going to be felt by developed countries but by developing countries that were more dependent on agriculture and more vulnerable to the spread of contagious disease. He anticipated that the biggest challenge would be to get the developed countries to care enough to do something about it.[80] Schelling had a curt response to economists who supported setting carbon dioxide-reduction goals and using markets to achieve them: "Yeah, that's no good."[81] Instead, he encouraged developed countries to commit to setting fuel-efficiency standards for automobiles or sequestering carbon from power plant emissions, in other words, helpful actions with known costs. He also suggested that developed countries might consider financially compensating developing countries for global warming because it would be cheaper than actually trying to prevent it.[82] These are certainly creative ideas although controversial. This may be what Robert Solow meant when he said, "The thing you've got to know about Tom is that his mind doesn't work exactly like other people's."[83]

Racial discrimination was another area that interested Schelling and his work in this area was cited by the Nobel committee. Using the very simple model of a checkerboard and some markers, Schelling reached a curious conclusion. In the words of the Royal Swedish Academy of Sciences, "even rather weak preferences regarding the share of the like persons in a neighborhood can result in strongly segregated living patterns."[84] In Schelling's model, individuals required at least one-third of their neighbors to look like themselves or else they moved. But if they moved into a neighborhood with more people like themselves, they might provoke one of their new neighbors to move, creating a cascading effect. What Schelling discovered was that only a little prejudice can create a lot of segregation or, according to the Swedish Academy, "no extreme preferences on the part of individuals are required in order for a social problem to arise."[85] This was an example of what would later be known as a *tipping point*.

Schelling also analyzed smoking addiction. He was aware of a 1988 article by Kevin Murphy and Nobel laureate Gary Becker that reached the unsurprising conclusion that the benefits of smoking must outweigh the costs, or else people won't do it.[86] Schelling didn't buy it. "I learned then that they don't know what they're talking about," he explained.[87] He knew first hand what it was like to try to quit smoking because he had been trying for twenty years. In his model, Schelling thought it was more realistic to think that people are not entirely in control of their own actions. Does it make sense that one part of you wants to flush cigarettes down the toilet hoping that the other part of you won't go out in the middle of the night to buy replacements?[88] This approach was described by Schelling in his essay "The Intimate Contest for Self Command," which was aptly summarized by one reporter as "a rational being at war with himself."[89] There was one surprising consequence of smoking that Schelling pointed out. Because smokers died relatively young and quickly, they actually save money for Social Security and Medicare. But the dire consequences are what concerned Schelling and he was a strong supporter of using high taxes on cigarettes to discourage smoking.[90]

As a Cold War analyst and a child of a naval officer, one might expect that Schelling would be a hawk on most issues. He, however, opposed the war in Iraq from the start. "It is not a good idea," he counseled, "for the United States to think it can unilaterally go into a country who might get nuclear weapons."[91] For the same reasons he considered the U.S. threat toward Iran to be a "potential mistake."[92] This wasn't the first time that Schelling opposed U.S. military actions when he believed they were wrong. When Nixon invaded Cambodia in 1970 he led a dozen colleagues to tell Henry Kissinger that they would no longer support or advise that administration.[93] As he reflected on what had happened in Cambodia, he explained, "We thought about it the way a lot of people think about Iraq now, that there was subterfuge, there was misuse or manipulation of intelligence information."[94]

Supporters of Schelling were sensitive to criticism that many of his ideas did not seem particularly unusual or profound. Michael Spence, a Nobel laureate and Schelling student, explained that "Once Schelling said this, everybody said, 'Of course.' But absolutely the best things in science and social science are the things that make everybody say, 'Why didn't I think of that?'"[95] This may be true but I suspect this reaction is more common in the social sciences than the sciences. I don't know anyone who wondered why they weren't the first to figure out the general theory of relativity, the double helix in DNA, or quantum mechanics.

After thirty-one years at Harvard, Schelling retired in 1990 and accepted a position at the University of Maryland. He retired again in 2003 but Maryland brought him back to help with fundraising after he won the Nobel Prize in 2005. He was eighty-four years old. The Nobel committee explained that Schelling was notified only moments before the official announcement was made in Stockholm because the committee had the wrong phone number.[96] Schelling couldn't believe it; he pointed out that he was in the phone book.[97]

Leonid Hurwicz, Eric S. Maskin, and Roger B. Myerson (2007 Prize Winners)

Ernest Hemmingway was quoted as saying, "No one that ever won the Nobel Prize ever wrote anything worth reading afterwards."[98] This was directed at winners in literature but it is relevant for economists if only because they are often well past their prime when they win. The record was established by Leonid Hurwicz of the University of Minnesota, who was ninety when he won the prize, almost fifty years after the publication of his key article. When informed of his award, Hurwicz confessed, "I didn't expect the recognition would come because people who were familiar with my work were slowly dying off."[99]

Also surprised were the traders at Entrade, a market created to predict future events like winning the Nobel Prize. In 2007, the market was betting on Eugene Fama of the University of Chicago. It was Fama who crafted the efficient market hypothesis that assumes the stock market properly values stocks by fully utilizing all available information.[100] If the stock market hadn't begun its devastating decline in 2007, it might have been Fama holding a check for $1.5 million instead of Hurwicz, Eric Maskin, and Roger Myerson, who were all notably missing from Entrade's list of likely winners.

Hurwicz pioneered the development of what is called *mechanism design theory* with an article in 1960, which was more fully developed by Maskin of the Institute for Advanced Studies at Princeton and Myerson of the University of Chicago. A reporter from the *Times* of London characterized them as "a relatively obscure trio whose work is highly abstract."[101] At its basic level, the theory is not too difficult. It simply assesses the likelihood that certain trading mechanisms will achieve their goals. For example, suppose you are trying to divide a pie between two people and you want the outcome to be what both consider fair.[102] One mechanism, called a *direct mechanism*, would be to ask them what they would consider to be a fair allocation. Neither party, however, is likely to be entirely honest if they believe their answer will affect the outcome. If they were both rational they would lie. A better mechanism, familiar to parents, is to let one person cut and the other choose. The resulting allocation is likely to be considered fair by both parties. Mechanism design theory essentially evaluates processes like these, but with a lot more mathematics.

To take another example, suppose June wants to sell a piano and will not accept anything less than $500. Jack wants to buy the piano and won't pay any more than $600. One mechanism for selling the piano is to ask June the minimum she will accept and Jack the maximum he will pay and set the price in the middle, $550. But if asked, both may lie. If their lies are big enough, no sale will take place, which is unfortunate for both. Mechanism design theorists have searched without success for a mechanism to ensure that the piano gets sold.[103] The unfortunate message for free-market advocates is that sometimes even the simplest exchange can be frustrated by strategic withholding of information.

Mechanism design theorists have also revisited the problem of public goods. In this problem, individuals may be willing to pay enough to provide a public good, like public radio, but when asked to reveal how much they are willing to pay, they may lie. As a result, public goods are often underfunded if they depend on voluntary payments, a fact confirmed by mechanism design theory. While the mathematical proof offered by design theorists may be original, the basic concept is not. One astute reporter noted that Adam Smith had it figured out in 1776 when he wrote that public works "though they may be in the highest degree advantageous to a great society, are however, of such a nature that the profit could never repay the expense to any individual or small number of individuals...."[104]

The Nobel committee concluded that "The theory of mechanism design currently plays a major role in many areas of economics and in parts of political science, and has led to many fruitful applications."[105] The Nobel committee offered one particularly precious example: They claimed that this theory explained why English agriculture was superior to the French.

Because the French relied on consensus to initiate public works, like draining a swamp, they found it difficult to make any progress. But the English voted on this kind of issue, making it easier for the majority to prevail and get the swamp drained. The abstract proofs of mechanism design apparently confirmed this insight.

It may be that these examples illustrate the challenge of developing an abstract theory first and trying to find meaningful examples later.[106] It is a reminder that mathematicians may not have had a real economic problem in mind when they developed their proofs.

Strategic Behavior

A lot of credit is given to the pioneers of game theory for a broad range of applications, many of which actually have very little to do with the lofty mathematical proofs of Nobel laureates. One reason for this confusion is the relationship between game theory and the broader economic analysis of strategic behavior. Ever since Adam Smith, economists have analyzed how individuals and firms react strategically to market conditions or bargaining situations. This strategic analysis has on one hand contributed to our understanding of a wide range of activities from auctions to the Cold War. Game theory, on the other hand, was born when mathematicians took this knowledge of strategic behavior and translated it into axioms and proofs. In return, it was expected that these proofs would reveal great insights for use in the Cold War and economic theory. Generally speaking, the results have been disappointing. Despite the Nobel Prizes, the actual contributions have often fallen short of the "greatest service rendered to mankind."

Even without esoteric proofs, it is often helpful when economists think through actions and anticipate possible responses. An example where this strategic thinking has been useful is the development of sophisticated auctions, like the one devised to sell off part of the electromagnetic spectrum. In 1994, the U.S. government held a number of auctions to sell frequencies for personal communications services (PCS) provided by mobile phones, pagers, wireless computers, and portable fax machines.[107] This was indeed a very carefully designed auction with several important innovations. Economists Preston McAfee and John McMillan have written about the development and the performance of this type of auction.[108]

Bidding for frequencies is particularly complicated because each frequency is both a substitute for other frequencies but also a complement. A combination of frequencies can be more valuable than the individual frequencies when they span across geographic regions. Some companies may go into the bidding with the goal of securing a single frequency across the United States, while other companies simply want to acquire additional frequencies in the same area. Consequently each party may be interested in different combinations of licenses and have different, complicated objectives.

Obviously it would be difficult for each party to get exactly the combination they wanted if there was a one-shot, simultaneous, sealed-bid auction for all licenses. A simple sequential bidding process with one frequency at a time would run into similar problems. In neither case could a company adjust its bids to take into account what it wants and what seems possible based on the other bids. A sophisticated solution to this problem is called a simultaneous, ascending auction and it was in fact the method used by the Federal Communications Commission in 1994. It is simultaneous because all frequencies are up for bid at the same time but the slow, steady bidding process allows parties to abandon their original strategy and move to another combination if necessary.

This auction was designed by economists with an understanding of game theory and competing parties apparently utilized game theorists to review their strategies. But the actual design of the auction is not a direct descendant of a Nash equilibrium or Selton's *subgame perfectedness*. It would have been virtually impossible to derive mathematically the optimum auction using game theory. The problem is simply too complicated. Instead, economists relied on the traditional approach of analyzing strategic behavior to anticipate how rational competitors would respond to different sets of rules. In summarizing the relationship between game theory and this auction, McAfee and McMillan conclude "that the real value of the theory is in developing intuition." Whether game theorists actually have better intuition is a difficult proposition to prove.

ELEVEN

General Equilibrium

Maurice F. Allais (1988)

Kenneth J. Arrow (1972)

Gerard Debreu (1983)

Economics and mathematics have become increasingly intertwined during the past few decades, a development that has been encouraged and rewarded by the Nobel Prize in economics. As a consequence it is sometimes difficult to identify a true economic idea among the accomplishments honored by the Nobel committee. Are these really economic insights or merely exercises in applied mathematics? Nowhere is this more evident than in the development of general equilibrium theory. What started with Adam Smith's description of market mechanisms has evolved into abstract proofs that are more likely to be described as elegant or robust than relevant.

Economics and mathematics are different in many ways. Mathematicians value abstract problems and solutions, while economics is ultimately about the real world. A good economic theory can explain and forecast economic events and contribute to better economic policies. But as economics evolved into more of a mathematical discipline, this practical purpose has faded. An early generation of economists translated economic theory into equations while the next generation formulated increasingly complex problems and solutions. The final result is sometimes barely recognizable as economics.

General equilibrium theory followed this evolutionary path. From Adam Smith and the classical economists to Nobel laureates Kenneth J. Arrow and Gerard Debreu, the description of a market economy has evolved from text to topology. Sir John R. Hicks played an important role in this evolution, as did Maurice F. Allais, a Nobel Prize winner who pioneered mathematical economics in France and was belatedly discovered by other economists and the Nobel Prize committee.

Not all of the work by these gifted economists was dry mathematics. All of them made other contributions, especially the brilliant Kenneth Arrow.

General equilibrium proofs may have made a name for him in economics, but his many insights have firmly established him as a key innovator in many fields.

Maurice F. Allais (1988 Prize Winner)

While France was under German occupation during World War II, a young French engineer, Maurice F. Allais, was in charge of mines, quarries, and railroads in the Nantes region. German control minimized Allais' administrative duties and allowed him time to read all the classics in mathematical economics then available in French. After reading the French economists Leon Walras, Augustin Cournot, and Jules Dupuit, Italian economist Vilfredo Pareto, and American economist Irving Fisher, he decided he could improve upon their mathematics. In 1943, two years and 900 pages later he published his first book on the subject, *In Quest of an Economic Discipline* (A la Recherche d'une Discipline Economique) followed by an 800 page sequel in 1947, *Economy and Interest* (Economie et Interet).[1]

Publishing a 900-page tome on mathematical economics would never be easy, but it was especially difficult in German-occupied France. Not to be deterred, Allais found enough subscribers committed to buy the book in advance so that a publisher accepted the manuscript and printed it in 1943. The second book, published in 1947, also required advance subscriptions to get printed.[2] In retrospect, it was fortunate for Allais that these books were published because they were cited as the primary reason for his Nobel Prize in 1988, then worth $403,000. Embedded in these 1,700 pages were some of the same results that were later "discovered" by other Nobel Prize winners including Paul Samuelson, Sir John Hicks, and Edmund Phelps. Like his American counterparts, Allais had recognized that more sophisticated mathematics from engineering and physics could improve upon the initial attempts by Walras and Pareto to convert economics into formulas. It is not surprising that the application of the same mathematical tools to the same economic theories would produce, in some cases, the same results.

Inspired by his readings in mathematical economics, Allais used calculus to show that markets assumed to be perfect in some ways – information, foresight, and competition – were also perfect in other ways, providing maximum profits and satisfaction.[3] When he turned to growth models and investment, he devised a simple model of two generations, young and old, that lived through two periods of time. Each generation produced only in their youth but consumed goods and services in both periods. This example illustrates how abstract models can sometimes be quite simple, except for the math. This particular model was similar to one developed by Samuelson that became known as the *overlapping generations model*.[4]

Allais also applied his mathematical skills to developing a formula for the demand for money. This was a simple model that had the intuitively plausible result that people hold less of their wealth as cash when interest rates are high. Obviously you would be foolish to keep all your money under your bed when the bank is offering to pay you interest. Based on this idea, Allais derived a specific formula that was later incorporated into work by economist William Baumol and Nobel laureate James Tobin. Only much later did they recognize the origin of this formula and belatedly credit Allais with its creation.[5]

There were other economic concepts that Allais took credit for discovering. He calculated the savings rate required for a growing economy to maintain the maximum sustainable income, which became known as the golden rule. He claimed, "I think I have given the first general and rigorous proof of this theorem."[6] Allais' models also differed from others because he was likely to include state monopolies, as these existed in the French economy.

Like many fellow mathematicians and physicists who transformed themselves into economists, Allais brought with him the high, abstract principles of a scientist studying inanimate objects. This attitude was evident in his Nobel lecture when he explained, "I have been gradually led to a twofold conviction: Human psychology remains fundamentally the same at all times and in all places; and the present is determined by the past according to invariant laws."[7] No one questions that predictable and consistent behavior is expected of celestial bodies and subatomic particles, but how relevant are these assumptions to human beings? Are humans subject to laws of psychology just as electrons are subject to laws of physics? Allais and his fellow mathematical economists had to believe so in order to apply the same optimization techniques to economics.

The type of psychology that most mathematical economists assume in their work is perfect rationality because it leads to consistent and predictable behavior, much like physics. Rationality is a convenient and plausible starting assumption and allowed work to move forward. But economics is only as good as its assumptions and in the real world, rational behavior is limited. There are simply too many examples of irrational behavior to ignore.

Allais himself stumbled onto a form of irrational behavior in the 1950s when he challenged an accepted principle of mathematical economics. The principle, originally proposed by mathematician John von Neumann and his colleague Oscar Morgenstern specified that individuals should not be influenced by factors that are essentially irrelevant to the choice before them. This so-called *independence axiom* is consistent with rational behavior and is part of *expected utility theory*. Allais didn't buy it. He constructed an ingenious series of lottery choices containing different payouts to test the hypothesis. Specifically, he offered individuals a choice between two specially designed lotteries. If they consistently chose the first option or consistently chose the second option, then the axiom held. All other patterns violated the axiom. Invariably, when Allais tested these choices with real people, the axiom was frequently violated.[8] Allais took this one step further and gave the test to top-flight theoretical economists at a meeting in 1952. The results indicated that the scholars themselves did not behave according to their own axiom![9]

What was the behavior that Allais discovered? He found that if a person held a lottery ticket that was almost a sure thing, it would cost a lot to convince that person to accept a 5 percent higher chance of losing. However, if the first lottery ticket had a low probability of winning, the same person would be willing to accept much less for the additional 5 percent risk. While this may sound reasonable to most people, it violated the independence axiom and is decidedly not rational. This so-called *Allais Paradox* left theoretical economists scratching their heads for a long time. Much later, behavioral economist and Nobel laureate Daniel Kahneman identified a related human behavior and called it the endowment effect. According to Kahneman, people seem to value things more when they have possession of them, even if that is economically irrational.

A Tree Falls in the Woods

Although Allais was clearly a pioneer in developing mathematical economics and a leader in the French marginalist school, his direct influence was insignificant outside of France. This effect had two causes. First, his work was written in French and by the time it was translated, the results were no longer new. The other cause was that his work was extraordinarily long. Even if you could read French, you might not want to plow through a 900 page book peppered with high-powered math. An editor of an American economics journal cited the time he received a paper submitted by Allais that ran 120 pages, far too long for any economics journal.[10] The length of Allais' written work also presented a problem for the Nobel committee, which suggested that his award was delayed because of the time it took them to review his books and his 1,500 scholarly articles.[11]

Unlike many other economists, Allais wasn't given the Nobel Prize because he started new fields in economics or provided "seminal" theories, but because he had produced some of the same proofs and equations that later earned Nobel Prizes for others. Paul Krugman noted this when he wrote, "It is a very interesting prize. You couldn't call the work seminal, because nothing changed as a result. On the other hand, it compares favorably with Hicks' *Value and Capital* and Samuelson's *Foundations of Economic Analysis*. It raises interesting philosophical issues, like the proverbial tree falling unheard in the forest."[12]

None of this should suggest that Allais himself was insignificant. Within France he taught and mentored students who were highly influenced by his ideas. Some of these students went on to run large state monopolies in France and were able to use the concept of *marginal cost* as the basis for setting prices. According to this concept, prices are most efficient if they are equal to the cost of producing one more unit. Marginal prices generally send accurate signals to markets about how costly a product really is.

Allais may not have influenced many Western economists but he did influence one French economist whose work was widely known. Nobel laureate Gerard Debreu explained that until he came across Allais' first book in economics, he had neither read much economics nor frankly had much interest in it. As he recounted, "Yet, upon reading a few pages, I became captivated by the author's determination, read through the forty page introduction, and gained enough motivation to devote three months of hard work to a study of the whole book. I emerged with a fascination for economics, that is, for mathematical economics."[13]

Winning a Nobel Prize is in itself sufficient evidence of talent that additional self-promotion is generally unnecessary. This was not true for Allais who wanted others to appreciate his accomplishments as much as he did. He regularly described his achievements in the most favorable light; no superlative seemed too strong. In his Nobel lecture he described one of his efforts as "the only case I know of in the entire history of econometric research where a model ... has been able to provide, in cases so numerous and so different, such good results, far better indeed than those of all the other theories proposed before or after its publication."[14] On another topic, he concluded that "The empirical verifications of my hereditary and relativistic theory of monetary dynamics are quite remarkable; indeed they are the most extraordinary ones that have ever been found in the Social Sciences, and this is in a field essential to the life of society."[15] Allais was clearly one of his own most enthusiastic reviewers.

Gravity

The name Maurice Allais was not familiar to most economists before he won his Nobel Prize, and he had little impact afterward. There is a possibility that he will be best known, not for his economics, but for a curious thing he observed related to a pendulum. In 1954, Allais was conducting an experiment testing the relationship between gravity and electromagnetic forces that involved measuring the frequency of a Foucalt pendulum. He observed a subtle but measurable anomaly; for a brief moment the pendulum accelerated as if gravity had momentarily increased. That moment coincided with the 1954 total solar eclipse. The same result was reported by two other laboratories and reproduced by Allais during the total eclipse of the sun in 1959. As Allais explained in his Nobel lecture, "In fact, all these phenomena are quite inexplicable within the framework of the currently accepted theories."[16]

While it would be easy to dismiss all this as simply more Allais bravado, it would be a mistake. Fifty years later, scientists have still not accounted for this anomaly.[17] Chris Duif, a Dutch scientist of the Delft University of Technology, has ruled out all the easy explanations for the Allais effect such as the effect of tides, air temperature, human movement, or tilting of the Earth's crust. None of these explanations alone can account for the anomaly. As reported in 2004, "Since that first observation, the 'Allais effect,' as it is now called, has confounded physicists. If the effect is real, it could indicate a hitherto unperceived flaw in General Relativity – the current explanation of how gravity works."[18]

But even before Duif's article, NASA was prepared to test the Allais effect during the August 11, 1999, total solar eclipse. In preparation for that event, NASA scientist David Noever, based at the Marshal Space Flight Center in Huntsville, Alabama, assembled a team positioned in various international locations, all armed with modern gravimeters and old-fashioned pendulums in an attempt to reproduce the effect. If the same phenomenon was observed, the diversity of locations and measuring devices could be used to help determine what was really going on. Prior to this validation exercise, the press widely reported the preparation and quoted Noevers, "It's unlikely but Allais could have stumbled onto something."[19] After the eclipse on August 11, however, the whole project mysteriously disappeared. While it was anticipated that the data would take some time to analyze, nothing ever materialized. The absence of any explanation for the disappearance of the study fueled rampant speculation on internet websites, including one writer who claimed that Noever had abruptly left NASA and taken his data with him, leaving everyone in the dark.

There was some speculation that the final resolution of the Allais effect may explain another gravitational anomaly perplexing the scientific community. Two spacecraft launched in the early 1970s, Pioneers I and II, were receding from the solar system slightly more slowly than calculated. The two phenomena may be unrelated to the Allais effect, but then again, they might be.

Allais' father owned a cheese shop in Paris but died four years after joining the French army and being taken prisoner by the Germans in World War I. Allais felt "deeply marked" by this experience, but he threw himself into his academic studies, usually finishing at the top of his class. In high school he studied Latin and science, and in college he turned to mathematics and philosophy. He continued his college education by studying mathematics at one of the top schools in France, the Ecole Polytechnique, again graduating at the top of his class in 1933. Interrupted by a year of military service he completed his education with two years at the Ecole Nationale Superior des Mines in Paris, which prepared him for his first career as a mining engineer in Nantes.

Before long, Allais started thinking about economics. He told reporters that his interest in economics was sparked by a visit to the United States in the 1930s during the Depression.[20] He saw widespread poverty and decided that economics was an important vehicle for improving social conditions. After World War II, Allais pursued an academic career and became a professor of economic analysis at the Ecole Nationale Superieure des Mines in 1948. He was as proud of his scientific work as he was of his economic writing. He received fourteen scientific prizes, including the prestigious French prize, the Gold Medal of the National Center for Scientific Research. He noted in his biography for the Nobel committee that he was the only economist to ever receive that award.[21]

Keynesian, Monetarist, or Nut

At the time that Allais won the 1988 Nobel Prize, the press thought that every economist had to be either a Keynesian or a monetarist, but Allais was a little hard to pin down. Although Milton Friedman described Allais as an old friend, he also described him as "tenacious" and "a little bit of a nut."[22] Allais proclaimed, "If you will permit me, I don't fit into any category except my own. I am not a monetarist and I am not a Keynesian. On certain points I agree with each."[23] Ignoring his protestations to the contrary, the *Wall Street Journal* chose to characterize Allais as an opponent of Keynesian policies in France and an advocate for free-markets who was "largely ignored by French leaders...."[24]

Because of his newly acquired fame from the Nobel Prize, the press solic-
ited Allais' views on a wide variety of subjects, and he was more than willing to oblige. Liberalized trade and a single European currency were big
issues at the time. Although Allais was described as a free-market economist, he still questioned the benefits of free trade for Europe, especially if
free trade put them into direct competition with lower-cost competitors.
Using particularly strong language, he warned that liberalized trade could
be "suicidal" for Europe. And while he supported the move toward a single currency in Europe, he was not pleased that Germany seemed to be
setting the conditions for France and others to consolidate their currency.
According to Allais, "For more than a decade, successive French governments have bent over backwards to obey fiscal standards imposed by Bonn
in order to maintain the Franco-German alliance as the cornerstone of
European integration. For the French economy and for ordinary French
people the result has been little short of disastrous."[25] Equally troubling for
Allais was the U.S. stock market, which he described as a "veritable casino."[26]
After reciting the institutional flaws in the market that encouraged speculation, Allais concluded in 1989 that "the weaknesses of Wall Street today are
the same as those that led to the crash of 1929."[27]

Allais did not limit his opinions to economic issues. The press especially
appreciated his uncensored opinions that challenged French orthodoxy. At
one point Allais took on those who believed that French deserved to be the
world language because of its clarity, logic, and special genius. Allais would
have none of that. He argued that the French language was not inherently
superior to any language. Dominance of a language in world affairs, according to Allais, is granted to those countries that are dominant in the world
economy. If French was receding in popularity as a world language, then so
was France receding as a world power.[28] On a different issue, Allais objected
to politicians putting pressure on academics to retire. As he said, "It's amazing that politicians think it's normal that they should not retire, while they
think it's normal to push scholars into retirement."[29]

Kenneth J. Arrow (1972 Prize Winner)

The Nobel Prize committee frequently recognized mathematicians who
translated familiar economic concepts into increasingly higher levels of
mathematics. While the Nobel committee thought this enhanced the scientific credibility of economics, it also had the effect of moving economic
theory further from the reality of actual day-to-day economic activity. One
of the outstanding practitioners bridging this gap was the 1972 Nobel Prize

winner Kenneth Arrow. A mathematician by training, Arrow provided formal proofs for social choice and general equilibrium.

Arrow was widely recognized for translating and generalizing an interesting phenomenon regarding voting patterns. As early as 1785, the mathematician Condorcet discovered that it was possible for a series of majority votes to be quite illogical, even if the voters themselves were perfectly logical and consistent. To illustrate this paradox, suppose that in one election a majority of voters supported financing a new football stadium, and in another, separate election, they rejected funding a new school. One would expect that if a vote had been limited to choosing between a football stadium and a school that the stadium would win. But according to Condorcet, that was not necessarily true. It is possible for the school to be preferred and win in a head-to-head election against the stadium. How could this be?

Condorcet's reasoning went like this. Suppose one-third of the voters rank their preferences in this order: football stadium (f), no project (n), and schools (s). That means they prefer the football stadium but if that weren't possible, they would vote for no project over schools. Suppose another third prefer the school but if that weren't possible, they would vote for the football stadium over no project (s, f, n), and the last third do not want either project but prefer schools over a football stadium (n, s, f). With these preferences, a majority of voters would vote "yes" to support a stadium, "no" to support a school, but would surprisingly choose schools over a football stadium. As Condorcet concluded, a series of majority votes may be irrational – more precisely, not transitive – even if each individual voter's choice is perfectly rational.[30]

One can conclude from the *Condorcet paradox* that majority voting cannot be counted on to produce a single "correct" ranking of social preferences. Arrow translated this into set theory and reached a similar but more general conclusion: It is essentially impossible to guarantee that any method of determining social preferences will always be logical. This became known as Arrow's impossibility theorem. The issue, Arrow concluded, does not just refer to voting but applies to any other approach to determine social preferences. The one exception was the case of a dictator who imposes his or her own preferences on society. The preferences of a dictator could be rational although not necessarily fair.[31]

This finding was disturbing to those who favored government solutions to social problems and, at the same time, was reassuring to those who didn't. But perhaps more is made of this result than is necessary. The impossibility theorem is not a proof that voting is always illogical, only that the outcomes may be odd under certain conditions. In that case, voting is not perfect and the results may depend on how the vote is structured. But few things in life are perfect, with the exception of competitive markets, which are only assumed to be perfect. And this was the topic of Arrow's other major contribution.

Adam Smith described how a single market can balance supply and demand by allowing the price of a product to rise or fall. If, for example, there is a surplus of wheat, the price should fall until the point that the market "clears" and the surplus is eliminated. It wasn't long before economists started wondering if this result could occur simultaneously for all markets. Was there a price for every good that would guarantee that every market would clear? The idea that you could prove the existence of this set of prices became something of a holy grail for mathematical economists.

In order to solve the puzzle, the realities of a real economy had to be set aside in favor of abstract equations representing perfect markets. The solution was complicated because a price change in one market can affect the demand for goods in another. Early eminent economists with mathematical skills started to consider the problem, including William Jevons, Carl Menger, and Leon Walras in the nineteenth century and John Hicks and Paul Samuelson in the twentieth century. But it was the mathematicians who really cracked the code, beginning with Abraham Wald in the mid-1930s who provided the first proof that a general equilibrium existed.[32] Wald's proof, however, was considered extremely complicated and only used calculus.

In the 1930s, the mathematician John von Neumann introduced new mathematics to economics, including combinatorial topology, which was refined by Shizuo Kakutani in 1941.[33] These new tools swept through the mathematics community as they applied them to old economics problems. Arrow applied the tool to general equilibrium in 1951 and reached the familiar conclusion that a competitive equilibrium was always the best solution for an economy.[34] But as Arrow noted, "the appropriate tool was clearly in the air" because Gerard Debreu came up with roughly the same proof about the same time while working at the Cowles Commission in Chicago.[35]

The coincidence continued as both Arrow and Debreu turned their attention independently to the task of applying the new tool to prove the existence of a competitive equilibrium. They had both demonstrated that a competitive equilibrium was the best solution but the challenge remained to use the new tool to prove that a competitive equilibrium actually existed, as Wald had done twenty years earlier using calculus. Arrow and Debreu realized they were working on the same problem again, but this time they teamed up and produced a single proof published in 1954.[36] The new mathematics simply reaffirmed what Adam Smith had observed 160 years earlier. Where Smith argued his case using examples such as the market for corn, Arrow and Debreu made their case by appealing to "semi-positive vectors" and "disjoint sets in the nonpositive orthant." As different as these two approaches were, they were both making the same point: Prices adjust until markets clear in perfectly competitive markets.

Did Arrow's proofs convince him to favor free markets, or was this just an interesting mathematical exercise? In fact, he seemed to have some reservations about markets. At one point Arrow explained that "markets are not, in my opinion, a full solution to any problem," especially if the goal is an equitable distribution of income.[37] In his Nobel acceptance speech in 1972, Arrow conceded that the actual balancing of supply and demand in a market system "is far from perfect," and pointed to the market failures during the Depression of the 1930s.[38] He went even further when he blamed the "decline in the welfare of the working poor" on the growing "market ideology in the United States and the United Kingdom."[39] And he complained that this increasing reliance on markets was not "unleashing tremendous productive forces."[40] In fact, he pointed out that "those European countries that have maintained social welfare institutions to a much greater extent than we have – Germany, France and, of course, the Scandinavian countries ... are not doing worse than the United States on an overall basis."[41]

Although Arrow was critical of an excessive reliance on markets, he wasn't about to give up on them, either. In an interview in 1995, he paraphrased Winston Churchill by describing capitalism as "the worst system except for any others."[42] Of course there are many types of capitalism and Arrow seemed to favor one with more liberal social policies.

Market Failures

Nearly 200 years after Adam Smith, economists were still relying on assumptions of perfect information for most of their mathematical analysis. It was, for example, a central part of Arrow's "proofs" in the 1950s. However, Arrow deserved credit for introducing other economists to the formal analysis of uncertainty and imperfect information. In 1963, Arrow wrote a very influential paper on medical care published in the profession's top journal, the *American Economic Review*. The article formally introduced the concepts of moral hazard and adverse selection that illustrated how markets broke down when information was not perfect. Arrow didn't really "discover" that markets were imperfect, but he was able to convince other economists that this was a legitimate topic for research. He was able to do this because he translated these concepts into mathematics and because he enjoyed something approaching superstar status in the profession for his general equilibrium proofs. Arrow's research on uncertainty and information inspired work by many economists, including one of his own students, future Nobel Prize winner Michael Spence.

Information problems are probably most obvious in the insurance market. Once people have insurance, they also have less incentive to try to avoid accidents, a problem that is known as moral hazard. The information problem arises because the insurance company cannot always know whether the insured are being careless or not. Another problem, adverse selection, occurs when only high-risk individuals sign up for insurance. Individuals will always know more about themselves and their circumstances than insurance companies.

Because of these problems with private insurance, Arrow was skeptical about the ability of a free market to solve the health care problem. He concluded, "I think we need basically a single-payer system...."[43] It may seem a little out of character for an economist who "proved" the superiority and existence of a competitive equilibrium to endorse a policy sometimes referred to as "socialized" medicine, but that is in fact the case. Arrow explained that there are significant savings to be achieved from the economies of scale associated with a single government insurer. He pointed to Medicare and the Social Security system as examples of the efficiencies that we could expect from a single-payer health plan. The other advantage of this system, he explained, is that it would eliminate the problems of adverse selection where high-risk individuals are the first to want insurance and low-risk individuals are forced to pay higher rates to cover them. According to Arrow, "If everybody's covered, there's no way of cherry picking, having plans that appeal to only particular groups, with all the distortions that accompany them."[44]

Arrow did not entirely abandon hope for some competition in health care. While he advocated a noncompetitive financing system, he still thought there could be competition by health care providers, including health maintenance organizations (HMOs). He would also allow individuals to buy more than the basic coverage which would encourage some competition and not entirely constrain individual choice.[45]

Arrow was a New Yorker who studied mathematics, graduating from City College in 1940 with a bachelor of science degree and from Columbia University in 1941 with a master's.[46] Initially interested in statistics, he was recruited by economist Harold Hotelling who claimed that the economics department at Columbia was more open to statistical studies than the math department and he sweetened the offer with a promise of financial support.[47] Arrow completed his doctorate at Columbia after several interruptions, including working as a researcher for the U.S. Air Force, briefly pursuing a career as an actuary, and working as a research associate for the Cowles Commission in Chicago.

Arrow shared the 1972 Nobel Prize and financial award of $98,000 with fellow theoretician Sir John R. Hicks. The most laudatory assessment of Arrow's contribution was probably offered by fellow Nobel Prize winner Paul Samuelson. Without denying the esoteric nature of Arrow's contribution, Samuelson insisted that it would someday have practical implications and predicted that his writings would "provide the new theoretical systems out of which legislation of the future will be shaped."[48] Arrow felt that theoretical work was often underappreciated because of the pressure "for relevance, seeking things like immediate action."[49] He especially appreciated the Nobel Prize because it encouraged theoretical work.

Samuelson also was most impressed with Arrow's impossibility theorem, which he claimed proved "once and for all that there cannot possibly be found such an ideal voting scheme: The search of the great minds of recorded history for the perfect democracy, it turns out, is the search for a chimera, for a logical self-contradiction."[50] In fact, Arrow pointed out the shortcomings of both a voting democracy and a market in the absence of perfect information. The real world, in case anyone doubted it, is not perfect.

Gerard Debreu (1983 Prize Winner)

In the nineteenth century, Leon Walras launched the effort by mathematical economists to use general, abstract equations to represent an entire economy. Gerard Debreu contributed to that effort on his own and in collaboration with Kenneth Arrow, initially by reaffirming that perfect competition was optimal and later by confirming the existence of a general equilibrium.

Debreu continued to elaborate on the basic general equilibrium model through much of his academic career. The original model he developed with Arrow did not include a government sector with taxes and spending, nor did it include natural resources that could be consumed and exhausted, or the possibility of many slightly different products or much of a financial sector. Starting with the basic general equilibrium model, economists asked whether equilibriums existed for all of these special cases and if they did exist, whether they continued to be optimal.[51] Debreu, having helped develop the first mathematical proofs with Arrow, led the way on many of these elaborations. There was no shortage of ways to tweak the models and incorporate additional economic concepts. In 1984, a quick survey of economic journals found 350 articles containing existence proofs of general equilibrium under slightly varying conditions.

Like Arrow, Debreu also studied uncertainty but his Nobel Prize in 1983 was given primarily for his work in general equilibrium. Most general equilibrium theorists are careful not to imply that any of this work has a direct application. The Nobel committee made a similar point when they explained that this research was not necessarily an endorsement of free markets. While Debreu and Arrow described a set of mathematical conditions that "are sufficient for economic efficiency," that doesn't mean that any real world economy actually achieves that level of perfection. The mathematical conditions are too abstract and too ideal to have any obvious relevance for an actual economy. But despite all the warnings about reading too much into this work, some economists still interpret it as support for free markets. The warnings on labels are sometimes ignored.

With limited relevance to the real economy, how useful is general equilibrium theory? The Nobel committee asserted that this approach to economics "yields a better intuitive understanding of the basic economics."[52] Better than what they did not say. Professor Karl-Goran Mäler added the enigmatic comment, "Although the math is more complex, it allows you to understand the problems more easily."[53] There is often some confusion about what Arrow and Debreu actually "proved." What they proved was that a certain mathematical problem had a solution as long as the necessary conditions held. The relationship to economics was that the model included sets defined as supply and demand.

Economist Robert Dorfman identified some of the limitations of general equilibrium equations as developed by Debreu, Arrow, and others. They generally had to assume that businesses could be equally efficient at any size. In other words, a small car manufacturer should be able to produce cars just as cheaply as Toyota or Ford Motor Company.[54] Although such an assumption seems implausible, it was typically included in general equilibrium models. The reason it was used was not necessarily because mathematicians thought it was realistic, but because it made the math work better. If the theorists had assumed that size was an advantage, then the perfect equilibrium proofs quickly fell apart. It can be a problem when the math requirements dictate the economic assumptions. That's clearly not the best way to create a useful economic theory. Dorfman identified a second limitation: Existence proofs merely showed that equilibrium prices existed in a perfect world, not that they would necessarily ever occur. To prove that would be far more difficult.

Gerard Debreu's interest in economics developed gradually. While studying mathematics at the Ecole Normale Superieure in 1943, he discovered the text by future Nobel Prize winner Maurice Allais. It was the first time that he had heard of Leon Walras and general equilibrium. With this new inspiration, he continued his studies in mathematical economics at the Centre National de la Recherche Scientifique for two and one-half years. The Centre allowed him to pursue this new interest because, as Debreu explained, they had an "impressive tolerance for the absence of tangible results."[55]

Debreu was awarded a Rockefeller Fellowship that allowed him to visit several American universities, including Harvard, Berkeley, Chicago, and Columbia. The visit to the University of Chicago resulted in another lucky break when he was offered a position as a research associate at the Cowles Commission starting in 1950. It was at Cowles that Debreu developed his analysis of general equilibrium. After holding several different positions, Debreu moved to the University of California, Berkeley in 1962. He was still there twenty-one years later when his Nobel Prize was awarded.

Debreu and Arrow were collaborators and friends. Arrow noted that Debreu was particularly impressed with American democracy when Congress impeached President Nixon for his political transgressions. Any government that could prosecute such high-level crimes, according to Debreu, was worthy of respect. He was so moved that he decided to become an American citizen in 1975.

Debreu was the first Berkeley professor to be awarded a Nobel Prize in economics and was later joined by four more.[56] Colleagues often described Debreu as polite, gracious, and even elegant. Despite being described as a shy person who protected his personal thoughts and feelings, he volunteered to coach the economics department football team in a challenge match against Stanford, coached by Kenneth Arrow in 1979. Debreu was clearly just being a good sport since he confessed that he lacked even a rudimentary understanding of the game. While football was not his sport, Debreu enjoyed hiking in the Bay Area as much as he enjoyed traveling and fine food. In 2005, Gerard Debreu died in Paris of natural causes at the age of eighty-three.

TWELVE

A World View

Amartya K. Sen (1998)

Sir W. Arthur Lewis (1979)

James E. Meade (1977)

Bertil G. Ohlin (1977)

Paul R. Krugman (2008)

Robert A. Mundell (1999)

Understanding the benefits from international trade has been an important objective of economists for centuries. As each new economic theory was developed, some economists soon applied it to questions about trade. For example, Sir John Hicks had only recently developed general equilibrium models when Bertil Ohlin added an international sector to them to explain why countries specialize in certain exports. And when Keynesian models were still relatively new in the 1950s, James Meade added an international sector to see how it affected macroeconomic policy. His student, Robert Mundell, continued to explore this question in the 1960s. Then, in the late 1970s, Paul Krugman introduced familiar models of monopolistic competition and economies of scale into trade models and created something of a hybrid. Each of these economists was a Nobel Prize winner who helped to draw attention to the importance of international issues.

Economists Sir W. Arthur Lewis and Amartya K. Sen were more interested in the problems of underdevelopment that led to widespread poverty, hunger, and occasionally famine. Many economists either ignored less-developed countries or simply assumed that they operated under the same principles as developed countries. Nobel Prize winners Lewis and Sen were not willing to ignore the plight of these countries. They wanted to understand the problems that made these countries different, problems that they had personally experienced; Lewis was from St. Lucia and Sen from India.

Amartya K. Sen (1998 Prize Winner)

Amartya Sen did not exactly fit the profile for a Nobel Prize winner in economics. Much of his major work did not involve advanced mathematics nor was it intended to promote the role of free markets. Instead he embarked on an unusual research agenda; he dedicated his efforts to understanding and attacking poverty, famine, and discrimination. This humanitarian focus was unusual for economists in general, and even more unusual for the small elite counted as Nobel Prize winners. It was no doubt these distinguishing features that prompted a member of the Swedish committee that selects winners to state in the 1980s that "Sen will never get the prize."[1] It was a poor forecast, and Amartya K. Sen was awarded the Nobel Prize in 1998.

What prompted the Nobel committee to break with convention? There was some speculation that the choice was an attempt to restore some dignity to the prize after the embarrassment of the previous year. In 1997 Robert Merton and Myron Scholes won the prize for their clever formulas related to financial instruments, only to find their hedge fund, Long-Term Capital Management (LTCM), collapse less than a year later. Its final throes were painfully chronicled in the pages of the business press and later memorialized in the book *When Genius Failed* by Roger Lowenstein. Amartya Sen and his humanitarian theories were not going to suffer the same embarrassment. Some people speculated that the Swedish committee intentionally selected Sen that year because they thought he could return some dignity to the burnished medallion.

One of the most profound contributions by Sen was his simple observation in 1992 that as many as 100 million women appeared to be missing in parts of Asia and North Africa – not missing in the sense of pictures on milk cartons, but missing from the columns of data produced by national surveys. If women are supposed to represent about half of a population – or more typically 1 or 2 percent more than men – why did certain countries show significantly fewer females? Sen described this as a terrible deficit linked to inadequate health care and nutrition for girls and women relative to boys and men. Few statistical reviews of national census data have ever produced such a disturbing conclusion. The claim was supported by other demographic studies that followed.[2]

In a follow-up to this discovery, Sen observed that in 2003 little progress had been made. There was one positive development; he found an improvement in the availability of health care and nutrition for females. Unfortunately, the improvement in this area was offset by the reduced birth rate for female babies, a phenomenon linked to "sex-specific abortions."

The introduction of the technology for determining the gender of fetuses had made this disturbing practice possible. Female birth rates in Singapore, Taiwan, South Korea, and China were all disproportionately low. Even allowing for the possibility that normal birth rates for females could fall 5 percent below that of males, the Chinese gap of 14 percent was more than a mere statistical aberration. Data for parts of India followed the same pattern that could only be explained by sex-specific abortions.[3]

This particular line of inquiry was typical of Sen's work. In another major research effort, Sen investigated the cause of famines, a topic largely ignored by fellow economists. After reviewing four major famines, he concluded that the problem was more than a lack of food. Equally important, or more so, was the inability to *buy* food. In what may seem obvious, he observed that food supply can fall without causing a famine. It is only when such events are accompanied by a sudden impoverishment of a segment of the population that the result is widespread hunger and starvation. For example, the Bangladesh famine of 1974 was precipitated by a flood that destroyed considerable food production and pushed up food prices. But the flood also depressed the incomes of agricultural workers who were the ones that starved.[4] Sen argued that efforts to improve the sustainability of food supplies would not be sufficient to reduce the risk of famine unless the poverty issue was also addressed.

This was more than an academic exercise for Sen. He was about ten years old in 1943, living in Santiniketan, India when the Bengal famine killed between two and three million people. The famine was horrific but did not directly affect him or his fellow schoolmates and their families who were economically well off. Even lower-middle-class families were spared in this catastrophe – the deprivation was almost exclusively concentrated among the very poorest families. This observation was consistent with the conclusions Sen reached later in his professional studies.

Another conclusion emerged from Sen's famine studies; he observed that famine had a political dimension. Democratic governments, he argued, are held accountable by voters and therefore more likely to prevent starvation. If a famine occurred on their watch, they could count on being turned out of office by the electorate. Such accountability did not apply to dictators who were sometimes indifferent to food shortages. This is the reason why Sen concluded, "famine does not occur in democratic countries."[5]

As a result of his famine studies, Sen encouraged advanced countries like the United States to support democracies, even if they didn't offer them any strategic advantage. Advanced countries should also practice fair trade, according to Sen, as another way to improve economic conditions that can prevent famine. He further supported global initiatives that would spread literacy and reduce illnesses, and even donated some of his Nobel Prize money for that purpose.[6] Sen established the Pratichi Trust to support projects in India and Bangladesh to promote literacy and basic health.[7]

Earlier in his career, Sen pursued more conventional economic research but even then he had a humanitarian agenda. He and some other academics were disturbed by Arrow's impossibility theorem because it denied the existence of a rational set of social preferences. According to Arrow, there was no way to be sure that public preferences, determined by voting, for instance, were rational. Without a credible method to determine national priorities, Sen feared that governments would not have the authority to address the important economic issues of income distribution and poverty. As Sen said, "How can we find any rational basis for making such aggregative judgments as 'the society prefers this to that,' or 'the society should choose this over that,' or 'this is socially right'?"[8]

A related issue in economics was the long-standing aversion toward making *interpersonal comparisons*. For example, claiming that taking food from a rich person and giving it to a starving person is a good thing involves an interpersonal comparison. Sen offered the example of Nero fiddling while Rome burned.[9] Isn't the survival of Rome more important than Nero's pleasure, or for that matter, food for the hungry more important than the idle diversions of the rich? For many economists this is forbidden territory because it assumes that one can objectively and scientifically compare the happiness or utility of one person to another. This type of interpersonal comparison had been ruled out of conventional economics for some time. In 1938, Lionel Robbins, an economist at the London School of Economics, expressed this position as "Every mind is inscrutable to every other mind and no common denominator of feelings is possible."[10] Eventually the prohibition of interpersonal comparisons took hold of the profession and neoclassical economists started purging any hint of it from their work. Arrow's impossibility theory, for example, did not allow for any interpersonal comparisons.

Sen thought that economists should be willing to use interpersonal comparisons. In fact, by applying them to a limited degree, he was able to eliminate Arrow's impossibility theorem. When interpersonal comparisons were allowed, there were social preferences that were consistently rational and transitive. But such a discovery was lost on most economists who were taught to avoid, at all costs, any such analysis. The vast majority of the profession remained indifferent to Sen's innovation.

Arrow's impossibility theorem merely stated that under certain conditions, a social welfare function may not be rational. Similarly, Condorcet simply showed that social preferences may not be transitive under some conditions. Rather than abandon hope that a society can express its preferences through majority voting, Sen and others explored the question in greater detail to determine the exact conditions that will result in a consistent set of social preferences. This wasn't a new area of interest. Duncan Black showed in 1948 that majority voting was consistent if the issue was one dimensional, such as school funding, and each participant had a clear, single preference.[11] Sen proved it was consistent under a more general condition that he called the *extreme value restriction*. For instance, suppose three people are voting on whether to paint city hall red, white, or blue. If you simply rule out one color from one ranking (i.e., no one ranks white the lowest) then the voting paradox goes away.[12]

This theoretical work was important for Sen because it gave him confidence that his opposition to poverty, hunger, and famine could be more than a private sentiment. By invoking interpersonal comparisons and the extreme value restriction, he believed that society as a whole could, on logical grounds, also be opposed to poverty, hunger, and famine. All this may seem a little obsessive to people outside academics but for someone like Sen, with a strong background in philosophy and economic theory, this was all quite necessary.

These ideas were by no means the grand sum of Sen's contributions to economics. He wrote some twenty books and about 250 articles by the time he won the Nobel Prize in 1998. One of Sen's many interests was to improve the quality of poverty statistics. The usual convention is to set an income threshold and count the population that falls below that level as poor. One problem is that this measure does not indicate how far the poor fall below the poverty line. Government programs that help the very poorest families but don't quite move them out of poverty would leave the poverty statistic unchanged, leading to the mistaken conclusion that they were ineffective. Sen's alternative measure was more complicated but started with the conventional method and then adjusted it based on how far people fell below the poverty level. Sen also proposed adjusting national income for the degree of income inequality. This method was intended to provide a better measure of economic well-being. Those countries with high national income and relatively high equality ranked higher on Sen's scale.[13] None of these measures were very widely used in practice although they stimulated considerable academic discussion.[14]

Poverty statistics are flawed in other ways. Two families with identical incomes may experience very different conditions if someone in one family has a costly illness. In a case like this, the level of deprivation is not accurately indicated by income alone. A better approach, according to Sen, was to think about poverty as a lack of capability "to lead a minimally acceptable life."[15] A lack of money certainly limits that capability but so do health problems and other financial obligations. This kind of thinking took Sen in quite a different direction than conventional microeconomists. Poverty statistics based on simple income thresholds are clearly inadequate measures of well-being if much of a person's income is dedicated to high medical costs or at risk because of a high crime rate or the threat of natural disasters.

The Nobel Prize committee's decision to honor a humanitarian economist may not have seemed unusual except to insiders who recognized this as a significant break from the past. If traditional economists objected to the selection, they didn't say much. However, one particular zealot for the business press did speak out. *European Wall Street Journal* editorial writer Robert Pollock was beside himself with outrage over Sen's Nobel Prize. How could the Nobel committee go from "sensible" selections like Milton Friedman and Friedrich A. von Hayek to Sen, who he claimed "has done little but give voice to the muddleheaded views of the establishment leftists."[16] Pollock complained that Sen promoted the misguided policy of reallocating income instead of supporting free markets. And, he complained, even "Where Mr. Sen's insights have been accurate ... they have been unremarkable."[17] He castigated Sen for "being an expert in the kind of quibbling or 'problematizing' on which far too many students base doctoral dissertations...."[18]

Most Nobel Prize-winning economists have an impressive academic pedigree, but in this respect, Sen was exceptional. He was the quintessential academic. Not only did he work at the top universities in the world, Harvard, Massachusetts Institute of Technology (MIT), Stanford, Berkeley, the London School of Economics, Oxford and Cambridge, but he was born in the 1930s on the campus of a combined college and school in Santiniketan, India. His father taught university chemistry and his maternal grandfather taught Sanskrit as well as ancient and medieval Indian culture. At the time of his Nobel Prize announcement, he had left his position at Harvard to become the Master of Trinity College of Cambridge University, a position analogous to a university president in the United States.

Sen's early education took place at a school in Santiniketan where he was insulated from most but not all of the hardships in the country. As a child he recalled a Muslim day worker coming to their house pleading for help after being knifed in the streets by partisan Hindus. The man had entered hostile territory in a desperate search for work to provide food for his family. Sen's father took the man to the hospital, where the staff was unable to save his life. The event left a lasting impression on Sen who recounted the story for his Nobel biography. He was devastated that a man could be put in the predicament of having to choose between watching his family starve and possible death. The fact that the hostility was motivated by religious differences was particularly disturbing to him.[19]

After his early education, Sen attended Presidency College from 1951 to 1953 in Calcutta and then Trinity College in Cambridge, where he completed a second bachelor's degree in economics in two years and began graduate studies. Keynes had died but Cambridge was still rife with academic turf wars. Joan Robinson and her colleagues pushed the development of Keynesian economics into more abstract theoretical territory and developed equally obscure criticisms of neoclassical economics. The battles between Keynesians and neoclassical economists were fought not just in academic journals and symposia but also in the hallways of Cambridge and in the elections to the Faculty Board. Sen did not much care for this unproductive jousting, and claimed that he "was lucky to have close relations with economists on both sides of the divide."[20] Sen described Robinson, his thesis advisor, as "totally brilliant but vigorously intolerant."

In 1963, Sen began his sojourn of major universities, beginning with the University of Delhi, a one-year visit to Berkeley in 1964, and the London School of Economics in 1971. In 1977 he took a job at Oxford until his wife died from cancer in 1985, leaving him with two small children, ten and eight years old. As a single parent, Sen continued his academic wanderlust. He and his children sampled more college campuses, including those already named as well as Yale, Princeton, UCLA, and the University of Texas at Austin. He settled for a while at Harvard, but in 1998 returned to Trinity College Cambridge.[21] The *Manchester Guardian* noted the irony of the economist with a Nobel Prize for his work on poverty and famine was the master "of one of the richest landowners in England – estimated to be worth up to 400 million pounds … a college legendary for its cuisine and wine cellar."[22]

Sir W. Arthur Lewis (1979 Prize Winner)

In 1979, the Nobel committee selected Arthur Lewis as its winner, who demonstrated a pragmatic approach to economics, drawing on his broad liberal arts background and marshalling a wide knowledge of economic theory, facts, and statistics. Arthur Lewis was most interested in why poor countries remained poor while rich countries grew and prospered. Other economists, especially in America, had almost lost interest in this topic. Either the plight of poor nations didn't interest economists from wealthy countries, or as some claimed, their abstract mathematical models couldn't unravel this stubborn problem. Lewis was different. He was from a poor country, St. Lucia in the Caribbean, and thus had first-hand experience with what it meant to live in a "less-developed country." Also, he had little interest in solving mathematical puzzles; he wanted to solve economic problems.

The first challenge for Lewis was to describe the key features of a developing economy. He started with the simple observation that there was a profound disparity between rural and urban areas. On one side was a large, economically inefficient agricultural sector with a vast pool of underemployed workers. On the other side was a more modern, urban sector with active commercial and industrial activity. Lewis insisted that any economic analysis of developing economies had to include both sectors. This concept became known as a *dual economy*. Whatever constraints existed on growth in the urban industrial sector, one of them was not a shortage of labor, which was cheap and abundantly available from the countryside. Although this may seem like a fairly simple concept, it was sufficiently accurate to provide a framework for future analysis of those developing economies that suffered from underemployment.

Lewis' second idea was again based on a relatively simple observation related to exchange rates although it never gained much traction in the profession. While many countries specialize in producing something, nearly every country produces food; it may be specialized, dependent on each particular climate, but it is still food. Consequently domestic food production competes with foreign food production and is therefore decisive in establishing exchange rates. According to Lewis, a country that is particularly inefficient in producing food will have a relatively lower exchange rate or, more precisely, worse *terms of trade*. Because most developing countries were relatively inefficient food producers, the concept also explained why they generally had relatively poor terms of trade. Such an idea is inconsistent, however, with the more venerable concept of comparative advantage, and did not generate much interest among economists.

Although these two concepts were cited by the Nobel committee, Lewis dedicated his Nobel lecture to a different topic. In 1979, Lewis was worried about how poor countries were going to sustain their current level of economic growth.[23] On average, growth had been strong in less-developed countries from 1953 to 1973, but Lewis was doubtful that it could continue. He reasoned that economic growth in these countries seemed to depend on growth in the more-developed countries, and with lower growth expected in the developed world, Lewis saw trouble ahead.

There was an easy solution, Lewis suggested, to helping the poor countries of the world. If the advanced countries would simply reduce barriers to imports they could help developing countries and help close the gap between rich and poor nations. But in his Nobel lecture, Lewis doubted this would happen. Instead, he observed what he called "a strange world" in which the advanced countries reduced trade barriers among themselves but raised them for poor countries. He feared that this would ensure that most poor countries would never catch up.

Economic events unfolded quite differently from Lewis' expectations for many reasons. The energy crisis ended in the 1980s and was followed by relatively low oil prices for twenty-five years. During this period some relatively less-developed countries experienced phenomenal growth, including China, Korea, Taiwan, and Singapore while others continued to flounder. And over an even longer time horizon, some advanced countries of the world did gradually lower trade barriers with less-developed countries.

Lewis earned a doctorate in industrial economics in 1937, and his path to that achievement was probably unlike many others. St. Lucia and other Caribbean islands may be vacation destinations for wealthy tourists, but they are also home to relatively poor native residents. One of them was Arthur Lewis whose situation deteriorated after his father died.[24] Fortunately, Lewis was a very good student and successfully qualified for government scholarships. Academic success, however, was not enough to allow him to study in his chosen field, engineering. Such disciplines were not open to young black students as there was little chance at that time that anyone would hire a black engineer. Instead, he pursued a business administration degree at the London School of Economics where he discovered economics.

Lewis began teaching in 1938 in London and worked his way up to become a full professor at the University of Manchester. In the 1940s, Lewis began his research in economic history, and by 1950 he was writing about developmental economics. Some of this research was inspired by another Nobel winner, Friedrich Hayek, who was acting chairman of the economics department at the London School. Hayek asked Lewis to teach a course about world economics between the wars, to which Lewis replied that he did not know much about that. Undeterred, Hayek suggested that this was then an excellent opportunity to learn the subject; Lewis accepted and expanded his expertise to include international issues.

Throughout his career, Lewis moved seamlessly between administration and academic positions. From 1957 to 1963, he worked in various capacities for the United Nations and later as Vice-Chancellor for the University of the West Indies. It was for this latter position that Lewis was knighted in 1963 by Queen Elizabeth II. That year he returned to university life, accepting an academic position at Princeton.[25]

When Lewis' Nobel Prize was announced in 1979, the chair of his economics department at Princeton noted that Lewis was "the perfect counter-individual to the maxim that nice guys finish last."[26] In many ways, Lewis was one of the few old-school economists to win a Nobel Prize. He was an astute observer of real economic activity and wrote clearly and convincingly on topics of poverty and underdevelopment. He did not prove a particular theorem, or found a field of economics, or develop a new statistical technique. He was a broad thinker who was motivated by big questions in economics, not the small, solvable variety. His approach required a broader understanding of history, politics, and even culture than the specialized training of his colleagues.

Lewis was not the first black person to win a Nobel Prize but he was the first to win one in a category other than peace.[27] He was quite aware of the barriers that he had to face as a black man in academics. Speaking to his fellow economists in 1938, he reportedly said, "I'm the kind of person you guys like the least; I'm an educated native."[28] Although he was a leading black scholar in the 1960s, Lewis was not particularly supportive of black studies programs on university campuses. It wasn't that he thought they were wrong; he just didn't think they were enough. He anticipated that it would take much more to eradicate the message of racial inferiority than a black studies program at a university. His preference was to counter racial stereotypes at an earlier age, long before students even thought about college.[29]

On the occasion of Lewis' death in 1991 at his home in Barbados, the *New York Times* eulogized that "Any scholar can wallow in infinite complexity. But it took Sir Arthur's insight to identify common paths to economic development."[30] The *Times* went on to explain that Lewis, "the only black economics laureate – never forgot that economics is foremost about people."[31]

James E. Meade (1977 Prize Winner)

International trade has always been relatively more important for European countries than for the United States, where trade is overshadowed by the larger domestic economy. This may be the reason that the first two economists recognized for their work in international trade were not Americans; they were James E. Meade from England and Bertil Ohlin from Sweden. Meade, like Ohlin, was a model builder, constructing equations that combined general equilibrium and Keynesian concepts. He also liked to describe his models in long scholarly texts for an audience he characterized as educated laymen. This style was not appreciated by conventional American economists who preferred to attend conferences, give papers, and publish in technical journal where they could communicate through equations rather than words. Harry Johnson of the University of Chicago was one of those economists who was not a fan of Meade's "large tomes." Johnson claimed that "students find it incredibly tedious to read his books and difficult to convince themselves that the effort is worthwhile in terms of knowledge gained."[32]

Nevertheless, James Meade won the Nobel Prize in economics in 1977 for work described in two of those "large tomes" published in the 1950s entitled *The Balance of Payments* (1951) and *Trade and Welfare* (1955). In these works, Meade expanded the evolving Keynesian macroeconomic models to include multiple countries and introduce trade and exchange rates. His goal was not just to achieve full employment, which he referred to as an *internal balance*, but also to achieve a balance of payments, which he called the *external balance*.[33] Meade was among the small group of economists who were interested in determining whether Keynesian policies continued to work properly within an international context. According to Johnson, Meade observed that there were "possible policy conflicts between external and internal balance under a fixed exchange rate system."[34]

Harry Johnson was not so sure that Meade was the first to combine successfully Hicks' general equilibrium and Keynesian economics. As he observed, "The required integration of Keynesian and Hicksian theory had been performed, with reference to exchange rate adjustment, more or less simultaneously and with rather more sophistication by Harberger and Laursen and Metzler at Chicago...."[35] Furthermore, Johnson insisted that the "policy targets and instruments had been worked out contemporaneously, with more mathematical rigour and comprehensiveness, by Tinbergen."[36] While much of Meade's work was perhaps not unique, he managed to combine familiar concepts in a unique way that provoked thought and controversy. He also taught some talented students at the London School of Economics, including Robert Mundell who also went on to win a Nobel Prize for international economics.[37]

The Nobel committee also mentioned Meade's work analyzing the effect of *customs unions* in the spirit of earlier work by Jacob Viner of the University of Chicago. Although it is an old term, customs unions themselves have become increasingly important and are better known as free trade zones such as the European Economic Community, a precursor to the European Union. Customs unions create free trade among its participants but maintain trade barriers with the outside world. Economists like Viner and Meade wondered whether customs unions move the world closer to free trade or further from it. The answer, as usual, depends on particular circumstances because the theoretical benefits of free trade within the union can be offset by barriers to trade outside the union.

Rather than explain his Nobel ideas during his prize lecture, Meade took the opportunity to revise his trade theory from the 1950s. During that decade, inflation was not much of a problem and thus most policy analysis, including Meade's, focused on maintaining full employment. That was the goal of his "internal balance." But from the vantage point of 1977, when inflation was rampant in world economies, full employment was clearly not enough. Most countries wanted price stability as well.

Meade blamed trade unions as the primary culprit for simultaneous inflation and unemployment, otherwise known as *stagflation*. He described a process where powerful unions force higher wages, which in turn force higher prices, creating the familiar wage-price spiral. Meade believed that higher wages and prices would cause unemployment and for that reason he argued that trade unions should be restrained. Despite being described as a Keynesian, Meade's diagnosis was more consistent with Milton Friedman's than John Maynard Keynes'. Keynes clearly argued the opposite case in the 1930s, but Meade explained that things were different in the 1970s and it would be presumptuous to claim that Keynes would not have understood that were he still alive. Trade unions, in Meade's view, caused both inflation and unemployment, requiring some kind of government regulation.

Meade concluded his Nobel lecture by examining different ways to restrain trade union power, including what he described as "the civilized approach." He proposed regulating wage demands by means of "impartial, outside tribunals" that would also take into account the broader national interest. Conceivably, such tribunals would restrain trade union demands and limit wage increases to achieve full employment and price stability.

While this approach appeared to be hostile to trade unions and consistent with a more conservative economic philosophy, that was apparently not what Meade intended. He was greatly concerned about the distribution of income and supported government efforts to create "the sort of free, efficient, and humanely just society in which I would like to live."[38] He thought that the distribution of personal income should be determined by government policies of taxation and social security rather than wage bargaining by trade unions. For the most part, other economists were likely to view Meade as a socialist, although one who did not adhere to any strict formula.[39]

In 1930, Meade worked with Dennis Robertson at Cambridge and, as he described it, "fell under the spell of Keynes." He also worked with the young Cambridge economists and became a member of the self-described "circus" of future Keynesians that included Joan Robinson.[40] At that time the circus was discussing Keynes' first major work, *A Treatise on Money*, a precursor to the *General Theory*. Meade was part of the inner circle and was invited by Keynes to dine at the High Table and even to lunch with him at his parents' residence in Harvey Road.[41]

Being part of the inner circle at Cambridge did not necessarily ensure acceptance of Meade's ideas. After returning to Oxford, Meade wrote his first manuscript for a book entitled *The Rate of Interest* and submitted it to Macmillan Publishers. Keynes commented on the manuscript describing it as "probably half-baked" and not particularly profitable although he continued to describe Meade as a promising young economist. Joan Robinson reviewed the book favorably when it came out but in a backhanded way when she commented on "the more comprehensible parts of the short book...."[42]

At the beginning of World War II, the British government thought that economists should be able to target key sectors of the German economy for destruction in order to disable the German war machine. This was exactly the kind of practical assignment where Meade's expertise in general equilibrium models and Keynesian macroeconomics was nearly useless. He transferred to another assignment within the War Cabinet Secretariat where he focused on solving Britain's own economic challenges. In this capacity, he again had contact with Keynes, who by then was at the Treasury and devising ways to organize the world economic system after the war. Meade had another small run-in with Keynes when the two differed on the role of monetary policy after the war. Keynes wanted low, stable interest rates to spur investment and contain the government's debt obligation, while Meade argued for more flexible interest rates in order to fine-tune the macroeconomy.[43] Keynes' arguments carried the day, at least in the immediate post–World War II era.

During his government assignment, Meade worked with Richard Stone in developing the first double-entry bookkeeping system for a national system of accounts that would later earn Stone a Nobel Prize. Meade also had a hand in designing the post–World War II institutions to govern trade and finance, including the International Monetary Fund, the International Bank for Reconstruction and Development (now the World Bank), and in particular, the General Agreement on Tariffs and Trade or GATT. Meade had been a solid advocate for floating exchange rates and free trade and GATT emerged as a powerful mechanism for moving the world in that direction. An obituary in the journal *Economic Record* referred to Meade as "one of the fathers of what eventually became the GATT."[44]

In 1947, Meade left government to join Lionel Robbins at the London School of Economics and later took a position at Cambridge. He retired in 1974 and won the Nobel Prize in 1977 at the age of seventy. He died eighteen years later. Paul Samuelson once wrote that "James Meade would give his cloak to a shivering beggar, not only because he feels it is right and fair to do so, but also for the reason that the beggar will receive more pleasure from it than a well-off professor of political economy."[45] Meade was respected by his peers for his intellectual honesty, which led him to conclusions that were neither exclusively Keynesian nor neoclassical.[46]

Bertil G. Ohlin (1977 Prize Winner)

One of the two economists honored in 1977 for working in the field of international trade was Bertil G. Ohlin. His name was familiar to economists who studied trade theory because it was the second half of the famous *Heckscher-Ohlin theorem*, an essential entry in every textbook on international economics.

Ohlin gained recognition by using a simple model that became the standard used by Nobel laureate Paul Samuelson and others. The model focused on the prices and quantities of imports and exports for two countries producing two products from two factors of production, labor, and capital. It was simple enough to manage mathematically and yet sufficiently detailed to illustrate basic principles of international trade.

For any country involved in trade, certain kinds of goods will be exported and others will be imported. But what determines whether Japan exports cars or the United States does? The most famous answer to this question was provided by David Ricardo in the early nineteenth century. According to his theory of comparative advantage, countries will export goods that they can produce relatively cheaper than other goods. In this example, countries have a comparative advantage in automobiles when they can produce them more efficiently relative to the production of other commodities, such as clothing. Countries with specialized expertise, including better technology and more highly educated workers, should have relatively more efficient production processes and therefore a comparative advantage.[47]

This theory created a problem for economists who subscribed to the standard competitive model. In this model, information is perfect so that every country is expected to have equal access to all available technologies and knowledge. What determines comparative advantage then? The answer to that hypothetical question came from Heckscher and Ohlin in the 1930s. Even if all countries have access to the same information and production technologies, there should still be an opportunity to specialize and trade. Their idea was related to the relative abundance of productive factors. Countries like the United States with a lot of capital, namely factories and machines, will export capital-intensive products such as airplanes, and import labor-intensive products such as clothing. You would expect to find the opposite for labor-intensive countries.

While this might seem like a simple answer, there were many complications. To begin with, it is difficult to measure accurately the level of capital intensity. In fact, it was nearly twenty years after Ohlin's book was published that that Nobel Prize winner Wassily Leontief used his input-output analysis to derive accurate measurements of capital intensity. When he applied this tool to test Heckscher and Ohlin's theorem, he found that exports from capital-intensive countries were not exclusively capital intensive. The evidence seemed to contradict Heckscher and Ohlin: The United States appeared to import capital-intensive products and export labor-intensive products.[48] This paradox generated a lot of interest, a lot of ideas, and a lot of articles, but in the end did not resolve the problem. A 1993 Harvard dissertation concluded that the Heckscher-Ohlin theorem explained trade patterns better before World War II than after, a period in which it simply did "not do all that well."[49] The theorem remained important for theoretical economists but seemed to have limited practical value.

Why didn't the Heckscher-Ohlin theorem really work? Like many of the models developed in the postwar years, it was based on perfect competition, which is not a terribly accurate model for macroeconomics or world trade. The United States today exports capital-intensive goods such as airplanes but it also imports capital-intensive goods like automobiles. The early trade models could simply not explain these patterns.

Not only does it appear that the Heckscher-Ohlin theorem has little to do with actual trade flows, it may also have little to do with Ohlin. In a review of Ohlin's work, Richard Caves of Harvard concluded that the theorem was "clearly stated in Heckscher's 1919 paper and hints appear earlier still in Wicksell's work."[50] Attributing even a small part of the theorem to Ohlin may have been overly generous.

Race to the Bottom

Ohlin borrowed another idea from Heckscher: a tendency for labor to receive equal compensation in all countries. Under free trade and perfect competition, compensation for comparable work should tend to be equal. Economists refer to this tendency as the *factor price equalization theorem*. According to this concept, wages in Mexico and China will eventually equal wages for comparable work in Sweden and the United States. This is a familiar concern of free trade critics, especially labor unions in high-wage countries. Free trade can certainly force wages down in developed countries, but will wages actually be equal throughout the world? Only in models with perfect competition and free trade does this seem to occur. In the real world where competition isn't perfect, trade isn't generally free, and there is a cost to transporting goods, wages for comparable work may tend to converge without actually being equal.[51]

Tariffs have been around a long time and for almost an equally long time, economists have been condemning them. Adam Smith did so in 1776 as did Ohlin in the 1930s. A tariff on automobile imports may benefit domestic producers and their employees, but in a general equilibrium model it will come at the expense of consumers and other domestic producers. Ohlin was able to show that the cost of a tariff is borne by other sectors in the economy because consumers will have less money to spend on everything else after paying more for automobiles.[52]

While John Maynard Keynes and his Cambridge colleagues were developing the concept of *aggregate demand*, a small group of Swedish economists in Stockholm, including Ohlin, were developing a similar theory. There were differences, but the two approaches shared some key features including a focus on the volatility of investment and the opportunity for government policies to facilitate economic recovery.

Despite the parallel development of Keynesian economics by the Stockholm school, Ohlin and Keynes were not always in agreement. In the late 1920s, Keynes and Ohlin disagreed about the likely effect of the war reparations placed on Germany after World War I. Keynes was concerned that an unrestrained effort to exact revenge by the Treaty of Versailles could place an excessive burden on the German economy. Harsh retribution, predicted Keynes, could backfire by creating an unstable Germany and increasing the potential for another war.[53]

The Keynes/Ohlin debate over reparations focused on a secondary issue. All could agree that reparations directly reduced German purchasing power but there was also a possibility that import and export prices could change as well, making it even more difficult for Germany to make its payments.[54] The question was whether reparations would also adversely affect Germany's terms of trade, thus increasing the already heavy burden on the German economy.[55] While the theoretical issue was abstract and remained unsettled, the actual impact of war reparations played out exactly as Keynes had predicted. Not only did the German economy become dangerously unstable in the 1920s, but that instability also helped to usher in a new wave of German nationalism and military aggression.

Keynes had an opportunity to see an early version of Ohlin's neoclassical trade model and was not impressed. While Ohlin was developing his model for his dissertation under Gustav Cassel in Stockholm, he sent a paper to Francis Edgeworth in 1922, the co-editor with Keynes of the *Economic Journal*. Edgeworth forwarded the paper to Keynes whose sole comment was, "This amounts to nothing and should be refused."[56] Ohlin's response was that Keynes was probably too busy to actually read the paper or he would have better understood both the paper and the German reparations issue.[57]

Ohlin's research slowed considerably in 1938 when he became a member of the Swedish Rikstag, and again in 1944 when he became the leader of the Liberal Party, a position that he held until 1967. Throughout those years, the Liberal Party was the major opposition party to the Social Democrats. Instead of writing journal articles, he wrote newspaper articles – lots of them. It was reported that he wrote 2,300 articles.[58] The Liberals and Ohlin opposed the "nationalization of Swedish industry or unnecessarily detailed state control of economic life."[59] He once explained what he most wanted to be remembered for in his political career: "I have long worked to bring about a favorable economic development in Sweden and to check the growth of socialization."[60]

Over the years, Ohlin became increasingly frustrated with progress in economics in general and trade theory in particular. He was not impressed by the research inspired by his theorem; it was all too technical and seemed to produce few insights. He was concerned that economists were too preoccupied with model building, or as he described it, "model mania," instead of exploring new practical approaches to economics.[61] Least useful, he believed, was the common practice of constructing economic models simply to demonstrate mathematical elegance without any actual problem in mind.[62]

To emphasize this point, Ohlin essentially ignored trade theory in his prize lecture even though it was the reason for his award. Instead he focused on a real economic problem, the slow economic recovery taking place at that moment in 1977. Bertil Ohlin died on August 3, 1979.

Paul R. Krugman (2008 Prize Winner)

The Swedish Academy of Sciences has occasionally been accused of being unduly influenced by current events, but when they announced the 2008 Nobel Prize winner, it seemed to some that they had picked the ideal economist for that moment in history. The United States economy had, by all indications, started a dangerous and precipitous freefall. The stock market was down about 40 percent from the previous year while housing prices plunged and foreclosures soared. More ominous was the announcement of major Wall Street bank failures, an event unseen since the Great Depression. Stunned by this sudden turn of events, citizens across the country were wondering if they hadn't been duped by charlatans selling deregulation and free markets. It would have been a bad time for the Nobel committee to choose another free market zealot. Instead, the committee picked Paul Krugman who was already famous for his willingness to challenge conventional wisdom.

What Krugman did for international economics was to breathe some common sense into it. Before Krugman, economists were still using a variation of David Ricardo's theory of comparative advantage from the early nineteenth century to explain who exports what. The theory was updated in the 1930s by Heckscher and Ohlin, but the idea was still essentially the same; countries specialize in particular exports based on whether they have a lot of labor, capital, or natural resources. Thus, France exported wine, Britain exported manufactured textiles, and India exported raw materials like cotton.

This theory worked well as long as you lived in the nineteenth century. Fast forward to the post–World War II era when trade really exploded and the theory failed to explain basic trade patterns. A problem arose because a single country often exports and imports very similar products with no apparent specialization. As the Nobel committee wrote, "A country such as Sweden, for example, exports and imports cars."[63] Volvos are shipped out and BMWs come in.

How did Krugman solve this puzzle? Very simply; Volvos are not BMWs and people prefer one over the other. As a group, consumers like to choose from a variety of vehicles. Furthermore, Krugman recognized that economies of scale allows cars to be manufactured more cheaply under mass production. As a result, Sweden specializes in the production of Volvos and Germany in the production of BMWs and then they trade. Not so difficult really.[64]

As the Nobel committee conceded, "The basic idea is rather self-evident," which begs the question why didn't other economists figure this out before 1979 when Krugman wrote his ten page article?[65] In fact, other economists did apply some of the same concepts to trade theory at about the same time and posited similar mathematical models.[66] And even before that, other economists had, according to Krugman, "pointed to the importance of economies to scale and imperfect competition in actual international markets."[67] But many of them were ignored. It was necessary to translate these intuitively compelling ideas into mathematics before the economics profession was willing to accept them. There was also the difficulty of finding sympathetic reviewers who were willing even to consider models based on something other than perfect competition. To his credit, Krugman was able to break through these barriers and discover something that already seemed familiar. As he described it, "For me, the biggest thrill in theory is the moment when your model tells you something that should have been obvious all along."[68]

Krugman was able to expand these ideas into a more general theory of trade and geography. We know, for example, that more than half of the world's population lives in cities and the rest live in more or less rural areas. Cities are where you expect to find large businesses and consequently more jobs, higher wages, and a greater variety of consumer goods and services. But why are most businesses located in cities? There are well-recognized advantages of being part of a large, concentrated industry in a single location. Obviously it helps manufacturers to be located closer to suppliers and customers in order to reduce transportation costs as well as the costs associated with communication, advertising, and contracting. Having a greater choice of suppliers should reduce costs and having access to a larger market should be more profitable. This is an older concept in economics called *external economies of scale* in which benefits of size accrue to an entire industry rather than a single company. Krugman adapted his ideas from international trade to this framework and expanded the list of the forces that tend to concentrate industries in a single city. For example, low transportation costs stimulate more trade and therefore contribute to larger businesses and larger cities.

Although he started out at Yale with a strong interest in history, Krugman switched to economics by his junior year when he became a research assistant for economist William Nordhaus.[69] He earned his doctorate at MIT with a specialty in trade. Although Krugman worked for a year (1982–3) as a senior economist at the Council of Economic Advisors during the Reagan administration, he never compromised his liberal values. Commenting on this period, he claimed that "I was then and still am an unabashed defender of the welfare state, which I regard as the most decent social arrangement yet devised."[70]

While a Princeton professor, Krugman devoted much of his time in the years prior to the Nobel Prize as a regular columnist and blogger for the *New York Times*. In this capacity he unleashed a punishing barrage of columns attacking the policies of President George W. Bush and later Republican presidential candidate John McCain. He developed something of a reputation for biting remarks, such as when he referred to Republicans as "the party of the stupid." While the Nobel Prize committee made it clear that his award was based on his academic research, they acknowledged his role as a "lively blogger and spirited columnist."[71]

Robert A. Mundell (1999 Prize Winner)

"Had the price of gold been raised in the late 1920s, or, alternatively, had the major central banks pursued policies of price stability instead of adhering to the gold standard, there would have been no Great Depression, no Nazi revolution, and no World War II," said Robert Mundell in 1999.[72]

The major central banks did abandon the gold standard in the 1930s but not quickly enough to avoid yet another economic collapse. To claim that this delay resulted in World War II by way of the Great Depression and the Nazi revolution sounds more like the ravings of a madman than a Nobel Prize winner. But these are the words of Robert Mundell, the winner of the 1999 Nobel Prize. The prize money, he told the immediate throng of reporters, would be used to restore an Italian castle that he had bought some years earlier from the Catholic Church. Here was someone that was clearly eccentric even by academic standards.

One would suspect that a man who blamed the Great Depression, the Nazi rise to power, and World War II on the gold standard would be opposed to the gold standard – but not Robert Mundell. He was a strong advocate for a return to the gold standard long after the concept had gone the way of top hats and coat tails.

All Nobel laureates are expected to provide a curriculum vitae but Mundell did not, which only added to his eccentric reputation. If he had, it would have been evident that his last publication in a major refereed journal was about thirty-four years earlier.[73] Mundell also failed to provide much of a personal biography for the Nobel Foundation. Other than being born in Canada in 1932, little has been reported about him before he enrolled in college. Hence his story begins as an undergraduate at the University of British Columbia where he fell in love with economic theory. Disregarding the advice of one professor to marry a rich girl for financial support, he borrowed money and went to MIT to study international economics. When it came time to write his dissertation, he worked with trade specialist and future Nobel laureate James Meade who was then at the London School of Economics.

Mundell took a position at the University of Chicago but left six years later after what was described as bitter feuding. A newspaper account suggested that the rigors of university life caused both his personal and professional lives to unravel.[74] He left Chicago for an obscure school in Ontario, the University of Waterloo, and about that time, bought his Italian castle. A couple of years later, however, Cambridge University invited him to give the prestigious Marshall lectures in 1973 and Columbia University hired him the following year. He was working there when his Nobel Prize was announced in 1999.[75]

Supply-Side Economics

Despite the reasons given for the Nobel Prize, Mundell was most famous for his advocacy of *supply-side economics* and a return to the gold standard. From its inception, supply-side economics seemed to be more of a political sound bite than a full blown economic theory and by 1999 had lost much of its glitter. It lacked mathematical models normally found in academic journal articles and research papers. What it did have was a political following in the Reagan administration and at the *Wall Street Journal*, namely editor Robert Bartley and his protégé, Jude Wanniski.

The supply-sider idea of cutting taxes to stimulate the economy was not an original idea. Keynesians had endorsed this policy for many decades. But the supply-siders didn't want to cut just any taxes; they wanted to cut taxes for the rich. This new twist appealed to wealthy benefactors but it had one problem: it lacked popular appeal. The solution was found in a theory proposed by economists Arthur Laffer and Robert Mundell. In their formulation, tax cuts had a positive effect on the economy but only if they were given to the rich so they could work harder and invest more. It also came with a risky prediction that any deficit created by the tax cut would soon vanish under a surge of economic activity. In practice, the deficits created by the Reagan tax cuts persisted long after they were supposed to end. It was the failure of this particular aspect of supply-side economics that left the notion with relatively few supporters. As Paul Samuelson and William Nordhaus wrote, the "Laffer-curve prediction that revenues would rise following the tax cuts has proven false."[76]

Major support for the supply side "revolution" was provided in 1981 and 1982 by Paul Craig Roberts, Assistant Secretary of the Treasury for Economic Policy in the Reagan administration. Roberts was a student of Nobel Prize winner James Buchanan and a columnist for *Business Week* from 1983 to 1998. His integral role in the supply-side "revolution" explains his unbridled enthusiasm for Mundell's 1999 Nobel award. Invited back by *Business Week* to write about Mundell's Nobel Prize, Roberts insisted that the award was the ultimate vindication of supply-side economics. Sounding like a victim of persecution, Roberts complained that the "American economic Establishment" had unfairly attacked the "handful of supply-siders." The attacks were even more painful because the critics used the phrase "voodoo economics," a term originally coined by George H. W. Bush when he was running against Reagan in the 1980 Republican presidential primary. In Robert's opinion, however, the 1999 announcement changed all that by making Mundell "the first supply-side theorist to win a Nobel Prize."

Readers of *Business Week* are to be excused if they thought that Mundell actually won the Nobel Prize for his work in supply-side economics. He did not. The 1999 Nobel Prize had no more to do with Mundell's supply-side theories than with the fact that he owned a castle. In fact, the Nobel committee didn't even mention supply-side economics in their press release or presentation speech. Members of the committee must have been aware of Mundell's role in supply-side economics in the 1980s but they completely ignored it, denying it the legitimacy that Roberts desired.

Mundell-Fleming

What, then, did the Nobel committee recognize as Mundell's contribution to mankind? There were two ideas, one an extension of Keynesian theory to include international markets and the other an analysis of a unified currency. The first contribution is referred to as the Mundell-Fleming model and can be described as a complementary amendment to the conventional textbook version of Keynesian economics.

In the Keynesian model, increases in the money supply can help stimulate an underperforming economy. It does this by lowering interest rates and stimulating consumer purchases and business borrowing.[77] Mundell noted that this policy also had an international effect that reinforced the outcome by indirectly stimulating exports under floating exchange rates.[78] Mundell worked this out mathematically for additional cases involving fiscal policy and fixed exchange rates.[79]

Mundell's conclusion was fairly simple: Monetary policy works under floating exchange rates and fiscal policy works under fixed exchange rates.[80] Whether this is true in the real world remains to be proven, but if Nobel laureate James Tobin is correct, it may not even be true in theory. Tobin modified some of the assumptions in Mundell's model and reached the opposite conclusion. The irony is that Tobin presented this contradictory model during his Nobel lecture in 1981, eighteen years before Mundell received his Nobel Prize.

Mundell's other achievement involved international currencies. Any two countries that engage in trade must exchange currencies at some rate. The world has experimented with many different approaches to setting exchange rates but by far the most simple is to adopt a single currency, as most of Western Europe now has done. Apart from eliminating tariffs and trade barriers, a single currency can be the surest way to promote more trade.

One of the best examples of a common currency area is the United States itself. It may seem obvious that the United States should have a common currency but that has not always been the case. While a national currency was introduced even before the end of the Revolutionary War, and gold was a reliable currency in the early decades of the country, there were also many forms of paper currency in circulation issued by banks and states. Ultimately the issuance of greenbacks in the nineteenth century and Federal Reserve notes in the twentieth century ushered in an era of a single national currency. In our modern economy, anything but a single currency for the United States would seem like a ridiculous inconvenience.

The political difficulties of convincing independent countries to adopt a single currency can be formidable. National pride alone can prevent a country from abandoning its own currency, a symbol of its independence. But what does a country give up economically if it accepts a common currency? Primarily, participants in a common currency policy give up the ability to use independent macroeconomic policy to fine tune an economy. If, for example, Louisiana suffered from high unemployment, it might favor a policy to increase the money supply, lower interest rates, and stimulate consumer demand. Of course Louisiana can't do this unilaterally because it doesn't have its own currency. This may represent the most significant impediment to the adoption of a common currency.

Mundell's consideration of optimum currency areas in 1961 offered the seemingly modest insight that this impediment is less important when labor is highly mobile. If the unemployed move from Louisiana to Texas or California where jobs are more plentiful, the problem of localized unemployment is eliminated.[81] While this may have been a narrow theoretical discovery, it seemed to become more important because of a major historical event. In the late 1990s, Europe did in fact create a multinational central bank and adopted the Euro as its single currency. Mundell had been a strong advocate for a common European currency and, by exploring these theoretical issues in the 1960s, he appeared to be ahead of his time.

Economists generally fall into two major camps, those who favor floating exchange rates and those who support common currencies. Mundell supported common currencies but in the particular form of a *gold standard*. If all currencies have a fixed value relative to gold, then gold becomes the common world currency. This position placed Mundell at odds with many economists including one of his former colleagues at the University of Chicago, fellow Nobel laureate Milton Friedman. One of the reasons for Friedman's award was his work supporting free-floating exchange rates, the alternative to Mundell's gold standard. Once again, the Nobel committee honored economists on opposing sides of a major debate.

The creation of the Euro has already sparked a fascinating discussion on the future of the world's money. Will the world evolve into three major currency areas centered on the dollar, the euro, and the yen? If so, will the exchange rates among these currencies continue to be volatile or settle down? Or will there be convergence toward a single world currency? Many different international financial systems have been tested in the real world and there is no reason to expect that we have all the answers on this important topic.

THIRTEEN

Numbers Guys

Ragnar A. Frisch (1969)

Jan Tinbergen (1969)

Trygve M. Haavelmo (1989)

Sir Clive W. J. Granger (2003)

Robert F. Engle, III (2003)

Daniel L. McFadden (2000)

James J. Heckman (2000)

The conversion of economic concepts into formulas dominated the development of economic theory in the post–World War II era. This was a great opportunity for mathematically inclined economists even though much of the work was fairly inconclusive. As soon as one group derived an economic principle, another group proved the opposite. What economists needed were actual numbers to determine whose theory was better. They hoped to find truth in statistics.

In the 1920s, statisticians borrowed techniques from physics and other disciplines to calibrate equations with actual economic data. The field of study became known as *econometrics* and involved general statistical techniques refined for use with economic data and models. The name econometrics implies its meaning, a combination of economics and statistics or metrics. Nobel Prize winner Ragnar Frisch is credited with coining the term and defined it as "the statistical verification of the laws of pure economics."[1] Frisch and his student, Trygve Haavelmo, developed the basic framework for econometrics while another Nobel Prize winner, Jan Tinbergen, started applying the techniques to systems of equations. The goal was to provide compelling explanations of economic events and more accurate predictions of the future.

A later generation of Nobel Prize–winning statisticians concentrated on problems of particular interest to economists. Sir Clive W. J. Granger and Robert F. Engle, III developed new methods to analyze data collected over time, Daniel L. McFadden created a better method to study choices made between discrete alternatives, such as buying a Honda Accord or a Toyota Camry, and James J. Heckman explored some of the problems of using groups of individuals to test economic hypotheses.

The standard approach taken in econometrics generally starts with a theory. For example, the quantity of automobiles demanded by consumers should depend on the price of automobiles. Data can be collected and analyzed with the expectation that the number of cars demanded will be lower when prices are higher. Searching for this statistical relationship can run afoul of a number of real-world complications. For example, the success of this approach depends on how precisely human behavior can be depicted by a formula. There is little room in this approach for caprice, spontaneity, or changes in tastes or values. Patterns of human nature have to persist long enough so that they can be measured and used for predictions. Techniques pioneered by Nobel Prize winners have provided valuable statistical tools to analyze these types of problems, but like economics, they are limited by assumptions that are not always met in the real world.

Ragnar A. Frisch (1969 Prize Winner)

Beginning in the 1920s, Ragnar Frisch dedicated his career to quantifying economics so that it would become an applied science. He had no patience for qualitative economics because "practically any 'conclusion' can be drawn and defended."[2] Instead he turned to quantifying everything he possibly could in his economic analysis. In the process, he helped to found the Econometric Society and the journal *Econometrica* for which he served as editor from 1933 to 1955. His major contribution was to convert economic equations into numbers.

This was an ambitious project, even more so because most of Frisch's work predated computers. There was no option other than to conduct the calculations by hand, which made even simple analyses extremely tedious. By necessity this forced researchers to limit their models to only the most important equations and variables but hard-driving personalities like Ragnar Frisch were always pushing the limits. He needed students to help with the calculations so he founded the Institute of Economics at the University of Oslo and secured funding from the Rockefeller Foundation. Student assistants did much of the tedious arithmetic until computers became more common in the 1960s.

Econometrics doesn't just involve collecting and analyzing economic data. Such an approach would be *inductive* and rely on real-world observations to guide the development of theories. Econometricians, including Frisch, typically rejected this approach. They insisted on starting with a well-defined theory with specific equations and then filling in the values with statistics. This took a more *deductive* approach. Frisch was very critical of the notion that facts could speak for themselves. As he said in his Nobel speech, "Facts that speak for themselves, talk in a very naïve language."[3]

A strictly deductive approach limited what economists could do. It would be useful to review economic events and data and then develop a theory based on a deeper understanding of historical and institutional contexts. But that was considered "unscientific." Instead the theories were often derived from assumptions of perfect information and complete rationality. It didn't take a deep understanding of the real world to derive these formulas; economists could develop them in their offices with a pad of paper and a pencil. An editorial in the *New York Times* in 1969 commended Frisch and Tinbergen for their scientific contribution but with the warning that the "pressure for mathematical precision can sometimes separate economists from real problems that cannot easily be quantified."[4]

The obvious way to evaluate economic models is to see how well they can account for past economic outcomes and predict future ones. On this score econometrics has had a mixed record. In the year Frisch won his Nobel Prize, an article in the *New York Times* reported that "econometricians themselves are the first to acknowledge they are still far from being able to forecast infallibly the course of the economy." Therefore, it suggested, that a better measure of success would be the prestige and salary levels of econometricians. Based on this measure of success, there was no question that "mathematical techniques in theoretical and applied economics have often paid off handsomely."[5]

Frisch estimated equations from both microeconomics and macroeconomics and, in fact, is credited with inventing these names to distinguish between the two. His contribution cited by the Nobel committee was primarily for macroeconomics, in which he created early versions of input-output models, trade-cycle models that showed boom and bust behavior, and dynamic models representing economic growth. Frisch went further than his colleagues by trying to estimate statistical models even when they included multiple equations. Through his work, Frisch laid the foundation for the massive macroeconomic models that would come to flourish during the computer age.

From the time of his birth in Norway, Ragnar Frisch was supposed to be a goldsmith. His father ran the family gold- and silverworks firm that

Ragnar's grandfather had established in 1856. In fact, his family ancestry could be traced back to a request in 1630 from King Christian IV to the Prince of Saxony for a team of mining specialists to exploit the silver deposits discovered at Kongsberg, Norway. Frisch completed an apprenticeship in 1920 that qualified him as a goldsmith, just about the time that his career took a detour.

Frisch's mother steered him to the college catalogue for Oslo University because she suspected that gold smithing was not the right career for her son. Together they picked the economics program because, according to Frisch, it "was the shortest and easiest study."[6] Graduating with a degree in economics in 1919, Frisch pursued advanced study in economics and mathematics, earning a doctorate in mathematical economics.

Frisch recounted that he was offered a position at Yale University after being invited to the United States by the American economist Irving Fisher. Even though the salary was five times higher than what he received in Oslo, he turned it down and returned home, never regretting the decision. Still, his life wasn't always easy in Norway, particularly during World War II. Although he seldom mentioned the experience, Frisch and other university professors spent a year in a Nazi concentration camp in 1943.[7]

Frisch was a prolific researcher, but he was not particularly disciplined when it came to turning his voluminous notes and mimeographed reports into published articles and books. His colleague from the University of Oslo, Leif Johansen, lamented this fact in an article documenting Frisch's academic work.[8] Johansen offered several examples where Frisch approached a problem in a very original way only to be ignored by the profession because the Institute report was either published in a Scandinavian language or not widely circulated.

However, enough of Frisch's work was published to earn him the very first Nobel Prize in economics, which was shared with Jan Tinbergen from Holland. He and Tinbergen were selected from thirty nominees and given a medal and a share of the $73,000 prize money. Frisch was unfortunately unable to attend the lavish ceremony in Sweden but sent a colleague in his place. The Nobel committee specifically cited his contribution to model building, mathematical programming, national income accounts, and launching the field of econometrics.

Along with his work in economics Frisch was a beekeeper but not because he particularly valued the honey or the experience of working with bees. His purpose was to study bee genetics and create more productive bees. He explained that he would not describe the activity as either pleasant or entertaining. It was, he reflected, "more in the nature of an obsession which

I shall never be able to get rid of."[9] Ragnar Frisch died in 1973 at the age of seventy-eight.

Jan Tinbergen (1969 Prize Winner)

In 1969 the Nobel committee announced that Jan Tinbergen would receive the first Nobel Prize in economics with Ragnar Frisch. His contribution to the development of econometrics and the art of large model building was specifically cited by the committee. They also mentioned his League of Nations study of the United States economy from 1919 to 1932, calling it a "pioneering work."[10]

John Maynard Keynes reviewed the same League of Nations study and complimented Tinbergen for his "brave pioneer effort" and commented that the labor involved to accomplish it "must have been enormous." But overall, Keynes was not impressed with Tinbergen's elaborate model building and statistical testing, describing it as both "alchemy" and a "nightmare." He concluded that "I have the feeling that Prof. Tinbergen may agree with much of my comment, but that his reaction will be to engage another ten computors and drown his sorrows in arithmetic."[11] Some of Keynes' criticisms were minor issues but others were fundamental.[12] The criticism must have stung because Tinbergen admired Keynes' work and believed that his statistical approach provided support for Keynesian theory.[13] At the same time, Tinbergen's work was criticized by other economists for being too Keynesian, which left him with few supporters.[14] But his approach was favored by at least one group that mattered, the Swedish Nobel committee.

Following in Frisch's footsteps, Tinbergen pioneered the intensive use of data and statistics to measure economic relationships, especially macroeconomic equations related to national employment, wage levels, and trade. Because there was little actual data available in the 1930s, he had to make do with what he had and became an inspiration for other model builders including future Nobel Prize winner Lawrence Klein.

As the director of the Netherlands Central Planning Bureau, Tinbergen was expected to have something useful to say about solving economic problems and achieving economic growth. Unlike some economists, Tinbergen's policy recommendations were not always to unleash free markets. More often than not, the outcome of his planning models would lead him to support regulating exchange rates, increasing public expenditures, or some other type of government action.

For Tinbergen, the quantification of economics was more than a profession; it was a crusade. He hoped to infuse economics with more quantitative and mathematical models because, as he explained, "they force us to present a 'complete' theory...."[15] At the same time he was dismissive of economics that was not mathematical, referring to them as "literary theories."[16]

One of those literary theories has to be the *cobweb model* that can be found in many elementary economics texts and ironically had a link to Tinbergen. The original version of the model explained why agricultural markets are often volatile. In the first year, farmers produce too much corn and the price falls. As a consequence, farmers independently decide to cut production the following year. But as they all lower production, prices and profits rise the next year. Subsequently farmers decide to increase production, and the cycle repeats itself. The model can either converge or break down depending on supply and demand, and in the process it traces out a pattern that resembles a cobweb. This model is a good example of how reasonable expectations can cause market volatility. In 1931, Tinbergen was one of the first to use this concept in an article to analyze a business cycle for the shipbuilding industry.[17]

Econometrics is no substitute for understanding underlying economic relationships, and Tinbergen understood this. At one point when he was testing different variables to explain the price of beef, he came across an odd relationship. He found that when feed prices for cattle were high, the price for beef itself was low. Now this didn't make sense because high feed prices should have made cattle and beef more expensive, not less. When Tinbergen looked into this puzzle, he found something that he hadn't expected. High feed prices put economic pressure on poor farmers who often had no choice but to slaughter some additional cattle to pay the higher cost. This put more beef on the market, which tended to bring down its price. This unusual result finally made sense, but only after Tinbergen had a better understanding of the actual market. He cited this example in his Nobel Prize lecture.[18]

Although Tinbergen had a doctorate, it was in physics, not economics. Why did he switch fields? He claimed that he took an interest in economics after witnessing the economic injustices during the Great Depression.[19] He hoped to use his scientific training to solve the problem of business cycles as well as poverty in underdeveloped countries. Referring to these efforts, economist Bent Hansen said that "As much as he [Tinbergen] is respected in the privileged world, he is beloved by the underprivileged, the underdogs."[20] Lawrence Klein echoed these comments when he cited Tinbergen's "good works in society towards peace and conflict resolution."[21] And Paul Samuelson simply called him a "humanist saint."[22]

Trygve M. Haavelmo (1989 Prize Winner)

Although most economists work in cloistered specialties, there are certain names that are generally familiar to the broader profession because of their popular writing, textbooks, or leadership roles in the American Economics Association or other professional associations. Most Nobel Prize winners fall into this category. But occasionally there is a winner who is largely unknown, even among economists. The 1989 winner from Norway, Trygve Haavelmo, was one of those. The *Wall Street Journal* ungraciously noted that of the twenty economists they called, five had never heard of him and several more recalled an article he may have written some fifty years earlier.[23] Since the Swedish committee highlighted his contribution to econometrics and large model building, a *Journal* reporter called Michael K. Evans, former member of the President's Council of Economic Advisors and econometric model builder, and asked for a reaction. He explained that Haavelmo's contribution was considered important some fifty years earlier but that little of it had survived. Samuelson was one of the few economists that came to Haavelmo's defense, explaining that his work was important and it was not appropriate to ask "What have you done for me lately?"[24]

Haavelmo probably didn't help matters either with his reaction to the Nobel Prize. When a reporter from Reuters called his home on the day his award was announced, Haavelmo told him "I don't like the idea of such prizes. I'm not going to talk about this on the phone, and I haven't thought it through. Don't write anything."[25] He added that the prize "is quite irrelevant to the real issues,"[26] and he didn't say anything more. He disappeared for the remainder of the day, probably going for a long walk in the woods, which was his habit. Unlike the calls from Sweden to the United States to inform Nobel Prize winners, European winners aren't called in the early morning hours so this couldn't have been the reason for his annoyance. His response made the press wonder if he was actually going to accept the prize and the $469,000 check that went along with it. He did; after all, he was an economist.

Perhaps it was the many years that had elapsed since his work was published, or perhaps it was his initial response, but for some reason the press was not particularly nice to Haavelmo. This was one of the few years that reporters pushed beyond the Nobel committee press release and standard quips from loyal colleagues. The *Wall Street Journal* reporter speculated about why Haavelmo really won the Nobel Prize. The anonymous reporter wrote that there "is a good deal of politics in the Nobel award," and the Swedish committee may have "stretched a little far to get non-U.S. and non-British winners."[27] MIT, they reported, had an annual pool to bet on who would win the prize, and in 1989 there was not a single winner. Assar Lindbeck, who was both head of the committee that selected Haavelmo and coincidently his personal friend, insisted that Haavelmo was "the father of modern econometrics," a characterization that didn't exactly fit, in part because it had already been used to describe Ragnar Frisch.[28]

The Nobel committee honored Haavelmo for highlighting two problems with the early use of economic statistics. The first one is the *identification problem*, which is best illustrated with an example. At the simplest level one can propose that the quantity of pigs demanded by consumers depends exclusively on their price. If economics was an experimental science, one could systematically change the price of pigs while holding everything else constant and record the number of pigs demanded. The outcome should show that consumers want fewer pigs at higher prices. Real world data, however, are unlikely to show that result because prices are determined by both supply and demand and neither are constant. Statisticians have struggled with this problem for a long time by trying to find the right number of equations and variables. The Nobel committee gave Haavelmo credit for recognizing this problem but a review by James Heckman noted that this problem was familiar to economists as early as 1915, long before Haavelmo.[29]

Haavelmo wrote about a related topic called the *simultaneity problem*. In the real world, variables that determine the demand for pigs may also affect the demand for cows and chickens, which can cycle back and affect the demand for pigs. Or a single variable, the price of corn, may affect both the demand for pigs and the supply of pigs. It can be difficult, if not impossible, to isolate any one relationship from this web of mutually interdependent relationships. Although Haavelmo was not the first to be aware of these problems or the last to propose solutions, he certainly added to the awareness of the challenge facing econometricians.

Another, more controversial contribution was the Haavelmo-Cowles approach to econometrics, which was widely adopted in the post–World War II period. This was a general approach to econometrics rather than a specific technique. It was based on the idea that there are two steps in econometric research. The first step was to develop a theory that explained economic behavior. The second step was to collect data in order to test the theory. A statistical test would be applied to determine whether the model was reasonably consistent with the data with less than a 5 percent chance of an error. In theory, econometricians mechanically tested theories and either accepted or rejected them. The belief was that this would make economics scientific and objective, just as the Nobel committee hoped.

While econometricians tried to follow this protocol for many decades, it wasn't especially successful. James Heckman, another Nobel Prize winner, claimed that Haavelmo-Cowles is the reason that "rigorous econometrics is often perceived to be irrelevant by empirical analysts who take a much more inductive approach to economic knowledge."[30] In other words, economists are more likely to look at economic information and then develop a theory. At the very least they often tinker with their equations until they find a better statistical result. Christopher Sims thought the idea of "sifting through theories" and mechanically "rejecting one false one after another until the truth crops up" did not appear to work in economics.[31] But more importantly, Haavelmo's method did not appear to have advanced our understanding of the economy. In his review article, Heckman asked "why the Haavelmo-Cowles program has not been empirically fruitful?"[32] While it produced a voluminous academic literature, rich in arcane details, it actually produced relatively few new insights.

For his part, Haavelmo thought the criticism was misguided. In his Nobel lecture he said, "Econometrics has to be founded on theories that describe in a reasonably accurate way the fashion in which the observed world has operated in the past." The problem, he explained, wasn't with econometrics but with the fact that "existing economic theories are not good enough for this purpose."[33] He went on to suggest that one of the shortcomings of economic theory is that it ignores the political and social conventions that govern human behavior. These so-called "rules of the game" are created to guide human behavior. Understanding these institutional features of an economy should, according to Haavelmo, produce better theories.

Trygve Haavelmo was the second Norwegian to win the Nobel Prize. The first was Ragnar Frisch, his mentor at the University of Oslo and later his supervisor at the Institute of Economics in Oslo. Some commentators have pointed out that it is not always possible to tell who had the ideas first, Frisch or Haavelmo, because the former "was notorious for not writing down many of his best ideas, at least not in accessible form."[34]

At the outbreak of World War II in 1939, Haavelmo left Norway for New York with the support of a Rockefeller fellowship and stretched the trip into seven years by working for the Norwegian Trade Commission and later the Cowles Commission at the University of Chicago. But he never truly adjusted to the United States and was anxious to return to his home in Norway. Paul Samuelson said, "He would have rowed home, if he could."[35]

Shortly after returning to Norway, Haavelmo "all but quit the field of econometrics."[36] As an alternative he tried to improve economic theory so that econometrics had better material to work with. The *Boston Globe* reported that "When Harvard econometrician Zvi Griliches visited Haavelmo in 1967, he found him more interested in trout fishing than in current economics."[37]

Sir Clive W. J. Granger (2003 Prize Winner)

The 2003 Nobel Prize in economics did not recognize any new economic principle or theory. It was granted in honor of a statistical method that gave econometricians another, more sophisticated tool for analyzing data collected over time called *time series* data. The new technique was a clever improvement over existing methods and sparked something of a resurgence in time series analysis.

Econometrics is not an exact science. James Stock, a Harvard economist, provided a simple example of the difficulty. He noted that U.S. national income has been growing significantly for at least the last 100 years, and at the same time Mars has been slowly but steadily getting closer to the Earth. Because of these two long-term trends, it is virtually guaranteed that a simple statistical correlation would support the hypothesis that U.S. national income is determined by the country's proximity to Mars.[38] The lesson of this example is that statistical analysis cannot be applied indiscriminately.

The nature of the data described in this example is a time series because the observations are made over time – annually, quarterly, monthly, etc. The problem described here occurs when time series tend to drift up or drift down over a long period of time, a characteristic statisticians refer to as *nonstationary*. If a time series is nonstationary, it typically doesn't have a fixed distribution or mean. Statistics was not originally designed to handle this kind of phenomenon, which unfortunately, is fairly common in economics.

It is important to remember that the original development of statistical concepts was not necessarily based on human economic behavior but on more objective biological or mechanical processes like flipping a coin. The percentage of heads in ten coin flips is a classic example of a random variable that is the foundation of statistical theory. The percentage of heads will closely adhere to the principles of statistics and forecasts can be made within well-defined levels of confidence. But is this also true for the stock market or consumer spending? These are clearly not like flipping a coin because they are influenced by human behavior, which produces its own unique patterns. The differences between economic variables and classical random variables were of great interest to the 2003 Nobel Prize winners, statisticians Sir Clive W. J. Granger and Robert F. Engle, III.[39] What Granger did was to recognize this difference and propose a more customized statistical approach.

It is no surprise that many economic variables such as population, gross domestic product, and productivity tend to drift up over time while others tend to drift down, such as the relative size of agriculture and the real value of a dollar. Because of these long-term trends, it is just too easy to find statistically significant correlations even when no real cause-and-effect relationship exists. Statisticians refer to this as *spurious correlation*. This problem made it difficult to use economic time series data to reliably test even the most basic economic theory.

Granger, a statistician by training, showed that economists could easily be duped by these nonstationary variables. Many years earlier, Keynes had proposed a simple idea that consumption spending for an entire economy was determined primarily by a single variable, national income. As national income went up, Keynes argued, so should consumption. This concept could be tested statistically by using time series data and one would likely find a strong statistical correlation because both national income and consumption have been drifting upward for a long time. But the evidence would remain suspect because it could also just as easily be a spurious statistical result since both variables are nonstationary.

As a result, some economists abandoned time series altogether while others developed simple techniques to avoid the obvious problems with nonstationary data. One approach was to consider only year-to-year changes in time series data. For example, one would expect the increase in income from 1945 to 1946 to cause an increase in consumption for the same period and so on for every other period. It turned out that this simple change, converting the data from levels to annual changes, was usually enough to avoid the problem. While this simple approach could work reasonably well, it was not very "elegant" or sophisticated from a statistical point of view. Granger came up with a related but more elegant solution in 1981.

Without specifying the exact form of Granger's innovation, the basic concept referred to is not so difficult. It can be illustrated with the following example. Suppose a person and a dog are free to wander in any direction and we track their movements. If the person and the dog are unrelated, then there may not be any apparent relationship between the two paths. However, if the dog belongs to the person, then their paths should coincide more frequently and Granger would say that the two paths are *cointegrated.*[40] Granger and his co-winner, Robert Engle, suggested statistical tests that attempt to identify the presence of cointegration. They then recommended better methods for estimating the relationships between these variables. For instance, if we knew that consumption and income were "cointegrated," then their relationship could be estimated with more appropriate techniques. Granger used the same idea to develop a test to see if one variable appeared to cause another to change, which became known as the *Granger causality test.*

Not all economists were enthusiastic about the new methods associated with cointegration. Nobel Prize winner Lawrence Klein, in particular, was concerned that the techniques could produce misleading results because they tested relationships that were not necessarily consistent with the original economic model. As he warned, "The technique of cointegration, ... I think can do damage.... Successive differencing, as it is done in cointegration techniques, may introduce new relationships, some of which we do not want to have in our analysis." While he conceded that the cointegration method "keeps the analysis simple," he also contended that "the world is not simple."[41]

Granger and Engle were certainly successful at highlighting an important problem that compromised earlier econometric techniques. But no matter how often a technique appears in the eminent journal *Econometrica*, the ultimate test is to explain historical patterns and accurately predict the future. By this standard there is no consensus on cointegration as with most econometric approaches. It is difficult to name any economic theories that have been rejected or accepted by the profession because of econometric results. As econometricians know, the latest statistical methods will eventually be replaced by even newer methods. With this in mind, modesty may be the best strategy when describing econometric innovations.

Granger and his mother spent the duration of World War II in Cambridge, England, living with his grandparents. His father, who fought in and survived the war, worked in sales for a company that sold jams, jellies, and marmalades. Granger did well in mathematics, but his overall school performance was sufficiently unimpressive that a teacher told his mother that he had no chance of success.[42] Not a very good prediction. Almost by accident, Granger decided to study statistics. When asked to state his career plan, he found that his stutter made it too difficult to say the word "meteorology" but "statistics" came out just fine. The first in his family to attend a university, Granger enrolled at the University of Nottingham with an initial major in mathematics and economics. By the end of the first year he dropped the economics part of his degree and concentrated on mathematics. He received his doctorate in statistics in 1959 with the completion of his dissertation on time series analysis, setting the stage for his later work.[43]

Granger was awarded a Harkness Fellowship that he used to travel to the United States and worked with Oskar Morgenstern on a time series project suggested by John von Neumann. Granger returned to Nottingham but later accepted an offer from the University of California, San Diego, which aspired to build a world-class econometrics program. They were successful – the econometric group at U.C. San Diego was eventually ranked third in the world.[44]

When the 2003 Nobel Prize was announced, Granger speculated about what it meant when someone like himself with so little economic training could win the Nobel Prize in economics. "Does this say something about me," he wondered, "or something about the field of economics?"[45] His only formal training was limited to a few months during his undergraduate days at the University of Nottingham. It was, of course, supplemented with additional reading in economics and interaction with economists, but this paled in comparison to his formal training in mathematics and statistics. He speculated that economics could have "less basic core material than is necessary for fields such as mathematics, physics, or chemistry." And yet the "common concepts and features" that characterize economic theory "may be quite simplistic and are not necessarily realistic."[46]

Robert F. Engle (2003 Prize Winner)

There are economists who are denied tenure at a university or advised not to apply for it, but few economists in this category go on to win a Nobel Prize. This happened to the 2003 winner, Robert Engle. According to Engle, "Although MIT promoted me to Associate Professor, it was clear that I would not get tenure there."[47] With that understanding, Engle searched for other employment, which he found at the University of San Diego. The move turned out to be fortunate for Engle because it opened up an opportunity to collaborate with fellow econometrician Clive Granger. Granger and Engle co-authored a number of articles and solved problems that were later cited by the Nobel committee.

Both of the 2003 Nobel Prize winners in economics were specialists in time series analysis and each of them focused on the particular problem of applying classical statistical theory to economic data. An important assumption in classical statistics is that random variables, like those generated by flipping coins or throwing dice, have a fixed mean and variance. The same assumption is applied throughout much econometric analysis, but economic variables don't behave like dice and they don't necessarily have a fixed *mean* or *variance*. Granger's work focused on the mean. Engle focused on the variance. If the variance isn't fixed, then conventional time series analysis is likely to give the wrong results unless corrected. Engle provided a correction in what was called the ARCH model.[48]

This may sound like a rather obscure contribution for a Nobel Prize, but Engle's work attracted a surprising amount of attention because variance is of great interest to one important sector of the economy, Wall Street. The value of any individual stock or combination of stocks, including the Dow Jones averages, NASDAQ, or Standard and Poor's 500, will bounce around over time, drifting in one direction for a while and then another. This movement is referred to as *volatility* and can be measured by variance. Sophisticated investors are very interested in the variance of stocks because they consider it a good indicator of risk.

In general, the variance for most stocks does not appear to be constant. Any graph of stock prices or rates of return is likely to show moderate fluctuations interspersed by distinct clusters of higher volatility. Because of this pattern, the variance will depend upon the time period selected and how many clusters of volatility are included. The clusters themselves appear to be almost randomly distributed but they are more common during market downturns. As Engle observed, "Volatility tends to be higher in bear markets."[49] This means that there is probably not a single, "correct" variance. The advantage of Engle's ARCH model is that it recognized that volatility was likely to be higher immediately following a volatile episode and that it allowed the variance to change over time.[50] This not only provided a unique estimate of current stock volatility but also provided a different way to forecast future volatility.

Engle's model was also related to the valuation of options. One of the variables that determine the value of an option in the Black–Scholes formula is the variance of a stock. With a new way to estimate variances, Engle's model also provided a new way to calculate the value of an option. There are, of course, other applications of the ARCH model for time series analysis, but it was the financial markets that made the most of it. This was one of the key innovations that led to the development of a new field of study called financial econometrics.

The goal in these efforts was to provide more accurate information about the risk or value of a financial instrument so that investors could make smarter choices. Despite its complexity, this approach does not necessarily guarantee success. Engle's statistical measure is based on historical patterns and constitutes only one factor, sometimes a minor one, in determining future stock prices or future volatility. Stock values may depend more on the performance of the chief executive officer, the degree of future competition, or the success of a particular marketing strategy. Statistics in this case may be interesting but have limited value.

Robert Fry Engle, III was born in Syracuse, New York. Like his father, he was fond of ice dancing and more importantly, science. Engle entered the doctoral program in physics at Cornell where he studied quantum mechanics with Nobel laureate Hans Bethe. Although he finished a state-of-the-art master's degree using nuclear magnetic resonance, he lost interest in physics and switched to the economics doctoral program at Cornell. Courses in microeconomics, econometrics, statistics, and probability were relatively easy because of his strong background in math and statistics. In 1969, Engle completed his dissertation, received his Ph.D., and married Marianne Eger all on the same day.

For the next five years, Engle worked at MIT specializing in urban economics, although his heart was in time series. It wasn't until he left MIT for the University of California, San Diego that he became part of what he called the "golden time for time series econometrics."[51] Engle, Granger, and the other econometricians at San Diego teamed up with the faculty of the London School of Economics to advance time series analysis. This collaboration led to results that were recognized by his Nobel Prize in 2003. U.C. San Diego came close to having two full-time Nobel Prize winners that year except that both Granger and Engle had just retired only months before the announcement. Engle had taken another position at New York University.

Engle may be the only economist to win both a Nobel Prize and awards for ice dancing. He and his partner placed second in the national adult skating championships in 1996 and 1999.

Daniel L. McFadden (2000 Prize Winner)

Econometrics has evolved considerably from the early twentieth century when the first attempts were made to use classical statistics to estimate economic equations. By the 1960s, with mainframe computers and a growing abundance of data, there was an explosion of statistical estimates of every conceivable type. Some economists specialized in estimating only demand functions, because they are so integral to economic thinking. One variation of this was the decision that individuals make when they choose one thing over another. As consumers we may decide to choose Coke over Pepsi, driving cars over mass transit, or retirement over working. This class of decisions involves making a selection, or what economists describe as a *discrete choice*.

Much of the data collected from personal surveys are based on discrete choices, such as which political party you favor, which product you prefer, or which mode of transportation you plan to use. Econometricians knew how to estimate equations based on prices and quantities, but discrete variables presented a different problem.

The key to estimating these relationships was relatively simple: Convert a yes or no variable into a probability. Because probabilities are continuous variables between zero and one, they lend themselves to more familiar statistical techniques. One of the two Nobel Prize winners of 2000, Daniel McFadden, made his mark on the profession by developing this idea. In 1965, a student at Berkeley asked McFadden for some help analyzing freeway routing decisions by the California Department of Highways. McFadden used probabilities to model the choices and published a report in 1968. Over the next few years, he and others refined this technique for estimating discrete choices.

The basic concept, however, was not invented by McFadden. Estimation of discrete choice models was pioneered by biostatisticians during the 1940s. Joseph Berkson introduced just such a model in 1944 and published it in the *Journal of the American Statistical Association*. By the 1960s, researchers were introducing models to describe situations where more than two choices were possible. Even earlier, in 1927, L. L. Thurstone, a biostatistician, introduced the basic framework for discrete choice, and it became known as the random utility maximization (RUM) model.[52] McFadden was familiar with discrete choice models created by psychologists, and he adapted these models using microeconomics. In his model, choices were determined by age, gender, occupation, marital status, and other personal variables.

McFadden employed another concept called *hedonic attributes*. To illustrate this idea, consider commuters who must decide whether to drive a car to work or take a bus. In a sense what they are really doing is evaluating specific attributes of driving a car, the shorter travel time, the greater convenience involved, the minimal amount of walking, the certainty of departure, and the cost. In his expanded analysis, McFadden factored in all of these other attributes. He claimed that this approach provided him with a better forecast of Bay Area Rapid Transit (BART) ridership than what the BART planners had devised.

Statistical analysis in economics is no better than the theory that is being estimated. Discrete choice models work best when, say, two thirty-five-year-old married lawyers with incomes of $80,000 owning a house in Richmond make the exact same choices. If these carefully enumerated two lawyers buy different products, vote for different candidates, or choose different modes of transportation, then the discrete choice model won't work so well.

McFadden generally limited his professional advice to developing statistical techniques except for a couple of instances that occurred after he won the Nobel Prize. In February of 2001, he contributed an op/ed article to the *Wall Street Journal* arguing against government intervention in the California energy markets. In the midst of the West Coast energy crisis, wholesale electricity prices were hitting all-time records of $1,000 per megawatt hour instead of the normal $40 to $50. California and the federal government were considering restricting prices, which dismayed many economists including McFadden. "The state," he argued, "is poised to repeat the mistakes of the last cycle of regulation."[53] While he admitted that the markets were simply poorly designed he stated his preference for a "dysfunctional partially deregulated market" over a "fully-regulated one that promises to be even more dysfunctional."[54]

After a long delay, the federal government implemented a price cap on electricity, despite McFadden's passionate opposition. Almost immediately, prices collapsed and the energy crisis subsided, leaving behind a huge debt for California and West Coast utilities. Only after the energy crisis did it become clear that Enron and other energy traders – who had pushed for deregulation – had systematically manipulated the market and pillaged consumers. The magnitude of the fraud was immense, costing Californians and other ratepayers on the West Coast billions of dollars in overpayments.

In another case, McFadden added his name in 2003 to a list of nine other Nobel winning economists who opposed President George W. Bush's tax plan. They objected to the fact that the tax cuts primarily benefited high-income earners, and McFadden added that they would result in chronic deficits that would force the government to cut spending.[55] Nobel Prize winner Milton Friedman and other conservative economists lined up on the other side of the issue expressing their support for the tax cuts. Like McFadden, Friedman thought the tax cuts would cause the government to limit future spending, but unlike McFadden, he thought that was a good outcome.

McFadden grew up on a remote farm in North Carolina with neither electricity nor running water, but he did have interesting parents. His father only had four years of formal schooling, and yet he was hired to work at a bank at the age of fourteen because he could add five-digit columns of numbers in his head. His mother was an architect who taught college before becoming a high school math teacher. With few neighbors, the family, especially Daniel, enjoyed reading as their primary form of recreation.

In order to keep Daniel challenged in the rural North Carolina public schools, his teachers let him read books and complete correspondence courses in algebra and geometry. At age sixteen, McFadden moved to Minnesota to work on his uncle's dairy farm and soon enrolled at the University of Minnesota. He graduated with honors at age nineteen with a degree in physics. His first plan was to pursue physics in graduate school at Minnesota, but he was drawn to a new interdisciplinary program in the behavioral sciences sponsored by the Ford Foundation.

After completing his degree, McFadden worked at several universities but was at Berkeley in 1991 when his Nobel Prize was announced in 2000. Despite living in the Bay area, he managed to reconnect with his rural upbringing by owning a small farm in the Napa Valley where his family grew grapes and raised a few animals.

James J. Heckman (2000 Prize Winner)

Anyone paying attention to the Nobel Prize awards in economics would have noticed an evolving trend. Prior to 2000, there were eight winners from the University of Chicago, about twice as many as their nearest rivals, Harvard and Cambridge.[56] Chicago, with its famously conservative and pro-market perspective, was hugely popular with the Swedish Nobel committee. A reporter noticed this and once asked James Heckman what it felt like to be at the University of Chicago without a Nobel. "After a while it starts to hurt," he confessed.[57] When he finally did receive the prize in 2000, he felt "relieved."[58]

Heckman was a graduate of Colorado College in Colorado Springs where he majored in mathematics and took courses in physics and philosophy. By reading classics in economics by Adam Smith, David Ricardo, and Paul Samuelson, he discovered he had an interest in social sciences. He was most impressed by a book on economic development written by Arthur Lewis, a 1979 Nobel laureate. "This book had it all," Heckman recounted and it inspired him to pursue economics.[59]

After a brief start in the economics program at the University of Chicago, Heckman transferred to Princeton, where he fulfilled his ambition to study development economics with Arthur Lewis. As Heckman's interests gravitated from international topics to labor economics, he conducted a good deal of econometric work with individual survey data. His first job after graduate school was at Columbia University, and he was invited to conduct research at the National Bureau of Economic Research (NBER) office in New York. Nobel laureate Gary Becker of the University of Chicago was a frequent visitor to the NBER, and Heckman learned much from him and other like-minded economists. In 1973 Heckman was recruited by Chicago where he was still working at the time of his Nobel award in 2000.

There was thus little reason to expect Heckman to be much different from his Chicago colleagues. He had briefly attended the University of Chicago after completing his undergraduate degree and found Milton Friedman "fascinating." His work combining microeconomics and econometrics into what would be called *microeconometrics* seemed ready made for Chicago. When he set out to show that government was either ineffective or sometimes harmful, he was clearly embracing a free market point of view. However, it would be a mistake to paint Heckman as a typical Chicago School economist, because he sometimes reached conclusions that contradicted his own earlier views as well as those of his Chicago colleagues.

In one of those early studies, Heckman decided to evaluate the effect of Title VII of the Civil Rights Act. "Being from the University of Chicago economics department which has a theoretical bias against government intervention, Mr. Heckman said he set out to prove that Title VII hadn't helped African-American workers."[60] Ten years later, the data didn't fit the conclusion. "I truly did want to show the government didn't have an impact," Heckman confessed, but in the end, he claimed to have no choice but to conclude that "it had a huge effect."[61] This hardly helped his standing among his fellow laissez-faire economists. "To be honest," he explained, "some of my colleagues at Chicago were very hostile to this finding, and remain so."[62] It took courage for Heckman to stand by his conclusions because they contradicted a good part of his professional training and troubled his academic colleagues. His results, however, were not inconsistent with his own personal experience.

Born in Chicago in 1944, Heckman moved at the age of twelve with his family to the South for a brief period. In Lexington, Kentucky, he witnessed racial segregation as it existed in 1956. He saw signs for "whites only" or "colored only" at drinking fountains and park benches. When he tried to sit in the back of a bus in Lexington in order to look out the big bay windows, he was told that was not where white people sat. He recalled the thinly veiled warning to his family from neighbors that the South was not Chicago and that they had "different ways down here."[63] The Heckmans' next move was to Oklahoma City, which was also segregated, a practice that left both James and his sister "dumbfounded." In an interview with the Minnesota

Federal Reserve in 2005, he described these experiences as the reason "the race issue fascinates me."[64]

Heckman's next experience with "the race issue" occurred in the 1960s. While a student at Colorado College, he and his roommate decided to take an extensive road trip during winter break to Louisiana, traveling through Chicago, Lexington, Birmingham, and Hattiesburg, Mississippi. Although Heckman would describe himself and his friend as simply "ignorant kids," they had an agenda. Heckman and his black roommate from Nigeria, Abiodun Afonja, were "curious" about the Jim Crow system of racial segregation and wanted to see it first hand. But because of the politically charged atmosphere of Birmingham and other cities, they were often mistaken for *freedom riders* out to change the system, not merely observe it. Only a few months before the two passed through Birmingham, a black church had been firebombed and four young girls had died.[65]

The two roommates were not disappointed in their aspiration to experience the Jim Crow system. In Birmingham, they were required to eat at different counters in a soda fountain, and they created some anxiety among the locals when they decided to stay together in a YMCA for blacks. In Hattiesburg, the local police asked them if they were trying to integrate their town and made sure that the two stayed in separate hotels.[66] Even in New Orleans they found themselves shunned by the club hawkers on Bourbon Street. Revisiting New Orleans seven years later during an economics conference, Heckman was "amazed" at the change. Any sign of segregation had been obliterated, and according to his research, the Civil Rights Act had a lot to do with that.

Heckman revisited the race issue when he reviewed the controversial 1994 book *The Bell Curve* by Charles Murray and Richard Herrnstein. The authors argued that IQ was a legitimate measure of intelligence, and in fact, was a good predictor of academic and economic success as well as criminal activity. Their most inflammatory argument was that whites had, on average, higher IQs than blacks, largely due to genetic differences. These arguments triggered a barrage of criticisms, including one from Heckman. While some critics objected to every conclusion in *The Bell Curve*, Heckman focused his criticisms more narrowly on the genetics issue. He pointed out that even the authors acknowledged that intelligence was the product of both nature and the environment and that no one could really place a precise weight on either of the two factors.

More than most reviewers, Heckman gave credit to the authors of *The Bell Curve* for their willingness to address the disparity of academic and economic success across ethnic groups as well other sensitive issues. His review, he acknowledged, was not as negative as others. He wrote that the authors "firmly and rather convincingly refute the critics of IQ and aptitude tests who claim that the tests are racially biased and unrelated to true productivity in schools or the workplace."[67] He agreed that ability is unequally distributed and that ability drives academic and economic success. What he did not believe was that ability is exclusively or even primarily driven by genetics or race. In particular, he claimed that there were no statistics in the book that "justified any theory of genetic determinism."[68] He concluded that the inevitable force of genetic determinism argued for in *The Bell Curve* was not backed up by statistical evidence.

Heckman also believed that motivation, attitude, and other factors are just as important as cognitive ability in determining success. Even more importantly, Heckman argued that all of these characteristics, even IQ, can be improved through "sustained high-intensity investments in the education of young children." He cited reading and responding to children as particularly helpful parental activities.[69] Although this clearly wasn't their thesis, Heckman observed that even "the authors acknowledge that there are strong indications that very intensive programs can be effective."[70]

Heckman's support for intensive, early childhood education was hardly newsworthy when he reviewed *The Bell Curve* in 1995 but it made the headlines shortly after he won the Nobel Prize. In 2004, Heckman released a paper that foretold of "a future of declining wages and lower productivity unless America increases investment in its preschool-age children."[71] He estimated the benefits of extending a particular preschool program in Ypsilanti, Michigan, the Perry Preschool, to the whole country.[72] His calculation of a 16 percent return on investment was very high, because he counted numerous benefits along with higher earnings, fewer teenage pregnancies, and reduced crime.[73] In another article in the *Wall Street Journal* in 2006, Heckman claimed that the Perry Preschool program could improve performance better than smaller classrooms, better than adult training, and better than attempts to rehabilitate juvenile delinquents. He enthusiastically endorsed this approach as the best way for society to "compensate for the accident of birth."[74]

Advocates for preschool education were grateful for Heckman's support because in many ways he was the perfect, credible expert. Not only was he a Nobel Prize winner but he was also from the University of Chicago economics department with a reputation for opposing public initiatives. Support from an unlikely source carries more weight and attracts more attention than from a likely source. Heckman supported government funding for preschool education, but that was as far as he strayed from the Chicago

School dogma. He was quick to suggest that the government could issue vouchers to finance privately run programs and promote competition and efficiency. There was no reason, he said, why the programs would have to take place in public facilities.

These examples may constitute more the exception than the rule, since Heckman spent much of his career applying econometric analysis to survey data in order to test microeconomic models. This involved typical Chicago School models that presumed rational, self-interested behavior. In the course of his work, Heckman focused on an important but underappreciated problem known as the *self-selection bias*. It was this contribution that was cited by the Nobel committee. Here is the issue. We can compare the average salary of college graduates to the average salary of high school graduates and conclude that the difference is due to college education. But did four years of college account for the entire difference, or were the two groups different from the start? Were the college-bound students smarter, more motivated, more disciplined, or were they from wealthier families with better job contacts? Students that choose to go to college may well be different from other students, and that can create a self-selection bias. As a result, this bias can account for part or all of the wage advantage of college graduates. A similar problem can exist for preschool programs, not because the children self-select, but because their parents do. Parents that place their children in preschool programs may provide other opportunities for their children as well. How much does this original difference account for the apparent benefit of a preschool program?

None of this analysis is controversial or surprising, and in fact it all could theoretically be resolved if we could measure the precise determinants of success. For example, if taller individuals are more likely to attend college and taller individuals earn more money, then we can measure everyone's height and account for this factor. The problem gets more challenging as the characteristics to measure become more abstract, such as motivation, attitude, reliability, or consistency. Many relevant characteristics simply can't be measured. These are referred to as *unobserved data* and are the reason that self-selection biases are difficult to correct.

There is only one really good way to avoid this problem and that is through *random assignment* experiments. If we took a population of students and randomly assigned only some to college, then we would have a good test of the benefits of college. This approach works because those unobserved traits would also be randomly distributed among the two groups, and with sufficiently large samples any bias would become increasingly irrelevant. The problem with the approach is that most people do not want a flip of the coin to determine whether they go to college. And even if some people were willing to participate in this kind of experiment, they may be unusual themselves and not representative of the population, creating yet another self-selection bias. The best statistical technique is thus typically not practical for many interesting questions in economics, including measuring the returns to college education and the benefit of preschool programs.

Short of random assignments there is no fully reliable way to resolve the problem of self-selection bias or the problem with unobserved variables. Heckman's major contribution was to define the problem and to ensure that researchers appreciated how it limited their conclusions. He also developed statistical techniques to provide some measure of correction for the biases. This was admittedly a difficult task because it requires making assumptions about the nature of unobserved variables. Whether such techniques are justified is hard to prove because the key information is, by definition, unobserved.

FOURTEEN

History and Institutions

Robert W. Fogel (1993)

Douglass C. North (1993)

Oliver E. Williamson (2009)

Elinor Ostrom (2009)

The Nobel committee has been so focused on rewarding economics that projects a scientific and mathematical image that it has often ignored more practical, historical, or institutional approaches. There have been exceptions, including two economists who focused on an institutional topic called economic governance. Oliver E. Williamson, a co-winner in 2009, explored the narrow question of why some activities are included within a firm and others are not. The answer to this question requires a deeper understanding of transaction costs.

An entirely different issue caught the attention of his co-winner, Elinor Ostrom, the first woman Nobel laureate in economics. Ostrom was interested in solutions to environmental problems known as common-pool resources. Economists had previously suggested solutions to this problem but they had largely overlooked the role of voluntary cooperative organizations. She found that cooperation, not competition, could sometimes provide a reasonably efficient outcome. Both of these Nobel laureates were more interested in institutional arrangements either within firms or within cooperative organizations, and both were linked to the prior work of Nobel laureate Ronald Coase.

The other two Nobel Prize winners in this category, Robert W. Fogel and Douglass C. North, won Nobel Prizes in 1993 for their work in economic history. Both used economic theory and techniques they learned from Nobel laureate Simon Kuznets to explore unsettled historical questions. The answers they found often surprised other economists and historians. In other respects, the two economic historians had different ideas and sometimes reached different conclusions. They did not, for example, share the same opinion about the importance of railroads in American history.

Robert W. Fogel (1993 Prize Winner)

The 1993 winner of the economics Nobel Prize, Robert Fogel, was no stranger to controversy. In the 1970s, he decided to investigate a question that few historians would think of: Was slavery economically efficient? In order to answer the question, the University of Chicago economist collected great amounts of statistical data, employed conventional neoclassical theory, and concluded that slavery was in fact efficient. He and co-author Stanley Engerman published these results in a best selling book in 1974, *Time on the Cross*. In addition to the finding that slavery was an efficient form of production – that is, after slaves were kidnapped in Africa and sold in America – he concluded that the material condition of most slaves was not all bad, either. The slave owners, he argued, had an interest in maintaining physically healthy slaves, and therefore provided a standard of living that "compared favorably with those of free industrial workers."[1]

While some reviewers questioned the purpose of even studying such a question, Fogel insisted that he was not racist and had no intention of trying to justify slavery. The criticism was so severe, however, that Fogel felt compelled to write another book twenty-five years later, *Without Consent or Contract*, in which he reiterated the point of condemning slavery by devoting more than half the book to antislavery ideology.[2]

The Nobel committee dealt with this awkward topic head on. Their spokesperson said "despite the moral heinousness of slavery, it was an efficient market solution."[3] It seemed to bother Fogel and Engerman that people would believe that slave plantations were inefficient. How could they be inefficient if they existed in a market economy? Wasn't the fact that plantations persisted for so many years sufficient evidence that they were economically efficient? One could almost hear Milton Friedman explaining the basic principle of free markets: If a firm survives in a competitive economy, then it must be efficient. To back up the argument, Fogel and Engerman compiled stacks of evidence to show that slave plantations were efficient and profitable. Fogel insisted, "If you want me to say it [slavery] was unprofitable or inefficient, I won't."[4]

Why, then, did reviewers find the book offensive? As Peter Passell said in the *New York Times*, Fogel "infuriated some commentators with what was widely viewed as an apology for pre-Civil War slavery."[5] Fogel had his own explanation: Readers simply had a hard time separating the larger moral issue from the economic issue. It was quite possible for something to be both immoral and efficient. For example, Fogel argued, you might be able to recover the cost of burying your parents by selling "your dying parents for dog meat."[6] While such a concept may be economically efficient, it still isn't done because, as Fogel explained, "the thought revolts us. There is such a thing as morality and morality is higher than economics."[7] In other words, as a professional economist he should be able to estimate the market price of recycling parents or the efficiency of slave plantations without facing the wrath of sensitive moralists.

Why is it important to know if slavery was economically efficient? After all, most people are not going to change their opinion about slavery based on whether or not it was profitable. That was not, however, Fogel's point. He concluded that if slavery were economically efficient, then it was not going to collapse on its own. The only way to eliminate a profitable industry such as slavery was through government intervention, which in this case, meant military action. Fogel didn't believe this finding justified slavery, but it did justify the Civil War. According to Fogel, the history of the Civil War should show that it was necessary to destroy a heinous social institution that was also a profitable business enterprise.

Where Fogel got into trouble was when he tested the hypotheses that slaves were lazy, inept, and unproductive, and that the brutal treatment of slave families undermined the stability of black families today.[8] Social scientists can choose any hypothesis they want to test, but why start with one that claims slaves were "lazy, inept, and unproductive"? Where did that idea come from? Fogel concluded that slaves did not have these characteristics but gave some of the credit to the slave owners. As Fogel and Engerman concluded, "The typical slave field hand was not lazy, inept, and unproductive. On average he was harder-working and more efficient than his white counterpart."[9] One reason for that, the authors suggested, was that "The material (not psychological) conditions of the lives of slaves compared favorably with those of free industrial workers."[10] Of course the work environment of free workers was not exactly comparable to slaves who faced the possibility of being sold, whipped, or killed.[11]

Once again, the slave owners were not necessarily acting out of any real compassion in keeping their slaves healthy; they were acting out of self-interest because a healthy slave was a more productive slave. Slave owners may have had no more compassion for their slaves than for their mules, but they kept both in shape for work. Furthermore, Fogel argued, keeping a slave in condition for work required a sizeable investment. From his research, he found that "the typical slave field hand received about 90 percent of the income he produced."[12]

In certain respects, Fogel and Engerman painted a rosy picture of the antebellum Southern economy. Incomes were growing faster in the South than the North during the twenty years before the Civil War, and farms were 35 percent more efficient in the South. But they may have gone beyond their data when they followed their argument to an extreme conclusion. They suggested that the stories of mistreatment may have been exaggerated. For example, the authors found that it was in the interest of slave owners to keep families together, unless of course the individual was "at an age when it would have been normal for them to have left the family."[13] It was language like this that incensed Fogel and Engerman's critics. It may have been normal for a teenager to leave the nest at age sixteen but was it "normal" that they be sold to the highest bidder?

Based on their historical research, Fogel and Engerman offered a controversial explanation for the social problems facing black families today. They claimed that the problems originated with antislavery critics who fashioned a "myth" about the horrors of slavery. According to the myths, African slaves resisted the coercion and violence perpetrated by the white planters by becoming "lazy loafers and bunglers."[14] These myths in effect became the spikes that held blacks on the cross long after they were freed from slavery. But by discrediting such myths, Fogel and Engerman believed that they were contributing to greater enlightenment. They wrote, "The belief that slave-breeding, sexual exploitation, and promiscuity destroyed the black family is a myth.... It was to the economic interest of planters to encourage the stability of slave families and most of them did so."[15]

Fogel seemed to be arguing that blacks had become martyrs based on a mistaken or exaggerated history of oppression. And as martyrs, they were unable to pursue productive lives of self-improvement, unfairly condemning the efforts of successful black professionals. Fogel and Engerman wrote that this "turned those who struggled for self-improvement in the only way they could into 'Uncle Toms.'"[16] The authors seemed to expect that their research would somehow liberate people from these destructive tendencies. They concluded, "Three hundred and fifty years on the cross are enough. It's time to reveal not only to blacks but to whites as well, that part of American history that has been kept from them – the record of black achievement under adversity."[17]

Before the debate ended, *Time on the Cross* was exposed to more attacks than most books of its kind. Berkeley economist and critic Richard Sutch simply stated "Their views have not survived."[18] The *San Francisco Chronicle* reported that Fogel's "conclusions are widely cited in standard textbooks, although most scholars do not fully share them."[19] Even a fairly sympathetic review from economist Barry Eichengreen concluded that the most enduring legacy of *Time on the Cross* was the research method, not the substance of the argument. In the process of writing the book, Fogel pioneered a new approach that combined sophisticated statistical and economic analysis with economic history.

Apart from his eccentric ideas on slavery, Fogel's approach to economic history was a familiar one. Systematic collection and organization of historical data followed by hypothesis testing was the hallmark of Nobel laureate Simon Kuznets. Fogel was directly exposed to this technique as a graduate student at Johns Hopkins University where he obtained his doctorate in 1963. As Fogel explained, "Simon Kuznets, who supervised my doctoral dissertation, was by far the most influential figure in my graduate training."[20] Kuznets, however, was rarely accused of reaching a conclusion that was not substantiated by his research.

Another area cited by the Nobel committee was Fogel's work on railroads. Here Fogel reached another controversial conclusion, although less emotionally charged. After years of comprehensive data collection and analysis, Fogel concluded that railroads were probably overrated as economic drivers. Economist W. W. Rostow, writing in the 1950s, had suggested that railroads in the nineteenth century and other new technologies in general could have a profound impact on economic growth. Railroads helped the economy "take-off," he argued, by opening up new areas for farming and expanding iron and coal industries. Joseph Schumpeter posited a similar theme with his concept of waves of *creative destruction*. But Fogel countered that most of these transportation needs could have been met by canals and horse and wagons with only about a 5 percent loss of GNP in 1890. All but 4 percent of agricultural land could still be served by other modes of transportation and at only a slight cost premium.[21] Fogel noted that because many of the rails were imported, the railroad industry never bought more than 10 percent of the domestic iron production before the Civil War.[22]

This was a typical Fogel approach to economic history, developing counterfactual "what if" cases. In other words, what if the railroad had never been invented? His answer: The economy would have been only slightly smaller. Economists were again impressed with Fogel's technique but not persuaded by his conclusions. The problem with counterfactual cases is that they require an almost perfect understanding of how economies work. How else do you rerun the course of history without major events and expect to know the outcome? Railroads were at the center of a rapid transformation of the American economy from 1830 to 1890, and even if canals and horse-drawn wagons could have moved goods at slightly higher costs, would they have offered the same quality? Would they have stimulated the same inventiveness, the same industries, and the same level of growth? Canals and

horses certainly weren't as fast as railroads, and yet isn't speed an important part of economic development? As many of his critics suggested, Fogel
probably undervalued the benefits of railroads.

Peter Passell, writing in the *New York Times*, suggested that Fogel's
work on railroads implies that government should not provide support
for new, emerging technologies.[23] If railroads were not indispensable
then, perhaps high technology isn't so important today. Are automobiles, computers, biotechnology, and other economy-transforming technologies overrated? But this line of argument may go too far. Should we
really consider abandoning public support of potentially transforming
technologies based on Fogel's controversial study of nineteenth-century
railroads? A little skepticism is well advised when counterfactual studies
are also counterintuitive.

With millions of dollars of funding and the assistance of many researchers, Fogel also launched an ambitious project to explore the relationships
among nutrition, health, mortality, morbidity, and economic productivity.
His team applied modern statistical techniques to obscure databases from
a multitude of sources, including orphanages, schools, and the military.
Other economists had studied investments in education, but Fogel focused
on a more fundamental investment in human capital – food consumption.
Historically, as people improved their food consumption, they increased
their average height and weight, thus improving their health, longevity, and
capacity for work.

Fogel summarized the state of this research, including the work of others,
in his Nobel lecture. He reported, "that during the eighteenth and nineteenth centuries Europeans were severely stunted by modern standards."[24]
Around 1790, an average thirty-year-old English male weighed 134 pounds,
but his French counterpart weighed only 110 pounds. These weights were
20 percent below modern averages for the English and 33 percent below
today's average for the French. Both eighteenth-century English- and
Frenchmen were about four inches (ten centimeters) shorter than their
modern counterparts.

Fogel noted both a cause and an effect behind these statistics. The cause
was inadequate nutrition, which contributed to this type of diminutive stature. The effect was that smallness allowed people to be more active than
they could have been otherwise. Caloric consumption was so low in the
eighteenth century that it was barely enough to allow for much work, and
if individuals had been any larger they would have required even higher
caloric intake. Fogel argued that if the English and French had been the size
of modern Americans, "virtually all of the energy produced by their food

supplies would have been required for maintenance and hardly any would have been available to sustain work."[25]

Fogel and other researchers also estimated the distribution of food consumption and concluded that the poorest individuals in 1790 did not have enough food to maintain a significant work effort, even if they wanted to. In France, for example, "the bottom 10 percent of the labor force lacked sufficient energy for regular work and the next 10 percent had enough energy for less than 3 hours of light work daily."[26] The conditions were better in England, but even there the poorest 20 percent probably could not have sustained an eight-hour day of light work.[27]

By comparing height and weight statistics with mortality and morbidity rates, Fogel was able to estimate the impacts of inadequate nutrition on these health measures. He concluded that the entire decline in death rates in England, France, and Sweden between 1775 and 1875 could be attributed to improvements in nutrition.

In America, better nutrition did not immediately translate into longer lifetimes. While modernization made the average person wealthier, it also created greater inequality and lowered the material well-being of the poor, causing the health of the average person to decline. It wasn't until the early twentieth century that the negative effect of modernization had largely run its course, and life expectancy in the United States increased, eventually returning to its 1790 level.[28]

Robert Fogel grew up in New York City and planned to study physics and chemistry at Cornell, but he found he had a greater interest in economics and history. During college, he gained some notoriety for his involvement in radical politics. An article in the *San Francisco Chronicle* reported that he had once been "a Communist youth organizer and was even featured in Collier's magazine in 1946 as a campus radical."[29] Whatever radical beliefs he once had were left far behind as he proceeded through his economics education. During graduate school at Columbia, Fogel learned about free-market economics from Nobel laureate George Stigler, and later at Johns Hopkins, learned how to collect economic data from Simon Kuznets.

Fogel met his wife when they both worked on Henry Wallace's election campaign in 1948. He credits his wife with caring for their children, helping with his research, and boosting his "self-confidence when my unorthodox findings provoked controversy and criticism...."[30] Probably because of the controversy over his slavery research, the *New York Times* noted at the time of his award that "Professor Fogel's wife of 44 years, Enid, a former dean at Harvard, is black."[31]

Douglass C. North (1993 Prize Winner)

A long-standing question in economics is why some countries are successful economically while others struggle to provide even a bare subsistence for many of their citizens. Parts of Asia and broad sections of Africa and Central and South America have missed out on the long-term economic growth enjoyed by many of the people of North America, Europe, and Japan. Conventional neoclassical economics has a simple answer to this question: free markets. Those that have them prosper and those that don't have them fail. The conventional answer to reducing underdevelopment is more economic freedom: lower taxes, less regulation, and less government.

None of this is quite right according to the 1993 Nobel winner Douglass C. North. There is more to the secret of economic success, and it starts with a very important function of government, the rule of law as it applies to businesses. Government can't simply step back and let free markets reign, because if it did, all would soon be chaos. In order for markets to work, government needs to define the rules of capitalism. What's more, government also needs to enforce the rules fairly and consistently. The notion that free markets mean the absence of government is just a fantasy, according to North. Political systems and the rules they develop and enforce are just as essential to a successful economy as free markets. Economists spent the first 200 years after Adam Smith echoing his call for *less* government to foster a better business environment. North slightly modified the message. He wanted *better* government to foster a better business environment.

How did North develop this idea? While studying how canals and railroads accelerated trade and regional specialization, he concluded that none of this could have happened without government support. As a result of railroads, the South grew cotton, the Midwest grew food crops, the Northeast manufactured goods, and the overall economy grew quickly as they all traded with each other.[32] Few academics would object to this familiar thesis except perhaps North's Nobel co-winner, Robert Fogel. Fogel tried to prove that railroads were far less important than historians believed. So were railroads important, as North claimed, or not, as Fogel argued? By honoring both men with Nobel Prizes in the same year, the Swedish Academy of Sciences seemed to hedge its bets.

Canals, like railroads, were a major force in transportation, and they demonstrated an important principle to North. Because canals were too expensive and too risky to be built by a single company or even a combination of companies, there was a need for public funding to supplement private investment.[33] This process required a new role for government that was not part of conventional economics; it required government to solve difficult political problems in order to pave the way for economic growth. In American history, the political process successfully solved the problem, canals were built, and the economy prospered. This was the original example that convinced North that political institutions were important and potentially useful.[34]

North was credited with another observation about how government can foster economic success: He concluded that England became an economic powerhouse in the nineteenth century largely due to the formidable power of the British Navy. The national fleet successfully protected its merchant ships from pirates, making British trade safer and more profitable then that of other countries. As a bonus, the higher security reduced the need to fully arm merchant ships, freeing up valuable space for even more cargo.[35]

European nations did not prosper equally in the mercantilist era. England and Holland both achieved early success in trade and economic growth while France and Spain fared less well. England and Holland were more successful, according to North, because they opposed monopolies and enforced patents and property rights, at least after 1600. These enlightened government policies gave them an advantage over France and Spain.[36] Frequently short of cash, the governments of France and Spain pushed harder for revenue and were quick to grant special deals to individual businesses that undermined general business activity. North even went so far as to speculate that Latin America would have been better off if it had been colonized by England rather than Spain because they would have inherited better government policies. Of course all governments granted special deals – look at the East India Tea Company of England – but North saw more favoritism in France and Spain than in England and Holland.

How do certain government regulations benefit the economy? An example would be a patent system that encourages creativity and innovation by temporarily protecting the fruits of these labors from competition. According to North, governments must also ensure the enforcement of contracts so that businesses and individuals can be held to their commitments. And there are property rights. If something can be sold then there must be assurance that it won't be stolen, usurped, or expropriated. Without these rules and some way to enforce them, any economy would suffer. Economic stability requires courts, prosecutors, constitutions, laws, legislatures, and political parties to ensure the economy works.

In addition to these formal institutions, North observed that we also need to pay attention to informal institutions. In order to develop and transmit values from generation to generation, societies need effective families, neighborhoods, churches, schools, and businesses. Each country develops its own unique informal institutions but only some will help economic growth. For example, does society value and reward creativity, individuality, hard work, honesty and material success, or do years of corruption and special privileges undermine the informal conventions that motivate market participants? Because institutions – both formal and informal – change, North insisted that economists must study history to understand fully the economy of any country.

Soviet Union

North also applied his theories to the collapse of communism in the Soviet Union and associated communist states. The question they faced was how to transform a state-run economy into a modern market economy. The best idea from traditional economists was to simply cut loose all enterprises from state ownership and let them succeed or fail. The important thing, they argued, was to make markets free. The rest – the rules of law and business conduct – could come later. This approach was called "shock therapy" and was expected to transform the heavily regulated Soviet economy into an efficient, well-functioning market economy. The result was disappointing. As economist Andrew Krikelas of the Atlanta Federal Reserve observed, "While many neoclassically trained economists have been asked to counsel the leaders of nations making the transition from centrally planned to free market economies, much of their advice has proved to be inadequate if not unhelpful."[37]

Why didn't shock therapy work? According to North, you need to have formal rules in place that guide market behavior, and those rules have to evolve from that particular society. For example, you can't expect free markets to be successful in an atmosphere rife with corruption and favoritism, and you can't export American institutions to another country that doesn't fully appreciate them. As North explained, "economies that adopt the formal rules of another economy will have very different performance characteristics than the first economy because of different informal norms and enforcement."[38] Shock therapy was not successful in the Soviet Union for the simple reason that it lacked political institutions to create and enforce essential business rules like patent law, contract law, and other property rights.[39] Alberto de Capitani of the World Bank said, "It's almost common sense, but it's a message not fully internalized by the economics profession."[40]

Africa

North applied the same idea to developing countries. Along with a few colleagues, he posed the question in an article entitled, "If Economists Are So Smart, Why Is Africa So Poor?"[41] The answer to the question, the authors concluded, was that neoclassical economists did not fully understand the importance of political institutions. When World Bank economists placed conditions on foreign aid, they often insisted on reducing government regulation, taxes, and subsidies with the intent of fostering free markets. Evidently much of this failed to work because Africa is still quite poor.

North and his co-authors thought that economists should stop neglecting political systems. Most African countries, they reasoned, needed better governments that would enforce contracts and never threaten to expropriate private assets. The authors cited Liberia, Nigeria, Burundi, and Zimbabwe as examples of failures where the political institutions were simply incompatible with capitalist economic development.

There were some countries in Africa, however, that did offer stable business environments according to the authors and these economies were more successful. The examples were Uganda under the authoritarian president, Yoweri Museveni, and South Africa under the apartheid system of racial discrimination. Others might have been a little embarrassed to hold up these two countries as success stories, but North and his colleagues commended these countries for their adherence to "the rule of law." They seemed more interested in who enforced pro-business regulations than who respected human rights or democratic values.[42]

North and his co-authors fortunately suggested some better examples including the American system of checks and balances. This model allows the federal government to keep the greed and ambition of political leaders in check. A similar check on power can come about through a system of federalism that disperses power and authority between states and the federal government. Both approaches tend to disperse power, thus increasing the chance that governments will provide the rules necessary for successful business activity.

In North's work there was an underlying theme that was skeptical of traditional neoclassical economics. While he was supportive of free-market activity, he was not impressed with the assumptions of perfectly rational behavior. Instead, his work emphasized the limits of neoclassical economics using the concept of bounded rationality developed by Nobel laureate Herbert Simon. North was once quoted as saying that the assumptions of rationality and self-interest were simply crazy.[43] He cited himself as an example. Would it be rational for him to give 40 percent of his salary to his employer, Washington University? Probably not, yet that is what he did.[44] Statements like that didn't endear him to market zealots. Commenting on North's work, Milton Friedman explained that "People time and again have professed to be moving outside the limits of neoclassical economics. In fact they really don't get anywhere. I'm very skeptical."[45]

Attending Berkeley in the early 1940s, North became what he described as "a convinced Marxist." Like his radical colleagues, he opposed war against Germany when the Soviet Union established a pact with Hitler in 1941. When Hitler invaded the Soviet Union the next year and American Marxists suddenly supported war against Germany, North broke ranks and continued to advocate for peace.

By his own account, North was a mediocre student at Berkeley. While majoring in political science, philosophy, and economics, he only achieved slightly better than a C average. He graduated and joined the Merchant Marine and became a navigator, deciding that was a good way to avoid having to kill anyone.[46] He did a lot of reading during his three years in the Merchant Marine, which ignited his interest in economics. After leaving the service, he fought an urge to become a photographer and enrolled in the graduate program in economics at Berkeley.[47] North received a doctorate but claimed that he didn't really understand economic theory until later in his career when he played chess with Don Gordon, his colleague at the University of Washington. The two would talk economics during their games and North found this enlightening.

During the 1956–7 academic year, North was hired as a research associate at the National Bureau of Economic Research. He enjoyed the work but he particularly valued the one day each week that he spent working with Nobel laureate Simon Kuznets in Baltimore. Like Fogel, North learned the art of data collection from Kuznets, who supervised his work on the tedious task of compiling the U.S. balance of payments from 1790 to 1860.

North was one of the founders of a new approach to economic history that emphasized theory and statistics. The group coined the term *cliometrics* after Clio the muse of history. North played a key role in promoting this new subdiscipline when he became the editor for the *Journal of Economic History*, which published the work of other economic historians, including his co-winner Robert Fogel. This endeavor was an important part of the reason that North won the Nobel Prize in 1993.

North may have rejected his radical youth and even became a Republican for a time, but he was not consistently conservative.[48] In 2003, North signed on with 450 economists, including nine other Nobel Prize winners (George Akerlof, Kenneth Arrow, Lawrence Klein, Daniel McFadden, Franco

Modigliani, Paul Samuelson, William Sharpe, Robert Solow, and Joseph Stiglitz), to condemn President George W. Bush's proposed tax cuts.[49] This complaint was directed at Bush's plan to accelerate income tax deductions and eliminate dividend taxes, a proposal that was hugely popular with high-income tax payers. The petition claimed that Bush's tax cut would worsen the deficit and do nothing for the economy.

Oliver E. Williamson (2009 Prize Winner)

It may evolve to be that one of the most important contributions of Nobel laureate Ronald Coase was to push the frontiers of economics beyond traditional microeconomics as embraced by the Chicago School. Although he became a pivotal member of the Chicago School, Coase encouraged academic economists to look beyond a world driven by prices to institutional factors, including property rights and transaction costs. Two of the economists who pursued these ideas in greater depth and shared the Nobel Prize in its forty-first year were Oliver Williamson of the University of California, Berkeley, and Elinor Ostrom, a political scientist from the University of Indiana.

Coase borrowed an important principle from free-market economics to develop his theory about why large firms exist: Businesses cannot exist in a free market unless they are efficient. This principle also applied to *vertically integrated firms*, those firms that expand beyond a narrow business activity, either upstream toward their suppliers or downstream toward their customers. Since vertically integrated firms exist, this principle suggested that they must also be efficient. For example, power producers were historically vertically integrated because some of them also owned coal mines to fuel their power plants and many also owned transmission and distribution lines to deliver the power. According to Coase's theory, these firms were efficient because they did not have to negotiate contracts with separate owners of the coal mines or the transmission lines, thus avoiding transaction costs.

This was a convenient explanation for the existence of vertically integrated firms, but what about firms that were not vertically integrated? If integration lowers costs for some firms, why not for all of them? The answer offered by Oliver Williamson involved two new concepts, *asset specificity* and *contract complexity*. When complexity and asset specificity were low, transaction costs were also lower and consequently independent firms could more easily negotiate contracts. In the opposite case of high complexity and asset specificity, transaction costs were higher, creating an incentive for either long-term contracts or vertical integration.

A good example of this was the electric power industry, where some power generators owned their own coal mines and others did not. Williamson explained this variation by focusing on the physical proximity of other power plants and other coal mines. In remote locations where there were no other competing plants or mines, the assets of the two operations were more closely linked or, in Williamson's terms, specific. Forced to deal with each other, both sides would be inclined to fight for the best price, which was less defined because of the lack of other competitors. Negotiating contracts in this setting, with high asset specificity, could be time consuming and costly but could also be avoided through long-term contracts or joint ownership. The example illustrates how asset specificity can contribute to vertical integration. Empirical studies supported this theory.[50] A similar outcome is possible when contracts are also more complex, again encouraging long-term contracts or joint ownership to avoid the higher costs of contract negotiation.

The Nobel committee asserted that these theoretical ideas had an important effect on public policy. According to the Royal Swedish Academy of Sciences, antitrust policy in the United States recognized that "most mergers occur for reasons of improved efficiency, and that such efficiencies are particularly likely in the context of vertical mergers."[51] They credited Oliver Williamson with contributing to this recognition and reducing antitrust concerns in the United States. In fact, government antitrust enforcement has subsided in recent years and one reporter noted that "During the [George W.] Bush administration, the Justice Department did not file a single case under antimonopoly laws regulating a dominant firm."[52]

In the real world, firms merge with other companies for many reasons, only one of which is to lower transaction costs. The challenge for public policy is to recognize all of the ramifications of these decisions, which includes more than just transaction costs; it also includes the effect on competition. When a firm like Microsoft dominates a particular industry, a decision to expand vertically can have major repercussions for competitors in the upstream or downstream markets. Williamson himself recognized that there were limits to activities that could be efficiently incorporated within a single firm. When firms include too many diverse functions they may lose the discipline provided by external competition. This could result in an abuse by the firm's executives, especially if they are inclined to make decisions based on criteria other than efficiency.

Even the efficiency of vertically integrated firms in the power industry has been controversial. Some economists and policy makers have advocated for more competition in this industry by restricting exclusive relationships between power transmission and power generation. Will this help efficiency by forcing more competition, or will it harm efficiency by raising transaction costs? The jury is still out on this question, but there is some reason to believe that transaction costs could be significant. Contracts in the power industry are very complex and assets are sometimes specific, and so there is potential that a competitive market would face high transaction costs.

The concept of asset specificity in particular appears to have other applications. Firms with assets that have a unique purpose or specificity may have more trouble raising capital from creditors. Why is this? If lenders are worried about bankruptcy they know that they are less likely to recover their losses from the sale of specific assets than from more general-purpose assets. Consequently, firms with high asset specificity may find it more difficult to raise funds from capital markets. By probing the meaning of transaction costs, Oliver Williamson provided economists with some useful concepts.

Elinor Ostrom (2009 Prize Winner)

It was clear from the moment of the announcement that Elinor Ostrom, one of the 2009 prize winners, did not represent Nobel business as usual. She was trained as a political scientist at the University of California, Los Angeles, and was the first woman to win the Nobel Prize in economics, forty years after it was initiated. Even her research style, which relied on case studies and a broad interdisciplinary approach, set her apart from many predecessors. There was also the fact that she was a Nobel Prize winner in economics who was more interested in understanding cooperation than competition.

The biologist Garrett Hardin popularized the notion that *common-pool resources* create environmental risks in his famous 1968 article "The Tragedy of the Commons."[53] Long before that, economists had seen that open access to common-pool resources can easily result in excessive exploitation, to the point of serious destruction. Uncontrolled access to fisheries, pastures, forests, water for drinking or irrigation, oil fields, and even air can lead to excessive use. Once the problem was identified, solutions were proposed that required government action. In 1920, Arthur Pigou suggested a tax on the activity and in 1960 Ronald Coase suggested privatizing the resource. There was a third way to address this issue – voluntary cooperative governance. In this approach, stakeholders create an organization to regulate themselves and if successful, optimize the use of the resource and ensure sustainability over the long term. There are many examples where cooperation has been attempted to solve the problem of the commons with varying degrees of success.

Elinor Ostrom's dissertation focused on a case study of one of these organizations, a water replenishment district in her hometown of Los Angeles. If not for the voluntary efforts of this organization, Los Angeles risked losing much of its fresh groundwater to saltwater. By studying this particular example, Ostrom came to understand the value of voluntary organizations. In this case, the commons were protected without government taxes or regulation and without privatization. A voluntary organization came up with the solution to inject fresh water along the coast and pursued legal channels to enforce the action.[54] About twenty years later, Ostrom discovered that there were thousands of case studies of other organizations committed to protecting common resources, and she launched an investigation to learn why some succeeded and others failed. In the end, she concluded that there were no hard and fast rules for success, but there were certain principles that helped explain how it could be achieved.

Any cooperative organization managing a common-pool resource must implement certain basic functions: allocate rights among users, clearly define those rights, monitor the use of the resource to ensure no one exceeded their rights, and punish violators. Some of Ostrom's observations were almost self-evident: Enforcement of fishing rules were easier and cheaper when those rules applied to fishing seasons rather than tonnage, and smaller groups were generally easier to manage. But some of Ostrom's findings were more subtle. She concluded that sanctions worked better when they were graduated, becoming stiffer for repeat offenders. She also thought that organizations were more likely to succeed when decisions were made democratically and when users with the most to gain from the program had proportionally greater responsibility. Other findings were more surprising. She believed that monitoring was best done by the users themselves, who understood the resource better, rather than by an independent third party.[55]

Ultimately these principles could improve the likelihood that a cooperative effort would succeed, but there were no guarantees. In some cases, cooperative processes simply didn't work as well as more conventional strategies involving government regulation, taxes, or privatization. Ostrom was concerned that her work would be interpreted as providing the secrets of successful cooperation when no panacea actually existed. Instead, she recognized that every case had a unique set of problems and a unique set of participants who could find their own solutions. As she said, "The problem with these cure-alls is that they presume that humans do not have the ability to craft, even though they have a system of law and the courts that provides an arena to do so."[56]

Ostrom followed a different approach from many economists because she relied on case studies to inform her work and analysis. This approach, described as inductive, set her apart from many of her fellow Nobel laureates in economics because she looked for answers in the real world. She was quite familiar with game theory and traditional economics but also looked to political science and other disciplines for insights. To provide more systematic access to scholars in other disciplines, she founded and fostered the Workshop in Political Theory and Policy Analysis at Indiana University.

FIFTEEN

Reshaping the Prize

After completing its fortieth year, what can we say about the success of the Nobel Prize in economics? Has it fulfilled its mission of honoring those economists who, during the previous year, have rendered the greatest service to mankind? Have Nobel Prize–winning economists – the financial economists, the libertarians, the micro minds, the behaviorists, the Keynesians, the Chicago School, the inventors, the statisticians, the historians, and all the others – made this world a better place?

Some Nobel Prize winners invented planning tools that have certainly enriched our lives. With national income accounts we have a much clearer understanding about how well the economy is performing at any given time, and with input-output models and linear programming we can answer interesting and important questions. In other cases, Nobel Prize winners have proposed ideas that reinforce and sometimes challenge our understanding of economics. Right or wrong, these ideas force us to think about important social issues. But do we agree with Gary Becker that criminals are rational human beings who methodically calculate the costs and benefits of crime? Is James Buchanan correct when he claims that government officials are unlikely to act in the public interest? And what about Daniel Kahneman: Are human beings easily misled by context when making decisions? Are these ideas consistent with our own experiences and what we observe around us? Are they right most of the time or just some of the time?

Good economics may confirm our beliefs, but even better economics forces us to see the world differently. Where we once saw business activity, we now see transaction costs, and where we saw simple consumer choices, we now wonder how framing strategies might have shaped those choices. When the Federal Reserve bails out an unregulated Wall Street bank we may think it's unfair, but we may also worry about moral hazard. Is the

Federal Reserve sending a signal to major Wall Street firms that they are too big to fail and can therefore take unnecessary risks with other people's money? With a simple word or a phrase, economists have given us a lens to see the world more clearly.

Room for Improvement

The Nobel Prize in economics has almost always recognized interesting ideas and occasionally great achievements. However, the Nobel Prize committee could do better if its goal is to consistently recognize the greatest service to mankind. Some of the greatest economists of the past century were honored during the early years of the prize, while others were made to wait. That backlog seems to be gone. The adage, "All the mighty firs have fallen; now there are only bushes left," has been used to describe the Nobel Prize in economics.[1] There are even suggestions that the Nobel Foundation might skip a year occasionally if there are no compelling candidates. If the prize is to continue to play a positive role in recognizing important economic ideas and to achieve its lofty goal of recognizing the greatest service to mankind, it will need to change.

Many of the Nobel awards honored theories based on rational behavior and yet we know that self-interest, as important as it may be, has its limits. Exceptions to self-interest can be found everywhere, even among economists. Mohammed Yunus is one of those economists who dedicated himself to the public good and still enjoyed considerable success. Yunus earned his doctorate in economics from Vanderbilt University in 1969 and returned to his home in Bangladesh to head the economics department at Chittagong University. While teaching abstract economic theories, he discovered outside the walls of his university a very different kind of economy. Here he found the poor of Bangladesh living on one or two dollars a day with no education and no prospects for the future. Many of these desperate people were indebted to money lenders, and even though the sums were miniscule, the terms were exorbitant and the payments excessive.[2]

Yunus offered to pay off some of these small debts, and before long he was making and guaranteeing loans. The amazing thing that he discovered was that these small financial transactions had a big impact on the well-being of families. The small loans either lifted families out of a crushing debt or created an opportunity to launch a small business. He also discovered that when the loans were made to women, most of the benefits accrued to the entire family, including the children. What's more, he found that the poor were particularly responsible in paying off their debts.

From this modest discovery, Yunus and some of his students created the Grameen Bank, or village bank. It grew steadily and over the years provided loans totaling about $6 billion today. Because the loans were granted in small amounts, the benefits reached nearly seven million poor people in 73,000 villages. The bank also launched a myriad of small businesses through its micro loans, built 640,000 houses, and supported tens of thousands of school scholarships and college loans. The model has spread to more than 100 countries worldwide, multiplying its direct benefits many times over. Here is an economist who arguably rendered one of the greatest services to mankind but he did not win the Nobel Prize in economics. Instead he won the Nobel Peace Prize in 2006.

Yunus expressed concerns in his Nobel lecture about traditional economics because it paints a one-dimensional picture of human beings that ignores the "political, emotional, social, spiritual, environmental dimensions of their lives."[3] As an alternative, Yunus recommended, "Our theoretical constructs should make room for the blossoming of those qualities, not assume them away."[4] This novel approach to economics is one that the Nobel economics committee has studiously avoided. The economics prize is still focused on transforming economics into some sort of physical or natural science and trying to prove that economists deserve an equal place on the stage with the Nobel scientists. In the process they have ignored economists like Muhammad Yunus who understand that economics is about human nature, and is not independent of it.

Too often, Nobel Prize winners have simply incorporated older economic concepts or familiar behavior into mathematical models without achieving any particularly new insights. The prize needs to move beyond the discoveries of Adam Smith, John Maynard Keynes, and John von Neumann. As economists create new fields and apply their sophisticated tools to new problems, they are not leaving behind a long record of successes. Most of the great economic problems remain, including poverty, severe recessions, volatile business cycles, currency crises, and debt crises. Speculation can still wreak havoc in virtually any market, whether it is for stocks, real estate, currency, precious metals, or energy. And we continue to debate the economic consequences of climate change, oil depletion, financial regulation, health care, and globalization. It is time to stop looking for clever solutions to interesting academic puzzles and instead start looking for real insights into actual economic problems. The Nobel committee for economics should refocus on more practical results if they intend to provide a more meaningful service to mankind.

As the Nobel committee starts choosing winners over the next forty years, they could seriously consider making a few changes. For instance, they could

- Stop trying to emulate the Nobel physical and natural sciences. There was a time when it was important to minimize and maximize functions to test whether this particular approach could solve economic problems. For the most part, it did not. Unlike physical or natural scientists, economists cannot prove their ideas or theories on a blackboard, or, for the most part, in a laboratory. For whatever reasons, applying the tools of physics did not provide a deep understanding of real economic behavior. The age of Samuelson, Solow, Hicks, and Debreu was certainly a golden age for mathematical economists, but that approach evidently has run its course. Good economic ideas do not have to be proven mathematically in a journal article.
- The prize in economics should be about economics. This may seem obvious but it is still unfortunately necessary to point out. More than one economic laureate has simply refined mathematical or statistical techniques. Some winners, like John Nash, believed they were solving mathematical problems and they were. Sir Clive Granger suggested that economics must be easy if noneconomists like himself can win the Nobel Prize. He was wrong. Economics is not easy and what he did was not great economics; it was statistics. Unless the Bank of Sweden wants to rename their Nobel the prize in economics, statistics, and applied mathematics, they would do well to refocus on economic ideas.
- Embrace diversity and accept the fact that economists will disagree. The Nobel Prize in economics already includes contradictory theories from monetarists and Keynesians, central planners and free-market advocates, and microeconomists and behaviorists. In one of the most striking contrasts, the Nobel Prize went to socialist Gunnar Myrdal and antisocialist Friedrich A. von Hayek, in the same year. But there is an even broader pool of economic ideas to choose from, and the Nobel Prize in economics should reflect that wider diversity. The recent awards for behaviorists and institutionalists is a good step in that direction.
- Accept the fact that some great economic theories have simply run their course. Classical economics originated 200 to 300 years ago and was based on simple, convenient assumptions. Revival of this theory in the second half of the twentieth century by Milton Friedman, Robert

Lucas, Edward Prescott, and others gained a following in the economics profession but provided few new insights. Classical economists will no doubt continue to resurrect new variations of this theory, but the Nobel committee should feel no obligation to reward it.

- Prioritize awards for important economic issues. Several Nobel Prizes have already been awarded for their potential to refine auctions, and while this topic may be interesting it is not the single most important economic issue. By concentrating on this issue, the Nobel committee diverts attention from important issues such as poverty, underdevelopment, financial crises, the business cycle, environmental degradation, discrimination, mass marketing, resource depletion, corporate power, and the costs of war. Rather than gravitate toward smaller, more manageable topics, the Nobel committee could prioritize topics that are most important to people.

- Recognize more work that has practical value. Some of the most creative and useful economic ideas came from Leontief, Kuznets, and Kantorovich who were all astute observers of the real world. Leontief once complained that his colleagues spent too much time staring out the window thinking up abstract problems and proofs and not enough time studying real economic problems. This same criticism applies to a number of Nobel laureates who were honored for inventing elaborate castles in the air. Practical value should be a criterion for a Nobel Prize in economics, not an afterthought.

- Broaden the nominating process so that it is not dominated by past winners. As long as past winners have a major role in choosing future winners, there will be little change. Some great economists have won the prize, but not all winners attained the same level of achievement. If the Nobel Prize in economics is to reward consistently the greatest service to mankind, it will need a new orientation for the twenty-first century. Only by broadening the nominating process can we hope to see significant change.

- Don't skip over great economists for political reasons. The Nobel committee lost opportunities to honor two great economists of the twentieth century when they failed to give the prize in economics to John Kenneth Galbraith and Joan Robinson. These two practitioners achieved luminary status in the economics profession and when they didn't win, the stature of the prize was diminished for many and raised questions about the objectivity of the selection process. If a formal posthumous award is not possible, at least the Nobel foundation should find some way to honor the lifetime contributions of these two great economists.

In addition to bestowing fame and financial rewards on economists, the Nobel foundation also sends an important signal about what is good economics. These signals influence graduate students as they choose fields of study and practicing economists as they select research topics. The awards are also important because both political leaders and the public value opinions of economists who have won Nobel Prizes. Because of the prestige and authority of a Nobel Prize, the committee needs to recognize important ideas consistently.

For the first forty years the Nobel committee disproportionately favored the economics department at the University of Chicago. This seems less a result of objective science than a preference for free markets advocated by Chicago School economists. While free markets and deregulation can be powerful and valuable tools, they aren't always perfect. By favoring a one-sided position on this topic, the Nobel committee has not provided a great service to the world. Where was the Nobel laureate who could explain why electric energy deregulation failed in California and the West coast in 2001? Where was the Nobel laureate who could explain the risk to the U.S. financial system in 2008 under the strain of subprime mortgages?

While there are many laureates who supported deregulating these markets, there is a conspicuous absence of those who raised concerns. Biases such as this, or of any kind, undermine the value of a Nobel Prize. For instance, if the prize had been won by post-Keynesian economist Hyman Minsky, we might have understood how "fragility" undermined the financial system in 2008. Or if Walter Adams, author of the *Bigness Complex: Industry, Labor, and Government* and other books, had won the prize, we could have anticipated the bailout of large banks and insurance companies because they were "too big to fail." These scholars developed important theories, but because they squarely addressed the limits of free markets, they evidently were not favored by the Swedish Nobel committee.

One of the most important benefits of a Nobel Prize in economics is the opportunity to educate the world about great and important ideas. This is an opportunity that should not be squandered. The award of a Nobel Prize in 2006 to Mohammad Yunus served this purpose because it informed the world about how micro lending has supported economic development in some of the most impoverished areas of the world. This was a Peace Prize but it should have been a prize in economics.

The Nobel Prize in economics should and can recognize major innovations and discoveries that lead to better economic performance. It has occasionally achieved this standard in the past, and with more focused effort it could consistently achieve this standard in the future. Economics is too important and affects too many lives for the Nobel Prize to reward anything less than the greatest service to mankind.

Notes

Chapter 1

1. Steve Lohr, "American Economist Gets Nobel: Public Choice Theory Cited," *New York Times*, 17 October 1986, 1.
2. Stephen Kotkin, "Aiming to Level a Global Playing Field," *New York Times*, 3 September 2006, 3.
3. David Leonhardt, "Two Professors, Collaborators in Econometrics, Win the Nobel," *New York Times*, 9 October 2003, C1.
4. Thomas Petzinger, "The Wall Street Journal Millennium: Industry & Economics," *Wall Street Journal*, 31 December 1999, R36.
5. Sylvia Nasar, "The Sometimes Dismal Nobel Prize," *New York Times*, 13 October 2001, C3.
6. This practice may have changed along the way because one of the early printed volumes referred to the economic prize lectures as "Nobel Lectures."

Chapter 2

1. Mont Pelerin Society website. Available at www.montpelerin.org
2. Ibid.
3. Ibid.
4. In addition to Hayek, Friedman, and Buchanan, other Nobel Prize winners associated with the Mont Pelerin Society included George Stigler (president), Gary Becker (president), Maurice Allais (member), Ronald Coase (member), and Vernon Smith (member).
5. Tom Redburn, "Economic Theorist of Public Choice School James M. Buchanan Wins Nobel Prize," *Los Angeles Times*, 17 October 1986.
6. Stephen Kresge and Leif Wenar, eds., *Hayek on Hayek: An Autobiographical Dialogue* (Chicago: The University of Chicago Press, 1994), 94.
7. Ibid., 125.
8. Ibid., 93.
9. Ibid., 89.
10. Ibid., 82.

11. Ibid., 83.
12. Paul A. Samuelson, "Nobel Choice: Economists in Contrast," *New York Times*, 10 October 1974, 69.
13. Kresge and Wenar, 145.
14. Ibid.
15. Sylvia Nasar, "Friedrich von Hayek Dies at 92; An Early Free-Market Economist," *New York Times*, 24 March 1992, D22.
16. Friedrich August von Hayek, "The Pretence of Knowledge," Nobel Memorial Lecture, 11 December 1974, *Nobel Lectures, Economics, 1969–1980*, Assar Lindbeck, ed. (Singapore: World Scientific Publishing Company, 1992).
17. Kresge and Wenar, 148.
18. Silk, 16.
19. Milton Friedman, "A Case of Bad Good News," *Newsweek*, 26 September 1983.
20. The Keynesian explanation was simple and direct – falling unemployment was a sign of rising demand which also causes higher prices and inflation.
21. George Wald and Linus Pauling, Letters to the Editor, *New York Times*, 24 October 1976, section IV, 14, and David Baltimore and S. E. Luria, Letters to the Editor, *New York Times*, 24 October 1976, section IV, 14.
22. "Americans Who Swept 5 Nobels Get $160,000 Prizes," *New York Times*, 11 December 1976, 3.
23. "Friedman Given A Nobel Award; 2 Share a Prize," *New York Times*, 15 October 1976, 1, and Milton Friedman and Rose Friedman, *Two Lucky People: Memoirs* (Chicago: University of Chicago Press, 1998).
24. Ibid., 399.
25. Ibid., 397.
26. Ibid., 594.
27. Ibid., 407.
28. Bernard Weintraub, "Friedman, in Nobel Lecture, Challenges a Tradition," *New York Times*, 14 December 1976, 55.
29. Ibid.
30. William Breit and Roger L. Ranson, *The Academic Scribblers* (New York: Holt, Reinhart and Winston, Inc. 1971), 209.
31. Ibid., 209.
32. Freidman and Friedman, 217–218.
33. Ibid., 219.
34. Leonard Silk, "Milton Friedman – Nobel Laureate," *New York Times*, 17 October 1976, section III, 16.
35. "Milton Friedman," Autobiography, in *Nobel Lectures, Economics, 1969–1980*, Assar Lindbeck, ed. (Singapore: World Scientific Publishing Company, 1992), 233.
36. Ibid., 239.
37. Ibid., 239.
38. "Prickly Laureate," *New York Times*, 15 October 1976, 30.
39. "Monetarism Reaps Its Own Reward," *New York Times*, 25 December 1976, 19, and "Prickly Laureate," 30.
40. Robert Hershey, "An Austere Scholar: James McGill Buchanan," *New York Times*, 17 October 1986, section IV, 1.

41. Ingemar Stahl, Presentation Speech 1986, in *Nobel Lectures, Economics, 1981–1990*, Karl-Gorän Mäler, ed. (Singapore: World Scientific Publishing Company, 1992), 329–330.

42. James Buchanan, "The Constitution of Economic Policy," Nobel Lecture, 8 December 1986, in *Nobel Lectures, Economics, 1981–1990*, Karl-Gorän Mäler, ed. (Singapore: World Scientific Publishing Company, 1992), 334–343.

43. James M. Buchanan and Richard E. Wagner, *Democracy in Deficit: The Political Legacy of Lord Keynes* (London, UK: Academic Press, 1977), 2.

44. Ibid.

45. Ibid., 4.

46. David Warsh, "The Skeptic's Reward," *Boston Globe*, 26 October 1986, A1, and "George Mason – Little School Got Big Name," *San Francisco Chronicle*, 30 October 1986, 11.

47. Redburn.

48. Warsh, A1.

49. Hershey, 1 and Warsh, A1.

50. Ibid.

51. Hershey, 1.

52. Lindley H. Clark Jr., "Critic of Politicians Wins Nobel Prize in Economic Science – James Buchanan Examines How Governments Make Decisions on Fiscal Policy," *Wall Street Journal*, 17 October 1986, 1.

53. "George Mason – Little School Got Big Name," 11 and Hershey, 1.

54. Michael Kinsley, "Viewpoint: How to Succeed in Academia by Really Trying," *Wall Street Journal*, 30 October 1986, 1.

55. Milton Friedman, Thomas DiLornzo, and David Shapiro, Letters to the Editor, Choice Remarks, *Wall Street Journal*, 10 November 1986.

56. Ibid.

57. Ibid.

58. "In celebration of Armen Alchian's 80th birthday: Living and breathing economics." *Economic Inquiry* 34, no. 3 (July 1996): 412–426.

59. Robert Lekachman, "A Controversial Nobel Choice: Tuning In to These Conservative Times," *New York Times* (Late edition, East Coast), 26 October 1986, section III, A2.

Chapter 3

1. Alfred Malabre and Richard Gibson, "Becker Wins '92 Nobel Prize for Economics," *Wall Street Journal*, 14 October 1992, B1.

2. Ibid.

3. Gary Becker, "The Economic Way of Looking at Life," Nobel Lecture, December 9, 1992" In *Nobel Lectures, Economics, 1991–1995*, Torsten Persson, ed. (Singapore: World Scientific Publishing Company, 1997), 28.

4. Ibid.

5. In other words, they have higher discount rates.

6. Gary Becker, "The Economics of Crime," Richmond, VA: *Cross Sections*, publication of Federal Reserve Bank of Richmond (Fall 1995).

7. Ibid.
8. Ibid.
9. "Gary Becker," Autobiography, in *Nobel Lectures, Economics, 1991–1995*, Torsten Persson, ed. (Singapore: World Scientific Publishing Company, 1997), 29.
10. Steven Mufson, "Economics Professor Wins Nobel: Chicago's Becker Cited for 'Human Analysis,'" *Washington Post*, 14 October 1992, F01.
11. Assar Lindbeck, Presentation Speech 1992, in *Nobel Lectures, Economics, 1991–1995*, Torsten Persson, ed. (Singapore: World Scientific Publishing Company, 1997), 23–24.
12. Gary Becker, "A Theory of Marriage: Part I," *Journal of Political Economy* 81, no. 4 (January 1973): 822.
13. "Gary Becker," Autobiography, 30.
14. Christopher Farrell, Michael Mandel, and Julia Flynn, "An Economist for the Common Man: Nobel winner Becker has applied economic principles to people's lives," *Business Week*, 26 October 1992, 36.
15. Jonathan Marshall, "U.S. Professor Wins Nobel for Economics: Gary Becker known for challenging orthodoxy," *San Francisco Chronicle*, 14 October 1992, A3.
16. Douglas Clement, "Interview with Gary Becker," Minneapolis: *The Region*, Federal Reserve Bank of Minneapolis, online, June 2002.
17. Ibid.
18. This could be measured properly only if a sample of students agreed to be randomly assigned to attend college or not. But this is, of course, impractical.
19. Marshall, A3.
20. Gary Becker, "When the Wake-Up Call is from the Nobel Committee," *Business Week, Economic Viewpoint*, 2 November 1992, 20.
21. Ibid.
22. Ibid.
23. Mufson, F01.
24. Clement, "Interview," and Mufson, F01.
25. Ibid.
26. Ibid.
27. Clement, 3–4.
28. Clement.
29. Clement.
30. Beth Belton, "Does crime pay? Economist's answer wins," *USA Today*, 14 October 1992, 4B.
31. George Stigler, "The Process and Progress of Economics," Nobel Memorial Lecture, 8 December 1982, in *Nobel Lectures, Economics, 1981–1990*, Karl-Gorän Mäler, ed. (Singapore: World Scientific Publishing Company, 1992).
32. George Stigler, "The Economist as Preacher: Reflections of a Nobel Prize Winner," *New York Times*, 24 October 1982, section III, 2.
33. Stigler, "The Process and Progress of Economics."
34. "George Stigler," Autobiography, in *Nobel Lectures, Economics, 1981–1990*, Karl-Gorän Mäler, ed. (Singapore: World Scientific Publishing Company, 1992), and Milton Friedman, "Biographical Memoirs: George Stigler, January 17,

1911–December 1, 1991." National Academy of Sciences. Available at www.nap. edu/html/biomems/gstigler.html

35. Friedman, "Biographical Memoirs."
36. "George Stigler," Autobiography.
37. Friedman, "Biographical Memoirs."
38. Ibid., 3.
39. Ibid.
40. Lars Werin, Presentation Speech, in *Nobel Lectures, Economics, 1981–1990*, Karl-Görän Mäler, ed. (Singapore: World Scientific Publishing Company, 1992).
41. Friedman, "Biographical Memoirs."
42. Ibid.
43. Richard Cottle, Ellis Johnson, and Roger Wets, "George B. Dantzig (1914–2005)," *Notices of the American Mathematical Society* (AMS) 54, no. 3: 349.
44. Nutritionists objected to the seven tablespoons of lard, pointing out that lard is high in saturated fat, a substance linked to the leading cause of the death in the United States, heart disease. A spokesman for the rendered lard products industry countered with the defense that lard had been around a long time and would continue to be around a long time in the future. Drew Sefton, "Professor, Nutritionists Chew the Fat Over Cheap But Lard-Heavy Diet," New Orleans: *Times-Picayune*, 21 April 2000, 6.
45. Friedman, "Biographical Memoirs," 5.
46. Ibid.
47. Stigler, "The Process and Progress of Economics," 263.
48. Ibid.
49. Werin, "Presentation Speech."
50. George Will, "Passing of a Prophet," *Washington Post*, 8 December 1991, c7.
51. Ibid.
52. Peter Passell, "George Joseph Stigler Dies at 80; Nobel Prize Winner in Economics," *New York Times*, 3 December 1991, B12.
53. Friedman, "Biographical Memoirs."
54. Sandra Salmans, "An Incisive Teacher: George Joseph Stigler," *New York Times*, 21 October 1982, section IV, 1.
55. Friedman, "Biographical Memoirs."
56. "George Stigler," Autobiography, 2.
57. Will, c7.
58. "Theodore W. Schultz," Autobiography, in *Nobel Lectures, Economics, 1969–1980*, Assar Lindbeck, ed. (Singapore: World Scientific Publishing Company, 1992).
59. Gale D. Johnson, "In Memoriam: Theodore W. Schultz," *Economic Development and Cultural Change* 47, no. 1 (October 1998): 209.
60. Peter Passell, "Theodore Schultz, 95, Winner of a Key Prize in Economics," Obituary, *New York Times*, 2 March 1998, A15.
61. Martin Weil, "Nobel-Winning Economist Theodore Schultz Dies," *Washington Post*, 3 March 1998, D6.
62. Passell, A15.
63. Johnson.

64. Mary Jean Bowman, "On Theodore W. Schultz's Contribution to Economics," *Scandinavian Journal of Economics* 82, no. 1 (1980), 86.
65. Theodore Schultz, "The Economics of Being Poor," Nobel Memorial Lecture, 8 December 1979, in *Nobel Lectures, Economics, 1969–1980*, Assar Lindbeck, ed. (Singapore: World Scientific Publishing Company, 1992), 251.
66. "Theodore Schultz," Chicago, Illinois: *The University of Chicago Chronicle* 17, no. 11 (5 March 1998).
67. Bowman, 85.
68. Schultz, "The Economics of Being Poor," 245.
69. Ibid., 246.
70. Ibid., 242.
71. Ibid., 250.
72. Ibid., 249.
73. Ibid., 248.
74. Press Release, Announcement of the 1991 Prize in Economic Sciences, Available at www.Nobelprize.org.
75. Peter Passell, "For a Common-Sense Economist, a Nobel – And an Impact in the Law," *New York Times*, Current Events Edition, 20 October 1991, 42.
76. Ronald H. Coase, "Banquet Speech," in *Nobel Lectures, Economics, 1991–1995*, Torsten Persson, ed. (Singapore: World Scientific Publishing Company, 1997), 17.
77. Ronald H. Coase, "The Institutional Structure of Production," Prize Lecture, (9 December 1991, in *Nobel Lectures, Economics, 1991–1995*, Torsten Persson, ed. (Singapore: World Scientific Publishing Company, 1997), 17.
78. Johnnie Roberts and Richard Gibson, "Friction Theorist Wins Economics Nobel," *Wall Street Journal*, 16 October 1991, B8.
79. David Warsh, "Nobel Winner Coase Blends Theories of Economics, Law," *Boston Globe*, 16 October 1991, 63.
80. David Warsh, "When the Revolution Was a Party: How Privatization Was Invented in the 1960s," *Boston Globe*, 20 October 1991, A33.
81. Paul Craig Roberts, "How Liberals Purged a Pair of Future Nobel Laureates," *Business Week*, 25 November 1991, 18.
82. Ibid.
83. Thomas Karier, *Great Experiments in American Economic Policy* (Westport, Connecticut: Praeger, 1997), 158.
84. Ronald H. Coase, "The Institutional Structure of Production," 19.
85. Warsh, "When the Revolution Was a Party," A33.
86. David Warsh, "Nobel Winner Coase Blends Theories of Economics, Law," 63.
87. Peter Passell, "Economics Nobel to a Basic Thinker," *New York Times*, Current Events Edition, 16 October 1991, D1.
88. "Nobel Prize News Catches Up to Coase," *USA Today*, 17 October 1991, 2B.

Chapter 4

1. "Merton Miller," Autobiography, in *Nobel Lectures, Economics, 1981–1990*, Karl Gorän Mäler, ed. (Singapore: World Scientific Publishing Company, 1992).

2. James Risen, "3 Americans Get Nobel Prize in Economics Award," *Los Angeles Times*, 17 October 1990, 1.

3. Later analysts added a caveat which is that different tax rates on dividends and capital gains can make a difference.

4. "Harry M. Markowitz," Autobiography, in *Nobel Lectures, Economics, 1981–1990*, Karl Gorän Mäler, ed. (Singapore: World Scientific Publishing Company, 1992).

5. "William F. Sharpe," Autobiography, in *Nobel Lectures, Economics, 1981–1990*, Karl Gorän Mäler, ed. (Singapore: World Scientific Publishing Company, 1992).

6. There is sometimes a misunderstanding that beta is an independent measure of risk for an individual stock. That is not entirely correct. The variance is probably a better measure of risk for an individual stock.

7. Risen, 1.

8. "Myron S. Scholes," Autobiography, in *Nobel Lectures, Economics, 1996–2000*, Torsten Persson, ed. (Singapore: World Scientific Publishing Company, 2003).

9. "Robert Merton," Autobiography, in *Nobel Lectures, Economics, 1996–2000*, Torsten Persson, ed. (Singapore: World Scientific Publishing Company, 2003).

10. Roger Lowenstein, *When Genius Failed: The Rise and Fall of Long-Term Capital Management* (New York: Random House, 2000), and "Nobel Laureates at Odds in Long-Term Capital Case: Joseph Stiglitz testifies in the hedge fund's tax suit that a transaction had no economic value," *Los Angeles Times*, 18 July 2003, C11.

11. "Merton, Robert," Autobiography, in *Nobel Lectures, Economics, 1996–2000*, Torsten Persson, ed. (Singapore: World Scientific Publishing Company, 2003).

12. Ibid.

13. Taking into account the interest on the $99 borrowed makes this less than 100 percent return.

14. Roger Lowenstein, *When Genius Failed: The Rise and Fall of Long-Term Capital Management* (New York: Random House, 2000), 35.

15. David Wessel, "Capital: Taxes Still Haunt the Ghost of LTCM," *Wall Street Journal*, 3 October 2002, A2.

16. David Wessel, "Capital: U.S. Scores a Win Against Tax-Shelter Abuse," *Wall Street Journal*, 31 August 2006, A2.

17. Ibid.

18. Eric Quinones, "2 Americans Win Nobel for Economics," New Orleans: *Times-Picayune*, 15 October 1997, C1.

19. Ibid.

20. David Dreman, "Nobel Laureates with Black Boxes," *Forbes*, 14 December 1998, 283.

21. Barbara Donnelly, "Efficient-Market Theorists Are Puzzled by Recent Gyrations in Stock Market," *Wall Street Journal*, 23 October 1987, 1.

22. Ibid.

23. Ibid.

24. Keith Devlin, "A Nobel Formula," Devlin's Angle, Mathematics Association of America, November 1997. Available at www.maa.org. Devlin appears to have mistakenly stated the market collapse was in 1978.

25. Ibid.
26. Ibid.
27. Ibid.
28. Dreman, 283.

Chapter 5

1. To illustrate this, consider a large increase in the price for home heating oil. There will be a *substitution effect* when people try to reduce their consumption of heating oil. But there is another effect, because a family that has to spend a lot more on heat will have less money to spend on everything else. The price increase acts like a reduction in income and can cause consumers to buy less of many other things including fuel. This is called the *income effect*.
2. They did this by presuming that there was a certain amount of money that would exactly offset any unhappiness caused by a price increase. It introduced the idea of compensation as an offset for price changes.
3. The value of this price reduction was approximately proportional to the reduced expenditure on current food purchases.
4. William J. Baumol, "John R. Hicks' Contribution to Economics," *Swedish Journal of Economics* 110, no. 6 (1972): 509. The reason that there are two measures has to do with the choice of compensating someone before or after a price change to maintain the level of contentment. For example, the amount you would have to pay consumers after a price increase to regain the same level of contentment as they had at the start was called "compensating variation" by Hicks. The alternative was to charge consumers before the price increase so they have the same level of contentment at the start as they will have after the price increase. He called that "equivalent variation." The two amounts of money, in a sense, represent the loss of value from a price increase, but they are two different numbers.
5. Hicks focused on one aspect of these equations that indicated how easy or difficult it was to substitute one input for another, which he called the *elasticity of substitution*. A high value, for example, indicated that a small increase in wages would cause a significant replacement of labor by machines.
6. Arjo Klamer, "An Accountant among Economists: Conversations with Sir John R. Hicks," *Journal of Economic Perspectives* 3, no. 4 (Fall 1989): 167–180.
7. Ibid.
8. Ibid.
9. Ibid.
10. "Sir John R. Hicks, 1904–1989," New School for Social Research, Available at www.cepa.newschool.edu/het/profiles/hicks.htm
11. Klamer, 167–180.
12. John R. Hicks, "The Mainspring of Economic Growth," Nobel Memorial Lecture, 27 April 1973, in *Nobel Lectures, Economics, 1969–1980*, Assar Lindbeck, ed. (Singapore: World Scientific Publishing Company, 1992).
13. Ibid., 237.
14. Klamer, 167–180.
15. Baumol, 523.

16. "John R. Hicks," Autobiography, in *Nobel Lectures, Economics, 1969–1980*, Assar Lindbeck, ed. (Singapore: World Scientific Publishing Company, 1992).

17. Klamer, 167–180.

18. "John R. Hicks," Autobiography.

19. R. Preston McAfee and John McMillan, "Auctions and Bidding," *Journal of Economic Literature* 25 (June 1997): 699–738.

20. David Lucking-Reilly, "Using Field Experiments to Test Equivalence Between Auction Formats: Magic on the Internet," *American Economic Review* 89, no. 5 (December 1999): 1063.

21. David Lucking-Reilly, "Vickrey Auctions in Practice: From Nineteenth-Century Philately to Twenty-First-Century E-Commerce," *Journal of Economic Perspectives* 14, no. 3 (Summer 2000): 183–192.

22. Ibid.

23. Ibid.

24. Although Fisher retired the same year that Vickrey enrolled, the two met and continued to correspond long after they had both left Yale.

25. Robert Dimand and Robert Koehn, "From Edgeworth to Fisher to Vickrey: A Comment on Michael J. Boskin's Vickrey Lecture," *Atlantic Economic Journal* 30, no. 2 (June 2002): 205.

26. Richard Holt, David Colander, David Kennett, and J. Barkley Rosser Jr., "William Vickrey's Legacy: Innovative Policies for Social Concerns," *Eastern Economic Journal* 24, no. 1 (Winter 1998): 1.

27. Ibid.

28. Robert Dimand and Robert Koehn. "Vickrey, Eisner, the Budget, and the Goal of Chock-Full Employment," *Journal of Economic Issues* 34, no. 2 (June 2000): 471 (7 pages).

29. Varian, C2.

30. "James A. Mirrlees," Autobiography, in *Les Prix Nobel, The Nobel Prizes 1996*, Tore Frangsmyr, ed. (Stockholm: Nobel Foundation, 1997).

31. Ibid.

32. Hal R. Varian, "In the Debate over Tax Policy, the Power of Luck Shouldn't Be Overlooked," *New York Times*, 3 May 2001, C2.

33. Ibid.

34. James A. Mirrlees, "Information and Incentives: The Economics of Carrots and Sticks," Nobel Lecture, 9 December 1996, in *Les Prix Nobel, The Nobel Prizes 1996*, Tore Frangsmyr, ed. (Stockholm: Nobel Foundation, 1997).

35. Ambrose Leung, "Nobel Laureate Urges SAR to Increase Salaries Tax Rate," Hong Kong: *South China Morning Post*, 8 October 2002, 3.

36. Jing Ji, "Expert Backs Preferential Tax Policy," *China Daily* (North American edition), 6 July 2006, 11.

37. James A. Mirrlees, "Banquet Speech," 10 December 1996, in *Les Prix Nobel, The Nobel Prizes 1996*, Tore Frangsmyr, ed. (Stockholm: Nobel Foundation, 1997).

38. Ibid.

39. "Vernon Smith," Autobiography, in *Les Prix Nobel, The Nobel Prizes 2002*, Tore Frangsmyr, ed. (Stockholm: Nobel Foundation, 2003), 8.

40. Lars-Göran Nilsson, Presentation Speech, 10 December 2002, in *Les Prix Nobel, The Nobel Prizes 2002*, Tore Frangsmyr, ed. (Stockholm: Nobel Foundation, 2003).

41. Vernon L. Smith, "Constructivist and Ecological Rationality in Economics," Nobel Prize Lecture, 8 December 2002, in *Les Prix Nobel, The Nobel Prizes 2002*, Tore Frangsmyr, ed. (Stockholm: Nobel Foundation, 2003), 511.

42. Jon E. Hilsenrath, "Nobel Winners for Economics are New Breed," *Wall Street Journal*, 10 October 2002, B1.

43. Michael Maiello, "Professor Bubble," *Forbes*, 10 November 2003, 190.

44. Ibid.

45. Smith, "Constructivist," 538.

46. Jeremy Clift, "The Lab Man," Interview with Vernon Smith, Washington D.C.: *Finance & Development* 40, no. 1 (March 2003): 6.

47. Smith, "Constructivist," 542.

48. Ibid., 540.

49. Clift, 6.

50. Smith, "Constructivist," 542, footnote 70.

51. Smith, "Constructivist," 519–520.

52. Rana Foroohar, "An Experimental Mind; Having Shaken the Ivory Tower and Reshaped Big Government, Vernon Smith's Ideas Are Revolutionizing Business," *Newsweek*, 6 October 2003, 46.

53. Ibid.

54. Smith, "Constructivist," 524.

55. Ibid., 525.

56. Ibid.

57. Peter Coy, "Laurels for an Odd Couple: A Psychologist and a Traditionalist Share This Year's Nobel," *Business Week*, 21 October 2002, 50.

58. Vernon Smith, "Banquet Speech," 10 December 2002, in *Les Prix Nobel, The Nobel Prizes 2002*, Tore Frangsmyr, ed. (Stockholm: Nobel Foundation, 2003).

59. Smith, "Constructivist," 551.

60. Clift, 6.

61. Ibid.

62. Foroohar, 46.

63. Ibid.

64. Maiello, 190.

65. Ibid.

66. Smith, "Constructivist," 526.

67. Ibid., 518.

68. Foroohar, 46.

Chapter 6

1. Bruce Bower, "Simple Minds, Smart Choices: For Sweet Decisions, Mix a Dash of Knowledge with a Cup of Ignorance," *Science News* 155, no. 22 (29 May 1999): 348.

2. Herbert Simon, "Rational Decision-Making in Business Organizations, Nobel Memorial Lecture," 8 December 1977, in *Nobel Lectures, Economics, 1969–1980*, Assar Lindbeck, ed. (Singapore: World Scientific Publishing Company, 1992), 277.

3. Roger Frantz, "Herbert Simon, Artificial Intelligence as a Framework for Understanding Intuition," *Journal of Economic Psychology* 24, no. 2 (April 2003): 265–277.

4. Ibid.

5. Ibid.

6. Ibid.

7. Ibid.

8. "Herbert A. Simon," Autobiography, in *Nobel Lectures, Economics, 1969–1980*, Assar Lindbeck, ed. (Singapore: World Scientific Publishing Company, 1992), 271. Also see Byron Spice, "Obituary: Herbert A. Simon/Father of Artificial Intelligence and Nobel Prize winner," Pittsburgh, Pennsylvania: *Post-Gazette*, 10 February 2001, 2.

9. Spice, 18.

10. Spice, "Obituary." Also see Byron Spice, "CMU's Simon Reflects on How Computers Will Continue to Shape the World," Pittsburgh, Pennsylvania: *Post-Gazette*, 16 October 2000.

11. Spice, "CMU's Simon."

12. David Klahr and Kenneth Kotovsky, "A Life of the Mind: Remembering Herb Simon," *American Psychological Society Observer*, News & Research 4, no. 4 (April 2001).

13. Spice, "CMU's Simon," 4.

14. Jonathan Williams, "A Life Spent on One Problem," *New York Times*, 26 November 1978, section III, 5.

15. Herbert Simon, "Rational Decision-Making," 290.

16. Ibid., 297.

17. Ibid., 299.

18. Ibid., 299.

19. Leonard Silk, "Nobel Winner's Heretical Views," *New York Times*, 9 November 1978, section IV: 2.

20. Bower, 348.

21. Spice, "Obituary." Also see Klahr and Kotovsky.

22. Klahr and Kotovsky, 5.

23. Malcolm Gladwell, *Blink: The Power of Thinking Without Thinking* (Boston: Little, Brown, 2005).

24. Daniel Kahneman, "Maps of Bounded Rationality: A Perspective on Intuitive Judgment and Choice," Nobel Prize Lecture, 8 December 2002, in *Les Prix Nobel, The Nobel Prizes 2002*, Tore Frangsmyr, ed. (Stockholm: Nobel Foundation, 2003), 451.

25. Matthew Rabin, "The Nobel Memorial Prize for Daniel Kahneman," *Scandinavian Journal of Economics* 105, no. 2 (2003): 162.

26. Kahneman, "Maps of Bounded Rationality," 470.

27. Ibid., 457.

28. Daniel Kahneman, "A Psychological Perspective on Economics," *American Economic Review* 93, no. 2 (May 2003): 164.

29. Rabin, 166.

30. "Daniel Kahneman," Autobiography, in *Les Prix Nobel, The Nobel Prizes 2002*, Tore Frangsmyr, ed. (Stockholm: Nobel Foundation, 2003), 13.

31. Rabin, 171.
32. Dan Lovallo and Daniel Kahneman, "Delusions of Success," *Harvard Business Review* 81, no. 7 (July 2003): 56–63.
33. Ibid.
34. Ibid.
35. Daniel Kahneman and Robert Sugden, "Experienced Utility as a Standard of Policy Evaluation," *Environmental & Resource Economics* 32 (2005): 170.
36. Ibid., 172.
37. Ibid., 169.
38. Ibid., 166.
39. Ibid., 166.
40. Rabin, 175.
41. Daniel Kahneman, Alan B. Krueger, David Schkade, Norbert Schwarz, and Arthur Stone, "Toward National Well-Being Accounts," *American Economic Review* 94, no. 2 (May 2004): 429.
42. Peter Singer, "Happiness, Money and Giving It Away," Bangkok: *Bangkok Post*, 17 July 2006, 1.
43. Kahneman, Krueger, et al., "Toward National Well-Being Accounts," 429.
44. Richard Tomkins, "Why Happiness Is Greater than the Sum of Its Parts," London, England: *Financial Times*, 10 December 2004, 13.
45. Daniel Kahneman, "Maps of Bounded Rationality," 460.
46. Kahneman and Sugden, 175.
47. Kahneman, Krueger, et al., 431.
48. Ibid.
49. Kahneman, "Maps of Bounded Rationality," 479.
50. Rabin, 172.
51. Ibid., 171.
52. Kahneman, Krueger, et al.
53. "Kahneman," Autobiography.
54. Ibid., 1.
55. Ibid.
56. Ibid.
57. Ibid., 5.
58. Ibid., 9, 14, and 18.
59. Ibid., 9–10.
60. Lars-Göran Nilsson, Presentation Speech, 10 December 2002, in *Les Prix Nobel, The Nobel Prizes 2002*, Tore Frangsmyr, ed. (Stockholm: Nobel Foundation, 2003).
61. "Kahneman," Autobiography, 14.
62. Ibid., 14.
63. Ibid., 13. Daniel Kahneman and Amos Tversky, "Prospect Theory: An Analysis of Decisions under Risk," *Econometrica* (1979). The name *prospect theory* was selected to refer to their ideas without any other particular significance.
64. "Kahneman," Autobiography, 16.
65. Kahneman, "A Psychological Perspective on Economics," 165.
66. "George A. Akerlof," Autobiography, in *Les Prix Nobel, The Nobel Prizes 2001*, Tore Frangsmyr, ed. (Stockholm: Nobel Foundation, 2002).

67. Ibid.
68. George Akerlof, "Behavioral Macroeconomics and Macroeconomic Behavior," Nobel Prize Lecture, in *Les Prix Nobel, The Nobel Prizes 2001*, Tore Frangsmyr, ed. (Stockholm: Nobel Foundation, 2002).
69. Ibid.
70. Ibid.
71. Paul Krugman, "Reckonings: Harvest of Lemons," *New York Times*, 14 October 2001, section 4, 13.
72. Ibid.
73. "Joseph E. Stiglitz," Autobiography, in *Les Prix Nobel, The Nobel Prizes 2001*, Tore Frangsmyr, ed. (Stockholm: Nobel Foundation, 2002), 3.
74. These included Nobel Prize winners Paul Samuelson, Franco Modigliani, Robert Solow, and Kenneth Arrow.
75. Eyal Press, "Rebel with a Cause: The Re-Education of Joseph Stiglitz," *Nation*, 10 June 2002: 11 (5 pages).
76. Krugman, "Reckonings."
77. Press.
78. "Joseph E. Stiglitz," Autobiography, 14.
79. Kenneth Rogoff, "An Open Letter To Joseph Stiglitz," Washington, D.C.: International Monetary Fund, 2 July 2002, 19. Available at www.imf.org
80. Ibid.
81. Charlotte Denny, "Interview: Joseph Stigllitz, Nobel Prize-Winning Economist: The Contented Malcontent," Manchester, UK: *Guardian*, 6 July 2002, 26.
82. Rogoff, "An Open Letter."
83. Ibid.
84. Ed Crooks, "The Odd Couple of Global Finance," London, UK: *Financial Times*, 6 July 2002, 11.
85. Press. Also see Robert Hunter Wade, "Joe Stiglitz's Bum Rap," Washington, D.C.: *Foreign Policy*, no. 139 (Nov/Dec 2003): 85.
86. Denny, 26.
87. Joseph Stiglitz, "Comment & Analysis: The Myth of the War Economy." Manchester, UK: *Guardian*, 22 January 2003, 18.
88. Joseph Stiglitz, "Odious Rulers, Odious Debts," *Atlantic Monthly*, November 2003, 39.
89. Kimberly Blanton, "Nobel Laureates Attack Tax Plan," *Boston Globe*, 11 February 2003, D1.
90. Alwyn Scott, "Nobel Laureate Says Jobless Recovery Remains a Puzzle," *St. Louis Post-Dispatch*, 12 January 2004, C1.
91. "U.S. Economist Suggests Japan Print Money to End Deflation," Tokyo: Jiji Press, English News Service, 27 March 2003, 1.
92. "Nobel Laureates at Odds in Long-Term Capital Case: Joseph Stiglitz Testifies in the Hedge Fund's Tax Suit that a Transaction Had No Economic Value," *Los Angeles Times*, 18 July 2003, C11.
93. Jon E. Hilsenrath, "Columbia Acquires Expensive Residence to House Professor," *Wall Street Journal*, 21 November 2002, 6.

94. Joseph Stiglitz, "Information and the Change in the Paradigm in Economics," Prize Lecture, 8 December 2001. In *Les Prix Nobel, The Nobel Prizes 2001*, Tore Frangsmyr, ed. (Stockholm: Nobel Foundation, 2002), 475.

95. A. Michael Spence, "Signaling in Retrospect and the Informational Structure of Markets," Nobel Prize Lecture, 8 December 2001, in *Les Prix Nobel, The Nobel Prizes 2001*, Tore Frangsmyr, ed. (Stockholm: Nobel Foundation, 2002).

96. Ibid.

97. Gene Epstein, "Economic Beat: The Great Unknown," *Barron's*, 15 October 2001, 36.

98. David, R. Henderson, "What the Nobel Economists Missed," *Wall Street Journal*, 12 October 2001, A14.

99. Although Spence's parents were residents of Canada, he was an accidental American; he was born in Montclair, New Jersey while his mother was on a trip.

100. Nina McCain, "Harvard Picks Economist, 40, as Faculty Dean," *Boston Globe*, 9 February 1984, 1.

101. Nina McCain, "Centerpiece; The Economist Becomes Dean; Harvard's Andrew Spence Gets Chance to Test His Skill at Management," *Boston Globe*, 15 March 1984, 1.

Chapter 7

1. Paul A. Samuleson, "How I Became an Economist," Nobel Foundation. Available at www.Nobelprize.org

2. Ibid.

3. Ibid.

4. Bernard Weintraub, "Samuelson, M.I.T. Economist, Wins a Nobel Memorial Award," *New York Times*, 27 October 1970, 1. Also see "Paul Samuelson," Autobiography, in *Nobel Lectures, Economics, 1969–1980*, Assar Lindbeck, ed. (Singapore: World Scientific Publishing Company, 1992), 265.

5. Leonard Silk, "Nobel for a Critic of Nixon Policies," *New York Times*, 1 November 1970, section IV, 2.

6. Samuelson, "How I Became an Economist."

7. "Paul Samuelson," Autobiography, 278. Also see Paul Samuelson, "Maximum Principles in Analytical Economics," Nobel Memorial Lecture, 11 December 1970, in *Nobel Lectures, Economics, 1969–1980*, Assar Lindbeck, ed. (Singapore: World Scientific Publishing Company, 1992), 279.

8. Assar Lindbeck, "Paul Anthony Samuelson's Contribution to Economics," *Swedish Journal of Economics* 107, no. 6 (1970): 345.

9. Ibid., 275.

10. "Samuelson's Economics," Editorial, *New York Times*, 27 October 1970, 44.

11. Paul Samuelson, "Maximum Principles in Analytical Economics," Nobel Memorial Lecture, 11 December 1970, in *Nobel Lectures, Economics, 1969–1980*, Assar Lindbeck, ed. (Singapore: World Scientific Publishing Company, 1992), 268.

12. Robert Reinhold, "Leader of Economic Mainstream, Paul Anthony Samuelson," *New York Times*, 27 October 1970, 8.

13. Mark Skousen, "The Perseverance of Paul Samuelson's Economics," *Journal of Economic Perspectives* 11, no. 2 (Spring 1997), 137.
14. Ibid.
15. Bennett Kremen, "Speaking of Books: Samuelson's "Economics," *New York Times*, 1 November 1970, section VII, 2.
16. Skousen, 137.
17. Samuelson, "Maximum Principles in Analytical Economics," 287.
18. Ibid., 287.
19. Skousen, 137.
20. Ibid.
21. Hal R. Varian, *Microeconomic Analysis* (New York: W.W. Norton & Company, 1978), 101–102.
22. Lindbeck, "Paul Anthony Samuelson's Contribution," 345.
23. Samuelson, "Maximum Principles in Analytical Economics," 279.
24. Leonard Silk, "Samuelson Contribution: Nobel Prize-Winner Has Demonstrated The Uniformity of All Economic Theory," *New York Times*, 28 October 1970, 67.
25. Silk, "Nobel for a Critic of Nixon Policies," 2.
26. Steven Greenhouse, "The Man Who Wrote the Book Suggests Econ 101 for Presidents," *New York Times*, Current Events Edition, 31 October 1993, 47.
27. Ibid.
28. Ibid.
29. Weintraub, 1.
30. "Robert Solow," Autobiography. In *Nobel Lectures, Economics, 1981–1990*, Karl-Gorän Mäler, ed. (Singapore: World Scientific Publishing Company, 1992), 278.
31. John Berry, "M.I.T. Economist Robert Solow Wins Nobel for Study of Growth," *Washington Post*, 22 October 1987, section C, 1.
32. Robert Solow, "Growth Theory and After," Nobel Lecture, 8 December 1987, in *Nobel Lectures, Economics, 1981–1990*, Karl-Gorän Mäler, ed. (Singapore: World Scientific Publishing Company, 1992), 280.
33. Ibid., 281.
34. David Warsh, "So Where Does Growth Theory Stand Now?" *Boston Globe*, 2 October 1994, 81.
35. Solow, "Growth Theory and After," 279.
36. Howell Raines, "Nobel in Economics to M.I.T. Professor," *New York Times*, 22 October 1987, section IV, 6.
37. David Wessel, "M.I.T. Economist Solow Wins Nobel Prize," *Wall Street Journal*, 22 October 1987, 1.
38. Ralph Vartabedian, "M.I.T. Prof. Robert Solow Wins Nobel Prize in Economics," *Los Angeles Times*, 22 October 1987, 1.
39. Ibid.
40. Warsh, 81.
41. Ibid.
42. Ibid.
43. Ibid. Also see "Robert Solow," Autobiography.
44. Feder, 6.

45. Vartabedian, 1.
46. Solow, "Growth Theory and After," 280.
47. Vartabedian, 1.
48. "Nobel Economist no Stuffed Shirt," *USA Today*, 22 October 1987, 2B.
49. Ibid.
50. "Valentine for an Economist," Editorial, *New York Times*, 23 October 1987, section I, 38.
51. Feder, 6.
52. Holcomb Noble, "James Tobin," Obituary, *New York Times*, 13 March 2002, B10.
53. Douglas Purvis, "James Tobin's Contributions to Economics," *Scandinavian Journal of Economics* 84, no. 1 (1982): 61–88.
54. Keynes explained this in comparison to bonds. When interest rates are low, bond prices are high and therefore likely to fall. In such situations, cautious investors would hold more cash.
55. Tobin thought that Keynes' explanation required investors to hold all cash or all bonds which they clearly do not do.
56. Purvis, 61–68.
57. Assar Lindbeck, Presentation Speech 1981, in *Nobel Lectures, Economics, 1981–1990*, Karl-Gorän Mäler, ed. (Singapore: World Scientific Publishing Company, 1992).
58. Ibid.
59. Ibid.
60. James Tobin, "Money and Finance in the Macro-economic Process," Nobel Memorial Lecture, 8 December 1981, in *Nobel Lectures, Economics, 1981–1990*, Karl-Gorän Mäler, ed. (Singapore: World Scientific Publishing Company, 1992), 333. Mundell's model showed that government tax cuts or spending increases were ineffective when exchange rates were floating. Using different assumptions, Tobin found the opposite, namely that fiscal policies were effective. Evaluating his new model, Tobin said, "Note, however, that – contrary to the classical Mundell (1963) conclusion that monetary policies work and fiscal policies do not in a regime of floating exchange rates – expansionary policies of both kinds are here effective."
61. James Tobin, "Money and Finance," 331.
62. Leonard Silk, "Portfolio Theorist: Tobin's Ideas on Investments Inspired Research on Effects," *New York Times*, 14 October 1981, D22.
63. Ibid.
64. Noble, B10.
65. "Tobin, Nobel Winner, Slams Reaganomics," *Boston Globe*, 16 October 1981.
66. Ibid.
67. "James Tobin," Autobiography, in *Nobel Lectures, Economics, 1981–1990*, Karl-Gorän Mäler, ed. (Singapore: World Scientific Publishing Company, 1992).
68. Ibid.
69. Ibid.
70. Alexander Stille, "Europeans, Wary of Globalization, Embrace American Economists Who Heed Social Needs," *New York Times*, 11 November 2000, B7.

71. Ibid.
72. Ibid.
73. Ibid.
74. "Professor James Tobin," Obituaries, United Kingdom: *Times Daily Register*, 14 March 2002.
75. Stille, B7.
76. John Vinocur, "Tobin of Yale Wins Nobel in Economics," *New York Times*, 17 October 1981, A1.
77. Karen Arenson, "Tobin Always 'Ahead of Field,'" *New York Times*, 14 October 1981, D1.
78. Noble, B10.
79. Arenson, D1.
80. Noble, B10.
81. Franco Modigliani, "Life Cycle, Individual Thrift and the Wealth of Nations," Nobel Lecture, in *Nobel Lectures, Economics, 1981–1990*, Karl-Goran Mäler, ed. (Singapore: World Scientific Publishing Company, 1992), 270.
82. In his 1985 Nobel acceptance speech, Modigliani made an intriguing reference to an unpublished and all but ignored article by Margaret Reid which provided "an important source of inspiration" for his own hypothesis but even more for Milton Friedman's competing explanation, the permanent income hypothesis.
83. Louis Uchitelle, "Economist Won Nobel Prize: Taught at MIT. Italian Immigrant Had Lifelong Hatred for Fascism," Montreal, Quebec: *Gazette*, 27 September 2003, C8.
84. Michael Hiltzik, "MIT Professor Modigliani Wins '85 Nobel in Economics," *Los Angeles Times*, 16 October 1985, 1.
85. Steve Lohr, "A Professor at M.I.T. Wins Nobel; Studied Market Shifts and Saving," *New York Times*, 16 October 1985, A1.
86. Uchitelle, "Economist Won Nobel Prize," C8.
87. "How Economic Policy Has Gone Awry."
88. Ibid.
89. Louis Uchitelle, "Franco Modigliani, Nobel-Winning Economist, Dies at 85," *New York Times*, 26 September 2003, A22.
90. "How Economic Policy Has Gone Awry."
91. Hiltzik, 1.
92. "Economist at MIT Awarded Nobel Prize, Blasts Reagan, Hits 'Disastrous' Federal Deficit, Urges Tax Hike," *Los Angeles Times*, 15 October 1985, 2.
93. Eric Berg, "Trailblazer and Team Player," *New York Times*, 16 October 1985, D1.
94. "How Economic Policy Has Gone Awry."
95. "Economist at MIT Awarded Nobel Prize."
96. Ibid.
97. Jonathan Fuerbringer, "Congress Hears Notes of Caution on Plan to Balance U.S. Budget," *New York Times*, 22 October 1985, 25.
98. Hiltzik, 1.
99. "Economist Wants People to Know He Did Not Paint the Sistine Chapel." *Seattle Times*, 27 October 1985, A5.

100. Ibid.
101. Ibid.
102. "How Economic Policy Has Gone Awry."
103. Uchitelle, C8.
104. Ibid.
105. Ibid.
106. William Robbins, "Father of Econometric Models; Nobel Winner Lawrence Klein 'Still a Teacher,'" *New York Times*, 16 October 1980, section IV, 1.
107. Deborah DeWitt Malley, "Lawrence Klein and His Forecasting Machine," *Fortune*, March 1975, 155.
108. Malley, 152–157.
109. Lawrence Klein, "Some Economic Scenarios for the 1980s," Nobel Memorial Lecture, 8 December 1980, in *Nobel Lectures, Economics, 1969–1980*, Assar Lindbeck, ed. (Singapore: World Scientific Publishing Company, 1992), 271.
110. John Vinocur, "Pennsylvania Professor Wins Nobel for Economics," *New York Times*, 16 October 1980, A1.
111. Leonard Silk, "Highly Regarded Klein Models Sometimes Falter in Predictions," *New York Times*, 16 October 1980, D6.
112. Ibid.
113. Malley, 157.
114. Ibid., 157.
115. R.J. Ball, "On Lawrence R. Klein's Contributions to Economics," *Scandinavian Journal of Economics* (1981), 89.
116. Ibid., 84.
117. Malley, 156.
118. Klein, "Some Economic Scenarios for the 1980s," 277.
119. Malley, 278.
120. Klein, "Some Economic Scenarios for the 1980s," 274. Inflation was based on the GDP deflator.
121. Malley, 277.
122. Robbins, 1.
123. Malley, 156.
124. Robbins, 1.
125. Malley, 152–157.
126. Robbins, 1.
127. Malley, 152–157.
128. Robbins, 1.
129. Ibid.
130. Ibid.
131. Paul Samuelson, "Nobel Choice, Economists in Contrast," *New York Times*, 10 October 1974, 69.
132. Erik Lundberg, "Gunnar Myrdal's Contribution to Economic Theory," *Swedish Journal of Economics* 112, no. 2 (1974), 477.
133. Samuel Brittan, "The not so noble Nobel Prize," London, UK: *Financial Times*, 19 December 2003, 21.
134. Another economist, Gary Becker, won a Nobel Prize for a much different, even contradictory, theory of discrimination that he developed in the 1960s.

135. Gunnar Myrdal, "The Equality issue in World Development," Nobel Memorial Lecture, 17 March 1975, in *Nobel Lectures, Economics, 1969–1980*, Assar Lindbeck, ed. (Singapore: World Scientific Publishing Company, 1992), 274.
136. Ibid., 278.
137. Ibid., 269.
138. Ibid., 272.
139. Ibid., 280.
140. Ibid., 280.
141. The others were Marie and Pierre Curie and Carl and Gerty Coris.
142. Samuelson, "Nobel Choice, Economists in Contrast," 69.
143. "Nobel Economics," Chennai: *Hindu*, 3 November 2003: 1.
144. Samuelson, "Nobel Choice, Economists in Contrast," 69.

Chapter 8

1. Martha Groves, "Economist's Former Wife Cashes in on His Nobel Prize: Thanks to her foresight in crafting a 1989 divorce agreement, Rita Lucas gets half of the $1 million award," *Los Angeles Times*, 21 October 1995.
2. Robert J. Barro, "A Rational Choice," *Wall Street Journal*, 11 October 1995, A14.
3. "Robert Lucas," Autobiography, in *Nobel Lectures, Economics, 1991–1995*, Torsten Persson, ed. (Singapore: World Scientific Publishing Company, 1997).
4. Robert E. Lucas, "Monetary Neutrality," Prize Lecture, 7 December 1995, in *Nobel Lectures, Economics, 1991–1995*, Torsten Persson, ed. (Singapore: World Scientific Publishing Company, 1997).
5. John F. Muth, "Rational Expectations and the Theory of Price Movements," *Econometricia* 29 (July 1961): 315–335.
6. Carl E. Walsh, "Nobel Views on Inflation and Unemployment," Federal Reserve Bank of San Francisco: *Economic Letter*, 10 January 1997.
7. Peter Passell, "A Nobel Award for a University of Chicago Economist, Yet Again." *New York Times*, 11 October 1995, D1.
8. Lucas, "Monetary Neutrality."
9. Barro, "A Rational Choice."
10. V. V. Chari, "Nobel Laureate Robert E. Lucas, Jr.: Architect of Modern Macroeconomics," Federal Reserve Bank of Minneapolis: *Quarterly Review* 23, no. 2 (Spring 1999): 2–12.
11. Ibid.
12. Edward C. Prescott, "The Transformation of Macroeconomic Policy and Research," Nobel Prize Lecture, 8 December 2004, in *Les Prix Nobel, The Nobel Prizes 2004*, Tore Frangsmyr, ed. (Stockholm: Nobel Foundation, 2005), 372.
13. Thomas Karier, *Great Experiments in American Economic Policy: From Kennedy to Reagan* (Westport, Connecticut: Praeger, 1997), 37–51.
14. John Kenneth Galbraith, *The Great Crash, 1929* (Boston: Houghton Mifflin Company, 1954), 99.
15. Ibid., 151.
16. Ellen McGrattan and Edward Prescott, "The 1929 Stock Market: Irving Fisher Was Right," *International Economic Review* 45, no. 4 (November 2004): 1003.

17. Prescott, "The Transformation of Macroeconomic Policy and Research," 390. Specifically, U.S. equities were worth less than the asset value of U.S. corporations, at least once you added in the value of intangible assets such as organizational capital, brand names, and patents.
18. Ibid., 390.
19. Ibid., 390.
20. In Prescott and Kydland's models, individual consumers know what their wage will be for the rest of their career so they can decide how much to work and consume every year of their lives. Once this is determined, their savings rate is also determined which in turn determines the rate of investment and most other macroeconomic variables. By folding microeconomic behavior into macro models, it is possible to wrap these loose ends into a neat little package.
21. Prescott, "The Transformation of Macroeconomic Policy and Research," 370.
22. Edward Prescott, Banquet Speech 2004, The Royal Swedish Academy of Sciences, Available at www.Nobelprize.org
23. Sergio Rebelo, "Real Business Cycle Models: Past, Present and Future," *Scandinavian Journal of Economics* 107, no. 2, (2005): 229.
24. James Hartley, "Kydland and Prescott's Nobel Prize: The Methodology of Time Consistency and Real Business Cycle Models," *Review of Political Economy* 18, no. 1 (January 2006): 18.
25. Ibid., 13.
26. Siddharth Varadarajan, "Business Cycles and Free Markets," Chennai, India, *Hindu*, 15 October 2004, 1.
27. Alan Bock, "Off the Charts. The 2004 Nobel Prize Winners in Economics Challenged commonly held models of economic behavior," Santa Ana, CA: *Orange County Register*, 28 November 2004, Cover page.
28. Hartley, "Kydland and Prescott's Nobel Prize," 22.
29. Prescott, "The Transformation of Macroeconomic Policy and Research," 383.
30. Ibid., 370.
31. Louis Uchitelle, "2 Mavericks in Economics Awarded Nobel," *New York Times*, 12 October 2004, C21.
32. Peter Coy, "Nobel Winners Without Much Impact," *Business Week*, 25 October 2004, 41.
33. Jon Hilsenrath, "American, Norwegian Win Nobel: Prescott, Kydland Honored in Economics for Research Crucial to Central Banking," *Wall Street Journal*, 12 October 2004, A2.
34. Because of all this mathematical training they should know better than to divide by zero. In his Nobel lecture Prescott defines an equation with sigma minus one in the denominator and then sets sigma equal to one. Edward C. Prescott, "The Transformation of Macroeconomic Policy and Research," Nobel Prize Lecture, 8 December 2004, in *Les Prix Nobel, The Nobel Prizes 2004*, Tore Frangsmyr, ed. (Stockholm: Nobel Foundation, 2005), 381. Also see, "Finn Kydland and Edward Prescott's Contribution to Dynamic Macroeconomics: The Time Consistency of Economic Policy and the Driving Forces Behind Business Cycles," The Royal Swedish Academy of Sciences, 19–20. Available at www.Nobelprize.org

35. John Havelock, "America Must Preserve Social Security," Anchorage, Alaska: *Anchorage Daily News*, 7 May 2005, B8.
36. Ibid.
37. Mike Meyers, Chris Serres, and Neal St. Anthony, "Politics Is Pain for New Laureate," Minneapolis, Minnesota: *Star Tribune*, 18 October 2004, 1D.
38. "Edward Prescott," Autobiography, in *Les Prix Nobel, The Nobel Prizes 2004*, Tore Frangsmyr, ed. (Stockholm: Nobel Foundation, 2005).
39. Ibid.
40. Ibid.
41. Ibid.
42. Ibid.
43. Ibid.
44. Ibid.
45. Uchitelle, C1.
46. "The Nobel Prize Market," Editorial, *Wall Street Journal*, 12 October 2004, A22.
47. Finn E. Kydland, "Quantitative Aggregate Theory," Nobel Prize Lecture, 8 December 2004, in *Les Prix Nobel, The Nobel Prizes 2004*, Tore Frangsmyr, ed. (Stockholm: Nobel Foundation, 2005).
48. Ibid., 352.
49. Ibid., 351.
50. Ibid., 354.
51. Kydland, "Quantitative Aggregate Theory," 353.
52. Varadarajan, 1.
53. Ibid. Prescott identified an important problem with his theory when he confessed, "We don't have a theory of what causes economy-wide productivity to change." One obvious theory is that business cycles cause economy-wide changes in productivity. In fact many economists would support the idea that changes in output and employment during business cycles cause productivity to change, not the other way around as Prescott and Kydland insist.
54. "Finn E. Kydland," Autobiography, in *Les Prix Nobel, The Nobel Prizes 2004*, Tore Frangsmyr, ed. (Stockholm: Nobel Foundation, 2005).
55. Ibid.
56. Charles Seife, "Macroeconomists Showed Why Good Intentions Go Wrong," *Science*, 15 October 2004, 401.
57. David Leonhardt, "Smart Money Is on Two For Nobel in Economics," *New York Times*, 8 October 2003, C3.
58. Louis Uchitelle, "American Wins Nobel in Economics," *New York Times*, 10 October 2006, C1.
59. Nobel Prize Press Release, 2006, The Royal Swedish Academy of Sciences, Available at www.NobelPrize.org
60. David Henderson, "Laureate Phelps," *Wall Street Journal*, 12 October 2006, A18.
61. "Edmund S. Phelps," Columbia University, Available at www.columbia.edu/~esp2/
62. Uchitelle, "American Wins Nobel in Economics."
63. Ibid.

64. Ibid.

65. In Phelps' model it was possible for a firm to reduce its wage and still hire more workers, something that would sound strange to most microeconomists.

66. "Edmund Phelps' Contributions to Macroeconomics," The Royal Swedish Academy of Sciences, 17, fn. 18. Available at www.Nobelprize.org

67. Ibid., 17, fn. 17. Intuitively the golden rule is not so difficult. Under the simplest of conditions, you should invest in capital until the last unit produces no additional output. That will determine the amount of capital that you would have for all future generations to produce the most consumption goods forever. The mathematics gets slightly more challenging as you introduce more realistic assumptions, such as capital depreciates, the population continues to grow at a steady rate, and there is a steady advance in technological growth.

68. Ibid., 18. fn. 19. Phelps, however, did some additional calculations describing how an economy can transition to the golden rule.

69. Ibid., 11. Phelps studied the behavior of firms with some monopoly power or ability to set prices. He noted that these firms can raise prices in the short run to generate profits but would quite likely lose sales and market shares in the future as a result. His work suggested that firms should consider an optimum strategy to set prices high enough to collect profits in the short run but not so high as to lose profits in the long run.

70. Ibid.

71. Henderson, "Laureate Phelps."

72. Ibid.

73. Ibid.

74. "Edmund Phelps' Contributions to Macroeconomics," 24.

75. Stefan Theil, "It's All About Attitude," *Newsweek (International Edition)*, 30 April 2007.

76. Ibid.

77. "Worthy Nobelist," Editorial, Washington, D.C.: Knight Ridder *Tribune Business News*, 17 October 2006, 1.

78. Donald Kalff, Letters to the Editor, Brussels: *Wall Street Journal (Europe)*, 21 February 2007, 14.

79. Mark Whitehouse, "Why Americans Should Pay More Taxes: A Nobel Winner View on Productive Economies," *Wall Street Journal*, 16 October 2006, A2.

80. Ibid.

81. David Henderson, "Laureate Phelps."

82. Ibid.

83. Ibid.

84. Whitehouse, A2.

85. Ibid.

86. Edmund Phelps, Banquet Speech, 10 December 2006, The Royal Swedish Academy of Sciences. Available at www.Nobelprize.org

87. Ibid.

88. Uchitelle, "American Wins Nobel in Economics."

89. Ibid.

Chapter 9

1. Vibha Kapuria-Foreman and Mark Perlman, "An Economic Historian's Economist: Remembering Simon Kuznets," London: *Economic Journal* 105, no. 433 (November 1995): 1530.

2. In this simple case, the contribution to gross product is the sum of valued added for iron ($1 million), steel ($3 million – $1 million = $2 million), and cars ($6 million – $3 million = $3 million), which again equals $6 million dollars. Either approach – final sales or value added – will get you the same answer.

3. Mark Skousen, "Business Europe: Chasing the Wrong Numbers," Brussels, Europe: *Wall Street Journal*, 16 July 2001, 11.

4. Steven Pearlstein, "New GNP Measure Tries to Take "Green" Approach," *Chicago Sun-Times*, 26 May 1993, 56.

5. Some described this pattern as Kuznet's U theory because the level of equality maps out something like the letter "U."

6. Alan Krueger, "When It Comes to Income Inequality, More Than Just Market Forces Are at Work," *New York Times* (late edition East Coast), 4 April 2002, C.2.

7. Kapuria-Foreman, 1530.

8. Ibid., 1525.

9. Ibid., 1527, and "Simon Kuznets," Autobiography, in *Nobel Lectures, Economics, 1969–1980*, Assar Lindbeck, ed. (Singapore: World Scientific Publishing Company, 1992).

10. "Harvard Economist Wins Nobel Prize," *New York Times*, 16 October 1971, 1.

11. Kapuria-Foreman, 1545.

12. Ibid., 1544.

13. "Passion for Truth," Editorial, *New York Times*, 17 October 1971, section IV, 10

14. Nicholas D. Kristof, "Simon Kuznets is Dead at 84; Nobel Laureate in Economics," Obituary, *New York Times*, 11 July 1985, B6.

15. Erik Lundberg, Presentation Speech 1984, in *Nobel Lectures, Economics, 1981–1990*, Karl-Gorän Mäler, ed. (Singapore: World Scientific Publishing Company, 1992).

16. Lindely H. Clark, and George Anders, "Briton Wins Nobel Economics Prize for Work on National Income Accounts," *Wall Street Journal*, 19 October 1984, 1.

17. Barnaby Feder, "Briton Is Awarded Nobel in Economics," *New York Times*, 19 October 1984, section IV, 1.

18. An increase in demand for coal will itself require increased production from many other industries that supply it, including the steel industry, which of course needs coal. This could get very complicated but the problem was elegantly solved by Leontief. By simply manipulating the original information, a new table is calculated that shows the total direct and indirect responses to a change in final demand. For example, if the table has .08 for total coal inputs to the construction industry, it means that every dollar of finished construction requires eight cents worth of coal, in this case, mostly to produce the steel that went into the buildings.

19. Each of these industries is paired with a major commodity category. Industries produce commodities and then these commodities in turn are used by various industries.

20. Robert Reinhold, "Economist Who Speculates in Ideas: Wassily Leontief," *New York Times*, 19 October 1973, 18.

21. Holcomb B. Noble, "Wassily Leontief, Economist Who Won a Nobel, Dies at 93," *New York Times*, 7 February 1999, 50.

22. Wassily Leontief, "Free Market has Crippled our Economy," *New York Times*, 11 March 1992, B3.

23. Noble, 50.

24. Leif Johansen, "L. V. Kantorovich's Contribution to Economics," *Swedish Journal of Economics* 78, no. 1 (1976): 61–79.

25. A plant operator may know, for example, what machinery is required to produce components for the final product and how many machine tools the plant is allowed. There may also be an allotment of electricity to the plant and other conditions that can be written as simple mathematical equations. Linear programming takes this problem and determines how many machine tools to assign to the production of each component in order to produce the highest output.

26. "Economist Leonid Kantorovich Dies at 75, Nobel Laureate Played Key Role in Reforms of Soviet Economy," *Los Angeles Times*, 12 April 1986, 7.

27. Leonid V. Kantorovich, "Mathematics in Economics: Achievements, Difficulties, Perspectives," Nobel Memorial Lecture, 11 December 1975, in *Nobel Lectures, Economics, 1969–1980*, Assar Lindbeck, ed. (Singapore: World Scientific Publishing Company, 1992), 266.

28. Ibid., 270.

29. Leonid V. Kantorovich, "Autobiography," In *Nobel Lectures, Economics, 1969–1980*, Assar Lindbeck, ed. (Singapore: World Scientific Publishing Company, 1992).

30. Ibid., 262.

31. "Economist Leonid Kantorovich Dies at 74," 7.

32. Ibid.

33. Julie Ingwersen, "Lauding our First Laureate," Colorado Springs: *Colorado College Bulletin* (April, 2001). Some of the other early participants were Lawrence Klein, Kenneth Arrow, James Tobin, Trygve Haavelmo, and Paul Samuelson.

34. Tjalling Koopmans, "Concepts of Optimality and their Uses," Nobel Memorial Lecture, 11 December 1975, in *Nobel Lectures, Economics, 1969–1980*, Assar Lindbeck, ed. (Singapore: World Scientific Publishing Company, 1992), 281.

35. "Tjalling C. Koopmans," Autobiography, in *Nobel Lectures, Economics, 1969–1980*, Assar Lindbeck, ed. (Singapore: World Scientific Publishing Company, 1992), 279.

36. Richard Cottle, Ellis Johnson, and Roger Wets, "George B. Dantzig (1914–2005)," *Notices of the American Mathematical Society* (AMS) 54, no. 3.

Chapter 10

1. "John F. Nash, Jr." In *Nobel Lectures, Economics, 1991–1995*, Torsten Persson, ed. (Singapore: World Scientific Publishing Company, 1997), 155.

2. Ibid., 156.
3. Ibid., 156, emphasis added.
4. Ibid., 156 and 162.
5. "The Work of John Nash in Game Theory," In *Nobel Lectures, Economics, 1991–1995*, Torsten Persson, ed. (Singapore: World Scientific Publishing Company, 1997), 162.
6. Sylvia Nasar, *A Beautiful Mind* (New York: Simon & Schuster, 1998), 71.
7. "The Work of John Nash in Game Theory," 164.
8. Nasar, *A Beautiful Mind*, 244.
9. Ibid.
10. Sadie J. Gillett and Joseph L Parham, "Game Theory," Projects for the History of Mathematics, University of Rhode Island, website, unpublished. Available at hypatia.math.uri.edu/~kulenm/mth381pr/HistTopics.htm
11. "The Work of John Nash in Game Theory," 161.
12. Nasar, *A Beautiful Mind*, 161.
13. Keith Devlin, "Mathematics: It's not only a game. Keith Devlin on the math pioneer whose work in 'game theory' netted a Nobel Prize," Manchester (UK): *Guardian*, 17 November 1994.
14. John Nash, "Non-Cooperative Games" *Annals of Mathematics* 54, no. 2 (September 1951): 295.
15. "The Work of John Nash in Game Theory," 165.
16. Nasar, *A Beautiful Mind*, 87.
17. Ignacio Palacios-Huerta, "Professionals Play Minimax," Brown University, unpublished manuscript, July, 2002.
18. Karl-Gorän Mäler, Presentation Speech 1994, in *Nobel Lectures, Economics, 1991–1995*, Torsten Persson, ed. (Singapore: World Scientific Publishing Company, 1997), 127.
19. Nasar, *A Beautiful Mind*, 88.
20. John F. Nash, "The Bargaining Problem," *Econometrica* 18, no. 2 (April 1950): 155.
21. Nasar, *A Beautiful Mind*, 350.
22. Karl-Gorän Mäler, Presentation Speech 1994, In *Nobel Lectures, Economics, 1991–1995*, Torsten Persson, ed. (Singapore: World Scientific Publishing Company, 1997).
23. David Warsh, "A Phone That Didn't Ring," *Boston Globe*, 12 October 1994, 45.
24. "If Life Is a Game, Why Not Play by the Rules?" Chennai, India: *Businessline*, 11 January 2003: 1.
25. "The Games Economists Play," *Economist*, 5 October 1994, 96.
26. Ibid.
27. Stuart Crainer, "Not Just a Game," London, UK: *Management Today* (July 1996): 66.
28. "John C. Harsanyi," Autobiography, in *Nobel Lectures, Economics, 1991–1995*, Torsten Persson, ed. (Singapore: World Scientific Publishing Company, 1997), 131.
29. The subtle distinction between incomplete information and imperfect information is the basis for Harsanyi's Nobel Prize. When players simply don't know with whom they are dealing in a game, the information is incomplete. However,

if each side knows the precise probability that their opponent is a particular type, the information is complete but imperfect. Harsanyi also introduced the idea of a lottery that reveals once and for all whether the Russian opponent is a hard liner. This simple idea converts the mathematical problem from one with incomplete information, and consequently unsolvable, to one with imperfect information and solvable.

30. "Nobel Laureate John C. Harsanyi, UC Berkeley economist and game theory pioneer, dies at 80." Press Release: University of California Berkeley, Haas School of Business.

31. Ben Wildavsky, "Berkeley Economist Shares Nobel; Research on Game Theory Shed Light on Complex Decision Processes," *San Francisco Chronicle*, 12 October 1994, A1.

32. Chris McGreal, "Calls Grow for Withdrawal of Nobel Prize: Israel Group Objects to Awards for 'Warmongers,' Game Theory Used for Political Bias, Say Critics," London, UK (Jerusalem): *Guardian*, 10 December 2005, 16.

33. M.J. Rosenberg, "Supporting Israel to death," *Jerusalem Post*, October 2006, 9.

34. McGreal, 16.

35. Hilary Leila Krieger, "He's Got Game," *Jerusalem Post*, 1 November 2005, 13.

36. Ibid.

37. Ibid.

38. In game theory analysis, a player is more likely to hold out for a bigger win if he or she places a high value on the future, or in economic terms, has a low discount rate.

39. Krieger, 13.

40. Rosenberg, 1.

41. McGreal, 16.

42. Ibid.

43. Ibid.

44. McGreal, 16.

45. Ibid and Krieger 13.

46. Krieger 13.

47. Ibid.

48. Ibid.

49. Tamara Lefcourt Ruby, "What Israel's Education System Can Learn from Aumann's Nobel," *Jerusalem Post*, 15 December 2005, 16.

50. "Robert Aumann," Autobiography, in *Les Prix Nobel, The Nobel Prizes 2005*, Karl Grandin, ed. (Stockholm: Nobel Foundation, 2006).

51. "Robert Aumann," Autobiography, 2.

52. Ibid.

53. Ibid.

54. Krieger, 13.

55. Robert J. Aumann, "Banquet Speech," 10 December 2005, in *Les Prix Nobel, The Nobel Prizes 2005*, Karl Grandin, ed. (Stockholm: Nobel Foundation, 2006).

56. Krieger, 13.

57. Michael Spence, "The Weekend Interview with Thomas Schelling: Mr. Counterintuition," *Wall Street Journal*, 17 February 2007, A9.

58. David Henderson, "The Great Game," *Wall Street Journal*, 11 October 2005, A16. Kim Clark, "In Praise of Original Thought; Tipping points and nuclear deterrence lead to the Nobel in economics," *U.S. News & World Report*, 24 October 2005, 52.

59. Kim Clark, "In Praise of Original Thought; Tipping Points and Nuclear Deterrence Lead to the Nobel in Economics," *U.S. News & World Report*, 24 October 2005, 52.

60. Ibid.

61. Louis Uchitelle, "American and Israeli Share Nobel Prize in Economics," *New York Times*, 11 October 2005, C2.

62. Thomas C. Schelling, "An Astonishing Sixty Years: The Legacy of Hiroshima," Nobel Prize Lecture, 8 December 2005, in Les *Prix Nobel, The Nobel Prizes 2005*, Karl Grandin, ed. (Stockholm: Nobel Foundation, 2006), 365.

63. Ibid., 367.

64. Ibid.

65. Jon, E. Hilsenrath, "A Nobel Economist Analyzes the Strategies of the Deadly Serious Games Nations Play," *Wall Street Journal*, 7 November 2005, A2.

66. Hilsenrath, A2.

67. Ibid.

68. Ibid.

69. "The Prize in Economic Sciences," Information for the Public, 2005, The Royal Swedish Academy of Sciences, 10 October 2005. Available at Nobelprize.org

70. Clark, 52.

71. Henderson, A16.

72. Ibid.

73. David Leonhardt, "To Prove You're Serious, Burn Some Bridges," *New York Times*, 17 October 2005, C4.

74. Ibid.

75. Uchitelle, C2.

76. Johan Lonroth and Maons Lonroth, "Game Theory Is Not Conceptually That Remarkable," London, UK: *Financial Times*, 21 October 2005, 12.

77. "Schelling Helped Stop the Cold War Turning Very Hot," Dublin, Ireland: *Irish Times*, 15 October 2005, 13.

78. Lonroth and Lonroth, 12.

79. David Washburn, "Nobel Winner, Other Discuss World Conflicts and Cooperation in La Jolla," Washington, D.C.: *Knight Ridder Tribune Business News*, 22 March 2006, 1.

80. Tim Harford, "Man with a Strategy for the Games of Life," Ontario, Canada: *National Post*, 24 December 2005, FW2.

81. Ibid.

82. David Henderson, "The Great Game," *Wall Street Journal*, 11 October 2005, A16.

83. Clark, 52.

84. "The Prize in Economic Sciences," Information for the Public, 2005. Available at www.Nobelprize.org

85. Ibid.

86. Harford, FW2.

87. Ibid.
88. Ibid.
89. Ibid.
90. Clark, 52.
91. Ibid.
92. Ibid.
93. Harford, FW2.
94. Ibid.
95. Leonhardt, C4.
96. Uchitelle, C2.
97. Harford, FW2.
98. Wolfgang Manchau and Nigel Hawkes. "Slavery Made Sound Economic Sense to Nobel Prize-Winner," London (UK): *Times*, 14 October 1993.
99. "The Week," *New York Times* (late edition, East Coast), 21 October 2007, section 4, 2.
100. Bill Barnhard, "Nobel Forecast Yields No Return," *Chicago Tribune*, 16 October 2007, 1.
101. Gabriel Rozenberg, "At 90, Hurwicz Becomes the Oldest Winner of Nobel Prize," London (UK): *Times*, 16 October 2007, 46.
102. David Cho, "3 U.S. Economists Share Nobel for Work on Flawed Markets," *Washington Post*, 16 October 2007, D1.
103. "The Prize in Economic Sciences," Information for the Public, 2007, The Royal Swedish Academy of Sciences, 3. Available at www.Nobelprize.org
104. Rick Wilson, "Real World Markets Act Differently," Charleston, West Virginia: *Sunday Gazette-Mail*, 21 October 2007, 1C.
105. Announcement of the 2007 Prize in Economic Sciences. Available at Nobelprize.org.
106. "Mechanism Design Theory," Scientific background on the Sveriges Riksbank Prize in Economic Sciences in Memory of Alfred Nobel 2007, The Royal Swedish Academy of Sciences, 9. Available at Nobelprize.org
107. R. Preston McAfee and John McMillan, "Analyzing the Airwaves Auction," *Journal of Economic Perspectives* 10, no. 1 (Winter 1996): 159.
108. Ibid.

Chapter 11

1. Ingemar Stahl, Presentation Speech, 1988, in *Nobel Lectures, Economics, 1981–1990*, Karl-Gorän Mäler, ed. (Singapore World Scientific Publishing Company, 1992), 344.
2. "Maurice Allais," Autobiography, in *Nobel Lectures, Economics, 1981–1990*, Karl-Gorän Mäler, ed. (Singapore: World Scientific Publishing Company, 1992), 374–375.
3. In particular, Allais showed that perfectly competitive markets were also socially efficient (Pareto optimum).
4. Robert Pool, "Market Theorists Gets Nobel Nod," *Science*, 28 October 1988, 511–512.

5. William Baumol and James Tobin, "The Optimal Cash Balance Proposition: Maurice Allais' Priority," *Journal of Economic Literature* 27, no. 3 (September 1989): 1160–2. Also see Maurice Allais, "An Outline of My Main Contributions to Economic Science," Nobel Lecture, 9 December 1988, in *Nobel Lectures, Economics, 1981–1990,* Karl-Gorän Mäler, ed. (Singapore: World Scientific Publishing Company, 1992), 22.
6. Allais, "An Outline of My Main Contributions," 378. Also see Pool, 511–2.
7. Ibid., 383.
8. Jean-Michel Grandmont, "Report on Maurice Allais' Scientific Work," *Scandinavian Journal of Economics* 91, no. 1 (1989): 24.
9. David Warsh, "Frenchman Wins Nobel in Economics," *Boston Globe,* 19 October 1988, 87.
10. Clark Jr., 1.
11. "A Prize Choice for France," Review and Outlook (Editorial), *Wall Street Journal,* 19 October 1988, 1. See also Warsh, "Frenchman Wins Nobel in Economics."
12. Warsh, "Frenchman Wins Nobel in Economics."
13. Jacques H. Dreze, "Maurice Allais and the French Marginalist School," *Scandinavian Journal of Economics* 91, no. 1 (1989): 8.
14. Allais, "An Outline of My Main Contributions," 380.
15. Ibid., 383.
16. Ibid., 348.
17. Alexandra Ravinet, "Solving the Enigma of a Total Eclipse," *Christian Science Monitor,* 5 August 1999: 14.
18. "Science and Technology: An Invisible Hand? Gravitational Anomalies," London, UK: *The Economist,* 21 August 2004, 74.
19. Ravinet, 14.
20. Clark Jr., 1.
21. "Maurice Allais," Autobiography.
22. Lindley H. Clark Jr., "Professor in France Wins Nobel Award in Economic Science – Maurice Allais' Contribution to Market Theory Cited 'Original' and 'Tenacious,'" *Wall Street Journal,* 19 October 1988, 1.
23. Arthur Max, "Maurice Allais of France Wins Nobel in Economics; First Frenchman Ever to Win Award," *Washington Post,* 19 October 1988, f01.
24. Clark Jr., 1.
25. Bernard Kaplan, "Europe Reluctant to let Germany Decide its Currency," Cleveland, Ohio, *The Plain Dealer,* 3 October 1995, 2C.
26. Dan Fisher and Rone Tempest, "Allais: 'Wall Street Has Become a Veritable Casino.' Nobel laureate Marice Allais says the weaknesses on the global exchanges are the same as those that led to the 1929 crash," *Los Angeles Times,* 26 October 1989, 1.
27. Ibid.
28. Keith Spicer, "French Nobelist Attacks the Noblest Language," Ottawa, Ontario, Canada: *The Ottawa Citizen,* 13 July 1989, A8.
29. Clark Jr., 1.
30. "Kenneth Arrow," *The Concise Encyclopedia of Economics,* The Library of Economics and Liberty, Available at www.econlib.org/library/Enc/bios/Arrow.html

31. Carl Christian von Weizsacker, "Kenneth Arrow's Contribution to Economics," *Swedish Journal of Economics* 110, no. 6 (1972): 498.
32. Kenneth Arrow, "General Economic Equilibrium: Purpose, Analytic Techniques, Collective Choice," Nobel Lecture, 12 December 1972, in *Nobel Lectures, Economics, 1969–1980*, Assar Lindbeck, ed. (Singapore: World Scientific Publishing Company, 1992), 219.
33. Ibid., 219–220.
34. The actual term he used wasn't best but "Pareto efficient" which is the best that an economy can do in the sense that no further improvement is possible.
35. Arrow, "General Economic Equilibrium," 223.
36. Ibid., 223.
37. Ibid., 209.
38. Ibid.
39. Ibid.
40. Ibid.
41. Klamer, 167–180.
42. Ibid.
43. Ibid.
44. Ibid.
45. Ibid.
46. "Kenneth Arrow," Autobiography, in *Nobel Lectures, Economics, 1969–1980*, Assar Lindbeck, ed. (Singapore: World Scientific Publishing Company, 1992).
47. Klamer, 167–180.
48. Paul Samuelson, "Pioneers of Economic Thought," *New York Times*, 26 October 1972, 71.
49. "Harvard and Oxford Professors Share Nobel Prize in Economics," *New York Times*, 26 October 1972, 1.
50. Samuelson, 1.
51. These standards were originally defined by Vilfredo Pareto.
52. Karl-Gorän Mäler, Presentation Speech 1983, in *Nobel Lectures, Economics, 1981–1990*, Karl-Gorän Mäler, ed. (Singapore: World Scientific Publishing Company, 1992).
53. Ibid.
54. Robert Dorfman, "A Nobel Quest for the Invisible Hand,"*New York Times*, 23 October 1983, section III, 15.
55. "Gerard Debreu," Autobiography, in *Nobel Lectures, Economics, 1981–1990*, Karl-Gorän Mäler, ed. (Singapore: World Scientific Publishing Company, 1992).
56. The other Berkeley professors were John Harsanyi (1994), Daniel McFadden (2000), George Akerlof (2001), and Oliver Williamson (2009).

Chapter 12

1. Sylvia Nasar, "Indian Wins Nobel Award in Economics," *New York Times*, 15 October 1998: C1.
2. Amartya Sen, "Missing women-revisited," London, UK: *British Medical Journal* 327, no. 7427 (6 December 2003): 1297.

3. Ibid.
4. Press Release, 14 October 1998, The Royal Swedish Academy of Sciences, 5. Available at www.Nobelprize.org
5. Amartya Sen, "Why half the planet is hungry," London, UK: *Observer*, 16 June 2002, 25.
6. Robert Pollock, "The Wrong Economist Won," *Wall Street Journal*, 15 October 1998, A22.
7. "Amartya Sen," Autobiography, in *Nobel Lectures, Economics, 1996–2000*, Torsten Persson, ed. (Singapore: World Scientific Publishing Company, 2003), 14.
8. Amartya Sen, "The Possibility of Social Choice," Nobel Lecture, 8 December 1998, in *Nobel Lectures, Economics, 1996–2000*, Torsten Persson, ed. (Singapore: World Scientific Publishing Company, 2003), 178.
9. Ibid., 188.
10. Cited in Sen, "The Possibility of Social Choice," 182.
11. This is sometimes called a single-peaked preference.
12. Kenneth Arrow, "Amartya K. Sen's Contributions to the Study of Social Welfare," *Scandinavian Journal of Economics* 101, no. 2 (1999): 166.
13. Ibid., 170.
14. Anthony Atkinson, "The Contributions of Amartya Sen to Welfare Economics," *Scandinavian Journal of Economics* 101, no. 2 (1999): 183.
15. Sen, "The Possibility of Social Choice," 194.
16. Pollock, A22.
17. Ibid.
18. Ibid.
19. Sen, "The Possibility of Social Choice," 2.
20. "Amartya Sen," Autobiography, 5.
21. Ibid.
22. Sabine Durrant, "Master of all he surveys, Amartya Sen is the new top don at the wealthiest college in Britain. But what does he actually do?" Manchester, UK: *Guardian*, 17 January 1998, 3.
23. Sir Arthur Lewis, "The Slowing Down of the Engine of Growth," Nobel Memorial Lecture, 8 December 1979, in *Nobel Lectures, Economics, 1969–1980*, Assar Lindbeck, ed. (Singapore: World Scientific Publishing Company, 1992).
24. "Sir Arthur Lewis," Autobiography, in *Nobel Lectures, Economics, 1969–1980*, Assar Lindbeck, ed. (Singapore: World Scientific Publishing Company, 1992).
25. Ibid.
26. Jeff Gerth, "Nobel Winners Focus on Poor Economies, William Arthur Lewis," *New York Times*, 17 October 1979, D18.
27. Crittenden, 1.
28. Gerth, D18.
29. Leonard Silk, "Human Capital Is Nobel Focus," *New York Times*, 17 October 1979, D2.
30. "A Down-to-Earth Economist," *New York Times*, Events Edition, 18 June 1991, A18.
31. Ibid.

32. Harry Johnson, "James Meade's Contribution to Economics," *Swedish Journal of Economics* 80, no. 1 (1978): 65.

33. Today, the challenge of achieving an external balance is less of an issue for those countries that have adopted floating exchange rates. But that was not the case in the early 1950s, when exchange rates were essentially fixed and only reluctantly changed. It was then possible for a currency to suffer from an excess of supply over demand, or a *balance of payments* problem, forcing a government to expend precious gold or foreign exchange to make up the difference. Today, a floating currency would simply depreciate, bringing supply and demand back into balance.

34. Johnson, 68.

35. Ibid.

36. Ibid.

37. Ibid., 66.

38. James Meade, "The Meaning of 'Internal Balance,'" Nobel Memorial Lecture, 8 December 1977, in *Nobel Lectures, Economics, 1969–1980*, Assar Lindbeck, ed. (Singapore: World Scientific Publishing Company, 1992), 318.

39. Johnson, 79.

40. Susan Howson, "James Meade," *Economic Journal* 110, no. 461 (February 2000): F123.

41. Ibid., 3.

42. Ibid.

43. Ibid., 10.

44. W. Max Corden, "James Meade 1907–1995," *Economic Record* 72, no. 217 (June 1996): 172.

45. "James Meade," Obituaries, Florida: *St. Petersburg Times*, 29 December 1995, 4A.

46. Howson, 1.

47. Assar Lindbeck, Nobel Nominating Speech 1977, The Royal Swedish Academy of Sciences. Available at www.Nobelprize.org

48. Richard Caves, "Bertil Ohlin's Contribution to Economics," *Scandinavian Journal of Economics* (1978): 91.

49. Antoni Estvadeordal, *Historical Essays on Comparative Advantage: 1913–1938*, Cambridge, MA: Harvard University, Dissertation, 1993, 189 pages.

50. Caves, 89.

51. Ibid., 90.

52. Ibid., 89. Samuelson, with the assistance of W. Stolper, spelled out the precise mathematical conditions for this effect.

53. American Economic Association, *Readings in the Theory of International Trade*, Selected by a Committee of the American Economic Association (Philadelphia, Pennsylvania: Blakiston Company, 1949).

54. Andrea Maneschi, Review of *A Centennial Celebration (1899–1999)*, by Bertil Ohlin. *History of Political Economy* 36, no. 1 (Spring 2004): 220. Also see Peter Debaere, Review of *A Centennial Celebration (1899–1999)*, by Bertil Ohlin. *Journal of Economic Literature* 42, no. 2 (June 2004): 505.

55. Richard Caves and Ronald Jones, *World Trade and Payments: An Introduction* (Boston, Massachusetts: Little, Brown and Company, 1985), 54–55.

56. "Bertil Ohlin," Autobiography, in *Nobel Lectures, Economics, 1969–1980*, Assar Lindbeck, ed. (Singapore: World Scientific Publishing Company, 1992).

57. Ibid.

58. Maneschi, 218.

59. "Bertil Ohlin," Autobiography.

60. "2 Nobel Laureates in Economics: Bertil Ohlin," *New York Times*, 15 October 1977, 33.

61. Maneschi, 221.

62. Caves, 93.

63. "Press Release," 13 October 2008, The Royal Swedish Academy of Sciences. Available at www.Nobelprize.org

64. "The Prize in Economic Sciences 2008," Information for the Public. The Royal Swedish Academy of Sciences. Available at www.Nobelprize.org

65. Ibid.

66. The other economists were Avinash Dixit, Victor Norman, and Kelvin Lancaster. "Trade and Geography – Economies of Scale, Differentiated Products and Transport Costs," Scientific Background on the Prize, Prize Committee of the Royal Swedish Academy of Sciences. Available at www. Nobelprize.org

67. Paul Krugman, "How I Work." Available at web.mit.edu/krugman/www/howi-work.html

68. Ibid.

69. Ibid.

70. Justin Lahart, "Paul Krugman Is Awarded Nobel in Economics," *Wall Street Journal*, 14 October 2008.

71. "The Prize in Economic Sciences 2008," 1.

72. Robert A. Mundell, "A Reconsideration of the Twentieth Century," The Royal Swedish Academy of Sciences, 1999: 230. Available at www.Nobelprize.org

73. David Warsh, "Coming in from the Cold," *Boston Globe*, 12 December 1999, E1.

74. Warsh, E1.

75. Ibid.

76. Mark Skousen, "The Perseverance of Paul Samuelson's Economics," *Journal of Economic Perspectives* 11, no. 2 (Spring 1997): 137.

77. John Hicks and Alvin Hansen rewrote economics in the 1930s and 1940s by devising equations and geometric curves to represent the relationships described by Keynes. The resulting IS-LM model provided a mechanical shorthand for analyzing fiscal and monetary policy in a Keynesian world. Keynesian policies, whether fiscal or monetary, are likely to cause changes in interest rates. This is the primary link to international markets. Domestic interest rates have to be comparable to foreign interest rates whenever capital can easily move across borders. Otherwise, investment funds will pour into countries with relatively high interest rates but comparable risk.

78. Lowering U.S. interest rates was likely to result in less demand for dollars which in turn would reduce the value of the dollar and stimulate exports. In the end, the increased production for exports would help stimulate the economy even more than originally expected.

79. The conclusion reached in Mundell-Fleming depends on whether the federal government attempts to maintain fixed exchange rates as the United States did prior to 1973, or whether rates are allowed to float as the dollar did after 1973. Under fixed exchange rates, fiscal policy is particularly effective when monetary policy is forced restore an exchange rate balance. For example, expansionary fiscal policy tends to raise interest rates, forcing the Federal Reserve to increase the money supply to suppress that tendency, thus adding expansionary monetary policy to the mix.

80. On the other hand, fiscal policy under floating rates and monetary policy under fixed rates have little domestic impact. In the first case, an expansionary fiscal policy simply drives interest rates and the dollar up, which undermines exports, offsetting the initial expansionary policy. In the second case, the Federal Reserve finds it impossible to expand the domestic economy under fixed exchange rates if lower interest rates are unsustainable. It then has to reverse course and cut the money supply to restore a balance between domestic and foreign interest rates.

81. As other economists also pointed out, even if labor can't or won't move, capital may not be so constrained. If investors build new factories and locate new offices in Louisiana to take advantage of the surplus labor force, the unemployment gap could still vanish. In either case the argument for an independent currency is effectively eliminated.

Chapter 13

1. Ragnar Frisch, "From Utopian Theory to Practical Applications: The Case of Econometrics." Nobel lecture, in *Nobel Lectures, Economics, 1969–1980,* Assar Lindbeck, ed. (Singapore: World Scientific Publishing Company, 1992), 225.

2. Ibid., 221.

3. Ibid., 220.

4. "Nobel Economics," Editorial, *New York Times,* 5 November 1969, 46.

5. Harry Schwartz, "Econometrics: Equations Not for Everyday Use," *New York Times,* 2 November 1969, section 4, 10.

6. "Ragnar Anton Kittil Frisch," Autobiography, In *Nobel Lectures, Economics, 1969–1980,* Assar Lindbeck, ed. (Singapore: World Scientific Publishing Company, 1992), 205.

7. Ibid.

8. "The First Nobel Prize in Economics," The Royal Swedish Academy of Sciences. Available at www.Nobelprize.org

9. "The First Nobel Prize in Economics," 206.

10. Robert M. Solow, "Progress in Economics Since Tinbergen," Leiden: *De Economist* 152, no. 2 (June 2004): 159.

11. Christopher Sims, "Econometrics for Policy Analysis: Progress and Regress," Leiden: *De Economist* 152, no. 2 (June 2004): 167. Keynes' reference to "computors" was about people hired to do calculations, not machines.

12. One reviewer opined that Keynes' comments "might suggest he did not understand how multiple regression worked." Sims, 167.

13. Lawrence Klein, "The Contribution of Jan Tinbergen to Economic Science," Leiden: *De Economist* 152, no. 2 (June 2004): 155.

14. J. Kol, "Tinbergen in De Economist," Leiden: *De Economist* 152, no. 2 (June 2004): 273.

15. Jan Tinbergen, "The Use of Models: Experience and Prospects," Nobel Lecture, in *Nobel Lectures, Economics, 1969–1980*, Assar Lindbeck, ed. (Singapore: World Scientific Publishing Company, 1992).

16. Ibid.

17. Bent Hansen, "Jan Tinbergen: An Appraisal of His Contributions to Economics," *Swedish Journal of Economics* 71 (1969): 327.

18. Tinbergen, "The Use of Models," 245.

19. Kol, 273.

20. Hansen, 336.

21. Klein, 155.

22. Paul Samuelson, "Homage to Jan Tinbergen," Leiden: *De Economist* 152, no. 2 (June 2004): 153.

23. "Norwegian Professor Trygve Haavelmo is Awarded Nobel Prize for Economics," *Wall Street Journal*, 12 October 1989.

24. Ibid.

25. David Warsh, "Economist's New Twist; A Nobel," *Boston Globe*, 12 October 1989, 1.

26. "Norwegian Wins Economics Nobel Prize Awards: The professor, however, calls the prize 'quite irrelevant to the real issues," *Los Angeles Times*, 12 October 1989.

27. "Norwegian Professor Trygve Haavelmo is Awarded Nobel Prize for Economics."

28. "Norwegian Wins Economics Nobel Prize Awards."

29. James Heckman, "Haavelmo and the Birth of Modern Econometrics: A Review of *The History of Econometric Ideas* by Mary Morgan," *Journal of Economic Literature* 30, no. 2 (June 1992): 876.

30. Ibid., 883.

31. Christopher Sims, "Econometrics for Policy Analysis: Progress and Regress," Leiden, *De Economist* 152, no. 2 (June 2004): 167.

32. Heckman, "Haavelmo and the Birth of Modern Econometrics," 883.

33. Trygve Haavelmo, "Econometrics and the Welfare State," Nobel Lecture, published in *American Economic Review* 87, no. 6 (December 1997): 13–16.

34. Marc Nerlove, "Trygve Haavelmo: A Critical Appreciation," *Scandinavian Journal of Economics* 92, no. 1 (1990): 17.

35. David Warsh, "Economist's New Twist; A Nobel," *Boston Globe*, 12 October 1989, 1.

36. Ibid.

37. Ibid.

38. Jon E. Hilsenrath, "Nobel in Economics Is Given to 2 Professors; Engle, Granger Developed Tools for Tracking Trends, Measuring Investment Risk," *Wall Street Journal*, 9 October 2003, A2.

39. C. W. J. Granger and P. Newbold, "Spurious regression in econometrics," *Journal of Econometrics*, 2 (1974): 111–120.

40. Peter Hans Matthews, "Paradise Lost and Found? The Econometric Contributions of Clive W. J. Granger and Robert Engle," *Review of Political Economy* 17, no. 1 (January 2005): 17.

41. Ibid., 23.

42. "Clive W. J. Granger," Autobiography, in *Les Prix Nobel, The Nobel Prizes 2003*, Tore Frangsmyr, ed. (Stockholm: Nobel Foundation, 2004).

43. Ibid.

44. Ibid.

45. Clive, W. J. Granger, "Time Series Analysis, Cointegration, and Applications," Nobel Lecture, 8 December 2003, in *Les Prix Nobel*, 363.

46. Ibid., 364.

47. "Robert F. Engle III," Autobiography, in *Les Prix Nobel*.

48. ARCH stands for autoregressive conditional heteroskedasticity.

49. Robert F. Engle III, "Risk and Volatility: Econometric Models and Financial Practice," Nobel Lecture, 8 December 2003, in *Les Prix Nobel*, 334.

50. This is called a conditional variance.

51. "Robert F. Engle III," Autobiography.

52. RUM stands for random utility maximization.

53. Daniel McFadden, "California Needs Deregulation Done Right," *Wall Street Journal*, 13 February 2001, A26.

54. Ibid.

55. Kimberly Blanton, "Nobel Laureates Attack Tax Plan Predict Drag on Growth, Damage to Middle Class," *Boston Globe*, 11 February 2003, D1.

56. Louis Uchitelle, "2 Americans Win the Nobel for Economics," *New York Times*, 12 October 2000, C1. Also see Charlotte Denny, "Nobel winner says New Deal doesn't work," Manchester, UK: *Guardian*, 12 October 2000, section 1, 24.

57. Uchitelle, C1.

58. Ibid.

59. Ingwersen.

60. Steve Liesman, "Two U.S. Economists Win Nobel Prize – Heckman, McFadden Cited For Analyzing Decisions Made About Lifestyles," *Wall Street Journal*, 12 October 2000, A2.

61. Ibid.

62. "Interview with James J. Heckman," Federal Reserve Bank of Minneapolis: *Region* (June 2005).

63. Ibid., 2.

64. Ibid.

65. Julie Ingwersen, "Lauding our First Laureate," Colorado Springs: *Colorado College Bulletin* (April 2001).

66. "Interview with James J. Heckman."

67. James J. Heckman, "Cracked Bell," *Reason Magazine* (March 1995).

68. "Interview with James J. Heckman," 3.

69. Heckman, "Cracked Bell," 5.

70. Ibid.

71. "Nobel Economist Sees Decline in Productivity Unless U.S. Invests in Preschool Programs," New York: *PR Newswire*, 3 December 2004, 1.

72. Heckman went on to say that he didn't count the Head Start Program among the "very intensive programs." In his view, it was "half-hearted." Heckman, "Cracked Bell."

73. "Nobel Economist Sees Decline in Productivity."

74. James Heckman, "Catch 'em Young," *Wall Street Journal*, 10 January 2006, A14.

Chapter 14

1. "Nobel Economists: On Institutions and Slavery," *Wall Street Journal*, 13 October 1993, A22.

2. Barry Eichengreen, "The Contributions of Robert W. Fogel to Economics and Economic History," *Scandinavian Journal of Economics* 96, no. 2 (1994): 175.

3. Lennart Jorberg, Presentation Speech 1993, in *Nobel Lectures, Economics, 1991–1995*, Torsten Persson, ed. (Singapore: World Scientific Publishing Company, 1997).

4. Lindsey Tanner, "Americans Win Economics Nobel, Slavery Impact, Property Rights Ideas Honored," New Orleans, Louisiana: *Times-Picayune*, 13 October 1993, C1.

5. Peter Passell, "Economic Scene," *New York Times*, 21 October 1993, D2.

6. Tanner, C1.

7. Ibid.

8. "Nobel Economists: On Institutions and Slavery."

9. Ibid.

10. Ibid.

11. Ibid.

12. Ibid.

13. Ibid.

14. Ibid.

15. Ibid.

16. Ibid.

17. Ibid.

18. Jonathan Marshall, "Novel Look at Economics Wins Nobel for 2 Americans," *San Francisco Chronicle*, 13 October 1993, A3.

19. Ibid.

20. "Robert Fogel," Autobiography, in *Nobel Lectures, Economics, 1991–1995*, Torsten Persson, ed. (Singapore: World Scientific Publishing Company, 1997).

21. Eichengreen, 172.

22. Peter Temin, "The Nobel Economics Prize, Explained," *New York Times*, 7 November 1993, F11.

23. Passell, D2.

24. Robert Fogel, "Economic Growth, Population Theory, and Physiology: The Bearing of Long-term Processes on the Making of Economic Policy," Nobel Lecture, 9 December 1993, in *Nobel Lectures, Economics, 1991–1995*, Torsten Persson, ed. (Singapore: World Scientific Publishing Company, 1997), 77.

25. Ibid., 76.

26. Ibid., 78.
27. Ibid.
28. Eichengreen, 176.
29. Marshall, A3.
30. "Robert Fogel," Autobiography.
31. Sylvia Nasar, "A Talent for Rewriting History," *New York Times*, 13 October 1993, D1.
32. Marshall, A3.
33. Johan Myhrman and Barry Weingast, "Douglass C. North's Contributions to Economics and Economic History," *Scandinavian Journal of Economics* 96, no. 2 (1994): 187.
34. Ibid., 192.
35. John Bremner, "An Economist Honored for his Unorthodoxy, Douglas North Receives Nobel Prize Today," *St. Louis Post-Dispatch*, 10 December 1993, 9D.
36. Myhrman and Weingast, 189,
37. Andrew Krikelas, "Review Essay – An Economist's Perspective on History: Thoughts on Institutions, Institutional Change, and Economic Performance," Federal Reserve Bank of Atlanta: *Economic Review* 80, no. 1 (January 1995): 28.
38. Douglass North, " Economic Performance through Time," Nobel Lecture, 9 December 1993, in *Nobel Lectures, Economics, 1991–1995*, Torsten Persson, ed. (Singapore: World Scientific Publishing Company, 1997), 9.
39. Nasar, "A Talent for Rewriting History," D1.
40. Amanda Bennett, "An Economist Investigates the Irrationality of People," *Wall Street Journal*, 29 July 1994, B1.
41. Douglass North, Stephen Haber, and Barry Weingast, "If Economists Are So Smart, Why Is Africa So Poor?" *Wall Street Journal*, 30 July 2003, A12.
42. Ibid.
43. Bremner, 9D.
44. Bennett, B1.
45. Ibid.
46. Ibid.
47. Ibid.
48. Bremner, 9D.
49. "Economists Attack Bush Tax-Cut Plan," *Houston Chronicle*, 11 February 2003, 2.
50. "Economic Governance: Scientific Background on the Sveriges Riksbank Prize in Economic Sciences in Memory of Alfred Nobel, 2009," The Royal Swedish Academy of Sciences, 12 October 2009, 4–5. Available at www.Nobelprize.org
51. Ibid.
52. Peter Whoriskey, "Monsanto Draws Antitrust Scrutiny," Spokane, Washington: *Spokesman-Review*, 29 November 2009, A6.
53. Garrett Hardin, "The Tragedy of the Commons," *Science* 162 (1968): 1243–1248.
54. Nick Zagorski, "Profile of Elinor Ostrom," *Proceedings of the National Academy of Sciences, U.S.A.* 103, no. 51 (19 December 2006): 19221–19223. Available at http://www.ncbi.nlm.nih.gov/pmc/articles/PMC1748208/

55. "Economic Governance: Scientific Background on the Sveriges Riksbank Prize in Economic Sciences in Memory of Alfred Nobel, 2009," The Royal Swedish Academy of Sciences, 12 October 2009, 11–12. Available at www.Nobelprize.org

56. Nick Zagorski, "Profile of Elinor Ostrom," *Proceedings of the National Academy of Sciences, U.S.A.* 103, no. 51 (19 December 2006): 19221–19223. Available at http://www.ncbi.nlm.nih.gov/pmc/articles/PMC1748208/

Chapter 15

1. Sylvia Nasar, "The Sometimes Dismal Nobel Prize," *New York Times*, 13 October 2001, C3.

2. Mohammed Yunus, Nobel Lecture, 10 December 2006, The Royal Swedish Academy of Sciences. Available at www.Nobelprize.org

3. Ibid.

4. Ibid.

Index